Austria and Other Margins

KATHERINE ARENS

AUSTRIA AND OTHER MARGINS: READING CULTURE

CAMDEN HOUSE

Copyright © 1996 by
CAMDEN HOUSE, INC.

Published by Camden House, Inc.
Drawer 2025
Columbia, SC 29202 USA

Printed on acid-free paper.
Binding materials are chosen for strength and
durability.

ISBN: 1–57113–109–4

Library of Congress Cataloging-in-Publication Data

Arens, Katherine, 1953–
 Austria and other margins: reading culture / Katherine Arens. – 1st ed.
  p. cm. – (Studies in German literature, linguistics, and culture)
 Includes bibliographical references and index.
 ISBN 1–57113–109–4 (alk. paper)
 1. Austrian literature—History and criticism. 2. Literature, Modern—20th century—History
and criticism. 3. Literature, Modern—History and criticism—Theory, etc. 4. Literature and
society. 5. Arts and society. 6. Cultural relations. I. Title. II. Series: Studies in German literature, linguistics, and culture (Unnumbered).
PT3822.A74 1996
809' .03--dc20   96–27663
                                                                                         CIP

Contents

Acknowledgments

I would like to thank two successive vice-presidents and deans of Graduate Studies of the University of Texas at Austin, William S. Livingston (now senior vice-president) and Teresa A. Sullivan, and the University Research Institute for two one-semester research leaves (fall 1989 and spring 1996), two islands of comparative quiet that enabled me to draft much of and reedit this volume.

Three of the chapters that follow appeared in earlier versions which have been subsequently much revised and updated: chapter 2 as "Mozart: A Case Study in Logocentric Repression," *Comparative Literature Studies* 23, no. 2 (Summer 1986): 141–69; chapter 4 as "Robert Wilson: Is Postmodern Performance Possible?," *Theatre Journal* 43, no. 1 (March 1991): 14–40; and chapter 6 as "Characterology: Hapsburg Empire to Third Reich," *Literature and Medicine* 8 (1989): 128–55.

Many further collegial and personal debts remain unacknowledged because they are so numerous. Thanks are due to my copyeditor, Jean W. Ross, and my anonymous reader from Camden House; they saved me from many errors. I would like to single out Andrea Winkler to thank for her comments about an earlier version of chapter 1 and Christa Gaug for her discussions on "Grillparzer's *Fiddler*." With help from Kinsky, William Russell has provided a consistent ear and moral support. Janet Swaffar remains the exemplary colleague and friend who has read more drafts of the bulk of what follows than anyone has a right to ask, let alone receive; her comments led me out of many dead-ends, but the errors which remain are my own.

K. A.
August 1996

Introduction:
Reading Culture, or the Critics' Text?

This introduction's title sets up an odd dichotomy. Who are the readers and critics it implies? To whom do they speak? What is their text? What separates these readers and critics from "reading culture," if anything?

The answer to "who is a critic?" will, of course, depend on who is asked and under what circumstances. Academicians, the "outside experts" working for publishers, armchair critics, newspaper commentators, and review editors all seem, on first glance, to fit the bill. But once one narrows the question to asking about a critic in the context of an academic publication rather than some other, more general type of critical reader, these options are quickly narrowed, and the potential ambiguities of reference for the term "critic" are quickly disambiguated: the academic critic receives a univalent referent, in Jean-François Lyotard's sense (*Differend* 39). This critic is neither an expert in all things nor a voice for popular opinion but rather a participant in a specialized chain of communication (39), a profession, or a discourse of mastery (Eagleton). In her or his role within the academy, the critic is "both ostensive (an object of perception) and nominative (an object of history)" (Lyotard, *Differend* 51).

In other words, today's critic is most often someone who can be viewed within the immediate academic context and someone who exists within a tradition and society of other academic critics and their views. Such a critic speaks for him- or herself and, at the same time, is a voice among voices, past as well as present — part of a tradition enclosed by its institutional history. The present collection of essays is, first and foremost, about such critical voices as participants in a historically grounded dialogue about the meanings available in culture. While its author stands within that academic tradition, her interest will, in contrast, be directed toward what today are most often called the "margins" of that dominant academic culture.

The concept of marginality is heavily in use in postcolonial criticism,[1] that branch of academic criticism that focuses on the impact of the nineteenth-century European colonial empires, particularly as those cultures exerted dominance over indigenous cultures and continue to do so in more subtle ways long after occupying governments and armies were removed. The present volume will use a more metaphoric sense of "marginality" and "dominance" to define the roles available to today's academic critics: each academic professional standing within an institution is part of a dominating academic culture, a culture that approves projects, publishes and gives grants in "areas of current interest," and celebrates its ever-renewed relevance in performances at professional meetings. The topics of the essays that follow are, in these contexts, often at the margins of these dominant academic cultures.

Two Margins: Culture and Criticism

The first set of margins to be exemplified below, the four studies that constitute section 1, are geopolitical ones, as those cultural geopolitics are enacted within the frameworks of today's institutional landscapes. Academic criticism (and the formal areas of study that engender it) today fails in large part to talk productively about intellectual disputes that reach across cultures. Academic departments and programs in the humanities are, quite conveniently, organized by "national literatures" and their accompanying languages or by the geographic units where their objects of study historically were found ("U.S. History," "Latin American Studies"). Historically, however, these "natural" units are anything but natural: nations may speak more than one language (officially or not); the history of a geographical region may be fragmented into areas of dominance that exclude some of its parts; literature in a single language may be produced in many nations. These divisions thus originate in the social and critical ideologies of particular historical and cultural moments and all too easily become self-perpetuating (see, for example, how departments of "Russian" turned into "Soviet" or "Slavic" institutes as geopolitics altered and what shapes they are assuming today).[2]

The four case studies presented in section 1 are views from margins created through such cultural-historical academic happenstance. The first two are from a tacit margin: from Austrian culture, which has been largely subsumed into "German" departments on the basis of language, while its geopolitics may often in many respects have more to do with other Western powers (France, Britain) or with Central Europe. The first is that of an Austrian romancier, Heimito von Doderer, who borrows his novelistic voice from Russia to elide Austria's shared twentieth-century historical past with Germany. The second follows an icon of Austrian identity, Mozart, from one narrative home in a nineteenth-century German novella, through a twentieth-century biography, and into its new international but Anglophone incarnation as Austria's national hero, *Amadeus*. At this margin, the question that is suppressed by dominant academic (and too often also political) cultures is a simple one: is Austria Germany? (Historians will rightly object that the name "Austria" never did refer to any official geopolitical entity.)

The third and fourth cases in section 1 are also artifacts of cultures in contact, cultures whose interdependence has also been isolated from too active consideration by those same departmental and geopolitical borders. In direction of cultural context, these two studies invert each other; yet each shows how one culture uses another, across language and geographical borders, to confront its own problems (war experiences of the twentieth century as crises of national hegemony and confidence). In the third study, we see how John Irving imports a German genre into the United States, while the fourth traces Robert Wilson's importation of U. S. popular culture onto the German stage.

Each of these four cases has been complicated by lying in the cultural or geopolitical margin. What an author knows of another culture is not always familiar to his readers or critics, so each study tries to span the artificial cultural boundaries that these authors themselves did not accept. Doderer looks to Russian history rather than to German or Western European history for a metaphor to explain his own situation; Irving looks to the novel that framed Germany's home front experience of the Second World War to find a way to have the U. S. confront Vietnam. "Mozart" was a historical entity, but one who is refashioned by authors seemingly at will once they try to overcome his pastness and make him relevant to various presents; the Second World War, Wilson points out, included Hollywood as well as Auschwitz, and the Western Powers are defined as much by their political alliances as by their early reliance on U. S. popular culture.

These first four studies thus are texts that exemplify cultural displacements, some successful, some less so — four studies in speaking against the grain of national cultures, or in speaking in two Germans, or in English and German at the same time. Yet while each essay speaks about a margin, each is also distinctly a "critic's text" because the questions asked are framed from the critics' points of view, consciously working their way out of existing sites of investigation and into less familiar, less comfortable terrain that does not yield comfortably or completely to such ill-fitting tools. Nonetheless, these studies connect cultures by looking to borrowings and rewritings of individual cultural traditions, recovering experiments and perspectives that have tended to vanish behind the more powerful images of dominant historical and critical points of view.

The second set of case studies, offered in section 2 of this volume, also work from the margins, but they have chosen more insidious, less easily reconciled margins than the more direct literary and cultural borrowings traced in section 1. These four case studies break lines between disciplines rather than those on the geopolitical maps, even though they share with the first four studies a common attempt to read the cultures that condition authors' writings. These margins are historical-cognitive ones rather than geographical or linguistic ones; they are often artifacts of U.S. academic history and its institutional habits, making them one degree more removed from the operative realities of more general history than those in section 1.[3]

Academic disciplines, like academic departments, are established on partially fictitious but nonetheless powerful grounds. Yet the boundaries between academic disciplines are considerably less easily interrogated than those between geopolitical entities. Each discipline has its professionals, who work in their appropriate fields in "approved" ways. Pierre Bourdieu points out that a field (discipline) is also a field of battle and a field of play: a region where individuals establish their independent domains and exclude others, exerting power over other players by legitimizing or invalidating others' parallel attempts at playing. This is a cruel vision: it functions only within what the public often calls academic turf, on which many of the players are approximately equal since they have equivalent credentials, equivalent access to professional venues, equivalent degrees of public trust.

Yet differences between "tiers" of academic employment, availability of grants or libraries, and access to professional organizations are less important to the authority of such academic critics outside the playing fields of the academy than they are within it. They create vicious internecine wars and (arguably) improve the "truths" generated by these professionals.[4] However, at the same time, such "professional differences" of site and support serve to turn each corner of an academic discipline into the margin for another — a completely relative designation that can shift with geopolitical changes much more rapidly than can the identities of nation-states. These margins are therefore very different from the margins enforced by the culture of nation-states.

Said most practically: the cultural margins enforced by geopolitics translated into the academy reflect (perhaps with a historical offset that has damaging effects) relative "truths" that place academic disciplines in specific relations to that dominant culture (as agents of its support, revolutionaries, or whatever). In contrast, the margins enforced between academic disciplines or by camps of professionals within the academy reflect the relative "truths" of the players' power, of their command of resources, status, and authority. Cultural margins thus tell us something about the relations of various power elites to the practical truths of everyday life; disciplinary margins, in contrast, inform us principally about the relations within power elites and only secondarily (and often through a glass darkly) about the everyday life of the culture that supports these elites. Cultural margins are "readings" of the dominant culture; disciplinary margins are "readings" of the dominant readers.

Moving back to the four case studies offered in section 2 of the present volume: these four essays, like their predecessors, attempt to speak from the margins, but they must do so by reclaiming the authority of the *reader* of culture rather than that of the professional critic. This requires a double attention to history, where the earlier studies arguably needed a single one, since these second essays must overcome not just the single fiction of dominant history but also the set of secondary fictions thrown off by that dominant history within the confines of academic disciplines.

The first of the studies in this section thus discusses a literary author (Adalbert Stifter) who has arguably been influenced by educational psychology as much as aesthetics; a second who is a physician-psychologist (Arthur Schnitzler); and a third who conceived of telling tales in scenes, as for the theater, even while he was writing prose (Franz Grillparzer). As written, each case projects a text back into its purported cultural context, which requires a crossing of disciplinary lines (between the social sciences and aesthetics, science and aesthetics, and two aesthetic norms formed by radically different cultural practices and institutions, respectively) and a reclaiming of those sets of cultural connections that were arguably available at a particular moment in history but have since been obscured (often because of the habits of formal academic disciplines). The fourth study focuses on a moment in cultural history (the 1960s and 1970s modern art scene in the West) and shows how two different players used the label "modern artist" to craft two very different careers, a difference that opens what other variables like nationality and gender can do on a common stage.

The second section of the present volume thus argues for a superseding of critical conventions in favor of critical readings of culture — to reclaim acts of reading from behind the historical conventions that have fossilized them as acts of academic criticism.

Reading Culture Critically: Displacing the Critic's Text

This two-part collection of case studies hopes to offer its essays as models for "reading culture" and for the critical practice of reading in cultural context — reading into the margins that have all too often fossilized as a consequence of the professionalization of academic criticism.[5]

The present critic would argue that such a shift of focus from criticism to critical readings of culture is a historical necessity today. Even as academics are becoming noted for ignoring each other within the university (in debates about "political correctness" from the right or the left, for instance), the resounding silence of critical appeal beyond those shelter walls is hollowing out the credibility of cultural studies in the public sphere. Today the academic critic appears in the public eye only as the object of satire (as in the *New York Times*'s yearly reports on the meeting of the Modern Language Association) or as one among many spoiled children arguing about vague ideological preferences with, seemingly, no real-world consequences (as when the debates on multiculturalism emerge onto the bestseller list). At the same time, diffuse, polarized accounts of these events and controversy are cast as central to the lives of professional academics in academy-internal publications such as the *Chronicle of Higher Education*, *LinguaFranca*, or *Heterodoxy*. Thus in versions purportedly "authorized" by academic professionals, the truth value of the critics' texts and the margins created and enforced by them is disseminated by publishers and television networks (Marxist critics would not say "disseminated by" but rather "originated in").

Yet culture will not allow its creations to be so negligent of its originators, so the "margins of culture" created as points of arbitration for critics have begun to trickle beyond their control and become public points of cultural reference. The debates that raged around E. D. Hirsch's *Cultural Literacy* can serve as a case in point: they demonstrate what happens when a "dominant" cultural perspective ensconced within the academy is con-

fronted by a margin or margins outside it. Hirsch's idea about teaching
cultural literacy as tied to U. S. antecedents in European culture was intended as a hermeneutic description of learning: showing how underlying
(in this case, often European) cultural schemata must be established in students' minds before the multicultural literacy necessary for today's U. S. environment becomes possible. He argues that the schemata underlying the
image of the hero in *Beowulf* are part of the tradition of the Western epic,
for example; without linking these schemata to those in *Gilgamesh*, a
reader will not see either the parallels or the contrasts between Eastern and
Western traditions.

    Whether one considers it a successful appeal or not (and most public
and academic critics seemingly did not), Hirsch's work was a plea for literature understood in a cultural and historical context. Yet in the subsequent debates on his book, his ideas were channeled into the public image
of the critic as ideologue, expressed and perhaps deformed in reference to
rubrics of normative "cultural literacy" to be challenged by a more desirable
"multiculturalism." Taking Hirsch's proposal as an ideological position, public debate reframed cultural literacy from one critic's original question about
the process of individual readers' acquiring cultural schemata in order to
orient themselves historically, to a free-wheeling public debate about cultural maintenance and repression. What Hirsch described as a process was,
then, taken as the product of his personal (and hence restricted) ideology.
What he described as a benchmark from which both the center and margins of U. S. culture were to be read (a starting point, not a norm) became
in the public mind the act of an elite critic trying to exclude less privileged
margins. The public remembered what too many critics had forgotten: critics' authority is not only vis-à-vis each other but also with respect to the
culture whose elite they are (or, in some cases, were once).[6]

    To try to reconcile these two spheres of authority (that of cultural his-
tory and that of academic criticism, albeit not in its present form), *Austria
and Other Margins* is an exercise in rejoining them by showing how cultures can be read rather than authorized, how texts can be reinserted re-
sponsibly into their own cultures by critical readers who are aware of the
historicity of their cultures. To accomplish this, as already noted, the volume's studies turn specifically to the margins of the dominant historical and
academic cultures to show how texts may have hoped to speak before
other, possibly more dominant, cultural reading strategies foreclosed their
voices. For simply because particular voices have been marginalized at
certain moments in cultural history does not mean that they will not
emerge again, reinvoked by academic critics, popular culture, or historical
accident.

    When Virginia Woolf delivered her 1929 call for *A Room of One's Own*
in an academic environment that excluded her, for example, her text delivered a critique about the hermetically closed academic atmosphere of her
age. Today that text lies firmly within the academy, not at its margins; it is
included in most "standard" feminist anthologies. That reuse inserts it into a

different sphere of culture than that in which it originally appeared — into a different "phrase regime," as Jean-François Lyotard would have called it (in *The Differend*), or into different disciplines (public culture versus academic feminism). Clearly, a noted contemporary author speaking at an academic event speaks with different resonance and power about a new feminist cause than does a canonical feminist enshrined a half-century later in a textbook, as part of an acknowledged feminist movement. The novelist's (even the feminist novelist's) "discourse of mastery" is simply different than that of the academic feminist and her students a half-century later: Woolf appealed to a public cultural elite, while the academic feminist has as her tribunal the established protocols of the academy. Woolf in play in a cultural reading now is therefore a potentially disputed object, entrapped in multiple phrase regimens and "in play" on a broad academic playing field multiply conditioned by the many cultural margins and centers. An object of culture (her text) has been transposed into an object of criticism; a margin has been moved to another kind of center.

The case of Woolf exemplifies the kind of critical reading of culture that can serve the interests of both a dominant culture and its margins. Her text is in play in Anglophone culture, but that play is by no means free. Critical cultural readings such as this volume offers can open perspectives on why she could be moved into a center of a later culture, out of its early margins. To be understood critically as an object of culture rather than an object of criticism, the text must be understood — read — both in its integrity and strategically, as an appropriate act of communication in its original context and as an artifact that subsequent generations can refashion to new purposes. The reasons for a text's afterlife are recoverable from a new historical vision of the original text and from the new site given to it to speak from. A single text thus participates in two cultural-historical truths; they are linked to each other only by chains of historical circumstance and cultural strategy, not by any absolute necessity. A critical reading of culture seeks these contextual conditions; an academic critic may more easily appropriate the text to her own purposes.

Traditional literary scholarship along nationalist lines also too easily leaves aside facets of these chains of historical circumstance and cultural strategy, such as when it identifies Woolf as a "(feminist) writer" and not as a cultural icon who participated in a particular transformation of British *culture* and *history* (not simply of British literature). Evolutions of cultural theory and criticism have, particularly since the 1960s, expanded the scope of their identifications of Woolf far beyond their traditional fiefs of literary history or aesthetics. The traditional definition of those fiefs' scope (the text as written word) has, as a matter of course, expanded to embrace the "text" of human experience: not only fiction but science, myth, ethics; not only high art but all aspects of popular culture as well. Yet these newer cultural critics have principally focused on drawing portraits of the various Woolfs left out of the original picture and have not looked at the other side of the cultural dynamics in which she and her work are enmeshed — the reasons that our contemporary culture would reappropriate and reread certain texts and not others.

Austria and Other Margins wishes, then, to open up the patterns of reading that have largely remained closed, marginalized, or oppositional because of today's tendency to isolate criticism from its various positions in culture. In consequence, the goal of the studies that follow is not to purvey particular readings as "truths" that exhaust their subjects but rather to explore how particular texts function within varied cultural systems, some more marginal than others. Each essay's reading is, to be sure, guided by a specific "theoretical premise" (a systematic reading strategy, possibly even identified with particular critics), but it tries to follow texts into cultural loci where they were read and which may need future rereadings. Each essay does not simply pull these texts into line under a single kind of critical ideological authority. Instead, each essay wishes to problematize rather than resolve an act of reading by opening connections between texts and cultures. Again, however, reading culture in this way, treating texts as cultural entities that function variously among their historical contexts, flouts current academic practice since each essay opens uneasy questions about marginal reading practices rather than offering a potentially authoritative reading.[7] The studies that follow may well offend on these grounds alone because they specifically aim to reclaim voices in each text which have been marginalized — by history, critical consensus, or public taste.

To clarify this claim in another way: consider the case of "popular texts." When cultural critics seek the echo of a text under the rubric "popular reception," their investigations have already accepted the way very specific cultural margins are defined today. In one instance, a critic could potentially conceive of "popular" science and "popular" fantasy writing as virtually interchangeable expressions of the public's sense of what matters and what is worth caring about. Yet "popular" may actually mean something very different in these two cases since "popular" fantasy tends to be read by academic critics as a set of purely literary conventions to be interpreted against a classic Western tradition of authorship, while "popular" science specifically tries to bridge the specialist and more general audience and so occupies a different place in culture. For today's critical reader of culture, the moral of this tale is that all popular texts need not be or have been popular in the same way — a difference that must be reclaimed if the reader is to be able to judge where the margins and centers of a culture may be and what their significance may be for the ways in which that culture tells its truths (or how the reader's own could do). This is, in short form, the major issue that the conclusion of the present volume will return to after the individual case studies.

Reading Culture Critically:
The Need for Readers, Not Critics

The question of margins also explains why the readings contained in this volume are necessarily discomfiting for the professional academic who too easily identifies professionalism with a particular sense of what is "naturally" in the center or on the margins of a particular culture — a strategy of reading that conflates cultures with political agendas or comprehensive ideologies. As noted above, the academy's ever-increasing diversity of critical camps has today all too often chosen to espouse this kind of reading to argue for each camp's authority in producing normative truth rather than admitting that even competing critics are speaking from a particular culture and (most often) from the center of this culture. Their theoretical claims to universality or comprehensive insight have today eclipsed the fact that *any* reading necessarily exists as a regional ontology, bounded by cultural and historical locations and requiring a clear acknowledgment that *then* is not *now*. Yet as more recent debates on multiculturalism reveal, few voices are raised to defend the notion that any one reading, even one that claims metatheoretical status, can do anything but speak for a particular margin or center.[8] Investigating this claim has not been done: *any* reader's reading can potentially do the same — professionalism is not a guarantee of a successful reading.

What *Austria and Other Margins* seeks to recommend, however, is that such nonprofessional readings of culture need to be examined, since their readings are not random or arbitrary, since even the most distant margins in which these other readers exist are formed *in conjunction with* the centers that critics occupy. *Otherness* is constituted in an opposition between margin and center,[9] and each act of reading now must necessarily incorporate (at least parts of) another time and another place — on the part of both the text to be read and the reader who is undertaking that reading. The professional critic pretending to be a naive reader might well interject here, "If reading offers no more than a culturally and historically bounded view, then why interpret? If all interpretation is based on individual conclusion and inference, where is truth?" A dedicated reader of cultures, however, would never fall into that trap — each reading reveals specifics of the context in which it appears, at least.

My answer to that disingenuous question is that, of course, cultural truth cannot be uncovered as such out of a text, but each reader must be sensitized to the fact that all truths are created by acts of will, according to the possibilities offered by history.[10] Even when an individual reader believes that he or she is reading "correctly," or "against the grain," that reader is simply weighting the margins and the center of a text against the historical and cultural frameworks we have inherited to read it against. To put it another way, readings simply provide consistent records of value systems as they are framed in a particular historical context. None of these records is an absolute truth, but each can be held accountable to one or more of those frameworks — to that of the text or that of the reader who uses the text for other purposes (professional or otherwise). They are never random. Moreover, the reader so engaged is involved not in "uncovering the text's truth" but rather in questioning the inviolability of one's own "natural" truth in a process of critical engagement that yields *a* truth (one that relates two discrete points in history, text and reader), not *the* truth; the reader produces results that document other readers' potential cultural choices and values without necessarily dictating them to others (as professional readers are wont to do).

To emphasize the act of reading a locus of culture rather than the authority of the critic, then, the case studies in *Austria and Other Margins* have been chosen as marginal cases: from Austrian literature as seen from the center of German culture and from situations where Anglophone culture meets the German-language cultural traditions. The texts chosen are by authors well known within their cultural spheres, occasionally less so outside them (or outside a small time window of more general visibility, such as that enjoyed by Doderer). All were not necessarily successes in their original context or since those times; the questions asked of each reach from a center in one academic sphere into another, more conventionally considered a margin to that first. These juxtapositions hope to highlight the importance of reading cultures *otherwise*, not just from one privileged set of margins or centers but in a dynamic, decentering way.

Notes

[1]"Post-colonial criticism" first grew out of English and French studies, when scholars turned to explore the relations among Anglophone and Francophone traditions within ex-colonies. "Marginalization" characterizes the positions in which intellectuals in such hybrid situations found themselves as representatives of neither an "indigenous" nor a "Western" tradition. Classic texts in the area are Edward W. Said's *Orientalism* and *Culture and Imperialism*; Gayatri Chakravorty Spivak's *In Other Worlds*, especially the essay "Subaltern Studies: Deconstructing Historiography" (197–221); bell hooks, *Feminist Theory*; Homi K. Bhabha, *The Location of Culture*, especially the essay "DissemiNation: Time, Narrative, and the Margins of the Modern Nation" (139–70); and Benedict Anderson, *Imagined Communities*. Other central names, such as Abdul R. JanMohammed, Chinua Achebe, Kwame Anthony Appiah, and Frantz Fanon, whose work is more representative to non-Western situations than those works just cited, are represented in Bill Ashcroft, Gareth Griffiths, and Helen Tiffin, eds., *The Post-Colonial Studies Reader*.

[2]The classic discussions on how national cultures were created in the nineteenth century by strategic rewritings of history are found in Eric Hobsbawm and Terence Ranger, eds., *The Invention of Tradition*.

[3]Gerald Graff, *Professing Literature*, offers an exemplary discussion on how English studies in the U. S. were modified in response to historical exigencies. For how the landscape of literary studies has changed in just over a decade, it is instructive to compare the two editions of Joseph Gibaldi, ed., *Introduction to Scholarship in*

Modern Languages and Literatures, put out by the Modern Language Association in 1981 and 1992. Each volume has chapters on major fields within the disciplines — an almost completely different map in each one. A similar point is made in Stephen Greenblatt and Giles Gunn, eds., *Redrawing the Boundaries*.

[4]Many such arguments reach the popular press, from the place of women's studies in the curriculum (highlighted at times in periodicals as diverse as *Atlantic* and *Mother Jones*) through the case of African-American studies at the City University of New York. Most recently (1995), David Remnick reported on the claims of television producer Steve Sohmer and scholar Mary Ann McGrail to priority in an intellectual property argument about the sources of *Hamlet* ("Hamlet in Hollywood").

[5]Perhaps the classic argument for cultural critics' acknowledging their links with general culture is made by Edward W. Said in his *The World, the Text, and the Critic*.

[6]In 1994 Harold Bloom attracted wide notice for trying to argue that critics should still have authority over that culture because of their ability to recognize and explain great literature; see *The Western Canon*.

[7]A historian and historiographer, Michel de Certeau, is particularly illuminating on how various cultures "reread" and offer new narratives of the "facts" about their historical situations. See particularly his *Heterologies* and *The Writing of History*.

[8]For a broad sampling of how such concepts are influencing literary and cultural studies today, see Lawrence Grossberg, Cary Nelson, and Paula A. Treichler, eds., *Cultural Studies*.

[9]The term "otherness" (or "the Other") is much in use in cultural studies today to indicate a member of a group other than that to which the speaker belongs, in a kind of defining dialectic of identity. The term was originally popularized by Jacques Lacan to refer to how an individual's ego is constructed. See *Écrits*, especially "The Signification of the Phallus" (281–91) and "The Mirror Stage as Formative of the Function of the I as Revealed in the Psychoanalytic Experience" (1–7).

[10]This position was, of course, also that of nineteenth-century hermeneutics. For an introduction to the problematics, see Kurt Mueller-Vollmer, ed., *The Hermeneutics Reader*.

Section I:

Literary Borrowings and Cultural Rewriting

1: *The Demons:*
Why Doderer Needs a Basement

Perhaps the greatest of Austria's postwar romanciers, Heimito von Doderer (1896–1966), had a career that was characterized by untimeliness. He had barely begun his breakthrough in the 1930s with *Ein Mord, den jeder begeht* (*Every Man a Murderer*, 1938); it was not his first work, but his first success. Within a very short time, however, his work proved unacceptable to the Third Reich's *Reichsschriftstellerkammer* (the Writer's Union, known as the RSK). In part, this may be due to the fact that his major theme was drawn from the Expressionists and from psychological theory of the 1920s: *Menschwerdung*, becoming human.[1] By the 1950s, however, works begun twenty years earlier were completed and established Doderer as a major voice in twentieth-century literature. Particularly two large novels, *The Strudelhof Steps* (1951) and *The Demons* (1956, begun as early as 1931), established Doderer, a historian by education, as a man who tried to tell "history in the form of [hi]stories" (Kramberg 391).

A joke told by Hans Weigel, an Austrian critic and cultural commentator, summarizes Doderer's reception as a modern novelist: "Doderer is writing a new novel. Its plot? Herr von X is crossing the Ringstraße. The first thousand pages are done already" (quoted in Weber, *HvD* [1987] 9). Doderer's style favors objective narration, yet eschews all causal connectedness in its meandering plots (Helen Wolff calls it "doderering," 379). This meandering is not an indication of lacking narrative control, since the novels were plotted carefully on extensive diagrammatic spreadsheets. In pride of accomplishment, Doderer responded to an English journalist who asked what differentiates Doderer's work from that of his compatriot, Musil: "I use [*sic*] to finish my novels" (Horowitz 13). Even Dietrich Weber, in his study of the structures of the complete novels, is forced to begin his chapter on *The Demons* by conceding: "The novel lacks a main theme, just as it does a main plot or a main character. To be sure, it has a main event (the burning of the Viennese Palace of Justice on 15 July 1927), but it by no means restricts itself to the representation of this field of events" (*HvD: Studien* 154). This dispersion is exemplary of Doderer's idea of "the total novel," not the collage or montage technique of Naturalist or Expressionist novels (such as *Berlin Alexanderplatz*); Doderer's works are based on an aesthetic of objectivity, a neorealism of its own sort.

Doderer believes that reality is created by individuals' apperception (or "resistance to apperception," *Apperzeptionsverweigerung*) of a reality that is much more diverse, circumstantial, and loosely connected than most narratives would have it. In a novel like *The Demons*, Doderer demonstrates how the public and private spheres interrelate in a recreation of a moment in history. True to his attempt to open and complicate a vision of reality that has been reduced by individuals' interpretations, Doderer's *Demons* focuses loosely around two figures who, in a moment of political turmoil and despair, establish themselves in parallel careers bridging their lives over the turmoil. Leonhard Kakabsa, a machinist who has taught himself Latin, is propelled by a typically random Doderer chain of events into an academic career as a private librarian for a prince. At the same time, a recently graduated historian, René Stangeler (Doderer's pseudonym for his own work written under the shadow of Nazi collaboration in 1946 and 1947), also finds a career: as a private librarian for a merchant who has inherited a castle with a peculiar library.

These two parallel lives will be the focus of this essay's investigation into "why Doderer needs a basement": to find out how Doderer really construes the interrelations between private lives and the political sphere, to assess how political his narrative really is. This will reveal the novel as a distinctive commentary on Nazism, as Doderer's attempt to describe world history as a psychological-cognitive construct. Doderer's ideas on history and the novel will first be sketched, then his personal situation, and finally the novel's characters, in order to find out what dimensions of political reality *The Demons* actually encompasses. Doderer's work simultaneously reflects and overcomes what Julia Kristeva called "the power of horror," the individual's need to preserve psychological orientation by falsifying the public domain.

Doderer and the Nazis

On 31 August 1939 Doderer wrote, "Yes, we had to sharpen up the abstractions and let their tracks run deep into us, in order to achieve a new form for our life. Now we have to get rid of the ghosts we called up" (Schmidt-Dengler, "HvD" 299). He was beginning his own inner revisionism that laid ground for his later apologetic stance about his wartime engagement: Nazis were the characteristic phenomenon of our time, but they "got away from us." Since the statement pointed the way toward a nominal "overcoming" of the Nazi experience (as revisionist history, stressing unknowing victimhood), Doderer's 1930s prose emerges again in the 1950s as a politically and personally viable artistic approach to twenty years of history. In publishing his great prose works of the 1950s, Doderer was not manufacturing a personal cover-up on the basis of hindsight, since he had already achieved a necessary psychological distance from the Nazi phenomenon while it happened.

Doderer's narrative revisionism was not exclusively a postwar undertaking. *Every Man a Murderer* reflects how constant revisionism was part of Doderer's whole approach to life, even in the 1930s. The hero unknowingly causes a murder, then runs up against its consequences years later. In reconstructing and recognizing his unknown deed, he becomes the agent of his own execution, administering his own punishment. This exemplifies how Doderer conceived direct and indirect guilt in a situation, which may explain his later reticence about his Nazi past — he had rethought his position personally, so he did not need to explain publicly. But the details of his life and Nazi engagement were not so easily put behind him,

Although the exact chronology of Doderer's Nazi party career is not ascertainable, its outlines are. He joined in April 1933 and seemed to become disillusioned quickly. His sister asserts that he left the party before the war broke out. The best possible chronology is that he stopped allowing himself to be carried as an active member in 1937 (one could apparently not leave the Austrian party officially); in 1941 he was excluded officially from the party. The reasons for his disillusionment are not clear: the standard interpretation is that he perceived the Nazis as enemies of culture (*ein Ungeist* [Horowitz 155]).

Wendelin Schmidt-Dengler puts another face on the matter in his discussion of Doderer's "retreat to language." As late as 1932, Doderer published pseudonymously for a left-oriented newspaper and wrote occasional historical pieces for larger daily papers (Schmidt-Dengler, "HvD" 292–93; Hesson, *Twentieth Century Odyssey*; Barker, "Heimito von Doderer and National Socialism"). These journalistic contacts were made, however, through his first wife, Gusti Hasterlik, the daughter of a Jewish doctor and Doderer's nominal fiancée for nine years before they married in 1930. Hesson believes that the failure of their relationship may have enhanced his anti-Semitism, which was directed primarily at the "Jewish press" (a common Austrian perspective). When they divorced in 1932, he lost these publishing contacts, which probably contributed to his decision to leave Vienna and go to Munich. According to Schmidt-Dengler, Doderer began to rework his aesthetics in light of Nazi racial politics (or perhaps his personal disillusionment and anti-Semitism). This phase is still evident in the national tone of *The Demons*: and in his working title for it: during its first major work period, 1930–36, Doderer called it *Die Dämonen der Ostmark*, using the Nazi name for Austria, and said its focus was the "Jewish world in the east of the German area [*Lebensraum*]" in a letter to Gerhard Aichinger of the RSK [Schmidt-Dengler, "HvD" 294]).

In private diaries, Doderer seemed to accept and then gradually withdraw from the Reich and its organizations, but he nonetheless maintained contact with individuals who, from today's viewpoint, were politically questionable. He even mentions his own "purity of blood" to Aichinger, which Schmidt-Dengler attributed to opportunism and to the addressee. However:

> I tried . . . to present the *theatrum judiacum* so to speak on *three levels*: on the level of family and erotic life, on the level of the press and the public sphere, and finally on the level of the economy, in the world of the big banks. (quoted in Schmidt-Dengler, "HvD" 295)

Doderer remained in contact with the RSK, but he reported on 27 August 1936 that its "giant bureaucratic machinery" depressed him (Schmidt-Dengler, "HvD" 295). The range of quasi-political writers or cultural organizations available in pre-*Anschluß* Austria would have made public engagement easy, but Doderer did not participate (see also Amann).

Ultimately the new German world he entered in 1936 Munich forced Doderer to withdraw inward: his letters, the themes of new works, and his diaries are telling either by their absence of commentary on the Nazi situation or in expressing his personal emptiness and loneliness. On 23 February 1937 he wrote about his surroundings: "the Bavarian population [the demographic term *Bevölkerung*, not the ideology-laden *Volk*] is divided into two parts, one smaller and one far larger. The first consists of those who are butchers by profession. The second, larger [consists] of those who only look that way" (quoted in Schmidt-Dengler, "HvD" 296). The lack of interest between Doderer and the RSK was mutual: Doderer could get permission to publish only his criminal novel, *Every Man a Murderer*, and not *The Demons.* Thereafter he seemed to lose interest in National Socialism: his rejection may have forced him into some inner distance from and outer respect for the previously scorned Austrian milieu. He couldn't follow the Nazi program, and they wouldn't follow him. Schmidt-Dengler expresses the essential distance between Doderer and the Nazis sympathetically:

> As paradoxical as it may sound, Doderer's unpolitical stance, especially his often crass misdiagnoses about the politics of the Nazis, protected him from falling so far into this *Weltanschauung* that the damage to his work would have been irreparable. At the same time, one may counter with the circumstance that they [the Nazis] didn't want this man, who had just about offered himself to National Socialism. What can be presented as Doderer's turn away from National Socialism, especially by pious hagiographers, is rather the many-layered product of a series of personal experiences, especially disillusionments, chance accidents (such as his publisher's contract and his difficulties in everyday life); only gradually does his critical insight set in against the Nazi regime. But even this [insight] was only acquired on a detour characteristic of Doderer: and this detour is the author's only achievement in the matter. He didn't go along with the recommended aesthetic programs, nor with the historical novel (whose central piece was to be a great, lonely hero), nor with earth-bound writing referring to the soil, nor with the war novel, nor with the panegyric praising the *Führer*'s personality . . . (Schmidt-Dengler, "HvD" 297)

Seen less sympathetically, Doderer was a *Mitläufer*, a fellow traveler, whose real stance was an ideology purportedly lacking ideology. As Doderer went along without open protest, he nonetheless continued to cite forbidden authors such as Jaspers. He returned to Austria in late 1938; by 1940 he had converted to Catholicism (Schmidt-Dengler, "HvD" 299).

When he became the elder statesman of Austrian letters after the war, the question of his political involvement remained unanswered publicly: he neither affirmed nor denied his involvement in the single greatest historical event of his day. His party membership may have cost him his chance at a Nobel Prize, and, as in the recent case of Paul de Man, it has led his later public to question the honesty of his artistic stance. But in Doderer's case, the lack of public comment need not lead to an automatic assumption that he had not assimilated the essential experience of his age.

Doderer's political ambivalence seems to have been reflected in the composition problems he had with *The Demons* since its characters (especially Stangeler, the historian) are partially autobiographical and its genesis encompassed the Nazi era (see Hesson). His source, Dostoyevsky's novel, correlated individuals' lives and history in a way that Doderer could not support in a narrative that spanned the Nazi era: Dostoyevsky dealt with politics, while Doderer was beginning to consider political or historical interpretation as secondary to lived experience. The divergences between Dostoyevsky's and Doderer's treatments clearly point to Doderer's growing conviction about the inadequacy of available narrative representations of history, particularly the history of his age. The comparisons between the two novels show Doderer's approach to a reproblematized history in narrative.

The Demons: Political Unrest

Doderer's *Demons* was conceived and begun in the 1930s, drawn from his reading of Dostoyevsky's work. It reconceptualizes the political sphere represented by Dostoyevsky's political radicals.[2] While Dostoyevsky drew on events in the Russian anarchist movement, Doderer transferred the setting to an Austrian event heralding the Nazi era in Austria (see Stieg): the worker's revolt of 15 July 1927. Where Dostoyevsky discussed planned unrest, Doderer's analysis of 1927 stressed that the revolt was probably spontaneous (generally confirmed by historians [Stieg 149]). Doderer's borrowing is colored by another source, Joris Karl Huysmann's *Là-Bas*, the story of a fifteenth-century child murderer, Gilles de Rais (Weber, *HvD: Studien* 205). Dostoyevsky's political demons are thus colored from the start of Doderer's adaptation into a new, more perverse "demonic" of his epoch. Instead of activism, Doderer shows how a blindness imposed by "ideologization" of the public sphere actually impedes psychic change (Weber, *HvD: Studien* 207); instead of politics, he'll show sexuality.

In general terms, the two novelists' stories are structured similarly in showing the emergence of "the demonic" in a period of political unrest; both focus on the intersection of middle-class and workers' lives in a general class realignment. In Dostoyevsky, the culmination of the work is the burning of a small town, attributed to radical anarchists; in Doderer, only the Viennese Parliament building is burned. Both events signify the end of a generation as that generation's essential character or demon emerges. Or, as Dostoyevsky's narrator phrases his personal view of a political tragedy:

> I have already hinted that all sorts of low-class individuals had made an appearance among us. In troubled times of uncertainty or transition all sorts of low individuals always appear everywhere. I am not talking about the so-called "progressives," who are always in a greater hurry than everyone else (that is their chief concern) and whose aims, though mostly absurd, are more or less definite. No, I am speaking only of the rabble. This rabble, which you will find in any society, usually rises to the surface in any period of transition, and is not only without any aim, but also without an inkling of an idea, merely expressing with all its strength unrest and impatience. And yet this rabble, without realizing it itself, almost always finds itself under the command of the small crowd of "progressives" . . . (459)

As we shall see, the "rabble" also rises as part of the demon of Doderer's age.

Dostoyevsky's demons are, though, less virulent and more personal than Doderer's: Dostoyevsky's Mrs. Stavrogin accuses Verkhovensky of being possessed by a "demon of irony" (197); and Dasha says to Stavrogin that he needs to be protected from his demon, which he calls "a nasty, scrofulous little devil with a cold in his head, one of the failures" (298). These demons are, in a certain sense, people who suddenly come into their own through the accident of chance opportunity; for good or ill, they show their essences in decisive action or inaction. Doderer reconceives the emergence of these demons as a moment when characters "become human" — a psychically much more serious change.[3] In each novel, one of these demons is a financial speculator; there is an older woman whose house builds the center of a salon; two younger couples try to solidify or break their relationships (Stangeler and Schlaggenberg; Stavrogin and Verkhovensky); a younger sister's fate is in the balance (Charlotte/Quapp or Lisa); and the tale is told by a chronicler, a "G--f" (Doderer's Geyrenhoff), who is peripherally involved. Despite these similarities, the narrator's position has shifted decisively between the novels. Dostoyevsky retains a degree of narrative control, while Doderer works against such overt direction of the narrative.

Doderer's demons are thus more than creations of the historical moment; they are also products of the false realities of individual apperception. In *The Strudelhof Steps*, Doderer has a character readapt a familiar quotation from Johann Strauss's *Fledermaus*: "Happy is he who does *not* forget." Doderer not only shows how characters emerge into the "real world"; his narrative dispersion stresses the gap between an individual's perception of the world and that world's realities — or even how an individual denies or "dodges" apperception (*Apperzeptionsverweigerung*).[4] Too often, Doderer feels, an individual organizes life around preconceived notions. Only if chance circumstance warrants is that individual forced to reconquer the outside world, to recapture the past by giving a retrospective meaning to a chain of previously unnoticed events. Yet again, even such an individual rereading of a chain of facts is only an apperception, not "real."

Any closed narrative, personal or historical, is automatically an ideologized fiction.

Dostoyevsky stresses that individuals do not see the overall pattern of their surroundings, but he believes that the author can relate history as sense instead of as an archive, as a narrative instead of as a pool of data for individual apperception. This assumption is anathema to Doderer: "Opinions are something like hemorrhoids of the spirit. Unfortunately, a writer also has opinions. But one does not constantly display such awful matters [in public]. Only building superintendents [*Hausmeister*] are always convinced of something or other" (*Dodererbuch* 353).[5] Doderer's writers are not supposed to have opinions (that is, a fixed narrative perspective), nor should they delude themselves that they are being objective: "Everything has two sides. But only when one recognizes that there are three sides does one grasp the matter" (*Dodererbuch* 354). In an aphorism under the title "Character-Demonology," Doderer identifies the error in having a fixed perspective: "Any person who realizes only his own character is demonic" (*Dodererbuch* 351). The writer must abandon his own stance, his birthright of assumed position: "The world breaks down into classes: from butchers to philosophy professors. The latter can't slaughter a calf, the former can't write a straight sentence. Only the writer holds them in proximity to each other: but only when he has given up his own birth class as beside the issue" (*Dodererbuch* 355).

Doderer thus believes that he has introduced his idea of historical diversity into the novel borrowed from Dostoyevsky. He does not seek to explain the genesis of an age's "demons"; he does not hold any political line in his narratives, although certain characters might. Instead, he shows how the demons of an age float among several streams of apperception that each might be designated "politics." By diversifying the reader's perceptions of "pseudological space" characterizing this historical moment ("Sexualität" 279), Doderer opens that space to the reader's reconceptualization of the political sphere depicted. Doderer's reconceptualization of Dostoyevsky's political world thus ultimately led to a new narrative style much less linear than that used in *Every Man A Murderer*. Dostoyevsky's narrator could still explain; Doderer eventually found that the questions of history could not be solved through the intrusion of a narrator who remained only peripherally affected by the demons of an age. When he found the narrative solution to his adaptation of *The Demons*, Doderer also found an approach to the Nazi era that allowed him to challenge his readers without explaining — through history, as a story.

Doderer's Narrator and History

Weber's 1963 study traces the genesis of Doderer's major works and provides the standard description of Doderer's theory of the novel, expanded in Hesson's 1982 study of the novel's origin. These expositions make it

clear that Doderer's novels were "writerly" (Roland Barthes's term [4]), intended for both the novelist and the critic to read and to dissect (*zerlegen*
[Weber, *HvD: Studien* 18]). I would argue that Doderer's self-identification
as a novelist supports a unique concept of history and shows how he intended to challenge (not perpetuate) inherited narrative norms.

Since realistic narrative presents historical flow and interconnections
rather than disjunction and scientific realism, Doderer describes himself as a
"naturalist," at least in technique. But this is not nineteenth-century naturalism (Weber, *HvD: Studien* 19):

> The world immediately surrounding us stands there so deeply and
> based on so much mystery that the most extravagant dreams seem like
> harmless, shallow things in comparison. This is my declaration of faith
> for naturalism and against romanticism, simply because I already find
> the former in the latter. (Weber, *HvD: Studien* 20)

Doderer's naturalism is based on modern theories of perception, not on a
belief in world process. For him, the world's objects are phenomena automatically subject to interpretation as they are perceived; the world in its reality is unseeable. The perceiver forms "concretions" out of individual phenomena, which then act as guideposts for individual action (concretion is
Doderer's term [Weber, *HvD: Studien* 21], echoing Ingarden's usage in phe-
nomenology). The unreachable "true" reality would have to unite an inner
and an outer world. This is impossible as a whole because an individual's
mind works in more restricted terms. Doderer terms the essential operation
of individual understanding "apperception," a productive activity in which
perceptions become objects of consciousness (Weber, *HvD: Studien* 22).
Unfortunately, as individual apperception continues, the concretions produced to orient and guide action also form a wall (what Doderer calls a
"second reality") between the individual and further perceptions
("Sexualität" 276).

Since understanding must be active, Doderer's ideal narrator is an
"essentially passive type" (Weber, *HvD: Studien* 23) who can suffer shocks
of recognition in recovering the past and the present and seeing more than
in the first experience. This ideal narrator will not prestructure reality for
readers, so they can use the narrative as their personal opportunity for apperception, not just to learn the narrator's point of view. Thus, as the novel
proceeds, both the narrator and the readers are subject to constant confusion about and reordering of apperceived "facts" as they try to put perceptions into language (*Sprachwerdung*, in parallel to *Menschwerdung*).[6] Apperception must be continual and tentative: the author "defends the
complexes and totality of life to the utmost, [and] . . . sits in the middle of
life and at the same time stands under the suspicion of having missed it
with his assertion that everything one sees exactly and exhaustively is all
beautiful" (Weber, *HvD: Studien* 25).

The narrator is therefore not supposed to present or transmit a world to
the reader. In actuality, he presents a monologue as data for the reader, ac-

companied by loose apperceptions that can even be second-guessed by the reader (Weber, *HvD: Studien* 25). Doderer's ideal novel thus has one form (by necessity, a linearity) and many contents — Doderer sticks to the plural of "content" (*Inhalt*). Its form offers a tentative structure subject to the reader's continuous rethinking — a "naturalist" reading strategy (Weber, *HvD: Studien* 29; Swales 371 ff.). Ultimately the writer must constantly strive "again to annihilate the composition — which enriches and structures itself continuously from the side of content — out of his inborn knowledge of the infinitude of the epic field, of the totality of life" (Weber, *HvD: Studien* 29).

For Doderer, then, the author has to overcome his own autobiography and the linearity of the narrator (Düsing 194) to force a series of associations for either the reader or a character in the novel: "*Interpretation* cannot be the function of an author! We'll leave that to Musil. Representation [*Darstellung*], though, must overcome its object, it must be more [than the object], *it must cast it into the dust!*" (Doderer, "Auszüge" 5). The artist only produces a work, not its interpretation; similarly, the storyteller is just a teller and shower, not an interpreter (Bachem, *HvD* 27 ff., for example).

While other modern novelists stress the active reader (Joyce) or the unreliable narrator (Musil, Borges, Fuentes), Doderer's position is unique because he believes that what applies to the artist should also apply to the historian. Like a narrator, a historian automatically becomes an ideologue if the history produced has a coherent narrative perspective or posited chain of cause and effect. At this point, the questions of narrative and history converge around a central problem of his life, art, and reception: why are most of Doderer's works set in the 1920s and 1930s and narrated from the 1950s point of view, while ignoring arguably the greatest historical phenomenon of the twentieth century, the Nazi era? As a historian by training, Doderer could not have ignored "historical continuity"; yet as a novelist, he refused to explain its facts. Instead, he reintroduces day-to-day experience into the abstract analyses of history, trying to follow his narrative imperative and pluralize the contents of concrete reality. Doderer the historian does not see history as causal or explanatory; he sees it as descriptive or representational.[7]

Both as an author and as a historian, then, Doderer does not feel empowered to "explain" the facts of the Nazi era. Such "explanations" are just intellectual shorthand that would block rethinkings of the era. But despite critics' assertions, *The Demons* does not avoid the Nazi era — it merely sets it in a bigger historical context of events leading up to and following from it. Doderer guides his readers into that era by showing the purportedly parallel lives of two historian-librarians, Leonhard Kakabsa and René Stangeler. The resulting narrative, however, is not a history but a chronicle: the narrator Geyrenhoff is so reliably unreliable that his narrative cannot possibly sustain being considered historical "explanation." *The Demons*, then, is intended to be more than a *commentary* on the Nazi era in Austria (or its "explanation" or "excuse"); it is intended to provoke readers to reopen the question about how that era emerged.

Nonparallel Realities: Historians and History

The Demons demonstrates all Doderer's objections to historical truth's being revealed in narrative determinism. Instead of tracing the politics of anarchism in a small town, Doderer diffuses politics among the experiences of a small group whose lives are intertwined against the confusing panorama of Vienna. Two of these lives barely intersect, but they run suggestively parallel: Leonhard Kakabsa and René Stangeler start from very different places but end up under the patronage of the rich, as historian-librarians whose lives reflect on their practice of history.

As the story begins, in November 1926, Stangeler is thirty (49), has finished the studies as a historian that he began in *The Strudelhof Steps* and is working more or less independently at the historical institute at the university (that is, he is unemployed in the bourgeois sense). He needs a position so that he can marry his love, Grete Siebenschein (98).[8] As Stangeler waits for a real academic appointment, he dabbles in the history community, hoping for a job in those days of scarce academic employment. This is, then, Doderer's alter ego, his historian *in nuce* who may have the vocation but not the profession.

The second major historian in *The Demons* finds his profession as historian before he finds his vocation, living a life that intersects Stangeler's at odd moments. Leonhard Kakabsa is introduced as "the tool and dye maker" from a strap-weaving factory. Initially his destiny is "to smell things" (121): he is portrayed as almost an animal who learns by smell, part of the "fauna of the bar" (*Gesamtfauna des Lokals*) in a working-class neighborhood (131). But one day Kakabsa outgrows his milieu spontaneously when he saves a girl falling off a ladder into an open bookstore window (140). By discovering the bookseller, the girl's father, he inadvertently discovers books. This discovery leads to Kakabsa's "becoming human" (*Menschwerdung*), his particular internal change. Kakabsa buys a Latin grammar (the high school standard) from the bookstore girl, Malva, who is enamored with him (152). He doesn't really know why, but once he has the book, he begins to engage it actively: to ask questions to understand the introduction, to buy a mythology reference book and a dictionary. This change is physical as well as mental: he designates a table as his desk and outfits it with bookends. "Leonhard, however, did not become conscious of the fact that he was riding around, mounted on words, in front of the portals of the spirit: already, therefore, on the only and correct vehicle by means of which one can pass through those gates" (160). After a period of contact with the bookseller, Leonhard begins to speak differently. One day he begins a sentence with a rhetorical gambit — "one must prove . . ." (161–

62) — and so he becomes aware that he is actually thinking differently, not just speaking differently to fit in with his new friends. Leonhard is a proto-historian who has become engaged with the work long before he knows what it implies.

Kakabsa meets two high school girls, Trix K. and Fella Storch, whose mother is ill, and is invited to the Storch house, where he meets the "troupe" (Stangeler's circle). Eventually he ascertains that he is reading the "right books" to keep his learning on the right track, as he begins to study with them and discovers that his Latin is better than theirs (524). Kakabsa also finds out that Latin is only the start — there is Greek, too (525 ff.). He only gradually becomes aware that his vocation has a social impact: he is disgruntled when he is identified as a "self-improver" (*Fortbilder* [529]; he hated the word [567]). This awareness forces him to rethink his old hatred of a schoolroom because his Latin grammar and change in the present have nothing to do with that past, repressive environment. Finally, a nightmare signals a decisive change in his thinking:

> And, in that, he recognized that he now began to think in a new lan-
> guage. Not Latin. But differently than before, in his native language. . . .
> His inner language stood at the threshold of outer [language] . . . , a
> decisive act which one could designate as nothing less than that cross-
> ing of the dialect barrier with which (at least in the center of Europe)
> every real life of the spirit begins . . . (531–32)

Shortly thereafter, he meets a group of worker-terrorists in the Burgenland and joins them when they plan an uprising in Stinkenbrunn; he becomes a spectator of a weird triangle involving sex and socialism (555). He recognizes how far he has come, on the one hand: "The authenticity of a movement of intellect is tested best through a material counterweight" (581). His vocation has decisively emerged through his inner change, but he still does not achieve a profession: Kakabsa still exists in a demimonde between would-be terrorists and a prostitute, Amy Gräven. The terrorist's self-designated "Republican Guard" (621) marched, got involved in a riot, and was mostly decimated. The remnants of the group were to be brought to trial in Vienna; this trial caused the civil unrest leading to the fire at the Palace of Justice (623–24).

Kakabsa's road to his profession and his real social stake is chance. Out of piety for his new friends, he has acquired a black suit so that he can visit properly (648), especially his friend Fella's apartment, where he meets her visiting Aunt, Mary K. (a heroine of *The Strudelhof Steps*). At one of Mary's gatherings, Kakabsa meets Stangeler, a "real historian." Afterwards, Stangeler has Mary K. give him a copy of Otto Weininger's *Sex and Character*, which "didn't hit as intended" (655). Stangeler probably intended to provoke him with this book's racist and sexist thinking (maybe even to insult him as lower class). What Kakabsa actually learned from it was that he could read real Latin texts, at least the Latin of Pico della Mirandola, an excerpt in Weininger's text (658–59). After his discovery, he went to the university library for the first time and learned how to use reference materials systematically (661–62). Stangeler's random shot thus backfires decisively: Kakabsa learns that Latin can be used for specific purposes (even social ones, as he discovers when he plays a game writing a Latin drinking song the next time he is at Mary's apartment [675]).

Leonhard's life takes an interesting twist that draws his life even closer to Stangeler's and to the profession of history (the chapter is entitled "A Short Curve"). He meets Karl Zeitler, a police officer interested in local history, and helps him translate some medieval documents (987). Since he uses library reference materials, he falls into a pattern of meeting Stangeler in the university library and walking him home in the twilight (988). One evening they go to see Grete, and Leonhard finds he actually is already connected to the "troupe": Grete lives in Mary's house, where he is a regular. His friend Zeitler is another connection, since he was the officer on duty in 1925 when Mary lost her leg in a tram accident (991–92).

After Leonhard becomes a regular in this set, his vocation begins to become a profession. With the Stangelers at a party with the troupe, Mary and Leonhard meet the Prince Alfons Croix, who feels them all out psychologically (1105). Stangeler feels Croix is a model of "clarity" (*Deutlichlichkeit* [1106]). Croix does not return the compliment, since he is specifically looking for someone who isn't bourgeois to educate as a future employee of his private archives — someone who doesn't "reek of general education," as Stangeler does. Croix recognizes the worker in Kakabsa (1108) and so offers him a job as personal librarian, including room, board, a stipend, and the chance to study, even as far as a doctorate (1110–11). Leonhard at first protests because he doesn't want to be untrue to himself or his trade (1111). Croix convinces him that accepting the job is not a compromise because it isn't calculated: accepting a chance offer does not mean you lose your freedom. "In the interim . . . Leonhard was already loosening couplings in the mechanics of his external life, stopped their merry-go-round and got off" (1113). After a few final difficulties, he is able to bid farewell to his district, his friends, and parts of his possessions to "cross the Rubicon" (1116–18). He has joined a profession, although its consequences are not yet clear to him.

René Stangeler's *Menschwerdung* happens while Kakabsa's does, and it is also tied up with his role as a historian — but with his profession, not his vocation. His "becoming human" is thus almost a parody of Leonhard's; it is no accident that Stangeler's historical institute originally smells oily to Leonhard (203). Early in the novel, Stangeler's fiancée Grete doubts his motivation about her and his work and so has thrown him out of his borrowed workroom in her parents' apartment. To drag him out of his depression about his apparent breakup, his richer friend Schlaggenberg drags him to a party with Geyrenhoff's troupe (another *Fledermaus* reference?). There Stangeler meets Schlaggenberg's sister, Quapp, and enters into a chain of events that make his eventual profession and life converge. At the party he meets Jan Herzka, the businessman who will inherit a castle with a library

in Stangeler's research field, witch trials of the seventeenth century (442 ff.);
he will ultimately become Stangeler's employer. Moreover, Stangeler's display of eloquence begins to patch up Grete's opinion of him, a gradual
cure that will culminate in her triumphant "He's really *not* stupid" four hundred pages later, when he negotiates a good employment contract (811).

The physical center of the book, a chapter called "The Trapdoor" (*Die
Falltür*), outlines the change in Stangeler's life, his "becoming human." On
16 May, the merchant Jan Herzka inherits Schloß Neudegg in Carinthia, an
unexpected bequest through his mother's family. Neudegg has been held
by the same family since the fourteenth century; as a Baronin Neudegg,
Herzka's mother was a cousin of the dead owner (678–79). Herzka does
not know how to sort out the purportedly valuable library, but he does remember the witch stories Stangeler had told (egged on by his own female
fantasies [683]), so he hires him on very good financial terms (688–93).

"Stangeler's ponderous, but not unmotivatedly functioning, intellect had
now completed the connection between Saturday's topic of conversation
(in which Jan Herzka had seemed to have strong interest) and the impending trip" (694). He goes back to his library carrel and gives up the
Merovingian documents he has been working on. René packs his bag and
explains his luck to his family, who think he has proved himself qualified
instead of only lucky (699). By 17 May, Herzka and Stangeler reach the
castle, scan the library holdings, and find the dungeons under the place
(743–44). In the process, they also uncover Quapp von Schlaggenberg's
parentage: Levielle, the financial manipulator, is her father, and another
Neudegg is her mother (718).

The library is a stunning assemblage of rare old volumes on demonol-
ogy, satanism, witch-hunts, and the like. A 1517 document about witch trials in the castle explains the dungeon and its Marquis de Sade peepholes.
They find the spyhole for the torturer in a hidden room after René reads
the document through to Herzka (744–48) on the day before the anniversary (19 May) of its writing (736–37). For this section of the novel, Doderer
has faked a long manuscript in early new high German, describing a no-
blemen's hunt that turns into a witch trial and a voyeur's orgy (757–93).
Herzka is naturally delighted to see a historical reflection of some favorite
perverse notions about women and so decides to keep the castle's collection intact and augment it in the future.

They leave for home on the castle document's anniversary, when history and sexuality converge in Herzka's and Stangeler's lives. Stangeler tells
Grete Siebenschein about his adventures, concluding with his job offer as
librarian, custodian, and acquisitions editor for Herzka's library (809). This
position will, of course, include buying trips to London, which pleases her
no end (810). When Stangeler signs his contract, he becomes a changed
person; his personal "becoming human" is "the mysterious chemical transformation of convictions into characteristics" (812). "He now had his occupation [*Praxis*]" (820). A celebratory walk leads him back to Dr. Dwight

Williams and Emmy Drobila, who can arrange an American publication for his work on witches (823).

Gradually Stangeler's life gets more complicated. He spends time in the library transcribing and researching the castle manuscript (1015). Too, he is caught between scientific respectability and a desire to profit from his discovery. He has an offer to publish it in the Library of Sexual Science (1016), which he declines, hoping for a sale to Harvard University. Later he ends up selling it to what is basically a scientific pornography firm in the United States, but he maintains his self-image of scientific dignity by requiring that the text be kept in German (1195). Rehearsing his sales pitch, he reiterates a philosophy about reality that approximates Doderer's. The library's owner, the medieval pornography collector, is very modern:

> Because something arose in him that our time has mastered: a second reality. It is erected next to the first, factual one, and [that is done] through ideologies. Mr. Achaz' reality was a sexual one: mature women, virtuous widows, crimes against his virtue, and so forth . . . . Mr. Achaz was an ideologue simply because he stretched out his hands towards experiences which can only — be bestowed. All ideologues do that . . . . a first-rate reality, no spirit world, just about like the constructed and arranged sexuality of Mr. Achaz. He had a program. (1021–22)

Achaz's "demon" overcame him and turned into a full worldview (*Weltanschauung* [1023]), which his relative Herzka inherits with the castle and library. This worldview has become Stangeler's livelihood, a choice which is publicly sanctioned when Grete visits the castle, her future husband's workplace (1051).

As the novel ends, Doderer (following his purported symphonic structure for its composition) not only draws his two historians back together (their vocations and their professions) but also inserts them into what is conventionally called history, to juxtapose their lives with reality — exposing to the reader the gaps in their professions, their ideologized "second realities" which aid their blindness about outside information. On the day the Palace of Justice burns, the troupe is invited to a garden party, where Lasch confronts Levielle about capital speculation, a sign of impending financial doom (1132). Or, as Doderer summarizes this moment in history: "Constellations explode and disperse themselves" (1152). Other members of the troupe are engaged in their own activities as its members hear the shots that turn a worker's demonstration bloody (1243–44). In a hotel, René is discussing his manuscript with his potential publisher and sees the demonstration as a threat to his personal treasure in his briefcase (1251). Quapp's car runs into a roadblock while she is trying to leave town, and her potential fiancé extricates her with his diplomatic credentials (1260 ff.). Geyrenhoff smells the building burn and sees the "felled trees" of lampposts from his window (1273). When René comes out of his hotel meeting, he wants to call Grete but can't because of the public works strike. Out of the historic moment, he retains only a jealousy about the privilege of Harvard professors and their easy lives (1316). Oblivious to the world, he returns to Grete's apartment as her family's hero.

The fire finds Leonhard in the prince's library; he becomes aware that something is wrong only when there is no heat, light, or phone; even that he only learns indirectly, through a servant's report (1216). He reacts out of concern for his new responsibilities, out of his new "second reality": he is in the (rich) Third District and is supposed to go and reserve some books in the university library for the prince. On his way there, his new life briefly converges with his old when he sees a workers' demonstration crossing the Ringstraße. Kakabsa's instinctual act is evidence that he has, indeed, crossed the dialect boundary: he saves the university by getting the custodians to lock the doors before they see the demonstration approaching (1226). He only wants to save the books, the "treasures" (1227): "This day was rich in so-called 'instinctual acts'" (1225). But Leonhard finds this day memorable only because it has disturbed his first chance to spend many continuous hours in the library (he has always just had one hour to himself, squeezed in between work and closing time): "[The sudden] . . . sense of the whole last period of his life almost struck Leonhard down. To him, it was as if the [library reading] room had become more heavily weighed down at the place where he sat; yes, as if his chair were sinking a bit into the floor" (1229). His new life has decisively displaced his old.

Leonhard finds out what is actually going on only when he goes to lunch at the buffet in the university (1287–88). Yet he has begun to evaluate all the facts from his new perspective; for him, the demonstration is a sign that the mob lacks intelligence (1290): "He did not believe that the electrical workers wanted to storm the [university] portals out of hate for intelligence [the intelligentsia? — deliberately ambiguous in German]. But that he understood absolutely nothing of this: that made him downcast" (1290). The narrator insinuates that Stangeler would have understood this situation, but "[l]ocked in, [Leonhard] remained closed out of everything that happened outside" (1291).

When Kakabsa is finally let out a back door and sees the fire (1306), he runs into his two worker friends, Niki and Karl, who plead: "Lead us out of this, Leo, we cain't [*sic*] take seeing no more of this. The scum [rabble, *Ruass*] is loose, all the scum from the Prater. Ya don't see a single worker any more" (1308). Leonhard, with the authority of the lettered but no real sense of the moment, manages to lead them out, finding his policeman friend's body in the process (1308). They carry the body out of the demonstration (1310) but part ways at Mary's house. He leaves them to enter her apartment and kiss her feet: through the shock of the day, Mary and Leonhard find each other as potential lovers, their future course purportedly determined (1322). Leonhard will spend his summer vacation in the Semmering mountain resort, near Mary (1334). When last we see him, long after that day, he has climbed the local mountain (literally), where the "light of God" enters into his heart (1335).

This is a 1930s human apotheosis, and, for the incautious reader, the end of the story. But it is not: their tale ends, but historical and institutional "facts" continue until the chronicle ends, in the 1950s. One story is over, but not the novel's reflection on history.

During the conflagration, both Kakabsa and Stangeler find their professions, one by leaving his milieu and the other by placating his fiancée with promises of Harvard professorial respectability (1193 ff.). Doderer has thus indeed shown how the demons come out then, the evil demons of the mob and the internal demon/genius of individuals. But which of these historians has "become human" with his demons? Possibly neither, since they both have entered the ideological space of distinct professional identities and established personal histories removed from the outside world. Each crystallizes (concretizes?) into a profession and life ideology, a fixed position and trajectory that make them lose their ability to resist history (we will be able to posit "how they'll behave under the Nazis" even though that is omitted from the book).

Stangeler is a member of the educated middle classes fighting to establish himself in a social position. He wishes to marry well, to have the purported ease of an academic lifestyle, and to enjoy general social respect as a "Herr Professor Doktor." What changes in his moment of "becoming human" is that his greed and social cunning awake: he learns how to write a contract with an employer who needs him, to sneak in perquisites, to impress his wife-to-be and his in-laws, to hold out for academic prestige (in this case, for Harvard University Press), and to be jealous of his seniors. His wife supports his social aspirations, not his work; she is complicit in holding out for the spouse who can insure that she'll be a "Frau Professor Doktor" with a chance to travel. This history has turned two lost young people into a couple of experienced social climbers.

Kakabsa's demon is more problematic: he is in the trades; his sister is a maid; he speaks dialect and has no particular social aspirations outside his neighborhood. He is a respected workman; his landlady likes him (a major accomplishment in Vienna [see McInnes, "Doderer versus Hausmeister"]); he is clean, decent, loyal, hardworking, and gifted with machinery. When he begins to be educated, he shares: he uses his Latin to help his policeman friend with local history. He has overcome a class boundary with his new language, his job, and his love for Mary K., but he leaves behind the simple piety of his landlady and his coffeehouse friends. Ultimately his Latin studies and history teach him that knowledge has a social function. He does not, however, tie knowledge to social power: he does not understand why workers would want to attack the university library. Such an act violates his class' traditional deference toward knowledge and order; the ideology of his class is still at odds with the ideology of his profession.

The reader is tempted to read these stories in terms of conventional class litanies. Kakabsa is a Horatio Alger story: a man who by virtue of his innate abilities has transcended his station. Stangeler is definitely middle-class, trying to "settle down" at a time when his profession is at a low; he attributes his success only to connections, vindicating his social sense of self. He has a shadow doppelgänger at the Institute for History, another young historian, named Neuberg (he is Jewish; see Hesson 25). Neuberg was trying to marry a commercial heiress; such a marriage would secure his social future while allowing him to pursue history (the nineteenth-century way of becoming a scholar [1017]). He is flabbergasted when he ends up with a job on the Monumenta Germaniae, a long-term medieval manuscript publishing project: "Since he had no connections whatsoever, he was thus forced to acknowledge that only his professional qualifications could have decided this issue" (1303). His realization also comes as he sees the flames from the Palace of Justice in the distance.

The contrast between Neuberg and Stangeler identifies the dilemma of the middle class: the pre-First-World-War system of protection and influence is diminishing in importance, but a meritocracy has not yet clearly replaced it. Jobs do not necessarily relate to ability or effort; luck and looks initially seem more important. These two historians, like Kakabsa, are subject to the random fates of 1920s Austria. But more significantly, the reader sees that there are historians with no sense of history, historians who do not try to pierce the complexity of history or the "great events" of their day. Perhaps their collective behavior reflects Doderer's point that great moments become great only in retrospect. These historians are not empowered to narrative, they are archivists, editors, and librarians — collectors and disseminators of purported facts. Doderer identifies their psychological need to make sense of their lives as narratives, but each lives an ideology he has not identified.

The complexity of this novel as historical representation is, however, not exhausted with these platitudes about the limitations of historians (whose vocations as historians yield professions as librarians, a significant distinction). What about Geyrenhoff, the chronicler? His narrative slips between the events of 1927 and those of 1955, when he wrote his chronicles, looking back to an age when he was "happy/fortunate" (*ein Glücklicher* [1337]). Until the last few pages, it has been easy for the reader to overlook that *The Demons* is a retrospective narrative. Suddenly the narrative falls into an enormous gap in history, between a reconstructed 1927 and 1955, the year the Republic of Austria was reestablished. Doderer's philosophy of history dismisses the need to trace causality in history, but Geyrenhoff leaves a hole in his narrative that leads the reader beyond the characters' blind desire for sense.

In light of what the narrative gap encompasses (the Nazi era), it is easy to say that Doderer was "covering up" for Austria. None of the events and few of the characters he depicts have been overtly political (and "party politics" are totally absent); nothing is proto-Nazi, and 1927 Austria encompasses only particular lives, not European history. Why, then, does *The Demons* play on these historically significant dates without exploiting their suggestiveness, and why does Geyrenhoff's chronicle make its gap so painfully obvious?

Why Doderer Needs a Basement

The answer to this question lies in Doderer's idea of false realities: the fact that people want a continuity or false reality to guide their lives. The gap in Doderer's narrative thus serves two distinct psychological purposes for the reader: the first is educational, the second, adaptive.

The gap in Geyrenhoff's chronology educates the reader indirectly. Doderer attempts to restore the historical specificity of an era by avoiding its historical myths, piercing the "pseudological space, that has become habitual, already drawn into one's psychic bookkeeping, organized" ("Sexualität" 282). However, Doderer realizes that there is no private space isolated from an ideologized political or social sphere (even if only unconsciously ideologized). He realizes that just showing the diversity of history, removed from its tendentious politics or interpretations, is impossible: even the private lives of characters are steeped in the social power transactions that a particular culture values. Although these power relations are unnamed, *The Demons* reflects them for readers familiar with the era, purportedly as subservient to individuals' "truths." Nonetheless, they reveal what Klaus Amann refers to as the "characteristic of political culture then: a very high degree of the ideologization of all realms of life" (133).

For example, the novel turns on the deeply entrenched class structure of 1927 Vienna, based on nineteenth-century notions about birth, ability, and position. On the most superficial level, these distinctions are shown as polite behavior. Kakabsa is almost universally deferent to the upper-class world, showing a deeply inculcated sense of where he does and does not belong. Doderer's narrator falls into this prejudice by portraying Kakabsa as distinctive in identifying people and places through smell, almost like a dog that keeps its quarters neat and hoards its toys. Stangeler's gift copy of Weininger's *Sex and Character* only confirms the narrator's tacit assumption that the upper classes are essentially different from the workers. The working classes are complicit: Kakabsa becomes a "Herr Doktor" to all the porters just because he uses the university library, and his former coworkers assume he knows what's going on in a political revolution because he can speak Latin. At the same time, the true upper classes (the aristocracy of birth, as opposed to the acquired nobility of the commercial classes) are utterly set apart from Geyrenhoff. Prince Croix moves through a different universe from the essentially middle-class world of the novel, although he can give his friends parties and pull strings (like *Fledermaus*'s Prince Orlofsky). Levielle, the fiscal speculator who brings them to ruin, has probably emerged from lower social status, and so also remains an outsider. These people are victims of an impassive social structure, in which parentage and inheritance are all that matters (for example, Quapp).

This class structure is also buttressed through an economic identification. As the demonstration leading to the fire collapses, Leonhard's friend Niki says that the workers are no longer involved or in control because the "scum from the Prater" (*die Ruass*) is loose. This rabble seems to be the unwashed unemployed, perhaps even street people in the modern sense. But the workers are trained to identify them as "other," as alien to their lives; they do not realize that they are but a paycheck away from that situation. And despite the fact that interwar Austria was characterized by a huge inflation rate and great unemployment, all Doderer shows is a pair of unemployed academics (Stangeler and Neuberg) searching for the right connections to get their jobs.

The middle classes in this story tacitly rely on investments and commercial money but attempt to hide that fact. Old money is based on land and property; that old money willingly turns to financial consultants when they require new-style economic managers. When the Holzbank collapses, it is because Levielle encouraged capitalism in its crudest new form, speculation (this parallels an actual bank collapse). The losers feel that their money disappeared because Levielle was dishonest; they do not question the whole investment system (borrowing and margins, which increase capital artificially and which were to culminate in the 1929–30 world collapse). Their gains and losses are also psychologically tied to their social stature, not to labor or honest work.

Just as class structure is tacitly rendered by Doderer, so are politics, in an interesting cross between politics and race relations. When politics emerge, these politics belong to the non-Germans (Hungarians, Serbo-Croatians, and other Slavs), not the German middle classes. Doderer's non-Germans are involved in terrorism and political publishing, yet they are evaluated by the troupe only in terms of their behavior. The reconfiguration of Central Europe after the First World War and the Austro-Hungarian Empire successor states are suggested by embassies in Vienna, but for the novel's characters, their ambassadors are still considered part of the Austrian social structure, not foreigners. They show, in general, no sense that lives changed at all after 1918 or 1938. Similarly, Geyrenhoff ignores the occupation and politics up to 1955, when the state treaty was reinstituted and Austria was restored as a republic. That Doderer referred to these social-historical facts without attempting to explain (concretize or ideologize) these facts may serve to educate the reader into seeing consequences of everyday behavior in historical retrospect: when not presented with a closed narrative, they may more easily recreate the ignored "facts" of 1927.

Doderer may have intended a second, psychological dimension to the gap in Geyrenhoff's chronicle: "The total state is nothing but the concatenation of innumerable pseudological spaces and their consolidation into a single, incredibly thick-walled [space], the consequence of which is the inexpressibility of all enclosed within it . . . the total state is consolidated denial of apperception [*Apperzeptionsverweigerung*], and thus a second reality" ("Sexualität" 293). By accepting a closed narrative, the characters have adapted to a situation beyond their capacity to comprehend or express. That individuals in this space (here, the novel) reject certain perceptions has an even worse consequence: "[to deny apperception] is to annihilate that which can no longer be perceived" (283). That is, ignorance is not bliss; it exacts a cost from those involved.

The cost is indicated in the novel by aberrant sexuality, which Doderer's essay identifies as the best example of the way that even private life is ideologized. Geyrenhoff reflects this aberration without confronting it: he cannot put a good face on Schlaggenberg's "Dicke Damen" fetish, and his reaction to the basement of Castle Neudegg focuses only on Quapp's parentage (social legitimacy). Sexual fetishes, inappropriate liaisons, the double standard, and a prostitute (naturally, with a good heart) inhabit this novel as a correlative to a disturbing but unfocused political reality (see Hesson 85 ff.). Even Stangeler's career-making witchcraft document is sexual perversion taken as history, resembling Schlaggenberg's fetish. Again, however, Doderer has inserted into the narrative more than Geyrenhoff confronts. While Herzka's manuscript relates the unholy practices leading to a witch trial and torture, it also confronts the abridgment of civil rights in face of the droit du seigneur, an abuse of the power of law over individual citizens. The witch trial is thus an early political cover-up, implicating retainers in an illegal use of power. After the event, they were bought off so that the appearance of a legal witch trial would be upheld (the details of the trial are historically adequate; for a brief history of the real Austrian witch-hunts of the period, see Evans 400 ff.).

Doderer forges this document, perhaps to emphasize the distance between novelist and historian. His chroniclers report on a collection of individuals interacting in chance situations, hiding historical realities behind perversions. The fictional Ruodlip von der Vläntsch describes his role in a witch-hunt in terms of his relationship to his lord; Geyrenhoff discusses the era only as embodies in a group of his friends. Ruodlip diffuses the emotional power of the legal experience into sexual threat and voyeurism; Schlaggenberg ignores his deteriorating social identity by cataloging his "Fat Ladies" as social, sexual, and anthropological types; is Herzka hiding the realities of the Nazis behind his "legitimate" collection? The veneer of their respective societies remains intact, while the sexual is left as purportedly free space for the individual. For Ruodlip, sexuality is confined to the basement, to an unseen unconscious into which individuals are forced against their will. Like Geyrenhoff's, his "history" is a chronicle of experienced data, not including the institutions, power, and social inertia/prestige reinforced by a repressive, inadequate class structure. The perverse sexuality of Ruodlip's testimony points to distinct power problems in that world — to the inadequacy of a description of history focused around the individual, accounting for the aura of personal power but not its structural source. He is behind the thick wall of Doderer's false reality.

In contrast to Ruodlip or Geyrenhoff, Doderer is honest enough to have included such a break in his narrative by adding his basement to his castle — quite literally, a peephole through a wall. His narrative reflects that, for most, Hitler was not a fact in 1927; by 1955 the Geyrenhoffs of Vienna had rewritten his existence in terms of their personal losses. But according to his own theory of history, Doderer is not necessarily acting in bad faith about the question of war guilt. The facts his characters refuse to see are behind a wall for them, but ·Doderer creates a psychological basement in his narrative to accommodate the emotional overflow of this era for the reader. Geyrenhoff dismisses this basement as a personal aberration, but there are psychologically more important interpretations for the gap in *The Demons,* an irreparable break in world meaning, showing the inexpressibility of the Nazi era.

Julia Kristeva, in *Powers of Horror: An Essay on Abjection,* confronts the issue of writers identified as Nazi sympathizers (dealing specifically with Céline) in a way applicable to Doderer's case. Her route includes a brief discussion of Dostoyevsky's *Possessed (Demons),* as a representative of what she terms "the abject," those "violent, dark revolts of being, directed against a threat that seems to emanate from an exorbitant outside or inside, ejected beyond the scope of the possible, the tolerable, and thinkable. It lies there, quite close, but it cannot be assimilated" (1). While an individual ego has its personal repression, its superego is characterized by this abject, which resists available representation as an ideology: "A 'something' that I do not recognize as a thing. A weight of meaninglessness, about which there is nothing insignificant, and which crushes me. On the edge of non-existence and hallucination, of a reality that, if I acknowledge it, annihilates me. There, abject and abjection are my safeguards. The primers of my culture" (2).

Kristeva's abject is thus what a culture repudiates, denies, or excludes from possible consideration, a level of repression beyond the individual unconscious: "a nonassimilable alien, a monster, a tumor, a cancer that the listening devices of the unconscious do not hear" (11). The abject causes the collapse of the individual's ego-construct and a return to primal being, to the authenticity of body and desire that cultural identification suppresses; it also causes terror — the "power of horror" that shatters societal judgment (15) and softens the superego (16). Doderer's characters and his narrator, Geyrenhoff, resist this authenticity; Ruodlip's basement acknowledges the terror of what the more modern culture does not acknowledge.[9]

When an author writes such moments of radical loss of meaning (and each will do so differently), he is sublimating abjection (Kristeva 26), substituting language for lost meaning in an attempt to reestablish the orientation of the person and his desires. As a nihilist and collaborationist, Céline reaches this point to fascinate us with the power of horror, the experience that is being denied (208): in Kristeva's version, there is an "essential struggle that a writer (man or woman) has to engage in with what he calls demonic only to call attention to it as the inseparable obverse of his very being, of the other (sex) that torments and possesses him" (208). Kristeva's abject expresses Céline's demons, which Doderer attempts to overcome in part by having a basement, an apocalypse (209), a return of the culturally repressed, a purported felling of the thick wall between an ideologized worldview and the facts of reality.

Conclusion: An Alternate Approach
to the Nazi Experience

Doderer's Geyrenhoff writes in 1955 to remember when he was "happy"; he joins his compatriots in denying his Nazi past, pointing only to his happy marriage. Yet he closes by acknowledging that he is sustaining a meaning that no longer exists, that he cannot stop time: "In these moments, I felt as if I would never see her [Quapp] or anyone else from the group again in this life, as they stood there with raised arms and waving hankies on the otherwise nearly empty train platform" (1345). As a consequence of his choice, Geyrenhoff has moved away from his current world and into a mansard atelier that had belonged to Schlaggenberg. He is dispossessed from the reality of 1955: his home by marriage, the Palace Ruthmayr, was destroyed in the war, and his wife died, probably before the war ("Her heart would not serve" [1337]).

In returning to his abandoned chronicle, Geyrenhoff has written himself close to an understanding of the gap in his own consciousness, to what lies beyond the wall of his apperception: "Thus ended for us this day, which, by the way, meant the Cannae of Austrian freedom. But no one knew that then, and we least of all" (1328).[10] Geyrenhoff, however, cannot bring himself to admit the total collapse of meaning of his world; he cannot face his personal guilt (mainly sins of omission by the silent) or the political situation in Austria that contributed to Nazism, cannot face the almost thirty years missing from his own narrative. His old pseudological space is disintegrating, but no new one has arisen to supplant it. He is lost conceptually, ideologically, geographically, and historically.

This conclusion to the book is, to be sure, underplayed, but it is not enough to consider this simply a psychological approach to history that Doderer uses to foreclose any further analysis of a difficult era in history.[11] This is not just a self-apology for possible collaboration, anchored in a self-serving theory of the novel. Kristeva offers another perspective on Geyrenhoff's experience, as Doderer took pains to delineate it: the Nazi experience has to his day (and perhaps not to ours) not achieved an objective correlative in language or history. Geyrenhoff, as a typical Austrian of his day, cannot face directly the abject of his culture, the places where its meaning broke down and allowed the Nazi demons to emerge (as part of it, as its internalized Other, the part of itself it denies or refuses to see as possible). As an author, Doderer cannot "explain" the guilt of Geyrenhoff or any other character without just erecting another ideological wall reducing the implications of the situation for each individual reader.

Instead of explaining, Doderer's historical narrative provokes by including an oblique reference to its own cultural unconscious. As Kristeva indicated, this cultural unconscious lacks a safe reference and so intrudes in the form of "horror," in Ruodlip's witch-hunt of perverse sexuality. Ruodlip does not deny his complicity in a perverse act that has aspects of politics and sexuality. Yet at the same time, Ruodlip, like Doderer, tacitly admits his later unwillingness to confront the oppressors: he writes his narrative to confess to later generations, not to communicate with his contemporaries or to charge his superiors with the abuse of power that would challenge the entire sociopolitical system of his day. Kristeva suggests the psychological validity of this stance (that it was not a pose). Ruodlip may have had a perverse enjoyment of his experience, but he knew it was not "right" on some level. Nonetheless, he did not wish to (or could not) confront the implications of his experience for his constructed worldview. Such a revisionist view of hegemony is often beyond the agency of an individual to effect; unless the perception is a shared perception, it will not be perceived. Those involved in a situation have a psychological need to protect themselves, so they can be driven as far as writing a confession. Yet they remain part of their false realities, retaining an ideological indebtedness to the constellation of the moment, no matter its inadequacy. Ruodlip may have been protecting his life in the face of a demented magnate; Kakabsa and Stangeler found their professions by remaining in a distinct ideological net, behind a wall that limited their apperception of reality. They therefore all have become complicit with the abuses of their epoch — they pass the moment in which refutation or course change is still possible and sell their freedom of agency to integrate into a sociopolitical system, even while denying a deep engagement with politics. This history and psychology of everyday life are, then, highly charged with horrors covertly tied to politics.

Doderer's history is purportedly a chronicle, a collection made without an overt ideology. Yet Geyrenhoff, the chronicler, admits that he has become a participant in the affairs of his troupe. When Geyrenhoff's situation is juxtaposed with Ruodlip's, the reader is led not only to analogize modernity with the Middle Ages but also to question the ethic hidden under the notion of historical causality. Doderer does not directly discuss "the truth" of the Nazi era, but he has opened up a reconsideration of its origins and its consequences by showing how everyday life correlates with historical truths.

In this sense, then, Doderer is a political writer of the Nazi era, more than just a meanderer or a proponent of "inner immigration." He allows the reader to see how individuals became involved with the Nazi spirit of the age, willingly or unwillingly, knowingly or unknowingly. But he is not forgiving or excusing their espousal of pseudological worlds — that is not the writer's (or the historians') task, in Doderer's opinion. His real task can be seen as highly political while not overtly politicized: he reestablished the links between sociopolitical structures and personal ethics or lives. Like Geyrenhoff, the individual is precluded by the "power of horror" to meditate on the Nazi era. But through the agency of the open narrative, which provides contexts for individual actions instead of explanations, Doderer reopens the Nazi question without answering it. This narrative, then, is highly political in a group-psychological sense: he is unconcerned with the stance of a particular individual or within an ideological construct but wishes to show the preconditions for various members of a group to be willingly made part of an everyday ideology that will ultimately lead them to their destruction. The truth about the public sphere, in Doderer's opinion, is psychological, not intellectual; "inner immigration" is a reaction, not an action; "history" is a result of false explanation, not of "historical process" or necessity.

Doderer thus stands apart from his contemporaries in his concept of the public sphere and of naturalism. He retains the power of a historical novel conceived on a scale that could recreate a world or explain a historical revolution, as Dostoyevsky had done, but changes its referent. Doderer's historians do not reflect or reflect on historical process, nor are they essentially imperiled by it. They and their contemporaries refuse to see, to consider any larger-scale implications of their actions; they are the willing agents for chaos because they refuse to realize that their personal lives have public consequences. Unlike the Expressionists, who portrayed how humanity was corrupted by society, Doderer shows how society and history are the results of a thousand individual acts, none of which can actually be considered a "cause" of the greater patterns that historians later purport to find. Seen this way, *The Demons* is definitely neither a modern novel nor a conventional historical novel: it is a political novel exposing the politics of everyday life and of self-identity.

Notes

[1] He is usually associated with the Austrian Expressionist painter and writer Albert Paris Gütersloh; his psychological theories are purportedly drawn from Hermann Swoboda.

[2] For the best description of the borrowing, see Horowitz 173 ff.; Weber, *HvD: Studien*, part 4; Weber, *HvD: Studien* 56 ff.; and Turner, *Doderer and the Politics of Marriage* 93 ff.

[3] Again, *Menschwerdung*; see Turner for an overview of recent work on *The Demons*.

[4] This treatment of characters may be based on Doderer's reading of Swoboda's psychology; see Düsing 182 ff. for an exact description of the interlinking of the perceptions that is to occur; see also Swales 372.

[5] All citations from Doderer have been translated by the present author. *The Demons* was translated by Richard and Clara Winston in 1961; the pagination in the 1993 reprint edition of that translation (Los Angeles: Sun & Moon Press, 1993) is always within five pages of the original German edition, to which I am referring here.

[6] For a discussion, see particularly Ivor Ivask 345 and Düsing 177 ff.

[7] This is not the interpretation of history offered in Symington, who, however, is arguing for a reinterpretation of Doderer's philosophy of history, not necessarily arguing historiography, as is being done here. Doderer's position would resemble that of Michel de Certeau, particularly in *The Writing of History.*

[8]His marital situation is a foil to that of another character from *The Strudelhof Steps*, Kajetan von Schlaggenberg, who is breaking up with his wife, Camy, and is showing a "fat women" fetish (82 ff.). As will be addressed later in the present discussion, Doderer explicitly ties sexuality and history together; see also "Sexualität und totaler Staat."

[9]For Kristeva, Dostoyevsky's *Demons* has the abject as its topic: "[I]t is the aim and motive of an existence whose meaning is lost in absolute degradation because it absolutely rejected the moral limit (a social, religious, familial, and individual one) as absolute" (18). As the fire burns, the egos involved lose their correlates and go into ecstasy at the very moment that human meaning is destroyed; it is a "collapse of paternal laws" (20) and a return to an identification with the mother's body as a possible reestablishing of a lost object of desire — a search for a new social role and ego security. The "return to the maternal" is a return to the first social construct of desire: that is, the child's ego finds its first outside correlate or mirror or transitional object in the person of the mother. Kristeva here draws on D. W. Winnicott and object-relations theory to propose an alternate construct of personal identity: while children use such objects to gradually build up their ego images, their desires are not necessarily fixated on a mother image but on whatever may satisfy these ego desires (which, in the present culture, usually is the mother).

[10]See also Symington for his interpretation of the "Cannae" reference; see Le Rider, "Variations," for his take on the *Anschluß* as a similar moment of political change.

[11]This is a very conventional strategy used to dismiss Doderer's work as a typical apologia for his purported Nazi collaboration: "The psychological implications of the historical situation, its relevance for the individual, interested [Doderer] more than the significance of the historical event as part of the historical process. Doderer did not see the task of the novelist as being to present a catalogue of facts. This is the task of the historian. The writer is not concerned with history in the abstract but with its relevance to everyday life" (Hesson 90).

Hans Eichner, in "Heimito von Doderer," finds this approach to Doderer completely unacceptable, in that it makes Doderer a paradigm for a too comfortable reading of the Nazi period for Austrians.

2: Mozart:
A Case Study in Logocentric Repression

Introduction

In speaking of Freud's work, Jacques Derrida creates a cultural concept analogous to that of personal psychological repression: logocentric repression.[1] While repression in the individual refers to the psyche's ability to retain experiences in the unconscious that have been suppressed from the conscious mind, Derrida's logocentric repression refers not to the psyche of an individual but to the patterns of conceptualization of cultures as representatives of groups of humans. His coinage refers, then, to a tension between the meanings that humans find in their (conscious and unconscious) worldviews and the meanings that are obscured by those worldviews and thus "deferred" from consideration. Mozart's genius is a sign that enables him to transcend class boundaries (Mörike) or create new values (Hildesheimer). Moreover, it can render its own earlier incarnations irrelevant to the text at hand (Shaffer). Shaffer's Salieri, the man of inferior talents, literally represses the public appearance of Mozart as genius. This repressed set of meanings is thus "deferred," put off, and considered extraneous to the unrepressed and consciously constituted systems of meaning.

In making this distinction between present meanings and absences with their traces, Derrida provides a definition of "difference" as "the pre-opening of the ontic-ontological difference" (*Freud* 198) — as the function of a meaning system projecting not only a set of acceptable meaning structures (its ontological facet) but also an inherent model of the Being of the world (its ontic facet, its innate concept of the structure of reality). This difference is a deferring action, a pressure by meanings present in the system on those that are seemingly absent but that in actuality have been forcibly closed out. Each element within a cultural meaning structure will, in consequence, correlate to a culturally relative locus of meaning as "a non-origin which is originary" (*Freud* 203), reflecting a cultural conscious as well as the unconscious, absent or deferred meanings that have left their traces on the system. When a culture sets up its characteristic differences, it will not only identify its worldview in a set of constituted relative meanings but will also necessarily prescribe boundaries to the meanings potentially acceptable to that system. These differences thus function as posited realities with an inherent ontic status that correlates to the ontology of the meaning structures assumed by their generating cultures. Such posited realities assume the status of ontic truths for their cultures as the points of genesis for the truths of their cultural-historical realities. Derrida's inherent program will stress, though, that each of these ontic-ontological meaning structures is in itself only a false reality that does not necessarily reflect an absolute truth.

Derrida's model of difference is formulated around notions of cultural signs and cultural meanings. The concept of sign and sign system embedded in this cultural model may be expanded and applied to other cultural data. Such an application would focus on the meaning systems in which signs function and on the ontic and ontological correlates of the present and absent or deferred meanings. More specifically, the logic of "difference" might be used to create a case study in logocentric repression — a study in the formation of loci of Being, of presences and absences within meaning systems — in several ways: (1) in explorations of the boundary values and generating premises of particular systems, as Derrida does in *Of Grammatology*; (2) in considerations of the systematic inclusionary-exclusionary pairs that systems allow, as Foucault does in *Madness and Civilization* or *The Order of Things*; or (3) in an examination of the systems that form around particular signs to see what is repressed in their formation, as Derrida illustrates in essays in *Writing and Difference*.

The present discussion will use the third option to trace the sign "Mozart" as the generating locus for a case study of the mutations of signs within meaning systems — the Mozart of Eduard Mörike's 1855 *Mozart auf der Reise nach Prag* ("Mozart on the Journey to Prague"), Wolfgang Hildesheimer's 1977–79 biographical *Mozart*, and Peter Shaffer's 1981 *Amadeus*. In each instance, the sign as the generating locus of meaning will be considered in order to exemplify three phases in the mutation of a cultural sign as the representatives of repressions in each of their eras. The results will trace the deferred meanings of each system to show the applicability of "difference" and its associated concepts to diachronic analyses.

Genius Deferred: Mörike

Eduard Mörike's *Mozart* is a sign in the cultural locus of the mid-nineteenth century, a sign whose creator is affiliated with the writers of the German Biedermeier. These authors found themselves between the Romanticism of the turn of the century and the Realism of the latter nineteenth century; born in the decades immediately surrounding 1800, the major authors of this period — Mörike, Franz Grillparzer, Annette von Droste-Hülshoff, and Adalbert Stifter[2] — were caught in the conservatism and repression of the Europe that resulted from the Congress of Vienna in 1814, as well as the supposed bourgeois revolutions of 1848. All in their prose were beginning to reject the fantastic imaginative literature of the Romantic movement and turn toward Realism: that is, to the class structure of their day, which in Austria and Germany implied the first rudiments of an educated middle class of civil servants, the latter phases in the development of the landed gentry (usually their decline), and the beginnings of an appreciation of the lower classes as a workforce, albeit in somewhat paternalistic form. They did not, as a group, take part in the activity surrounding 1848, although they individually supported various reforms (particularly Stifter, in his work in school reform) and rights for the emerging middle and lower classes. Yet they themselves reflect the education of their own generation. They look toward the benevolence and potential role for the nobility, to their religious backgrounds (although they were not necessarily believers), to the ever-increasing prominence of the cities over the country, and to a tacit support of a Romantic or Hegelian notion of world history — that change was inevitable but out of the control of the individual.

Eduard Mörike's *Mozart* is a creature of 1855, intended to be a "small portrait" (*Kleines Gemälde* [*Mozart* 80]) by its series title and a novella by its subtitle. Such a designation sets up the locus of the audience's reactions and expectations: a piece that will be part of the nineteenth-century convention of the "feuilleton," the literary essay (in this case of a subtype "conversations with famous people"). Yet for the reader of 1855, such a locus is somewhat spurious since that genre should apply to a contemporary and to contemporary mores and personality types. The primary tension between "portrait" and "conversation," between fictional novella and potentially realistic feuilleton, continues throughout the work to make a figure out of the past seem contemporary for the reader. Mörike's correspondence indicates that he was consciously filling a journalistic absence in addressing such a piece to the public on the event of Mozart's 100th birthday — "the first of its kind, as far as I know" (letter to Cotta, 6 May 1855 [*Mozart* 80]).

Mörike's novella as a system of meaning was therefore a conscious product of the author's stance vis-à-vis his cultural milieu. The interpreter of this meaning system, in following Derrida's desiderata for delineations of logocentric repression, must then begin to isolate the significant signs on which the text is built, in order that the repressed or deferred meanings be uncovered. For Mörike, the questions of genre and the audience as a social bellwether for the piece remained central, just as they prefaced the whole.

Because Mörike highlights a juxtaposition of genres, the system's first "difference" is that of the variance between historical periods: the personality of Mozart remains viable as a "real person" to the readers of Mörike's age, while certain of the stage settings (coach styles, dress styles, modes of entertainment) are consciously marked as outmoded. This assumption of continuity of essential humanity tacitly conditions the formulation of other central tensions in the work and forms the bridge over the historical periods. Mörike's primary cultural text is thus a depiction of the "essentially human" as illustrated in a matrix of practical and impractical behaviors of the characters involved. These at first seem to the reader to be the individual characteristics of Konstanze and Mozart, but they are ultimately tied to the inclusionary and exclusionary social expectations of class distinctions that have shifted between the time in which the novella was set and that in which it was written.

The first scenes of the work, in setting up the boundaries of the matrix of individual behavior, present a picture of Mozart and his wife Konstanze as a married couple plagued with financial troubles. In 1787 they are on the way to Prague for the premiere of *Don Giovanni*, but in a borrowed coach and with an obvious need to penny-pinch: "a full bottle of real 'Rosée d'Aurore' [cologne] emptied out to the bottom! I saved it like gold," is Konstanze's first lament (4). The trait to be juxtaposed with this is one of Mozart's — his unconcern with such matters, shown in his translating material need into spiritual capital: the spilled cologne lifted their spirits; "the whole coach seemed immediately cooled" (5), allowing them to enjoy the Indian summer day despite its heat. This pair of traits (pragmatic versus impractical, or practical manager versus dreamer) runs through each reported pseudoconversation of the pair in the text.

Yet Mörike is the feuilletonist as well as the fictionalist: he not only delineates the characteristic tension within the structure that interprets Mozart's personality but also weights it for his readers:

> Here the painful observation is prematurely forced upon us that this unbelievably receptive person, receptive to each stimulus of the world and to the highest an intuiting disposition can achieve, did indeed lack a constant and purely satisfied sense of self for his whole life, no matter how much he experienced, enjoyed, and produced out of himself in his short span. (8)

The rest of the author's first excursus extends this evaluation that Mozart lacked constancy and a sense of his own role. Mozart attended parties, which he needed to amuse his genius and rest his mind but through which he fell into financial hardship and eventually undermined his health — he also had to work hard giving lessons and conducting rehearsals, without ever earning enough money for his basic household needs (11). Equally damaging, in Mörike's eyes, was Mozart's innate lack of pragmatism, which led him to be frustrated by bad students, to be used by enemies in the theater, and to lend money out of the goodness of his heart to a series of deadbeats without thinking of the consequences.

The reinforcement to this authorial excursus evaluating the juxtaposition of characteristics establishes the novella as a series of scenes, each of which contrasts Konstanze and Mozart: Konstanze discusses the contractual and financial details of the production of *Giovanni* as well as Mozart's career potential away from Vienna and "the cursed, poisonous, yellow-black [the colors of bile and the Habsburg flag] Salieri" (18). In so doing, she fantasizes about their possible life in Berlin as a court composer and his wife — a life that would definitely be "living up to their proper status in society," complete with garden, coach, and imperial audiences. Here again, the pragmatic is shown to the reader as preferable — it would bring the tangible rewards of position in society and domestic comfort that the middle-class reader of 1855 would find desirable. Moreover, the pragmatic is further identified with middle-class domestic virtues and respectability, while the impractical is characterized as essential to the flagrancy of the upper classes. A quiet house and garden provide an ideal work atmosphere; the court is only a strenuous social tribute to be exacted of the composer who wishes to live quietly.

The second juxtaposition introduced by Mörike is contained in the narrative material about the orange tree and the aristocratic family Mozart is brought into contact with when he accidentally plucks its fruit. This juxtaposition is an inclusion/exclusion of class surrounding the person of the artist; it shows the reader how the impractical Mozart himself will look practical when his behavior is compared to that of the upper classes — Mörike's social hierarchy of values transposed into tensions of practical or impractical lifestyles and what they include or exclude for people, beyond their original definitions.

To the aristocratic household, Mozart is an enigma: the gardener who finds him as an intruder and marauder in the orangery cannot quite identify his position since his clothing is not of first quality (Mozart is wearing traveling clothes; Konstanze has carefully preserved the better garments for the receptions in Prague — excluding social appearances for traveling, including financial considerations appropriate to the middle class, even for an artist). Yet his demeanor is definitely that of a person of upper-class society, appropriate to a Mozart who had grown up visiting the courts of Europe. The liveried servant reports to his master: "I don't think he's right in the head; he's also very proud [*hochmütig*]" (24). The Count, on hearing about an anonymous "Moser" (the servant's mispronunciation), assumes he is a vagabond. When other members of the family properly identify "Mozart" and explain who he is, the dubious aristocrat retains traces of his original attitude: "Well, if that's true — and I'm taking you [his wife] at your word — we'll want to show the odd fellow [*Querkopf*] all possible honor" (25). His formal welcome to Mozart then turns into a game, giving the impression of utter familiarity with Mozart's person and status ("You are so little a stranger to us that I can say that the name Mozart can hardly be mentioned elsewhere as often and with more enthusiasm" [26]). Mozart has thus been included into the heights of the social hierarchy on the basis of his disposition, yet the possibility of exclusion because of his personal appearance and circumstances remains.

After this introduction, the implications of inclusion into or exclusion from the aristocratic class are explored by the author through a series of Mozart's actions and anecdotes. Each shows the values present in the expectations of members of particular classes and suggests which values they exclude from their purviews. Mozart, for example, admires the piano playing of the young bride Eugenie: "straightforward, unadorned and warm, indeed so complete" (28), showing the musician's personal taste for the natural and simple. The author demonstrates that Mozart's valuing of simplicity is not included in the disposition of the aristocratic audience by commenting that it is they who are privileged to enjoy the presence of the artist's person: "the unending satisfaction which lies in the unmediated contact

with the person of the artist and with his genius within the confines of familiar domestic walls" (29). They exclude his sense of nature within their
walls while including the decorative aspects of his person.

As a counterpoise image from the aristocratic sphere, Mozart describes a
mythological pageant he had seen while a youth in Italy, showing the full
grace and decorative sincerity of the entertainments of a high rococo court.
Mörike embellishes these beauties by adding a noble genealogy to the tale
of the tree that brought Mozart into the house — this orange tree adds a
historical dimension to the advantages of aristocracy: it originally belonged
to Mme. de Sevigny and has been preserved in the family for generations
(42). The party ends in an opera finale toast to Mozart: "Such pure charm
[*reines Entzücken*] . . . at the pinnacle of convivial [*gesellig*] enjoyment" (49).
Thus despite Mozart's initial insistence on the value of simplicity and the
author's insistence on aristocratic domesticity, the high life and decorative
existences led by the upper classes with their wealth still present enjoyment
to Mozart's soul, regardless of his liking for simplicity.

Konstanze again brings out the contrast: the simple life of the middle
classes and their definition of domesticity. She tells the women of the party
a series of anecdotes about Mozart as a simple man: about his experiments
with exercise using a proper gentleman's walking stick (a middle-class or-
nament intended for the use of someone on foot) and his establishment of
domestic tranquillity for a young couple whose marriage was inhibited by
financial woes and impediments to the man's career. A rake and sundry
household items were the trophies Mozart brought back from this adventure. Konstanze's story is tailored to her audience to include the virtues of
the artist's spirit while excluding the middle-class milieu in which the tale
originated.

Mozart had actually been wandering through the streets of Vienna because he and Konstanze had fought over a flirtatious student (who was
trying to entice Mozart — Konstanze assured herself it was the girl's fault).
The household gifts were peace offerings, not souvenirs. In this mood, Mozart would love to set up a simple household in the country and become a
farmer with his Konstanze. Yet while Mozart was able to aid the young
couple, he could not help himself. Mörike adds that Haydn had hoped at
this time that his Esterhazy patrons would set up regular financial support
to ease Mozart's position. But nothing was to come of it because of Mozart's impracticality — he did not pursue the introduction. After her anecdotes, Konstanze offers her countess-hostess one of the items as a personal
memory — a gift that will be repaid in kind by their host, since he will give
them a coach and horses of their own. The pragmatic Konstanze again
knows how to play her audience for financial gain. She must, moreover,
play by the rules of the upper classes — she is playing for patronage here,
not for middle-class domesticity. Both she and Mozart, then, know the exclusionary social roles to which they are subject: domesticity and middle-
class ills are excluded from the upper class's perception of the artist.

These scenes show the essence of the juxtaposition of aristocracy and middle class, the second tension around which the novella's structure of meaning is built. Middle class simplicity and respectability are contrasted with aristocratic mores and with the necessity of aristocratic patronage to keep the artist alive. The person of Mozart as artist is caught in a dichotomy between his affinities and thus between classes. He feels spiritually in tune with the grace of the nobility and with the simplicity of nature and the servant and craftsman classes in touch with it; yet at the same time, he needs to affiliate upward in order to survive financially. He can only call up the influence of patronage to save the young couple; he cannot move freely within the system, even though his disposition spans its poles. Because he is both included and excluded, he cannot act freely to save himself.

Beyond these two evaluations of social structure that Mörike provides, the third tension in the novella's structure of meaning characterizes Mozart as genius — as creator. The first element of evidence for this role is Mozart's explanation that the sight of the orange tree had evoked a memory of a mythological pageant, which in turn allowed his mind the free play necessary to remember the melodies that had vaguely been running through his head for the peasant wedding scene he needed for his opera (37–38). Yet here again, Mörike has not provided a pure description of creativity. Mozart recognizes that his temporary insensibility to class has resulted in an offense that must be atoned for in socially acceptable terms: this noble house is celebrating a wedding, so the damage he has caused might be mended by a gift of music. This purportedly creative response is thus initiated by an innate fear of the wrath of the upper classes; even their gardener, who had caught him, had "a face like iron . . . If the servant looked like that, I thought, how could His Grace himself look?" (39; an anticipation of the apparition of *Don Giovanni*). Mozart's creativity, then, has pragmatic initiating circumstances and may be disturbed by potential enemies — the real ones, such as the nobility with whom such as Mozart might not be able to deal, as well as (in this case spurious) artistic ones, such as Salieri, the court composer of the Habsburgs, called in jest "Monsieur Bonbonnière" by a Mozart who cannot take him seriously (48).

In contrast to these physical or practical limits on his creativity, Mörike provides evidence of the boundlessness of Mozart's musical imagination. During the performance which shows Mozart in "a condition unendingly different from our relationships" (65), Konstanze says that her husband still has something secret in his pocket — the ending of *Don Giovanni*, the writing of which had delayed their trip to the Esterhazys in Eisenstadt and jeopardized the patronage that Haydn had arranged. The author again intrudes to evaluate the pair of characteristics of genius, limits and boundlessness, emphasizing that Mozart's music is a door to "that beyond our senses [*übersinnliche*]" (68) and an "uncontained power of nature" with "blind greatness" (69). Mozart confirms this description for the reader by reporting on the feelings that drove him to stay up all night and finish his score: a sense that God had given him a ripe fruit — a finished melody —

which he had to record in case he should die overnight and not be able to complete his task:

> [I]f in the long or short run, another was given your opera to finish — maybe even a Frenchman — and he found everything all cleanly or- ganized from the introduction to No. 17, with the exception of one piece, all ripe fruits dropped into high grass that only needed to be gathered; and if he found there, unhoped for, that considerable stum- bling block already removed to such a degree, that he might laugh through his teeth! He might be tempted to betray me for the honor. But he'd burn his fingers on it; there would be a small band of good friends who know my mark and would honestly assure me of what is mine. (70)

This tension between the boundlessness of the creator and his prag- matic limits are reached in Mörike's conclusion to the work: hospitality and the breath of the spirit (*Geistesodem* and *Gastfreundlichkeit*) form a contrast that will make the artist "too much for this earth" (73–74) and will neces- sarily lead to the premature death of such a one as Mozart — a death ex- ploited to dramatic effect in Eugenie's fears and in the folk ballad she un- covers that closes the work, "Think thereon, O my soul" ("Denk es, o Seele").

Mozart auf der Reise nach Prag is thus a structure of meaning revealing a cultural text predicated on the three tensions already outlined: practi- cal/impractical, middle class/upper class, and limits/boundlessness. The structure of meaning underlying the novella is constructed by means of components of whole stories traditional to the ontology of the sign "Mozart" and weighted by the author using the discourse space given to Mozart himself, to his partners in conversations (especially Konstanze), and to authorial commentary. This structure within its double genre frame thus generates a cultural text with greater implications than that of the typical feuilleton: a text that reflects the tripartite class tensions of the day — the tenuous position of the middle classes (the couple who cannot get married, or Mozart and Konstanze's own inability to set up an independent life in the country), the disintegration of the nobility, and the insecurity of the newer educated classes of the nineteenth century. The count, for example, admires the "grand style, the familiar emperor's style, the inimitable, for which I have always admired the Josephs and the Fredrichs," which he himself lacks because he has many social doubts (30). In contrast to this clear predilection is the predicament of the educated classes (like Mozart, a new spiritual nobility) who have affinities split between the two poles. Each system excludes the other, with the educated class needing both the upper and lower classes to survive in the new world. Such a system is re- flective not of the eighteenth century, which the author purports to charac- terize, but rather of the post-Restoration Europe of the mid-nineteenth century: in Foucault's terms, a product of this later *episteme*.

What is deferred or closed out in this meaning structure; what traces of unanswered or unaddressed problems remain? Since the locus of this text's origin in class structure in two centuries is a sign whose reference is one of the greatest composers of all times, the deferred question is one of genius and art itself: how it could actively relate to the class system, and not how it is limited, as Mörike has shown. The final poem of the novella contains the most explicit traces of this unfulfilled discussion: the genius as shoes on a horse throwing sparks, with a perspective on both the woods and the garden — an entity representing a "loose element" in the system that perturbs its customary distinctions and spans the range from nature to culture that is so central to the eighteenth century but bound to pass away with the development of the nineteenth. Such a description of genius as a world force again does not discuss the effects the genius may have on the social system. Had Mörike done so, he would have introduced a projection of potential *change* into the tripartite logic structure of essentially static description on which the work is built — to suggest which of the three tensions would ultimately become dominant as the social-historical situation changed. Thus the text that seems to question the position of the artist with respect to the upper classes actually is excluding or deferring the larger question of social change in the nineteenth century — a central motif in Biedermeier art. The dual time frame of the novella therefore serves to obscure the effects of the revolutions of 1848 and to defer the 1855 reality of the ascent of the middle classes.[3]

Mörike, then, accepted the propriety of his chosen genre and audience and did not address the issue of genius in other than the terms of society versus nature: changing this choice would necessarily require a discussion of Mozart as social innovator, not as a class-bound creature, or perhaps even as an artistic or social rebel. The presence of the social structure as the overriding anchor for the structure of meaning of the cultural text underlying the novella thus requires a concomitant absence: the absence of a consideration of the nature of art in the world, or of the genius as innovator who can overcome social expectations. That potential meaning in the novella is left as a trace, an element held constant as the assumption that allows Mörike's consideration of Mozart as a valuable cultural sign for two centuries but remains in itself incommensurate to a social discussion. The ultimate sign of the genius in the eighteenth century, the figure of Mozart as creator, is thus transformed in the nineteenth century to the sign of the social victim, deferring the question of what genius mediates to the world that traps him.

Genius Deconstructed: Hildesheimer

The second historical locus in which a "Mozart-sign" of note emerged was the world of Germany after the Second World War. Wolfgang Hildesheimer chose to begin work on *Mozart* in 1956 — after spending the war years in

England and Palestine and returning to Germany to be an interpreter for the Nuremberg Trials. Such an experience was typical for his generation — the notion of having to return to his country or to reintegrate the German war experience into the international scene unknown in Germany. He, like his more famous contemporaries Günter Grass and Heinrich Böll, had to both "catch up" on the English modernists (Joyce, Hemingway) and French Absurd or Existentialist literature (Beckett, Ionesco) as well as forge a modernist style in the German language.[4] Moreover, in order to create an international literature for Germany, a literary scene and market had to be created that was under German writers' control even during the Allied Occupation. The collective of publishers, critics, publicists, and writers known as Group 47 filled this need, with public meetings at least yearly, press coverage, readings, and prizes, all of which introduced a new generation of writers to the international scene as well as reintegrating those writers who had been in exile or "underground" during the Nazi period.[5] The effect of such a group on the international public dovetailed with the occupation policy of the Western Powers: the establishment of "business as usual" and the reintegration of Germany into the West through an "overcoming" of the Nazi past (often mainly a declaration that it was no longer relevant). The literature that resulted from this context acknowledges the psychic and physical work that was needed to rebuild Germany yet tends to underplay the explicit history of the immediate past.[6] The literary norm in which an author of the postwar generation found himself was one stressing the individual and the value of individual experience in the face of mass culture and history — not the value of analyses of larger patterns of culture or history. In a figure such as Mozart, then, Hildesheimer's episteme will almost demand to be represented by an individual rather than a historical constellation.

Wolfgang Hildesheimer treated Mozart at least four times over a period extending from 1956 to the book-length biography of 1977–79. Yet the novelty of Hildesheimer's work is his methodological foreword, in which he warns his readers that he will not be giving them a standard biography — his Mozart is not the hero-genius of popular and romanticized legend but rather a fleeting image who has offered virtually endless material for popularizers and purveyors of popular culture (even of "high" culture), who have, however, never been able to present a biography that gave a sense of their object. Their work has rather served only to display their own prejudices and cherished self-projections, so it only represents "a notable example of the eternally failing" ("ein augenfälliges Beispiel des ewig Scheiternden" [Hildesheimer 7]).

Hildesheimer thus is fully cognizant that he is working in a cultural sign when he approaches the figure of Mozart. To be sure, the inordinately rich potentials that such a sign offers to the biographer or historian constitute its attractiveness to both scholar and reader. Yet as a sign, it represents a facade of reality at best, which will not be adequate to the Being of Mozart who left so little direct evidence of his person or personality. The role of the new biographer of Mozart is thus one of a virtual deconstructionist, pointing up the limits and inadequacies of the extant variants of the Mozart sign which serve as the loci of cultural meaning for his predecessors:

> an answer to a challenge, an experiment in the restoration, in the cleaning of a fresco which has been painted over many times in the course of the centuries. The restorer does not proceed systematically, but rather helps piece by piece, always at that point where a flake of earlier layers begins to loosen itself. That is not always easy, because the fragility of the picture stands mostly in contrast to the durability of the materials with which it is painted over. (7–8)

This author is thus attempting to deconstruct the various facades of pseudo-meaning that have been erected around the sign Mozart in order to explore the potentials of the trace, to see the breadth of interpretation to which this sign can be subjected instead of the limited vistas that have been presented traditionally: "The activity becomes an end unto itself and naturally also for self-enrichment, strengthened by the hope that it will also enrich others" (8).

In this procedure, Hildesheimer is aware that he as biographer is thus at best working in the conditional, or in realities modified at all points by a "maybe" (8) — not only did the person Mozart seem to consciously avoid leaving personal documentation, but even his contemporaries and coworkers did not see fit to document their reactions until after his death. Or from another perspective, the prospective biographer is revealing his own psychology through his fashion of thinking *about* Mozart: Mozart as a figure of inner projection or imagination ("Gestalt der Vorstellungskraft, . . . der Ein-bildungskraft" [9]), as a sign in which the boundaries between fact and conjecture must be unclear in the meaning construct assembled around it.

> He remains in conformity with accustomed norms of myth-generating biography-writing. However, the fact that precisely he — namely, the Viennese Mozart — coined a model, that *he* is the exemplary case who extended the categorical concept of "artist," this fact gets left out or suppressed through commonplaces. (9)

This coinage of the stereotype posits a Being behind the trace of genius embodied in the culturally bound meaning structures that the standard biographies have offered. Depending on their historical positions, biographers have only offered a Viennese genius, a henpecked husband, or a victim of an uncaring world. Hildesheimer realizes that he cannot transcend these boundaries, but he will at least attempt to counter the reader's tendency to focus on the message of such a constructed biography (the mediation, *Vermittlung*). In so doing, Hildesheimer realizes that the reader ignores the truer content of the work, the grafted-over psychology of the author (the mediator, *Vermittler* [10]), secured through the commonplace assumptions of what constitutes "typical reactions of a human psyche":

> Popular biographies find one-track explanations for everything within the boundaries of the probabilities corresponding to the radius of our

experience. The primary source is identical with the motive: wishful thinking. (11)

Such a biography represents at best a "receptive breakdown" (15) of the reader or biographer in the face of even the little information that exists. The goal of Hildesheimer's new approximation of Mozart is then to show "the unbridgeable distance between the inner life of Mozart and our deficient conception of its nature and its dimensions" (16) — that is, to reveal the scope of the ontology posited behind the trivialized facades.

Although this sounds like a program that could lead to the complete deconstruction of a cultural sign and the demonstration of its emptiness, Hildesheimer rests the feasibility of his program on an assumption that is considerably less radical: a concept of genius as extant in a scope and quality of emotion and disposition that are greater than those of the ordinary person — "He [Mozart] had an enormous synthetic-emotional register at his disposal; behind it he could assume many forms or even hide himself completely . . ." (14). This description is drawn, according to Hildesheimer, from the work of K. R. Eissler on genius, which found perhaps its fullest form in *Talent and Genius:*, a book about another historical figure around whom central myths of culture have been generated.

Eissler's central contention is that talents extend extant knowledge, while genius changes the rules on which knowledge is based, serving to generate "an inner evolvement of new paradigms" (275), the "creation of new values," and "the creation of a new universe presuppos[ing] not only a profound dissatisfaction with the world as it is, but also the ability to black out its appearance . . . as an obstacle" (281). This genius is, moreover, not self-reflexive or able to reveal his own inner life, and he carries with him a "dimension of fatefulness" (*Schicksalsschwere*) that precludes a revelation of the personal at the cost of his innate focus on the work itself. "It is one of the hallmarks of the works of genius that they are the outcome of the reverberation of the total personality" (278). Because of this, the work the genius produces cannot always be interpreted in the light of typical human patterns of cause and effect or personal motivations — this will not work for the interlocked and often unconscious motivations of the genius.

Because of his belief in Eissler's definition, Hildesheimer acknowledges Mozart as a genius. And instead of deconstructing the concept, he assumes the existence of such a category in ontic reality and shows how its complex and unknowable nature generates a series of conflicts that are the acknowledged or known facts of its existence. The course of Hildesheimer's biography thus elucidates a series of accepted stereotypes about Mozart and then juxtaposes them with facts that tend to get edited out in the establishment of "wish-fulfilling" biographies by earlier writers. An extensive series of juxtapositions is presented:

Mozart was reputed to be poor, but he had table silver until almost the end of his life (*Mozart* [1979] 25).

His childhood was supposed to have been unnatural and hard, driven by an unrelenting father. But Haydn suffered more real privations (35), and Mozart retained happy memories of England (supposedly his most difficult trip) until the end of his life (37).

Mozart was purported to have preferred certain key signatures for different moods, such as joy or tragedy — yet virtually all keys come up in equivalent works at all points in his life, not tied to biographical correlations (53).

The contrast of the age was the "Classical" Mozart, with his quiet genius, versus the "Romantic" Beethoven, with his tempestuous demeanor. Yet Goethe suggested that only Mozart could have composed adequate music for *Faust*, despite popular assumptions that the expansiveness of the Faustian man could be captured only by such a tormented soul as Beethoven's was reputed to be (50).

Hildesheimer contends that Mozart the man tends to be glorified through Mozart the musician. Yet the former wrote a series of canons with marvelous opening lines such as "Leck mir den Arsch fein recht schön sauber" ("Lick my ass right fine clean"; K. 382d, 1782) and "Leck mich im Arsch" (K. 382c, 1782) — which his publisher altered to the more salable and lofty "Nichts labt mich mehr" ("Nothing satisfies me anymore") and "Laßt froh uns sein" ("Let us be happy"). Mozart the Jovian musician did not have such scruples as would override these tendencies of Mozart the man.

Mozart was purportedly the victim of court intrigues, but he did not cease asking for (or receiving) help from friends and courtiers, no matter to what end: "He used his surrounding world where it promised to offer him something or to communicate something to him" (65), whether entertainment or contracts, and did not consider himself cut off.

He may have been a rebel in choosing libretti such as *Figaro*, a banned play — yet he sought to serve Absolutist rulers of his age, complaining only when they limited his personal development, as happened in Salzburg (66).

In contrast to traditional work-biographies, which find a turn toward melancholy after 1778 in the music, Hildesheimer suggests that Mozart's life may have changed not because of his mother's death but because it was the first time in his life he was able to negotiate his own artistic and personal affairs, since his father was not in Paris with him (99–100).

In contrast to the picture of the child genius, Mozart as early developer (*frühreif*) actually turned out a body of work that was a set of workmanlike studies in established form (particularly the formulaic operas) and did not emerge into originality until later (148).

Mozart was reputed to be "cold-hearted" and capable of turning Constanze's labor pains into the anguish of the quintet of *Don Giovanni* (by her report [173]).[7] But it appears rather that he was "a fallible people-reader" (134) who could show the motivations of people on stage to the fineness of a hair's breadth but seemed to be unable to gauge his own effect on people, to project himself into his surroundings without alienating people.

Other claims recur, such as "Vienna rejected him, while Prague accepted him with open arms": but Prague was a city with considerably fewer cultivated listeners (190), while Vienna had pronounced tastes — which did not include operas about servants (*Figaro*) or about topsy-turvy social situations (like the *Abduction from the Seraglio*) (192).

"The works of his genius are complete and cannot possibly be altered" — yet he altered acts of *Giovanni* down to the last minute (243) and often rewrote scores out of his head rather than refind them in his nonexistent filing system (243).

Constanze was supposed to be somewhat of a peasant, or "below him." As the later widow of Banker Nissen, however, she was reported to be a great lady who had no trouble purveying the Mozart legend to its patrons (269–75).

"Everyone turned away from him in his last years" — yet Haydn was actively convincing the Esterhazys to send gifts and possible contracts (308), which Mozart did not follow up on.

His downfall was caused ultimately by putting the Freemasons into the *Magic Flute* — yet it was debatable how much control he had over his own libretto, since it was a contract work. It was, additionally, not his great testament to humanity but rather "unmozartian-strange" (*unmozartisch-fremd*), and unique in his oeuvre in its strange mixture of keys and unresolved plot lines (338).

If he did indeed die a broken man, perishing slowly of starvation and hardship, then why was his productivity undiminished in these last years (354)? Moreover, he had a good general constitution (surviving several epidemics over his life), and his last illness seems to have gone relatively quickly (365–68). He may rather have died of mercury poisoning due to his treatments for kidney failure and a uremic coma (368–69).[8] And despite the divine image of his music, he seemed not to have been a churchgoing man except when he could use the church as a source of contracts (374).

These, then, are the binary oppositions that constitute Hildesheimer's deconstruction of the stereotypes around the sign "Mozart." Hildesheimer's biography assembles a structure of meaning as a panoply of such binary oppositions based on the clichés of Mozart's life. He leaves his readers with the sense of genius as trace and absence in his deconstruction of the sign — as a human presence whose essence was something different from that of the ordinary mortal, as Eissler stated. He closes by saying that

> here the mortal remains of an inconceivably great spirit were carried to the grave, an un-earned gift to mankind, in which Nature produced a one-time, probably unrepeatable — at least never repeated — work of art. (377)

Hildesheimer's Mozart is thus a sign whose presence pleads for the reader's acceptance of individuality and that defers questions of the validity of the world that caused its essence to be deferred as a structure of meaning. The genius is other and not subject to the ordinary rules of history or society. When they finally accept genius through its traces in biography, society and history have only generated clichés as structures of meaning represented in the popular biographies of man. They cannot communicate the ontic Being of genius that lay behind the appearances, and in fact, they only increase the distance of "genius" as an ontic-ontological construct and locus of relative meaning. Such popular biographies represent, then, only relative ontologies of motivations and of cultural prejudice. The assumed ontic status or Being of genius, Hildesheimer intimates, is the trace of genius obscured between the facts — outside of the constraints of society and history, working according to rules not constrained by the historical present. Hildesheimer's deferring structure of the essence of genius thus designates society as a presence whose norms close out the meaning of individuality and of ultimate value or worth, and the messages of Nature, with a Divine ontology beyond the ken of men.

Hildesheimer's Mozart also represents a cultural text of postwar Germany, familiar to the modern reader from the works of Group 47 and of more prominent individual authors such as Heinrich Böll. Because of recent German history, the literature of the immediate postwar era presents a locus of meaning that must necessarily lie outside historical reality, which tends itself to be turned into surface clichés that wrong the truths lying behind discardable cultural realities. As with any historical truth, Hildesheimer wishes to make the case, the truth of the cultural text is an absence, or at best a trace, outside of the meaning structures of society and their trivial biographies. Hildesheimer, like his contemporaries, sought in his Mozart a rejection of purported historical realities in favor of the celebration of the infinite potentials of humanity that they suppress.

Genius Reflected: Shaffer

The third locus in which the sign "Mozart" appears is the contemporary world of London's West End and Broadway theater: the world of the "theatrical success story" of the playwright Peter Shaffer, who since 1958 has had a string of critical and financial successes (*Five Finger Exercise* [1958], *The Private Ear and the Public Eye* [1963]; *The Royal Hunt of the Sun* [1964], *Equus* [1973], and *Amadeus* [1979]).[9] Turning to a play rather than to a further prose work to follow the development of a cultural sign involves finding another set of constraints in its evolution: the more intense financial pressures of stage productions and the necessity of the "full house" that condition the run and life of a play. While prose relies on the publishing market and the author's awareness of his public (claims that may be made for both Mörike and Hildesheimer), a playwright in the postwar era writes under the exigencies of creating a public success (to fill seats) rather than a critical one so that the investments in the productions can be recouped.

Books may sit on the shelves a month before they begin to sell; the cast of a play production cannot wait for the play to find its public. Shaffer's work meets this criterion while still fulfilling critical criteria. He produces plays that are read and filmed and will likely enter a modern canon of literature, not merely spectaculars that will fill one theater and then disappear. Under these constraints, the sign "Mozart" will turn into Shaffer's *Amadeus* — a new twist on old material that at one and the same time is able to capitalize on audience expectations and fill the theater, yet still offer something new to the critic and the reader.

Hildesheimer almost predicted the appearance of the "Mozart" that would form the basis for Peter Shaffer's play and movie *Amadeus*: "[T]he infamous rivalry between Mozart and Salieri is a product of literature and has had the effect of encouraging literature — only through the opposition of the envious rival does the hero win his true and full virtue" (19). The second point that factors into Shaffer's creation is the name itself: "[He] . . . called himself 'Wolfgang Amadé Mozart.' 'Amadeus' he never called himself, except in jest: Wolfgangus Amadeus Mozartus" (19).

Shaffer follows these dicta to produce scripts for a play and film that focus on the reflection and reaction of the court composer Salieri to the genius Mozart. Shaffer's program, like those of his predecessors discussed here, still rests on a notion of genius applied to Mozart and uses clichés to generate the surface structures of meaning for making his point. In a *New York Times Magazine* article written to celebrate the opening of the film, Shaffer quotes his idea of Mozart's genius, encompassed in a line of Salieri's cut from both his versions: "The God I acknowledge lives, for example, in bars 33–44 of Mozart's Masonic Funeral Music" ("Paying Homage" 22). "The apprehension of the Divine is aesthetic," and "No one suffered more than Mozart from sentimental misjudgment" (22). Shaffer wished to convey the relation of genius to the Divine and still avoid this trap of lapsing into cliché: to show "the shadowy and shining kingdoms in collision within one man" (27).

Yet one enormous difference from the notion of genius used by earlier writers emerges in both these statements and the scripts: whereas Mörike and Hildesheimer believed in the personal mission of the genius, Shaffer speaks only of the Divine, not of genius — the person of genius is only a tool of something in Nature beyond the normal ken of man (again in words that sound like those of Salieri in the play): "to be the Magic Flute at the lips of God . . . . He died after gigantic labors of sublime transcription, because the Player had finished playing with him: that is all. How lucky to be used up like that, rather than, as most of us are, by the trillion trivialities which whittle us away into dust" ("Paying Homage" 38). A variant of this statement is placed into the mouth of Salieri at various times in the script as the goal of his life and of all his professional activities as confined within the pact with the Deity that started his career.

The script that Shaffer creates thus emerges as a kind of cultural text around the underlying sign "Mozart/genius" different from the other texts we have examined — a change engendered not only by the choice of a dramatic form rather than prose. While even Hildesheimer agreed that the essence of genius can be approached only obliquely, in its activities and traces, he was still led to make the person of Mozart the center for his work — making the sign "Mozart" the central presence in his deconstructive analysis. Shaffer agrees that genius can be approached only obliquely to avoid cliché, but to do so, he cannot use a person of genius for the center of his logical pattern. He believes that the Divine may exist but cannot be named "genius" by the ordinary man: such a designation is itself a cliché. Those who are commonly designated so are for Shaffer conduits of an impersonal Divine force in Nature that exists outside of the ordinary scope of humans and that fairly arbitrarily chooses its vehicles with little or no regard for their persons and personalities. When they are used up, they disappear, and the Hand moves on.

Working from this assumption, Shaffer gives the stage not to Mozart, the trivialized sign, but rather to Salieri, the less familiar (albeit equally trivialized) enemy, in order that something new be presented to the audience. This shift generates a theatrical text that shows the *effect* of genius on the (purportedly) only person who realized his greatness during his lifetime — the *manifestation* of the otherworldly in this world, seen through the eyes of a would-be genius. Shaffer strengthened this concept between the 1979 London and 1980–81 New York versions of the play, and then finally in the 1984 movie, by making Salieri ever more active in Mozart's decline and fall and depicting Mozart as the ever more inadequate tool (Shaffer ix).

The play opens on the night in 1823 when Salieri plans to commit suicide in order to "substantiate" his claim of murdering Mozart and win himself the lasting fame that his music could not grant him. Before he goes, he is invoking the audience as the "Ghosts of the Future" (5) ("I was taught invocation by Gluck" [7]) because they are needed as witnesses if his plan is to be carried out. The film moves to a more literal interpretation of this moment, opening with Salieri's failed suicide attempt, and then introducing a father-confessor in Salieri's madhouse-hospital as a witness instead of the absent theater audience. This priest recognizes none of Salieri's music and much of Mozart's, and he must be convinced of Salieri's deed in lieu of the theater "ghosts."

The title of the work, *Amadeus*, "loved by God," could potentially have referred to Salieri himself, who prayed to the Lord from his youth on that he might rise above the mediocre and become a composer: "*Signore*, let me be a composer! Grant me sufficient praise to enjoy it. In return, I will live with virtue. I will strive to better the lot of my fellows" (8). He is given a sign (either a miraculous reaction by a statue of the Lord, or his father's death, in the two versions) and sets out on his successful career. But in each case, Salieri will "present to you — for one performance only — my last composition, entitled *The Death of Mozart; or, Did I Do It?*" (8).

Salieri sees Mozart as the "Creature," not appropriate to his conception of the role of a composer: "We [composers] took unremarkable men —

usual bankers, run-of-the-mill priests, ordinary soldiers and statesmen and their wives — and sacramentalized their mediocrity . . . The savor of their days remains behind because of *us* . . ." (10–11). Mozart, much later in the play, reflects the opposite interpretation in defining his role as a tool of the Divine, not as a genius:

> making a sound entirely new! . . . I bet you that's how God hears the world. Millions of sounds ascending at once and mixing in His ear to become an unending music, unimaginable to us! That's our job! That's our *job*, we composers: to combine the inner minds of him and him and him, and her and her — the thoughts of chambermaids and Court Composers — and turn the audience into God. (57–58)

Salieri, however, is looking for God on earth, among men, not only in His oblique reflection, as Mozart was: "I had heard a voice of God . . . the voice of an obscene child" (19). Salieri needs to find the music together with the person; Mozart knows that the music must be greater than the individual.

This is the dramatic tension of the entire play for Shaffer. Genius cannot be confronted; its effects can only be gauged. The Divine deigns to reveal itself on earth; it cannot be summoned by a "prolific composer" (31) like Salieri who prayed to God, "Let Your voice enter *me*" (19). In exhibiting the consequences of Salieri's position, Shaffer follows the hackneyed career of Mozart through Salieri's eyes, from the early Mozart of the "clever" (19) scores before the individual musical voice had emerged, through his confrontations with contemporaries who could not or would not help him further his career at court because of his fixation on German operas and "the German virtues" of "manly love" (23), which led to works offending the court, such as the *Abduction from the Seraglio.*

Salieri reacts to the threat Mozart represents to him — the loss of his position as the composer of his age — while seeing clearly the greatness of Mozart's music. He first tries to destroy the personality — for example, by encouraging Mozart to marry without his father's permission (30) — but then realizes that he himself is "growing rotten . . . because of *him*" (44): "You put into me perception of the Incomparable — which most men never know! — then ensured that I would know myself forever mediocre" (46). The court composer thus turns his vendetta away from Mozart as a person and toward God:

> What use, after all, is man, if not to teach God His lessons? . . . I'll tell you about the war I fought with God through his preferred Creature — Mozart, named Amadeus. In the waging of which, of course, the Creature had to be destroyed. (47)
> My quarrel now wasn't with Mozart — it was through him! Through him to God, who loved him so. (51)

Salieri must then alter his bargain with God: he seduces his student to void his oath of virtue and then resigns from his committees for the benefit of musicians to stop aiding his fellow man (51–52). The surprising result: he is rewarded not with God's fury, as he expected, but rather with success, and "a house filled with golden furniture" (54). "My own taste was for plain things — but I *denied* it! The successful lived with Gold, and so would I" (55). Paradoxically for the audience and for himself, Salieri sees that God seems definitely on his side: although the Emperor appeared unexpectedly to aid the restoration of Mozart's score of *Figaro* over the theater director's objections (and sabotage plans), these advantages are canceled by the ruler's yawn in the middle of the first performance, which effectively kills the work:

> The Creature's dreadful giggle was the laughter of God . . . . Reduce the man to destitution. Starve out the God. (70)
>
> I had just ruined Mozart's career at court. God rewarded me by granting me my dearest wish [the position of Kapellmeister] . . . . I was now truly alarmed. How long would I go unpunished? (72–73)

Still, as the final blow, Shaffer's Salieri is the one who convinces Mozart to put the Freemasons into the *Magic Flute*, thereby alienating his last patron and last source of income, van Swieten (72).

After engineering Mozart's fiscal ruin, Salieri also finally completes his psychological ruin by haunting him in the cloak and mask of the "iron guest" from *Don Giovanni* and either intimidating Mozart into finishing the requiem mass he is working on (the ghostly countdown outside Mozart's window in the play) or by actually commissioning it and then playing secretary to Mozart so that he works himself to death (the film version). The psychological pressure leads Mozart to state, "I've written nothing finally good!" (87) and to be thrown into final despair. Salieri gloats: "The profoundest voice in the world reduced to a nursery tune" (89). He reveals what he did in "poisoning" Mozart to death: "God does not love! He can only *use*! . . . He cares nothing for whom he uses: nothing for whom He denies! . . . You are no use to Him anymore . . . . All you can do now is *die*!" (88). In his self-assessment, he says:

> I weakened God's flute to thinness. God blew — as He must — without cease. The flute split in the mouth of His insatiable need . . . (91)
>
> I sought only slavery for myself. To be owned — ordered — exhausted by an Absolute. Music. This was denied me, and with it all meaning . . . . Salieri: Patron Saint of Mediocrities! And in the depth of your [the audience's] downcastness you can pray to me. And I will forgive you . . . . Mediocrities everywhere — now and to come — I absolve you all. Amen! (95–96)

Yet the whispers of the public (in the play) or the madmen (in the movie) echo these lines at the close of the action to show that, despite his plans, Salieri will remain a "deluded old man" who has indeed become extinct, as Salieri says of himself (96). When the voices of scandal die down within one human generation, so too will Salieri's name die — that is, until this play and movie resurrect him.

Shaffer's Salieri sets up a locus of meaning that reflects not only Mozart's genius but also the false cultural notion of genius itself. Shaffer juxtaposes mediocrity to genius, the chosen of God to the unchosen, and shows Salieri's confusion when the paths of material success do not match those of musical greatness. Musically, Mozart is indeed the "Amadeus"; fiscally, Salieri is — until he outlives himself. He was "created an ear" while Mozart was created God's flute. Following Salieri, the audience sees the Amadeus through the cracked glass of the would-be Amadeus and must be thrown back on its hackneyed notions of genius to be satisfied about the conclusion. The audience feels that Divine justice triumphs — their genius (their human-centered definition of genius) is avenged when his nemesis outlives himself.

The juxtaposition of material success with artistic ability thus allows Shaffer to use the structures of personal and professional success familiar to the audience to exploit the Mozart legend clichés for good theater and to paint a dual tragedy: that of Mozart, as the genius used by God whom the system of patronage and influence of the eighteenth century destroyed; and that of Salieri, as the man of the system who succeeds but loses what soul he ever had in forcibly ignoring his real gifts (perhaps those of politician or manager). The audience realizes that Salieri willed himself to be a composer, which he was not in any lasting sense — he was not chosen to be God's flute, to convey some of the sense of the Divine to his audiences and to turn them into God, as Mozart had desired to. He was chosen to be God's ear, to be the one who really understood greatness and who could have possibly turned the system to Mozart's use were it not for his personal ego and his personalized image of God, which led him to rely on a bargain that the Deity would not have made. The fallacy was Salieri's: he assumed that God would answer — although he did recognize the truth that God only uses to throw away.

The cultural text and meaning structure that underlie this theatricality, however, deliver an antihumanistic message. For the *New York Times*, Shaffer admits that he doesn't feel that man has made much of himself and his world. The theatrical text juxtaposes mediocrity and genius. The work, however, holds a question deferred by the culture at large: the person and society as structured knowledge, versus the randomness of Nature. Shaffer's Mozart shows us the Divine in his music but acts like a social disaster; Shaffer's Salieri is the successful man of system but an egomaniac and second-rate artist who believes in the Christian work ethic and its innate rewards. Because of their respective failings, neither of these characters shows a culturally traditional cause-and effect relationship with the Divine, since the God of the audience has not really rewarded the good and punished the evil. The theatrical structure of meaning is thus an ontology deferring the audience's discussion of the relation of God to the Divine: the former is man's concept of the rationale of the latter. The audience is appeased by the outcome of the struggle, but the steps in the development of the final crisis show only the unfathomability of Shaffer's Divine, normally obscured by conventional pictures of God.

Mozart's music is a fact for the audience and for the playwright, but one without reason. The fates of the two men seem just and unjust in variable measure, depending on the audience's personal definitions of "virtue" or "value" — and, of course, on the fact that the Mozart of the cliché, as Hildesheimer demonstrated, has to be the hero. In order, then, to use the audience's expectations for dramatic effect, Shaffer, like his predecessors, did not address the question of why a genius such as Mozart did not have enough sense to deal with his contemporaries on a more mature or "business-like" level since he had the absolute sense of the dramatic success that should have made him the ideal theater composer of the period. Here deferred is the question of individual who is both pragmatic and impractical, a question that was at the heart of Mörike's work, but with a larger absence: the deferred world of the unknown Divine Shaffer's Salieri attempts to deal with under his personalized invocation of "God" is senseless, does not operate in terms of human logic (either his or Mozart's). "God" seems a creation of the individual ego, will, and strength to carry a program through. In contrast to Salieri's God, the Divine in the universe has no human sense, is "heartless," and recognizes only strength to do the job or not.

This absent discussion of the relation of God and the Divine in the universe means, too, that Shaffer has largely deferred the question of the value of genius and has relegated it to the level of a cliché theater battle between Mozart and Salieri. The character of Salieri reflects the audience's assumptions that Mozart's music is valuable and that it shows us some of the world beyond, yet defers the question of that value. The concept of genius is the cultural cliché that explains Salieri's bitterness in theatrical terms — but what is the logic of a purported gift that destroys? In essence, then, Salieri is only the inverted reflection of Mozart's genius cliché, strong and resourceful and evil where Mozart is weak, helpless, and victimized in his näiveté. Shaffer's inverting mirror of the theatrical text, however, cancels out or defers an underlying cultural text that questions the utility of assuming that genius and humanity exist in a social creature such as Mozart.

Mozart is the "Creature" to Salieri; Salieri builds for himself "the altar of sophistication" (55), the overt appearance of humanity while representing evil. The deferred God is a "Versager" and can be said to "break down" in the audience's terms because He kills Mozart; the reflected genius polarizes the world against him and dies. The great absence is the sense of the Divine outside the known dicta of man and society. God is not dead; the sense of human organization that generated the concept is. "God" saves the play yet does not explain Divine justice. The late twentieth-century viewer of this play is ultimately being asked to question the norms and values of the culture that guarantees the theatricality of the play and that simultaneously creates the conditions of reward and punishment in which the stage characters exist.

Conclusion

The three texts discussed here have been presented as three structures of meaning that all use the sign "Mozart" as the locus of their presentations of interpretations of culture: a locus from 1855, one from postwar Germany, and one from late-twentieth-century England and America. Each structure thus correlates to a variant of Being as an ontology correlated to an ontic status, with its associated presences, absences, and deferred meanings. None particularly offers a "Mozart" who would be recognized in Austria, today or then.

Mörike's text presents a cultural text of greater scope stressing the presence of social forces around the locus of Mozart, and the tensions that defined the positions of his life as their correlates. The mixed genre and time frame of the piece, however, cloud the cultural text in deferring the question of change in the juxtaposition of the two historical eras involved: the 1780s of Mozart's life and the 1850s of the narrator and his public. The sign "Mozart" includes the tensions of these poles in portraying the genius who spans their breadth yet is virtually an absence in terms of impact. In Mörike's deferred terms, "genius" could function in more than a passive interrelationship with the environment: this genius could potentially be more than a stabilizing factor in the cultural text that became the structure of the literary work's ontology. The genius here spans the social classes available and thus defers for the reader the larger question of cultural upheaval that its social locus must necessarily suggest. As both a victim of and a profiteer from the class system, Mozart could echo messages of 1848 for the audience of 1855 but does not. The social destabilization of the mid-century has been deferred by the novella.

Hildesheimer draws a structure of meaning with the essence of genius as its central locus, in contrast to Mörike's choice of the social role of genius. In this choice, he presents a deconstruction of the opposing characteristics of this genius as represented in popular cliché and the recoverable historical reality, however poor that reality may seem in comparison to the phenomenon in question. The presence in Hildesheimer's cultural text is the social, personal, and cultural essence of genius beyond the ken and scope of ordinary men, as it stands in a tension with the biographer's or historian's tendency to level this otherness in an application of ordinary human norms. The absence within this structure is a discussion of what that expanded scope of genius is to offer mankind: why it is important for the reader to recognize the tension that the concept "genius" yields in this world and why the social and cultural structures that did not recognize a contemporary Mozart as valuable could still have glorified him in a backward glance or even have been interested in this phenomenon. The celebration of the individual is achieved in this structure, yet not the necessity of the individual on a level other than the emotional one for readers. Through his deconstruction of the social unrealities of trivial biographies, they are led by Hildesheimer to see the individual as a gift from God, not

as a social necessity who can initiate change. Yet in not addressing the social and historical issues of his own stance as a biographer, Hildesheimer
reflects the assumption of postwar Germany that modern society is bankrupt and cannot serve or encompass the historical veracity of the individual.

Shaffer chooses to create a reflecting structure to focus the central locus
of meaning in his structure on the presence of the Divine in the world. To
do so, he reflects and inverts the holy genius Mozart in the patron saint of
mediocrity, Salieri, thus creating for the audience a cultural locus that confronts them with both their heroes and their antiheroes or villains at once,
with examples of their inherently opposing cultural and artistic values —
inherently opposing if modern standards of success are to be equated with
the values associated with the sign of the genius replicated here as the cliché Mozart. The result is a text structure that not only includes these two
poles but also adds the potential tension of thwarted or fulfilled audience
expectation vis-à-vis their personal definition of the absent God. The Divine
that is in Nature emerges into this world through Mozart, but the tension
between "good" and "evil" that the audience believes is playing out between the characters of Mozart and Salieri actually serves to defer the ultimate questions associated with present cultural values. "God" is not just, as
Salieri notes. In relying on God's justice, then, the audience may be carry-
ing on a debate that is in itself only a repression of the relativity of its own
values since the terms in which the actors deal are not validated by the
presence of an anthropomorphized God who could confirm the audience's
judgment and reactions — and who could give sense to *any* of the human
activities and values in a consistent pattern of cause and effect. Instead,
random chance seems to be at the heart of the Divine. The audience's expectations make the play work, while simultaneously declaring as bankrupt
the twentieth-century popular psychology on which they rest — God, like
Salieri, has outlived himself in causal terms.

These three cultural texts arrange themselves into a progression marking the changes in logocentric repression for the last 150 years in Western
thought — the changes in the acceptable logics and sense-giving structures
and their concomitant assumptions for the shape and progress of the cultures that are their generating loci. Genius is first divided by society into the
sensibility of the upper classes in conflict with the sense of the middle
classes; then it is considered unexemplifiable by that which is present in
the norms of the culture in which it appears; and finally, it is relegated to a
superficial phenomenon of relative cultural expectations, dependent on the
audience's interpretation, not correlated in any necessary fashion to the Divine that is in its product — genius as an unimportant tool for a larger, un-
fathomable and impersonal power on patterns other than the human or
cultural norm.

Translating these repressions into the terms of an archaeology of the
shifts in concept of the human role in this world reveals a similar progression. Mozart's ilk existed with an ability to change society (as a sign threatening conservative elements) in the nineteenth century. This ability to effect

change became a wistful goal for the twentieth, which wished to escape the cultural and historical restrictions imposed on the individual by evolving under the term "genius" the ultimate cult of personality, individuality, and its value. And finally, the sign "Mozart" hollowed out into a pseudo-ontic concept as part of the value designations of culture, reflecting an attempt to personalize and control that which is essentially impersonal and beyond human control: the onto-ontology of the lived world. For the late twentieth century, Mozart the sign has disappeared into the mediocrity of each individual and into the value of the product, not the producer.

Notes

[1] See Jacques Derrida, "Freud," especially 197.

[2] Grillparzer (1791–1872) and Stifter (1805–1868) were both Austrians, while Mörike (1804–75) was German. Grillparzer was noted in his day for plays, both comic and tragic, that were staples of the Imperial Theater in Vienna, until he withdrew from public life in 1838 after the failure of the play *Weh dem, der lügt* (see also chapter 7) The main body of his works consists of history plays (drawn from Habsburg history, such as *Ein Bruderzwist in Habsburg*, 1872) and mythology or fairy-tale plays (such as *Des Meeres und der Liebe Wellen*, 1831, on the Hero and Leander material).

Stifter was known primarily for his work as a pedagogue in the Austrian school system (see chapter 5) and for his prose: the *Bildungsroman Der Nachsommer* (*Indian Summer*, 1857), the series of novellas known as the *Studien* (1844–50), and the children's stories *Bunte Steine* (1853). Mörike, a Protestant pastor educated at the Tübinger Stift (1804–75), and Annette von Droste-Hülshoff (1797–1848), an independent noblewoman, were known both as poets and secondarily as prose writers: Mörike for the novella under discussion here and for his fragmentary *Bildungsroman Maler Nolten* (1832), and Droste-Hülshoff for her 1842 novella *Die Judenbuche*.

Jeffrey Adams, as editor of *Mörike's Muses*, collects and translates an excellent selection of secondary literature on all phases of Mörike's production, a first-rate introduction to the field. In German, the same service is done by Victor G. Doerksen. Helga Slessarev's *Eduard Mörike* introduces the author. Other articles of note are Michael Perraudin's "*Mozart auf der Reise nach Prag*," an overview of the author's political situation, and Carol Wootton, "Literary Portraits of Mozart," which also mentions Shaffer.

[3] Another signature text of the Biedermeier, Franz Grillparzer's *Der arme Spielmann* (*The Poor Fiddler*, 1847), displays another class-bound musician's fate — a would-be musician perishes rejected by his class as well as by the music he loved; see chapter 7.

[4] Hildesheimer (1916–91) was well known for his work in both fiction and nonfiction. One of his early popular novels was *Paradies der falschen Vögel* (1953); his most famous piece of biography was *Marbot* (1981). *Mozart* was translated in 1982. For reasons of detail, that translation is not in use here. For overviews of his work, see Volker Jehle, ed., *Wolfgang Hildesheimer*, for a collection of secondary literature and contemporary responses to his work; and Patricia H. Stanley, *Wolfgang Hildesheimer and His Critics*, which presents reactions to the work, and *The Realm*

of Possibilities, in which "The Avant-Garde Mozart Biography" (31–74) discusses the narrative strategy of *Mozart.* Marion Faber discusses just the *Mozart* in a brief article.

[5]For a history of Group 47, see particularly the "in-house" report by the critic Hans Werner Richter, included in *Hans Werner Richter und die Gruppe 47,* ed. Hans A. Neunzig, and also Friedhelm Kröll, *Die "Gruppe 47."* For a more recent introduction to and overview of the Group 47, see a 1988 museum catalogue done by Peter Härtling et al., *Dichter und Richter.* For an insider's perspective, see also Hans Werner Richter's anecdotal *Im Etablissement der Schmetterlinge.* For a classic collection including excerpts from prizewinners, see Hans A. Neunzig, *Lesebuch der Gruppe 47.*

[6]Contrast, for example, the Nobel Prize-winning novel *Gruppenbild mit Dame* by Böll (1971, for the 1972 Prize), with Grass's *Die Blechtrommel* (1959) to see the prominence of the nonhistorical or nonpolitical in the evaluation of world critics.

[7]Hildesheimer uses this spelling of her name, which seems to have been variably spelled with *C* or *K*.

[8]Francis Carr has turned this idea into a biography, *Constanze and Mozart,* which contends that Mozart was poisoned by a jealous husband and the evidence covered up.

[9]Peter Shaffer (b. 1926) and his forty-year career have been the subject of many discussions, with major projects reviewed in virtually every periodical. For overviews on the author, see C. J. Gianakaris, *Peter Shaffer,* and Dennis A. Klein, *Peter Shaffer.* For discussions of the works, see Gianakaris, ed. *Peter Shaffer: A Casebook,* which gives an overview of the career; Eberle Thomas, *Peter Shaffer: An Annotated Bibliography*; and Gene A. Plunka, *Peter Shaffer: Roles, Rites, and Rituals in the Theater.* Interesting articles on *Amadeus* include: Werner Huber and Hubert Zapf, "On the Structure of Peter Shaffer's *Amadeus,*" a detailed study of the drama's construction; Daniel A. Jones, "Peter Shaffer's Continued Quest for God in *Amadeus,*" discussing the play intertextually to other Shaffer works; William J. Sullivan, for a psychoanalytic view of *Amadeus* subtitled "The Making and Un-Making of the Fathers"; and Martha A. Townsend on the film transformation.

3: John Irving, Günter Grass, and *Owen Meany:* The Gender-Sensitive *Bildungsroman*

In the flurry of reviews following the appearance of John Irving's *A Prayer for Owen Meany* in early 1989, R. Z. Sheppard in *Time* pointed out the obvious: "For graduate students there is the fact that Meany shares more than initials with Oskar Matzerath, the runt hero of Günter Grass's masterpiece, *The Tin Drum*" (80).[1] This acknowledges more reciprocal influence than do most critics, who stress Irving's reliance on Dickens and religious imagery.[2] At the same time, many critics (for example, Epstein) dismiss the novel as the latest in Irving's series of popularizing pastiches. This essay will take a different stance: that Irving, like Joyce Carol Oates, actually reinvigorates and parodies genres (as Oates does the romance novel in *Bellefleur*). In this case, the German *Bildungsroman,* the educational novel, the hallmark genre of nineteenth-century Germany, is the target of the borrowing: the genre refigured by Günter Grass in the 1960s and 1970s and imported into the United States by John Irving for his own purposes.

In tribute to the graduate student in all of us, I will discuss the Irving-Grass connection as an example of conscious literary borrowing. Irving's *Meany* borrows heavily from Grass in both plot and characterization (as well as from other authors — *A Christmas Carol*, for example, figures prominently in the plot). However, Irving's choice of genre implies a series of other issues surrounding his borrowing, especially the question of male-female reciprocity in social development. To specify what Irving and Grass share — the development of a modern "anti-*Bildungsroman*" — this discussion will first trace Irving's similarities to Grass, then outline the *Bildungsroman* in general and in Grass's permutation, and then discuss *A Prayer for Owen Meany* as a particular type of modern anti-*Bildungsroman*, a gender-sensitive or perhaps even feminist one.[3]

The Irving-Grass Connection

On the surface level, Grass and Irving share a sense of what constitutes a narrative: within a conventional linear or retrospective narrative (which converges with the present near the end of the tale's telling), they populate their worlds with figures of epic grotesqueness, with actions of cosmic preposterousness, and with mutilated humans who teach the merely human narrators about their humanness (for instance, Irving's Jenny Garp or Franny Berry, or Grass's Joachim Mahlke or Oskar).

The similarities between the authors is, of course, intentional. John Irving has provided us with an outline of what he sees in Grass in a review of *Headbirths* written for a 1982 *Saturday Review*.[4] Grass is the "King of the Toy Merchants," a reference to the toy seller Sigismund Markus from *The Tin Drum*, provider of Oskar's toy instruments of power, who died and "took all the toys in the world away with him" as the Nazis overran Danzig. Grass is valorized as "forever young" since "he exercises no discernible restraint on the mischief of his imagination or on the practical, down-to-earth morality of his politics" (61/399). Mischief, child-like tenacity, and breadth of narrative are the qualities valued most by Irving, who recognizes that "Grass also knows how to be harsh" (65/406). More particularly, in this review Irving repeats the recommendation that would come up in *Owen Meany*: that *Cat and Mouse* is the best introduction to Grass (67/409) — "[Y]ou can't be called well-read today if you haven't read him. Günter Grass is simply the most original and versatile writer alive" (68/412). Irving's interest in Grass goes back to the time Irving was writing his first novel, *Setting Free the Bears*, from 1963 on (McCaffrey 181), especially because of Grass's imaginative narrative (188).

Other interviews by Irving echo this praise and the terms in which it is given, since many characteristics of Grass's prose have been incorporated into Irving's aesthetics. For example, Irving, like Grass, points out that he is not concerned with good taste because it is "too contained" ("The Narrative Voice" 88). More importantly, "narrative momentum must override description, must restrain all our pretty abilities with the language." This program creates a narrative voice that Grass also chooses; this narrative voice demonstrates "a tone of legend" (89). Too, while both authors start with autobiographical elements, they move beyond the personal: Irving says that one uses up strict autobiography (McCaffrey 178–79).

Moving beyond the issue of style, Irving's borrowing from Grass may also extend into other realms, most notably into politics, social stance, and authorial intent in use of genre. Grass introduced a discussion of history into postwar German literature, into what he called "the time of fabrication" (Willson 24). Moreover, Grass's use of grotesque "fabrications" ties him in with the tradition of the picaresque novel (see also Rickels, Mouton, McElroy), with fairy tales, and with mythology (what Abbott calls "a realistic novel about myth" [218]). Nonetheless, he remains also in the tradition of the developmental novel (*Bildungsroman*) or, in more recent estimation, with the *Heimatroman*, or European regionalist novel (see Pott, *Literatur und Provinz*). Each of these characterizations warrants separate examination in order to outline the intentionality of Grass's prose.

When Grass critics speak of his mythic narrative voice, they refer to what corresponds to Irving's notion of the "voice of legend." Irving tries to assume a fairy-tale, never-never-land voice that Grass introduced to frame and enable a retelling of the horrors of German history. This never-never-land voice is represented in Oskar's story about the toy maker Markus, in the *Flounder* by a fish who narrates events from the war between the sexes, and in the multiple storytellers from *Dog Years*. This estranged narrative stance distances the narrator from his materials. His narrative schizophrenia does violence to conventional narrative as well as to the myths he writes about. (Irving agrees that violence is part of reality and that when he narrates such realities, violence is not gratuitous but is there in the world he depicts; see "Humans Are a Violent Species").

That Grass adapts the modern European *Heimatroman* is also relevant to a discussion of Irving. While the term formerly referred to genre novels (regional versions of what we in the United States know as costume or romance novels), it is assuming a cultural-political dimension for current German writers, referring to novels with regional settings that reflect real and more generalized sociopolitical issues (Pott includes the works of Grass and Siegfried Lenz in this category). Irving's works correspond to the narrative conventions of these novels: they reflect the New England landscape and often Vienna. But while Grass uses regionalism to address the "unconquered past" of Germany history and its unexpiated war guilt, Irving seems to avoid the political aspects of his environment. Even in *Owen Meany*, the hero dies while trying to get into combat, as only an indirect casualty of that war. Yet both writers share a narrative mode that presents the larger scope of history through the eyes of the small — quite literally so in the cases of Owen and Oskar of *The Tin Drum*.

Irving can match Grass's grotesque characters in many of his works. Owen Meany is an amalgam of Oskar of *The Tin Drum* (the size of a three-year-old, with a voice that shatters glass) and the adolescent Joachim Mahlke of *Cat and Mouse* (with the protuberant Adam's apple, the soldier-hero who talks to school classes for the Nazi government): all three share an overidentification with Christian figures (Mahlke with the Virgin Mary; Owen and Oskar with the Baby Jesus). Like Grass's Oskar, Lilly in *The Hotel New Hampshire* did not grow; where Grass favors black German shepherds in *Dog Years*, Irving favors bears; each shows the cruelty of packs of boys (the "Dusters," or Sunday school classes); each world is populated with midget entertainment troupes (who entertain Grass's troops, but buy Irving's Hotel), anarchists, and wars. Children emerge from blankets of fat in rain or "Tauwetter" (as a ballet dancer for Grass, who married one, or a wrestler for Irving, who was one). Males have uniform fetishes (Frank in *Hotel*; Mahlke's fascination with Nazi war medals) or psychic difficulty with virgin-Jesus identifications. And both authors are able to draw on the history of the Nazi takeover (as direct experience for Grass and as history for the Irving who studied in Vienna in 1963–64; see Reilly, "The *Anschluß*").

Irving borrows more than his narrative frame and regionalism from Grass's conception of the novel: he also tacitly borrows the high literature tradition of the *Bildungsroman*. While Irving is most often discussed in terms of Dickens, Dickens' most familiar works are, in German terms, developmental novels (*Entwicklungsroman*) or picaresque novels (*Schelmenroman*), not *Bildungsromane* per se. Like Oliver Twist, the typical Dickens character becomes what he is by finding himself, not by essential change. In contrast, the prototype hero for the German *Bildungsroman* is Goethe's Wilhelm Meister, a character who changes in response to educative pressures, like the narrated Rousseau of the *Confessions* or *Émile*. Through experience of the world, such characters alter fundamental facets of character to eventually integrate into the world of the upper bourgeoisie.

Grass takes the overall developmental plan of the *Bildungsroman* and uses it as a vehicle for social criticism. Through a double embedding of narrative frame (in the case of *The Tin Drum*, a juxtaposition of "I-Oskar" and "He-Oskar" as the narrator looks back on his life), Grass casts doubt on the reliability of the narrated truth. These multiple narrators often contradict each other; direct quotations do not bear the interpretation that their reporters make of them. In addition, a grotesque character like Oskar is not only the developing hero but also identifiable as a picaro, a rogue whose purpose is to throw the prejudices of a society back on itself. The "education" in *The Tin Drum*, then, becomes antieducation, in which one of the narrators (I-Oskar) progressively learns to question the master narratives of culture that the other (He-Oskar) embodies. This education becomes a lesson in the fundamental schizophrenia of modern culture, revealed in retrospective retellings of history from different perspectives.

In Grass's most pronounced version of this intentional narrative schizophrenia, I-Oskar sits in jail retelling the story of He-Oskar through the war, then emerges, during a second growth fever at the very close of the novel, into You-Oskar, a self-reflexive narrator who recognizes two realities simultaneously, one in the war and one since its close. Like Irving's standard characters, then, Grass shows victims of the educational process of life. In *Cat and Mouse*, Mahlke dies; his narrator does not and so is left to synthesize his experiences with those of Pilenz, his left-behind friend. Berry and Oskar attain some growth in narrating their stories but remain essentially stunted — they are educated away from society, not into it.

The traditional educational novel has an omniscient narrator keeping perspective on the heroes' growth. Using a dual perspective strategy, Grass's antieducational novel or regional novels undermine the narrators' reliability in order to make them participate in the educational experience, a tactic Irving takes over — the narrators are antiheroes, not models, for the reader. Too, the traditional educational novel ends with some assurance of the hero's integration into society, as a happy end that this novel shares with Dickens's developmental genre. For Grass and Irving, this integration is less than an apotheosis: their heroes are often maimed, or walking wounded, or killed just before success, or get used up and fade away, or integrate by relinquishing their real souls in favor of a soul lent them by society. (John Wheelwright in *Owen Meany* ends a Canadian dutch uncle and celibate, not a father. Oskar Matzerath's first attempt to grow, after the death of his putative fathers at the end of the war, turns him from a cute miniature into a misshapen dwarf; his second leaves him fevered, and we do not know how he will "turn out" until *The Rat*, many years later.) This irony or ambivalence refracted through multiple narrators is the key to

Grass's distinctive antieducational novel, an inversion of the values encompassed in the original genre. The fact that war, not peace, represents the ultimate development for the protagonists in *The Tin Drum* and *Owen Meany* emphasizes the novels' antieducational character.

The reference to the traditional *Bildungsroman* also immediately raises the issue of gender. The traditional developmental novel focuses on the hero. To be sure, women play key roles in facilitating his social integration, but many are ultimately discarded or left behind as "unacceptable" or "unavailable" types (Mignon in *Wilhelm Meister*, Rousseau's countess, and others); the women remain sacrifices or fond memories enhancing the depth of the youthful hero. Grass follows this vision about the place of women: Oskar, for instance, is left only with Bruno, his warden. While women like Oskar's grandmother and mother play crucial roles in his life, they ultimately recede in favor of Oskar. The women remain guideposts, with conflicts left unresolved by the narrative; their voices are interpreted by Oskar's, who gives only his version of their meanings without heeding their lives as coherent wholes.

On this point, Irving diverges from Grass's practice. Irving's antieducational novel is unclear about who is actually being educated since his heroes are even less in charge of the narrative than Grass's are. Irving treats the educational dynamic as a question of the group represented, not as a question of the individual hero. To illustrate: Grass, in *The Danzig Trilogy*, treats the war as an "unconquered past" that leaves psychic scars on isolated characters. Irving, in contrast, uses the Vietnam War as a problem for the family unit within society, not only for individuals. Where Grass uses stunted characters to expose society's inability to educate the individual (and, in this sense, "heal scars"), Irving transforms the antieducational novel by exploring the education required by communities of men *and* women together, not just one schizophrenic narrator. What in Grass remains a male literary genre (in the high German tradition), then, Irving construes as a gender-sensitive genre, even while acknowledging men's unreliability as narrators of women's voices.

Irving thus undercuts his narrator's reliability to question not only male development but also women's roles in society: both sexes are victims of a prevailing social construct, of which each sees only a part. Where Grass displays the antieducation of male characters, Irving has males acknowledge that women are antieducated along with their brother, fathers, and sons — a feminist gesture overlooked in popular analyses of his work.

The New Feminist Educational Novel:
Men Who Misjudge Women, and
How Women Survive

Irving's critics are unanimous in overlooking his narrators' unreliable perceptions of the social sphere. Doane and Hodges are typical in asserting that in *Garp*, "truth is structured in such a way as to guarantee paternal authority and to silence women no matter how much they seem to speak" (68). Such an assertion overlooks Irving's own stance as a writer and self-commentator. Irving never claims to speak for women; instead, he looks at the contemporary family as a social unit encompassing women.

Early in his career, Irving stated that his ideal unit of social commerce is the family (Miller 176–77). He admits that, while the men in his stories achieve some sort of growth, the women do not, in general, except insofar as they join a family unit (186–87). "Those who have read my work," he states, "know I regard the family as the greatest haven humans have invented" ("Humans Are a Violent Species" 71). Families seem "to mean less" these days, particularly in the city, and the "possibility of travel" is their greatest enemy because mobility reduces necessary contact: "People probably would leave their wives and husbands less frequently if they knew they couldn't move away, if they knew they had to simply take the house across the street or down the corner or on the west side of town" (71). Critics who charge him with patriarchal nostalgia overlook the fact that the families that Irving supports are definitely not "traditional families."[5]

The "traditional family" acts in Irving's world as an instrument of social repression, creating both male and female casualties. Women in traditional families do not grow, but in Irving's novels the nontraditional family units they engage in at least allow them to achieve stature (and perhaps, by the date of *Owen Meany*, some growth that the men do not recognize as such). Irving is noted for portraying nontraditional yet stable family units, often headed by single fathers, "heroes" like Garp and Berry who are "mother-men" (Sheppard, "Life into Art" 51). Transsexuals, prostitutes, anarchists, lunatics, rape victims — all can participate in ersatz family units that may be more effective than the socially familiar one. The son-narrators of Irving's stories have difficulty in accepting their families' emotionally satisfying (yet nontraditional) solutions in the face of social pressure. Nonetheless, they recognize alternate forms of nurturing that do not rely solely on the women — men can and do nurture in many Irving works (Garp's book was originally going to be titled *My Father's Illusions* [*Garp* 563]).

Yet Irving is bringing up another issue that he (perhaps because he is male) cannot resolve: the narrators ask why the women tend to be the victims, why they do not seem to "grow" as the men do. In contrast to his narrators, though, Irving as an author very clearly indicates that his women do indeed grow. As children of traditional families, in contrast, Irving's narrators are not in the position to perceive or communicate that growth. Critics do not, in general, accept any distance between Irving and his narrators (who so often share his name). But their identification is by no means assured. For example, the title *The World According to Garp* is assumed to refer to the narrator, T. S. Garp. Yet his mother, Jenny Garp, is also a writer with a worldview. Like Lilly in *Hotel New Hampshire*, Jenny Garp lives a life out of the mainstream, and dies — on first glance, both seem ineffectual. But Irving the author is careful to show that these women's books are ultimately more successful than those of their male counterparts, so why cannot Irving the author be showing Jenny Garp's world, while T. S. Garp believes he's the narrator? Even *Garp*'s original working title, *Lunacy and Sorrow*, can refer to Jenny's life as easily as it does to T. S. Garp's.

Is this a damnation of the woman's access to the writer's sphere instead of to society, as Doane would have it? Within Irving's conception of the family, it seems, such marginalization again need not be assumed: virtually everyone in Irving's fictional families is a writer. These women may be victims of society, but not of their families. Irving has commented, "I've often said that a novel is a search for a victim, or victims — that a novelist's moral and social responsibility is to show who the victims of the stories are. In my books, they tend to be women and children" ("Porn and the Novelist" 28). While critics eschew making this point, the actresses starring in the film versions of Irving novels seem to realize that his version of woman's victim status is interesting to play, even if it is incompatible with "hero" or star-level roles (Glenn Close in *Garp*, Jody Foster in *Hotel New Hampshire*).

Nonetheless, Irving's choice of a genre drawn from another narrative tradition helps obscure his point. The *Bildungsroman* is a German genre, sustaining Grass's "tone of legend" ("The Narrative Voice" 89) but favoring the male point of view. As altered by Grass for social-critical ends, the anti-*Bildungsroman* presents an uneven narrative voice with a problematic tension rendering the narrative opaque, as Anglophone critics find problematic in Irving's works:

> [O]ther 'socially relevant' themes (e.g. racism, feminism, anti-Semitism, terrorism) frequently intrude so forcefully into the otherwise fantastic world of the novel that they become preeminent and, at least temporarily, confuse or obfuscate the tones and rhythms of romance. Irving himself reinforced the difficulty of reconciling the elements of romance with those of social consciousness when he described (inaccurately, we think) Franny as the protagonist and hero of *Hotel*.
>
> (ABC Television interview quoted in Harter and Thompson 124)

The analysis of Irving's work as an adaptation of the *Bildungsroman* would, however, allow Franny to be the real hero of an Irving antieducational novel. Characters who participate in positive socialization are the protagonists in the developmental novel. In *Hotel*, Franny, not the male narrator, develops as a result of her social *Bildung*. By the same logic, Jenny is the hero of *Garp*. Because women and children are most seriously challenged ("victimized") in Irving's novels, they become the beneficiaries of the proffered education, not the narrating males who do not adequately perceive their lives. This suggestion is not made lightly: in virtually all of Irving's novels (even the father-son drama of *The Cider-House Rules*), the women dominate in more than the domestic sphere. Their deaths, their decisions, or their triumphs (like those of Susie-the-Bear among the walking wounded, or Hester-the-Molester, the *Madonna* clone of *Owen Meany*) figure prominently in the social sphere.[6] His women live their own lives, surviving society's oppression in unique ways, living their educational novel before they (or their sons or spouses) narrate it.

But again, these narrator-sons and -husbands do not know how to appreciate these women's survival tactics — in general, they are only able to say that these women did as well as they could (perhaps better than may have been expected, once the circumstances emerge). For example, Homer in *The Cider-House Rules* realizes that society is enforcing an unfair option for women: making orphans or abortions. Berry sees that his father (totally blind and somewhat befuddled) is the most suitable male to provide therapy for the battered women at the new hotel-shelter, perhaps because he can approach these women out of a position with virtually no remaining stake in society.

Irving thus has added a dimension to his version of the antieducational novel. His men do not only learn through women, as in the classical genre; they learn that they do not and cannot understand women. They even suggest obliquely that they may never have really seen a woman, but only society's conception of one; maybe they, as males and as sons, fathers, and brothers of these women, have been victimized by cultural stereotypes in ways they do not perceive because they are not the overt victims. However, Irving's narrators remain marginally more successful as gender role models: they are able in some way to establish the family units Irving values, while the women either thrive alone in or flee from the social environment. The men achieve compromises (negative social integration), while the women are forced into extreme positions without resolutions (marginalization or nonintegration).

These dilemmas of gender-specific education are illustrated in *A Prayer for Owen Meany*, Irving's most Grassesque novel. Here, Irving substitutes the Vietnam War for Grass's equivalent European crisis of faith, the Second World War. Both wars permanently changed the social texture of the nations involved. And the notion of a social crisis of faith is appropriate since religion is the superficial glue that strains extant social roles. Nonetheless, the social revolution of family structures and the relations between the male and female educable remain at the heart of the work. This novel questions the paths to social integration available to both men and women, and is thus a social critique beyond those offered by Grass and his male-dominated novels.

Owen Meany and the
Unreliable Male Narrator

The narrator-hero of *A Prayer for Owen Meany* is John Wheelwright, illegitimate scion of an old New England family. He tells the tale of growing up between his family of strong women, his cousins (especially Hester), and his best friend, Owen Meany, son of the owner of the dying local granite quarry. John and Owen grow up into the Vietnam War era as they play off their competing sensibilities, their respective image systems of what makes themselves and their successes. These lives are determined by the American cultural stereotypes of the 1950s and 1960s: popular narratives setting Catholic versus Protestant, high church versus low church, family versus rootlessness, war versus peace, hero versus draft dodger (versus "4F" — Owen Meany cuts off Wheelwright's finger so that he cannot physically qualify for the draft). These two characters (one narrator, one quoted yet nonetheless narrated) weave a tale about each boy's involvement in an unreliable world construct, forcing them into a particularly Irvingesque unknowningness about society and women.

In setting these conflicts, Wheelwright reports on a friend who is in almost every way his antithesis (he need not be schizophrenic like I-Oskar and He-Oskar). While Wheelwright is of old New England stock, Owen knows his family is poor working Irish-Catholic stock. John's mother is dominant in his emotional life; Owen's mother barely exists, covered over with the granite dust of the family quarry and closeted away from the town and from Owen because of her allergies. In consequence, Owen is always looking for a mother: John's mother Tabitha (in life or as a dressmaker's dummy after he accidentally causes her death) or the Virgin Mary (when he plays the Baby Jesus in the Christmas pageant). Owen knows too much about his mother, who is rigidly conventional; Tabitha Wheelwright, in contrast, goes into town once a week for singing lessons, always wears black, and conceived John out of wedlock (she calls him "my little fling"). The contrasts between these lives become intertwined through guilt: Owen Meany has his first hit ever in little league, and the fly ball kills John's mother.

The most important aspect of the boys' education is highlighted in their religious contrasts since they are alternately drawn to and repulsed by the trappings of each other's churches. In fact, Wheelwright frames his whole tale in his opinions about the relative merits of churches.[7] Wheelwright began Congregational, turned Episcopalian when his mother married (as he finds out later, because his unknown father was the Congregational minister), and ends up teaching at an Anglican academy in Canada. Even at the end of the book, he wishes to be buried in the severe Anglican rite of the Book of Common Prayer. The first result of his religious education, then, is the realization that religion correlates with lifestyles.

Wheelwright's notions of appropriate doctrine actually correlate religion with lifestyle, not epistemology: Catholics do certain things and live in ways that Protestants do not. A further, regional distinction is even drawn to expand these parallels: Congregationalists, Wheelwright asserts, are less like New England Puritan stock than are Episcopalians or Canadian Anglicans, and so Wheelwright is ultimately drawn to Puritanism. This religious imagery has been the reviewers' chief focus (a typical title is Kazin's "God's Own Little Squirt"), but they do not realize that the novel is not about theology in the narrowest sense. Wheelwright is, indeed, "doomed to remember a boy with a wrecked voice . . . because he is the reason I believe in God" (13), but even at his most religious, he is interested in religion only as a daily ritual. Thus Wheelwright claims only that he understands prayer, not the Bible or doctrine — the Book of Common Prayer, the text that helps believers get through the day.

The book's end, however, confirms that the religion issue only covers for questions about life: "We did not realize there were forces beyond our play. Now I know they were the forces that contributed to our illusion of Owen's weightlessness; they were the forces we didn't have the faith to feel, they were the forces we failed to believe in — and they were also lifting up Owen Meany, taking him out of our hands" (543).

This conclusion, however, is negative for the narrator, who has engaged in a profound act of antieducation about religion and regional lifestyles — he has moved to Canada, dodging not the draft but a lifestyle and an engagement with the contemporary United States. Ultimately, religion and life are left unseparated in a narrator who refuses to make distinctions about the sources and abuses of social power.

Because he cannot question the social questions lying at the basis of his religious obsession, Wheelwright puts down his skepticism with mythic analogies that console him, interpreting his life in terms of religious symbolism (ignoring the lifestyle issue to which the images point). Wheelwright lives in the family configuration of Jesus Christ: he had an adoptive father and a "virgin birth" when his mother won't admit the name of his actual father. In envy of John's situation, Owen works hard to achieve the same mythic role for the Christmas pageant (including choosing his "Virgin Mary" because of the size of her breasts, and asserting his own, purportedly "virgin birth" [473]). John's Puritan streak also draws him to his unreachable cousin Hester, with whom Owen Meany lived and who mocks the trappings of Catholicism when she becomes a rock star like the real Madonna of today's pop fame (with her name out of *The Scarlet Letter*). Ultimately Owen's self-declared Messianic mission leads him to death as he saves a group of Vietnamese orphans. Whether Owen is the Messiah is less important than his belief that he is, and so Wheelwright's flight to Canada is also evidence that he has accepted Owen's religious myths as the substance of his life, a simulacrum of Christ. In killing Tabitha Wheelwright, Owen had given Wheelwright his father back, reuniting a family through sacrifice and death.

Predictably, Wheelwright's focus on religion does not resolve his ambivalence about everyday life. But in his pervasive unwillingness to understand religion as a life choice, Wheelwright overlooks the parallel implications of religion for the women in his life. In Canada, he finds a personal messiah in the Reverend Katherine Keeling, an Anglican minister and mother, who, thanks to the rite of her church, can be a mother who serves God. In a gesture of affirmation and love, she lets Wheelwright play "Dutch uncle" to her children to share the love of her family with him. Yet here

Wheelwright reveals himself as an unreliable narrator because he inadvertently shows more to the reader than he himself can realize.

In earlier Irving novels, the women are almost uniformly victims of physical violence. In *Owen Meany* they are victims of what the reader (and not the narrator) recognizes as psychic violence: of anorexia, a disease that reflects women's need to control the only thing society lets them control, their own bodies. The two most significant women in Wheelwright's life may be anorexic. Katherine is too thin, Wheelwright says offhandedly. Is she ill, or is it only the narrator's preference for women who are zaftig? Similarly, Hester's proclivity to throw up at crucial moments is interpreted by John as her reaction to drinking too much — but he doesn't report seeing her drink. These women may be exhibiting a total physical response to the illusions controlling their lives. Both women's careers are based on the correlation of religion to lifestyle (one as a minister, one as an antireligion satirist), but both are nonetheless trapped in the restrictions of these socially acknowledged lives.

John Wheelwright is ultimately blind to the implications of religious imagery and stereotypes for women's lives. This is, however, not his only area of blindness. John's and Owen's lives are set into opposition to teach not only the relation of religion and life but also the limitations imposed by conventional definitions of manhood — the United States' "other religion" of success and power.

Just as both boys' lives are narrated in a way that reflects religious tropes (such as that of the Holy Family), they are also narrated to reflect current concepts about war and the conventional symbols of manhood: size, voice (written or spoken word), and potency. Owen Meany is as unlikely a wielder of power as was Grass's Oskar Matzerath, but both share the power of the voice, for example. Oskar can shatter (or etch) glass with his; Owen irritates vocally (and typographically, since his words are printed all in capitals), yet he achieves his strength as the feared contributor to his prep school's paper, *The Voice*. Wheelwright, in contrast, is dyslexic (273), and he becomes addicted to the word only in Canada, when he can't live without his newspaper (389). John's father is also vocally impaired, nursing a stutter until he admits his paternity (479). These men achieve their power only as adults, when they espouse conventional lifestyles (father, critic, warrior) — some of the tropes or "master narratives" of culture that guide individuals into life niches. In this case, these narratives about war and manhood exclude women utterly (unlike the religious tropes), just as they entrap the men into doomed lives. Too, these tropes of manhood entrap men just as inexorably as the religious ones may have done to Irving's women (a conclusion hinted at but not drawn by the willfully unknowing Wheelwright).

Owen arranges his ultimate proof of manhood (or the fulfillment of his vision, his self-delusion) when he stands on his toes and achieves the height necessary to enlist in the Army (365). However, he cannot scale the obstacle course wall, so a choice combat assignment in weapons is denied him (411). Instead, he becomes the honor guard for bodies being shipped home (perhaps another allusion to Grass, to the half-mad gravedigger in *The Tin Drum*). Nonetheless, Owen fulfills his self-declared destiny as a hero (ultimately being blown to bits to save some children). Yet while Owen lives out one narrative of manhood, he expresses a certain degree of doubt about it in counseling Wheelwright on draft dodging. Owen's advice, however, is couched in an alternative male discourse of the day: John should become a member of the peace movement to "get laid" by all the women there, move in with Hester (a folk singer at that time), and ultimately move to Canada as a political statement, as a pretend draft dodger.

On the face of the narrative, Owen is the only one to live out the male nightmare of the age, becoming a soldier in Vietnam. John already has his deferment on political grounds; one cousin (Simon) is 4F because of his knees, and the other (Noah) joins the Peace Corps. Ultimately, though, John Wheelwright is also shown to be a victim of these master myths of male behavior because he has been disenfranchised from free social choice. Because he is physically deformed, he does not achieve the military-hero status that Owen does. The impact of his deferred trial is so great that he must eventually even withdraw from the company of males. He consciously chooses, for example, to withdraw from the education of boys and become a "Mr. Chips" for the Bishop Strachan School, a girl's secondary school. With his withdrawal from the United States to his more comfortable religious myth, then, John Wheelwright has essentially removed himself from a male role except as an adoptive uncle to children. To the Reverend Katherine, in consequence, he seems to be a "nonpracticing homosexual" (375), a nonmale.

In Canada, John tries to substitute the women's choice of master social narrative (religion) for those of the American male, but he knows he lives a lie. Wheelwright doesn't even have the satisfaction of being a real draft dodger or of playing an active role in the peace movement, as Hester did. In consequence, he can't even express his own reaction to Vietnam, when even Hester can (she wrestles Owen to the ground when he asserts he's going to war [421 ff.]) — his move to Canada deprives him of a "true male voice" (no matter how inadequate that voice is) and the ability to craft a life according to its socially acceptable tropes. He is thus left in the company of women, as a man who can narrate women's downfalls from a nonparticipatory distance. No wonder that his thesis is a sympathetic treatment of Thomas Hardy's women.

The education that Wheelwright ultimately refuses is thus a deeper lying social narrative: the relation of males and females in his culture. The war narratives about manhood explicitly exclude women, while they trap men; but the religious narratives onto which John falls back serve only to mask gender conflicts as religious ones, conflicts among Catholics, Anglicans, and Puritans. Again, religious tropes about women pervade the novel and add to Wheelwright's inability to learn about and integrate himself into his society. In the novel, Wheelwright and Owen "grow out" of Catholicism by the time they reach college and try out a new set of narratives about manhood to guide their lives. They have tacitly discarded their earlier Holy Family fantasies but still retain odd notions about women and virginity compatible with their new public myths of maleness. Primary among these is a virgin-whore dualism conditioning males' evaluation of women. While Catholics use the nun or virgin-whore dualism to encompass the good and bad sides of females, the equivalent Protestant trope is virgin-magdalen (that is, reformed prostitute, not whore per se). Both Owen Meany's and John Wheelwright's lives constantly spiral around these tropes. For example, Owen disarms and beheads a statue of Mary Magdelene in the churchyard; later, and without Wheelwright's knowledge, he attaches the scavenged arms to Tabitha Wheelwright's dressmaker's dummy, which becomes his personal fetish — a symbolic synthesis of the two most important women in his life. Through this appropriation, Owen has synthesized his own virgin and whore fantasies, leaving open the question of whether his primary motivation was religious or sexual.

Where the reader sees Wheelwright's inability to resolve the ambivalences between religious and male narratives in his culture, the novel also reveals how little he sees about how these narratives obscure and trap the women in his life. Unconsciously, Wheelwright continuously identifies the women around him in terms of these damaging tropes or master narratives, again deferring the core of the education his world could offer him.

Each woman plays a part in the dance between religion and maleness, virgin and whore. First among these coded, lost women is Wheelwright's grandmother, Harriet, representing the Protestant matriarch of old stock. She upholds family honor in the town at all costs; because she cannot accept any restructuring of her rigid notions about the family, she condemns her daughter to dissimulation to preserve appearances. Instead of finding out what her daughter needs emotionally, she worries about the town's opinions. Similarly, as the town's grande dame, she puts the brilliant but underprivileged Owen Meany through school. What ultimately sustains Harriet after the death of her daughter is television: Owen watches with her, and they share mass culture delusions about how the world works. Her favorite fare is old movies in which the world as she knew it still seems intact, promising her the social power that can no longer be wielded.

Where Harriet is the "good woman," Tabitha Wheelwright plays the "bad woman" or Hester Prynne of the story, dressing in black and living like a nun to preserve her mother's delusion of respectability. Publicly, she plays the happy magdalen (repenting of past sexual crimes and devoting her chaste life to the welfare of her son), but in private she preserves an alternate life in a red dress: she becomes a third-class lounge performer, singing chiefly old Sinatra songs in a pleasant but weak voice (318). She is thus actually an unrepentant magdalen, upholding the social order to save her son financially: her mother will support them if she seems to behave — an important fiction, because she cannot support herself. Tabitha even postpones her marriage to Dan Needham for four years because of the tacit social pressure prohibiting the revelation of John's real father, the married Reverend Merrill (486). Yet her voice, both really and metaphorically, is not strong enough to allow her to survive with her son alone by writing a new master narrative valorizing her life. Symbolically (in John's religious interpretation), her death is caused by the deceit of her position since she may have presented her temple to the baseball — the weapon of her destruction when she turned to see the Reverend Merrill instead of watching the game. Tabitha was thus sacrificed to her mother, her son, and the morals of the town — to socially acceptable narratives.

That these master narratives of religiously and socially acceptable womanhood are disintegrating is glimpsed by the reader in the fragmentary story of the novel's real Hester, John Wheelwright's cousin. This Hester was not brought up to accept female narratives docilely. She grows up a tomboy, constantly running to catch up with her older brothers, who torment and taunt her. She eventually does catch up, since she graduates with them — she skips a grade, while one brother is put back. In any of the standard roles available to her, she cannot effect society to her satisfaction. For instance, as a folksinger (a 1960s trope), she has a voice that is physically just not loud enough to protest the war effectively.

In private, Hester can be more effective, if seemingly less consistent: she enters into a relationship with Owen Meany yet quite happily punches him when he begins to speak like a macho war hero. While John is "neutered" by his oppositional experience of Owen (453), then, Hester is sexually radicalized by her (probably platonic) relationship with him. John drops from public sight in moving to Canada; Hester inverts his silence and becomes a rock star, "Hester the Molester" (her brothers' childhood name for her when they teased her ruthlessly). In her personal sadistic reverse of male stereotypes, she specializes in seducing young male virgins as her way of practicing "safe sex" (453). In this negative, inverted role, she has achieved a public voice that Wheelwright as narrator does not understand: her rock videos appeal both to young females and to the Reverend Katherine, intercutting black-and-white images of sex and war with songs (453).

John Wheelwright is ultimately unable (or unwilling) to learn from Hester's choices. When Hester declares that she will have no children, since Owen wouldn't father them, John considers her damaged, almost mad (508). But again the chronology of her story makes clear *to the reader* that losing Owen freed her to have a public career on unconventional terms — she is protesting the inadequacy of the narratives available to her (and to the males in her life). In this evaluation, John relates to her only in terms of the male bonding he had with Owen; he runs off after Owen's funeral. When he abandons her, he loses his ability to learn about women. He will not understand that Hester, as a rock star, parodies the symbols on which he and Owen patterned their lives, reclaiming as a source of strength the Catholic whore image that the boys had discarded in their politics in favor of the Puritan or Anglican magdalen. In inverting her "approved" social myths, Hester reclaims passion and a relation to the public sphere. Because

Wheelwright cannot show us the coherence of Hester's new life, readers do not know if she is happy or emotionally damaged; we see only that she knows how to get her message out to the public.

Together these three generations of women are marked by the virgin-whore differential in different ways, as part of the great pattern of social narratives that have created John and Owen. The older generation, represented by Harriet, claims voice and power by first excluding men and then excluding the social and psychological realities of new epochs. The middle generation, embodied by Tabitha, dies — typical for Irving's 1950s mothers. These two mothers recede into silence because they have nothing they can say (remember, too, that Oskar's mother commits suicide by eating eels because she cannot deal with the conflicts between her German husband and her Polish lover). Tabitha reaches out to men with only limited public recognition (a Wednesday night booking in a third-class nightclub under an assumed name). She remains, like her dressmaker dummy, essentially headless.

The youngest generation of women in the novel is represented not only by Hester the Molester but also by the Reverend Katherine. They have power in the social sphere, but they pay for it. Hester may remain childless, but she exerts great influence on young girls (echoing again Irving's Susie-the-Bear, who adopts Franny Berry Jones's child but will not have her own). Katherine is principal of the school at which John Wheelwright works, she has a large family of her own, and she is able to serve the Lord, as already noted. While Hester has, then, largely renounced the acceptable configuration of home and family, Katherine lives the life of the double burden — sanctified and self-sanctifying by upholding both religious and social tradition.

The inability of Owen Meany to address the women and John's inability to articulate the pain of their positions mirror Grass's narrators. But Oskar's insensitivity to his eel-eating mother and his midget lover are simple egotistic absences. Irving's narrators remain more fundamentally unreliable than Grass's because they are enmeshed in a vague tangle of images from religion and society. Oskar is an egotist; John Wheelwright is confused and unable to confront the narratives of his culture.

What remains most crucial, and what differentiates Irving's ideological criticism through narration from Grass's, is this unreliability of his male narrators vis-à-vis women's lives and feelings. Only in Irving's novel are male social spheres explicitly juxtaposed with "men's illusions about women." These men think they control their lives, but, as the traditional educational novel recognized, women shape their lives. Unlike Grass's women (or those in the traditional *Bildungsroman*), however, Irving's women don't "go away" when the men grow beyond them. Behind the control of the male narrator, Irving's women are seen obliquely, trapped in the same "forces shaping our lives" (Irving's starting lines). This social world is a reciprocity between male and female; Irving's males sense that, but they cannot comprehend all that it implies. John Wheelwright appreciates women and fears them. This point of view is not feminist — he does not purport to speak for women or their rights. It is, however, decisively social-critical in revealing current gender constructs as creators of frightened males and damaged females.

The Feminist Antieducational Novel

Moving back to the question of the genre he borrowed, the *Bildungsroman*, we see that what renders Irving's narrative point of view unique is that he allows his narrators not only to tell their stories but also to show what confuses them. Particularly the women confuse Irving's narrator: they educate him by unsettling his assumptions and by showing how little he knows about them. Men like Wheelwright underestimate women consistently: "Thus we invent our lives" (*Hotel* 427). He is shocked, for instance, when he finds about Tabitha's alternate life, and he cannot approve of Hester the Molester's rock videos. Nonetheless, these women emerge for the readers as true, three-dimensional characters in those moments when they (often out of silence) explode into their sons' or lovers' consciousness. The narrator records their telling gestures or words, although these are not always conveyed in the sense in which they were enunciated. The women occupy social spaces that do not give them voices that the men can hear. That is a loss for the men, one that also wreaks violence on the women.

The unreliability of the narrator is crucial to the genre Irving has inherited, yet that narrator transmits a different message from Grass's. Both Grass and Irving intend their unreliable narrators as vehicles for political critique. Yet only Irving critiques gender constructs. Grass's antieducational novel shows the narrator recapturing his past, leaving the reader to second-guess the degree to which the narrator may or may not realize the growth of education and assimilation into society. Since the narrator is unreliable, pieces in the narrated growth pattern are missing. Readers are led to ferret out missing information but not necessarily to question this narrator out of their own experiences; they cannot identify with Oskar's grotesque, abnormal life, for example.

Irving's antieducational novel has larger claims: his narrators fail, but the novelist hopes to show us more, to suggest where we might look to identify with the narrated lives and find the *source* of their problems. For this reason, Irving's narrators are often more typical products of the dominant culture and less consciously the dropouts or exceptional figures that Grass chooses. Irving's reader knows more than the narrator and can second-guess his growth The truth of Irving's antieducation is thus not in the male voices of his narrators; it lies in the dynamics of what they see and what they do not. In each of the major novels that may be classified as antieducational novels — *The World According to Garp*, *Hotel New Hampshire*, *The Cider-House Rules*, *A Prayer for Owen Meany*, and *A Son of the Circus* — at least one woman grows parallel to the man within the same society; each is glimpsed by a sympathetic male narrator as a social construct (a "victim") but not necessarily comprehended.

Irving's criticism thus stresses personal identity constructs, while Grass construes politics in largely ungendered terms. Irving's figures end up in compromised lives that indicate clearly the constraints of their social roles. As he stated, women and children are the victims of the most violence in today's world, but half those children grow up to be men, who carry with them the damage done to and the strengths represented by the victimized women who bore and raised them. John Wheelwright does not purport to explain why Hester is the way she is: he only shows what she does. His narrator cannot even approve of or understand her voice. Implicitly, the narrator in *Owen Meany* fails in creating his life to the degree that he fails to explain hers. In very real terms, Irving is using his open narrative structure to echo the ongoing dialectical relationship that exists between men and women in today's society. For every damaged woman, there is at least one confused man: a brother who admires a sister's strength while deploring what was done to her, her pain his failed masculinity; a son who buys into a false image of his mother, dispels it, and then cannot find a viable image in his social environment for further relationships with women.

Irving has thus taken a genre and a narrative technique from Grass and expanded them through his own social agenda about the family, an agenda that he presents as integral to any subsequent political agenda. Individual lives are important, not the illusions fostered by socially acceptable narratives. Instead of educating his heroes into the truth of their society, as the classical educational novel did, or questioning that education in an antieducational novel, as Grass did, Irving educates his men in their own ignorance about women and in the interrelatedness of the sexes in terms of mutually constraining gender roles. Here Irving not only suggests alternatives to the patriarchal family but also demonstrates the mutability of gender roles. In this sense, he has bypassed a partisan feminist critique for a gender critique of society, suggesting the need for new educations for both men and women. The traditional education novel traces the hero's integration into society. Grass's antieducational novel shows the impossibility of this integration because society has become schizophrenic. But Irving's work stresses that not only individuals but family units, not only men but also women, are being denied by this new social (not just narrative) schizophrenia.[8]

Notes

[1]Good general introductions to Grass in English are Richard H. Lawson, *Günter Grass*, and Michael Hollington, *Günter Grass* (with a very useful bibliography). A set of plot summaries of the major novels with commentary is provided in Alan Frank Keele, *Understanding Günter Grass*. Fine collections of critical essays in English introducing the major problematics of Grass's work and conception are Patrick O'Neill, ed., *Critical Essays on Günter Grass* (which includes John Irving's review of *Headbirths*); Siegfried Mews, ed., *"The Fisherman and His Wife"*; and Gertrud Bauer Pickar, ed., *Adventures of a Flounder*. In German, an equivalent volume is edited by Manfred Durzak. A collection of reviews of *The Tin Drum* is edited by Franz Josef Görtz under the title *"Die Blechtrommel."* An overview of scholarship on Grass is found in the book by Volker Neuhaus.

For general introductions to John Irving's work, see the book by Gabriel Miller and that by Carol C. Harter and James R. Thompson; see also the 1985 bibliography by Edward C. Reilly. Two central essays in which Irving acknowledges his reliance on Dickens are reprinted in his *Trying to Save Piggy Sneed*: "The King of the Novel" (347–81) and "An Introduction to *A Christmas Carol*" (383–94).

[2]For example, Towers in the *New York Review of Books*; Kazin in the *New York Times Book Review*, who denies that the book has any irony; Wall in the *Christian Century*; Pritchard in the *New Republic*; and the most recent by Page (who calls it a *Bildungsroman* and traces its religious imagery) and Shostak (who gives it a Freudian interpretation).

[3]For aspects of Grass's U.S. receptions, see Patrick O'Neill, "A Different Drummer." The most useful introduction to *The Tin Drum* is Walter Jahnke and Klaus Lindemann, *Günter Grass, "Die Blechtrommel,"* which offers individual analyses of various symbol systems in this extremely dense novel. Arker, *Nichts ist vorbei*, is a German dissertation that offers the most complete discussion of the novel.

[4]This review has been reprinted in John Irving, *Trying to Save Piggy Sneed* (397–412), together with expanded "Author's Notes" commenting on his continuing engagement with Grass.

[5]Even his 1994 novel set in India, *A Son of the Circus*, treats nontraditional families.

[6]As Jane Bowers Hill points out, Irving exploits the *ingredients* of soap opera in showing the social exploitation of women, but that doesn't make the resulting books soap operas: "Irving employs the sub-genre that best embodies the popular mindset of our time, uses soap opera, . . . to expand the boundaries of the novel to life size again, to combat the contemporary novel's anorexic tendencies" (42–43).

[7]John Wheelwright's name may even be a play on that of the literary critic, Philip Wheelwright (1901–70), who was interested in the symbolism of religion and ritual in art. Grass's use of religious symbolism is broadly acknowledged (for example, by Guidry).

[8]This conclusion moves *A Prayer for Owen Meany* beyond the critiques offered in Irving's earlier works. The withdrawal into the family that characterized the endings of *Garp* and *Hotel New Hampshire* doesn't work for people without immense personal resources. In *Owen Meany*, Irving states firmly that we can't all move to Canada (see Edward C. Reilly, *Understanding John Irving*, chapter 8, which comments

on the Canada connection). Even if we did, we would still be addicted to the news. Like Wheelwright, we can deny the existence of our problems, but that doesn't mean we're solving them — the social revolution of the 1960s has not had deep effect on available social narratives.

4: Robert Wilson: Postmodernism in Cultural Contact

"Postmodernism" is a term from literary criticism that has entered more general usage, appearing in everything from *New Yorker* cartoons to architecture. It is the rubric applied to the most modern, trendy, and witty performances to signal the kind of art and social practice that claims to have freed itself from the shackles of tradition. In fact, says Hal Foster, "In art and architecture neoconservative postmodernism is marked by an eclectic historicism, in which old and new modes and styles (used goods, as it were) are retooled and recycled. In architecture this practice tends to the use of a campy pop-classical order to decorate the usual shed . . . indeed, the classical often returns as pop" ("(Post)Modern Polemics" 67). The postmodern is thus where cultures meet: where the sensibilities of different ages and nations are brought into contact so that the viewers or readers are startled out of complacency and required to rethink what they have considered "natural."

In the world of contemporary theater, the role of the postmodernist par excellence is played by playwright, director, and designer Robert Wilson, whose work has been familiar to audiences in Europe and New York for over two decades. His work first attained broader notice in the flurry of publicity surrounding the privatized funding of the 1984 Olympic Games in Los Angeles. As part of the festival around the games, Wilson's *the CIVIL warS* was originally scheduled (or rather, a production uniting its several sections, each a multi-hour program produced in a different European location over the preceding years).[1] The funding could not be found. Despite such setbacks, Wilson has remained prominent throughout the United States and Europe, particularly as a stage designer.

As an artistic citizen of two continents, Wilson shocks and amazes audiences on both, most often by stark juxtapositions of cultural references that destroy conventional narratives of history, occasionally in ways that offend the audience (see Lipman). His theater also calls traditional theater practice into question since his role is often closer to impresario or ringmaster than to playwright or director — Lehmann calls him a "scenographer" (Lehmann's usage to denote a parallel to choreographer). And his greatest recent successes have been as an opera designer and director, perhaps because audiences for opera (especially in Europe) are more tolerant of the avant-garde and of postmodern irreverence than was the U. S. Olympic Committee.

One of the most thoroughly documented Wilson pieces, *Death, Destruction, and Detroit* (1979, referred to as *DD&D*), provides perhaps the

best index to how Wilson's work exploits his awareness of working between national traditions. *DD&D* is also one of the last full-scale pieces that
Wilson did without a collaborator (he has often collaborated with contemporary minimalist composer Philip Glass or, more recently, Heiner Müller),
and with a professional cast (the actors of what was then the Schaubühne
am Halleschen Ufer in Berlin.[2] It was also unusual in that it was not a staging or adaptation of material written by others. In what follows, I will trace
the demands made on the audience and on theatrical infrastructure by the
text, the cultural-historical materials on which it is based, and the actual
performance practice employed. The explicitly political material on which
DD&D draws also allows this work to function as an index to the historical
and cultural blind spots between the two cultures (Germany and the United
States) on which Wilson was playing and which conditioned the relative
success or failure of this quintessentially postmodern, culturally-critical
work. *DD&D* was perceived to be a postmodern questioning of the "grand
narratives" of Western history (Lyotard xxiii), a play written to enhance the
audience's "incredulity toward metanarratives" (xxxiv) and their skepticism
toward the institutions or systems that live off these narratives.[3] But as we
shall see, *DD&D* was a participant in other types of cultural dynamics as
well, which make its role as the work of an intercultural artist much more
crucial than its aesthetics. That is, by adhering to critics' and audience's expectations about postmodernism, Wilson and *DD&D* stage not just an aesthetic confrontation but also a confrontation of cultures for audiences and
critics alike.

Modernist Critics, Postmodern Theater

The stereotype about postmodern artists is that they hope, by shattering traditional referential contexts for discourses, to aid in dissipating the oppres-
sive power of these traditions over individual members of society. Perhaps
in following this stereotype, recent critics have pursued Wilson's work as a
kind of counterhegemonic, antitraditionalist theatrical practice.

What is interesting about Wilson's recent canonization as a postmodernist, however, is that critics have always defined his work differently from
the way he does. When he speaks in his own voice, Wilson usually defines
his own aesthetics in relatively simple terms. At other times he seems to
conspire with his critics to express a public "party line" about the works —
to support a critic's drawing of a public profile for "a Robert Wilson spectacle" infamous in its own right. This public profile rests on critics' attempts
to establish public expectation about Wilson's works and impact. In this
sense, the critics are participating in what Hans Magnus Enzensberger has
called "the consciousness industry": they define a reality for an audience by
their practice, creating a horizon of expectation (Jauss 22–23) that makes a
Wilson play comprehensible to that audience.

Most critics recognize that Wilson's works question standard assumptions about theatrical space, performance, and audience reception. His techniques for doing so are taken from the canon of modernist minimalism (not surprising, since a number of his most successful pieces have been collaborations with Philip Glass; even his graphic works are exhibited in modernist galleries). In fact, Wilson was first presented to his audiences in Europe as a prototypical modernist, in an "Open Letter to André Breton," written by Louis Aragon and published in *Les Lettres Françaises*, 2–8 June 1971. In this article, the Paris production of *Deafman Glance* was touted as a miracle, "une extraordinaire machine de la liberté," including the freedom of the body and mind (quoted in Brecht 438). This statement echoes the myth of the modern artist-creator-genius whose individual strength and vision can liberate a generation from the weight of the past.

Stefan Brecht, a major Wilson proponent, describes early Wilson productions in similar terms in *The Original Theatre of the City of New York . . . The Theatre of Visions*. Brecht set the patterns for future discussions by theater professionals and aficionados about a growing body of unusual work; he describes the works from the perspective of a participant actor who has found his theatrical messiah, his artist-liberator myth. He tries to explain (rationalize?) what went on in a production like *Deafman Glance* by describing the various layers that went into it (visual, musical, verbal, movement); he explains that the apparent chaos of the production has a deeper unity, an appeal to both the left- and right-brain cognitive centers of the audience.

In essence, Brecht takes the line that Wilson's works are so far off standard theater practice that they must be the work of a genius, conveying an alternate, liberating experience to an audience trapped in traditional expectations. Each production is described as a process; Brecht refuses to specify any "message" inherent in them. Overall, his comments make a Wilson work sound like modern minimalism, a tradition represented, for instance, by Philip Glass and John Cage, who try to alienate the audience into accepting a piece on pure terms, purportedly removed from any cultural conditioning. However, Brecht's reports are not commensurate with Wilson's transcribed interviews from the same period, included in the same volume. These indicate that Wilson is strikingly nonverbal; he speaks in fragments, in trailing sentences, and in "ready-made" paragraphs of explanation about what he does with visual materials, comments which do not necessarily fit what went on before or after in a particular sequence of exchanges.

The "ready-made" paragraphs that Wilson uses may well be borrowed from previous critics, not evolved out of his own aesthetic philosophy; he seems to use his critics as this first sounding-boards to develop a verbal and conventionally-acceptable explanation for the public about what he just does instinctually. Such borrowings are commensurate with the kind of critique of institutionalized and official artistic practice considered characteristic of postmodernism, emphasizing "found" materials and cultural context.

Nonetheless, Brecht persists in "introducing" Wilson as a modernist, a liberator of theatrical practice.

Yet other (and less partisan) critics provide performance reviews that may be more instructive about Wilson's stage pieces, revealing them as something beyond (or less than) modern minimalism in the theater. Taken together, these reviews call the identification of Wilson's work as modernism into doubt; they also suggest what their audiences come to identify as a new generation of *postmodern* theater, exercising a new kind of cultural critique. Samuel Lipman's commentary on *Einstein on the Beach* at the Brooklyn Academy of Music in 1984 is typical of criticism later than Brecht's. Yes, *Einstein* sold out the house, but Glass and Wilson were putting their audience on, disguising monstrous pretense as important modern creativity — "yet another example of the European readiness to be charmed by American simplicities at once eccentric and divine" (16):

> There is no point in attempting to describe the story line of the knee plays [*sic*], for it is part and parcel of Wilson's aesthetic that there is none. Instead, the watcher is confronted by a motley assortment of symbols drawn from the stock inventory of emotionally charged detritus floating about in every half-educated intellectual's mind . . . . It was all creaky, and its minimalism extended well beyond its conception of its craftsmanship. (17–18)

Other choice adjectives include "boring" and "amateurish " (18); Glass's score is even dismissed as "pre-performance doodling" (20).

This judgment is particularly interesting because Lipman clearly knows the performance history of this material (he recognized sections from earlier productions, the first set pieces that would recur in *the CIVIL warS*); he is not reacting out of ignorance. This was, in his estimation, a bad performance of a work in an intolerable genre that degrades theatrical practice. To counter such negative reactions, other critics preferred to describe the piece as a minimalist religious experience (see, for example, Rockwell, "Stage"). But Lipman disparages this Wilson production as recycled late 1970s theater:

> The verdict on *Einstein* as an artwork must be that, as a collaboration, it represents a vastly more interesting work than either [Wilson or Glass] has been able to achieve on his own. (22)
>
> It is equally clear, it bears repeating, that neither Wilson nor Glass, working separately, has been able to achieve the success on his own that they have earned together. (24)

Lipman prefers to believe that Wilson's publicity is the Brooklyn Academy's marketing coup, not reflective of a new voice in the theater at all. Lipman gives the audience leave to pan the performance utterly.

Lipman has never been alone in assessing Wilson as failed because he does not provide a coherent artistic critique or program for a new generation. These themes pervaded reviews of the 1970s and early 1980s. Günther Rühle, in a German review of *DD&D*, says that there are, in general, many vague critical comments "out of purely not knowing what to say" about the piece (7). When critics cannot uncover a unitary artistic program in Wilson's work in terms they recognize, they also simply designate it a "failure." The typical Wilson review describes scenes and images that stick in the mind and outline the "star turns" that make certain scenes memorable (in the case of *DD&D*, these were almost all due to one actor, Otto Sander). At best, the average critic in the early 1980s identified Wilson's work as "postdramatic" (Lehmann 559) — as minimalist theater with all plots removed.

More recently, since the mid-1980s, a repeat collaborator, Heiner Müller, has had great success in working with Wilson and in formulating his program on other terms, as have the various opera houses for which he has worked most recently in the 1990s: "I was interested in doing almost anything together with Robert Wilson, simply because he's something foreign" (Wilson and Müller 45–46). Originally, in working on a sequel called *DD&D II*, Müller was given a batch of material by Wilson to make into a text; he decided it was a "family story." Müller's open letter to Wilson on *DD&D II* (reprinted in the text program) confirms that the piece did not achieve closure as a text or as a critique in modernist terms:

> For a week I've tried to manufacture a text which can serve as a center of gravity for your production of *DD&D II*, a construction which consists of its own explosion, more than your earlier works do. The attempt has failed. Maybe the explosion had already flourished too broadly, the degree of acceleration become too great (I don't mean in the clock sense) for a text (which necessarily means something) to be able to write itself into the whirlwind of the detonation. (Müller, unpaginated)

This statement is paradoxical: is Müller criticizing Wilson, or is he admitting he is not up to the task of making a text for the piece, to doing what Wilson himself did not do for *DD&D II*? Calling Wilson's piece an "explosion," though, identifies it indirectly as a postmodern play (one that resists a unified interpretation).

As a practicing playwright, Müller was clearly not happy with all of Wilson's spontaneity and willingness to improvise. Müller wanted to make a text, while Wilson wished to play with the theater space, with the actors, and with found visual materials. Yet while Müller retained certain doubts about Wilson (and placed some distance between himself and Wilson for the German audience for that production), Wilson was delighted to work on *DD&D II* with a German playwright — language was not a barrier for a theater concentrating on space (*[der deutsche Teil von] the CIVIL warS* 51–53). As they worked, Wilson felt that Müller would follow the lead he set, trying to match tones or words, not necessarily "sense." Wilson thus firmly tied himself (in what was then then West Berlin) to perhaps the most eminent East German playwright of the generation, but not necessarily in terms of traditional playwriting.

Except for Müller, though, critics through the 1980s generally refused to approach Wilson's works with new eyes. In contrast, Wilson's stagings of Müller's plays have been consistently well received (especially *Hamletmachine*), as were those of Philip Glass' works (most notably *Einstein on the Beach*), the early 1990s U.S. tour of *the Knee Plays*, a work with David Byrne (who contributes considerable popular visibility), and his work with the major opera houses of the world.[4] Yet any Wilson success, even a staging rather than an original work, still runs the danger of being considered a hoax by critics. As early as 1979, *Theater heute* offered three articles on the original *DD&D* in 1979 under the section heading "Robert Wilson: Genius or Bluffer?" These European critics were expecting a critical modernist expressing a great message in his works, and they did not find him (they found the play particularly humorless since it consumed public art funds to make what they considered trivial allusions to the German Nazi past).

By the time *the CIVIL warS* debate hit the popular press in the United States and the world, Wilson's unique theater practice and international reputation even contributed to the debacle. Yet by the mid-1980s, a new critical perspective had also finally entered reviews, which now stressed not his personal genius but rather a new kind of historical critique at the basis of his work:

> With *the CIVIL warS*, Robert Wilson's theater has grown up. The visions of the childlike dreamer are tied to the reins of language, literature, historical consciousness, meaning. That makes them stricter and more serious, that is disenchantment. Even Wilson's theater does not create any worlds of its own any more, but points complainingly to the familiar, poor one that we already have. ("Mein Vater" 162)

From a theater director's point of view, Wilson was still dangerous: "It is common for people to walk out of a Wilson production halfway through, even halfway through a short (for him) work of two or three hours. They tend to leave glowering and muttering to themselves about obscurantism" (McLaughlin 57). But Wilson had finally repeated seminal elements of his productions often enough to make it seem as if he had a consistent aesthetics. Critics weren't sure yet that Wilson was a genius, but he was no longer simply a bluffer.

What may also have come into play here is the fact that audiences were beginning to enjoy looking at Wilson spectacles even if they did not understand them. Critics' reviews from the late 1980s still identify Wilson's recurring ready-mades, call them kitsch, and ask whether he has lost his touch (Matussek 255; Lieberson 21). At the same time, however, audiences began to come to see his "stunning flops" (Lieberson 21) as the kind of "explosion" that Müller identified. And owners of theaters had moved beyond the Olympic Committee into a phase of capitalizing on Wilson's reputation (or notoriety) when they hired him to stage standards, always with a twist. By the mid-1980s in Europe and the United States, Wilson had become marketable — as an event if not as an artist with a vision.

Where the critics lagged behind the theater owners and the public is in acknowledging that an artist like Wilson has a distinct profile, whether or not that profile is part of any official aesthetics. That profile, however, is itself a work of art. As we shall see, Wilson has been very active in creating this new horizon of expectation about his own creativity — he has, in fact, changed his official images periodically in order to continue his theatrical practice almost without change for twenty years.

Wilson's Postmodern Aesthetics

In the 1970s, as noted, Wilson said very little to critics like Brecht, who were trying to frame him as a modernist. In contrast, by the 1980s Wilson began to present himself actively in ways that echo postmodernism's general critique of representation. In an interview, "About Video," given on 2 July 1986,[5] for example, Robert Wilson stresses that he pulls apart traditional assumptions about his medium, particularly by isolating various dimensions of a particular piece or performance. His statements about video seem to apply to his work in all media:

> My purpose in this method of working is to emphasize the importance of each separate element . . . . In many of my pieces, what you see and what you hear do not go together. The video and the audio are meant to stand on their own. If you closed your eyes you would still be able to appreciate the program, and the same would be true if you turned off the sound and just looked. What I am trying to do is give individual lives to both sound and picture. (2–3)

The separating of "tracks" in his videos indicates that he sees the piece as a type of collage, not as an integrated whole in the traditional sense; in it he works to isolate strands of meaning (words, images, music) instead of integrating them — he removes them from their traditional functions as "master discourses" in video productions and forces the audience to consider them in a new here and now. Wilson's theater pieces have almost always followed this pattern as well, detaching text from image from music from audience reaction.

Wilson consistently ties up his comments on his aesthetics with the persona he projects as an artist. He creates an "origin myth" for himself that stresses the social outcast (a far cry from the modern artist-hero). The story seems to vary slightly in each telling (that is, in each interview), which again makes the "meaning" of his biography shift freely. In effect, though, this makes him a moving target for critics: he is subverting expectations about himself at every turn.

Some facts are indisputable. Wilson grew up in Waco, Texas. As a child, he had a severe stutter that was alleviated (never cured) by his working with a ballet teacher, Byrd Hoffman (Stearns [2d ed.] 32). Hoffman used slow rhythmic patterns as a form of physical therapy for those with speech impediments. Through rhythmic gymnastics, she taught students to synchronize their minds and bodies. It worked for Wilson. In memory of what she did, he named his first theater group in New York after her: The Byrd Hoffman School for Byrds (and Foundation); his performers were nicknamed "Byrds." While he was doing his first theater pieces, Wilson continued her work as well as his, doing consulting work with disabled children; reportedly, he was gifted in establishing rapport with them on their terms (Stearns [2d ed.] 32).

This origin story may be true as raw facts, but it has undergone significant revisions for various audiences. Its most compelling mythic dimension for the 1970s critics (the modern artist searching for, and eventually finding, his voice and his theater) may have been a marketing gambit originating in Europe. Its probable source was his agent, Nina Karlweiss, who purveyed Wilson's approach to performance into an artistic phenomenon that became a necessary part of European festivals in the 1970s (Iden 15). There is no public documentation on how Wilson's image was created, but he acknowledges Karlweiss's part in his first success in France (Prikker 32, 34). In any case, becoming a fixture at major European festivals was a necessary part of a modern artist's image in the 1970s. Such visibility would have guaranteed gallery space and invitations in the United States — and hence sales or funding for further projects. (See the discussion of Christo and Chicago in chapter 8 for more information on the 1970s art scene.) We may never know how conscious this mythmaking was in Wilson's case, but one should not forget that, aside from speech therapy, Wilson did study marketing at the University of Texas.

A comparison of interviews given over more than a decade reveals some interesting examples of Wilson's sensitivity to market forces in art. An obvious example is the relationship he claims between his stage work and the contemporary dance scene. Wilson's 1970s interviews stress that he was influenced by the way Merce Cunningham manipulated stage space and floor patterns with his dancers' bodies; by 1980 George Balanchine had become his source — a shift obviously parallel to Balanchine's growth in national visibility. Wilson gains a little in popularity by shifting his attributions and demonstrates a real gift for keeping abreast with "the scene," whatever that may be. A later interview provides another example of his willingness to play with his own image. In it he repeats and refutes his own origin myth: "I was spastic, blind, and deaf and dumb until I was 17, and through a divine miracle I learned to talk and walk — and that's not true!" (Kelleher 37). By calling his own master myth into question here, he is trying to get his interviewer to see his work in a new way, not through the filter of prior critical assumptions. Such well-placed "candor" would be out of place in a pure artist-hero biography but completely in tune with a postmodern critique of that kind of art.

Reviews also describe Wilson's working in terms that fit the interviewers' points of view rather than a fixed aesthetics. In the earliest of these, which try to rescue his art but not necessarily as theater, Wilson is identified as a graphic artist who "finds" some visual material — often a picture, or his own image of how someone sees (usually encompassing some distortion or an extreme way of seeing). Wilson then "stretches" the visual material to fill space and time, turning an image into a theater performance. This conversion happens first by means of a series of scene sketches looking not unlike tanagrams or minimalist art, each of which will be blown up into stage backdrops for individual scenes. These backdrops are minimalist series, often based on pairs of objects or fields (such as foreground-background reversals); the forms' progress through their transformations ties the performance together.[6]

While the scene sketches emerge, accounts continue, Wilson "finds" either music or a text from the time period he wishes to highlight in the piece.[7] If it is music, he lets it play freely through the time period of the production; if it is a text, he fragments it as a minimalist musician would, breaking it into units that will be freely varied like the phrases in Philip Glass's music. Often, too, the text is not spoken by the actors present but presented as a voice-over on tape, to which the actors move and mime. Wilson thus treats words as objects, not as meaning units. A 1971 press conference announced Wilson's feeling for words. As Calvin Tomkins reports, "he simply repeated the word 'dinosaur' over and over, for twelve hours, while cutting an onion the whole time . . . [he said] 'I wasn't sure whether I was *saying* other words, but I knew I was *hearing* other words, like *disaster* and *soaring*'" (Stearns [2d ed.] 93). In a similar vein, Wilson evolved the *Knee Plays* out of a telling pun. That title sounded like Noh theater (which suggested a legitimate historical references for the stylized motion Wilson employs), but the plays also serve functionally as the transitions or "joints" between the larger set pieces of *the CIVIL warS*.

If one traces Wilson's works backward, looking behind these descriptions, it is clear that his minimalism was indeed principally a backdrop for his careful self-representation. His primary identity was as a person who was always more concerned with redefining the space of the theater in ways that subvert modernist conventions by appealing to the audience — a description, if you will, of a critical postmodernist. This description leads the audience to perceive Wilson's theater as a staging area, a special space invaded by a series of oddly displaced everyday objects. Several productions, for instance, have had proscenium-height cats' legs walking through (Stearns [2d ed.] 19); dinosaurs, zeppelins, and oversize furniture frequently colonize the performance space Wilson has created. This theater space is thus neither spatially, dimensionally, nor temporally closed in ways familiar to regular theatergoers. In fact, it is not aesthetically closed either since many of its objects and visual projections recur between Wilson productions, with no predictable other coherence than the resources of the production staff. In the case of *DD&D*, for instance, it seems that up to half the visuals used had appeared in earlier works. Similarly, the *Letter for Queen Victoria* was about civil war, although it predated *the CIVIL warS* by a decade (reported in Marranca 40). Most importantly Wilson's stage objects are not to be taken to represent anything outside that theater space. As he summarizes: "I hate naturalism . . . it kills the mystery" (Graham).

Wilson's preferred definition of his stage is as a space that is not intended to represent other spaces but rather to be a space in use on its own terms. It relates to itself, to the audience and actors on a particular night, and to Wilson's sense of what that space may suggest in a certain time or geographical location. The audience is led to believe that actors enter the theater space to emphasize its inner rhythms, progressions, and hidden coherences. A sound-over provides an overall pulse to each scene, against which actors or objects appear and execute stylized movement patterns including everything from therapy rhythms through what looks like rhythmic gymnastics to Chaplin walks (one of Wilson's acknowledged sources [Prikker 34]). Each scene generally encompasses one cycle or progression, conceived as minimalists might have done: actors get from point A to point B; the music goes so far; the lighting goes from light to dark and back; a particular quoted text loop is completed.

Stefan Brecht documents Wilson's edict that the actors are not to play to the audience or to each other; they too have to have a new vision inculcated into them. Instead of relating, they are to play into whatever rhythm pattern evolves onstage, be it slow motion or a nightmarish hypertrophied walk. Wilson admonishes his actors, "Be more reserved vis-à-vis the public" (Lehmann 562). Wilson confirms how he works: "For me, the best way to [hold theater open as a forum] is [to do] something totally controlled and mechanical. And then there's freedom. Ideally, one would be a machine at work, one must become totally mechanical to become free" (quoted in Lehmann 563). His actors are thus forbidden to identify with anything but the present system he sets into motion.

Wilson establishes this narrative about his theatrical space in order to critique conventional theatrical practice. He asserts, for example, that he loved the ensemble he had to work with for *DD&D* (the Schaubühne am Halleschen Ufer; Stearns [2d ed.] 23), but he doesn't think actors should have to work so hard to please the public, as they were trained to do ("Märchenspiel" 208). In fact, Wilson claims to choose actors for the quality of their movements rather than for acting ability. This assertion encompasses a measure of historical truth, since Wilson's earliest collaborators were dancers. Later he turned to disabled people (a deaf boy who used visual communication in lieu of sound; an autistic savant who played with words the way the savant in cinema's *Rain Man* did with numbers). Still later, Philip Glass's minimalist music anchored Wilson's visual rhythms (see Shyer). But such a framing imposed on these truths also undercuts the importance of the official theater in which he was visiting. In *DD&D*, Wilson went so far as to invent the idea of a "found person" to parallel the older notion of "found objects": an old woman's face interested him on the street, so her face in a pinspot became the centerpiece of the ballroom scene that opened act 2. This "found person" got as much time on center stage as a star actor did.

Wilson's most common statements about his works are thus designed to keep his audience from expecting to see a play when they enter his theater. A Wilson audience is supposed to find its way gradually into the rhythm of the performance space rather than into other kinds of narrative coherence. Through this space, Wilson claims to alienate viewers from their presuppositions and thus "free" them — his ultimate self-created horizon of expectation about his theater. The Wilson of the 1970s and 1980s underscored this image of being interested in the theater as a space or even by claiming not to be interested in the work he has produced but rather in a pattern evolving in rehearsal. In a real sense, then, there are no real Wilson works with fixed structures whose effects on the audience may be calculated or learned; there are only Wilson productions, designed to leave the audience's reactions "free." And thus he himself is a new kind of artist, true to found objects (to process), not to the product of creation (what he terms his "classicism"), and one who is audience-friendly since he "never tried to be avant garde" (Graham).

Clearly, Wilson is trading simultaneously on the expectations of modernist critics (with their emphasis on originality and creativity) and on the audience's eagerness to subvert that kind of aesthetic authority and approach a theater space on other terms. It is a theater practice set in opposition to most critics but in full awareness of their function in the theater world. The "official" theater world has had its revenge. For example, that Wilson's productions don't have a final "book" has been noticed, to his detriment: *the CIVIL warS* was overwhelmingly voted, then denied, the Pulitzer Prize in 1986 because the work had never been performed (see the history of production in Stansbury 84). The work did not exist because it never has been performed except as four different twelve-hour "fragments" in Europe; there also was no "text" since the committee did not accept Wilson's explanation that it had a "visual book," Wilson's sketches for the production (Graham). Legally it doesn't exist, either: without a book, it could not be copyrighted as a play.

Such reactions are not detriments: Wilson argues that he is not really doing plays and that his productions and operas "don't have plots, they are architectural constructions in time and space " (Graham). He can even assert that he "never liked theater"; he only liked ballet because it is architectonic, "a temporal and spatial arrangement" (Lotringer 39). Or he can say, "I don't like the theater much. But I love the abstract, fluttering visual patterns of ballet, and I think that is basically what I've done in theater: architectural landscapes that are structured" (quoted in Walsh 85). To circumvent the "legitimate theater," then, Wilson embraces the theater as audience experience while not writing plays and not liking any of the traditional conventions of word-based theater pieces.

As Wilson's works have become more popular, these critics need to save face, and so they occasionally (but rarely) point to his explicit reliance on a whole other set of theater conventions, including Busby Berkeley and the Ziegfeld Follies (see, for example, Quadri 17). When Wilson calls his pieces operas, even when they rely on declamation rather than singing, critics react by referring to Wagner's *Gesamtkunstwerk*, thereby linking Wilson with another misunderstood and controversial genius who created a new stage form, unifying all the arts in a new way. Marranca even cites Wagner to emphasize that a Wilson performance is "a spiritualized state of clairvoyance" relying on mysticism, illusion (39), and "universal archetypes" (40). In an attempt to reposition Wilson in relation to more traditional theater, Marranca dubs Wilson's stage space a "prelinguistic world" (43), implying not only its dreamlike quality but also a certain juvenile quality. Yet when Wilson calls his *A Letter for Queen Victoria* an "opera," he simply does so because "everything in it happens at once, the way it does in operas and the way it does in life" (quoted in Marranca 49).

There is an active game going on between Wilson and the critics, one from which audiences are largely excluded, although both parties are lobbying for the ability to create that audience's horizon of expectation. At best, Wilson plays to several audiences at once. For critics, he plays into their myths of what artist-creators do; for audiences, he stresses the found wonder of a certain kind of experience. Over the twenty years of his career he has brought many critics over to his side: he has sold his works to them as a new kind of theatrical experience growing out of modernism and minimalism, out of art and music and dance, and out of a whole nonnaturalistic aesthetic. All of that, however, may "not be true," as he comments about his own life. Müller may have hit the Wilson aesthetic most squarely by calling it an explosion — Wilson's exploding prior expectations imposed upon him by anyone trying to force him to do anything conventional.

Over the twenty years of Wilson's notoriety, these critics have definitely helped to convince the elite or "arty" audience that Wilson is worth looking at (even if they are not particularly clear why or not eager to look), and so he is now a box-office draw, especially as an opera designer. But it is now time to turn to *Death, Destruction, and Detroit*, a piece that was the high point of the first two decades of his career, and the moment when he tried to bring his subversion of the traditional theater together with the support of that theater. As we shall see, the "event" that Wilson crafted for the audience of the avant-garde Berlin theater scene may well have shown the point at which his purported freedom from traditions actually ran headlong into those traditions in a way that neither audience, critics, nor Wilson himself may have anticipated. He ran into a clash of cultures that almost spun beyond his control.

Postmodern Performance: *DD&D*

Death, Destruction, and Detroit grew out of Wilson's entire 1970s corpus, even anticipating *the CIVIL warS* (see Quadri 22). According to publicity, its

main theme was couples in relationships. However, the actual performance
was considerably more complex. *DD&D* dropped on the Berlin public like
a bomb (in both good and bad senses), especially when the public decided
it needed to work out its "hidden meaning" or "covert program," in the best
tradition of European theater audiences, who tend to link avant-garde performance with a political gesture.

The more Wilson confirmed that *DD&D* was a love story (Kelleher 36),
the more the German public preferred to see blatant politics. For example,
he reported:

> The German public confuses me, I don't understand it . . . . in Ger-
> many, suddenly all these people sat there, looking serious, and no
> young people. I was very astonished, because I didn't know why. I
> can't read German, but I had the feeling that they were only looking at
> things, they worked too hard to understand things . . . . I don't even
> understand what the actors say. Yes, I wrote the text [of *DD&D*], but I
> forgot what I wrote. (Kelleher 37)

Such statements can be read as honest bafflement but also as one particular
author's attempt to reclaim the theatrical space that he had defined as his
own for a decade — and to do so in an alien landscape, in a heavily-
endowed legitimate European theater in Berlin, the home of Germany's
avant garde.

To that end, early Wilson publicity offered this hyperinterpreting German audience his own version of the work's origin — a description of how
his art progresses, in terms like those that he used in the United States. He
described how he found a photograph in the Berlin flea market that
showed uniformed prisoners using minesweepers (metal detectors with
long handles), and one of these prisoners was Rudolf Hess (Stearns 41).
The publicity machine instantly turned such statements into the key
"political secret" of the play — a gambit that Wilson may not have originally intended for the first *DD&D* but that was highlighted in the later production of *DD&D II*, which was marketed from the very first as "Kafka
meets Hess" ("Märchenspiel" 5), as John Rockwell reports:

> The "central" character in *DD&D* was Rudolf Hess, a fact kept carefully
> masked in Berlin for fear of misinterpretations intruding on a proper
> appreciation of the play . . . . [as typical for Wilson,] the 'action' [is] a
> series of more or less direct reflections on the figure, his impact and his
> resonances through his time to ours . . . . The final scene of *DD&D*, for
> instance, found an old woman standing outside a wall and, in essence,
> lamenting her personal loss. But she did so in a broken recitative full of
> memories of Hess's private idiosyncrasies. It was intensely moving —
> especially if you knew the woman was Mrs. Hess and the wall was a
> replica of Spandau Prison where Hess is incarcerated. ("RW's Stage
> Works" 27)

It is doubtful whether Wilson had originally intended to tell the Hess story
when he started the project. And he found the ensemble itself difficult in its

professionalism: he mentioned working to break the actors' rapport with the audience, because they were used to telling a story — exactly what he didn't want to do (as reported in Stearns 105).

That the Hess reference was a great secret in Berlin while *DD&D* was in rehearsal is also dubious since the story was revealed just after the premiere, while performances were still running, in the April 1979 edition of *Theater heute*, the major German-language theater review (the information was publicized by Andrzej Wirth, who had access to Wilson). By the time of the first performance, the audience also had plenty of immediate cues to the provenance of Wilson's "found" visual readymades as well. One section of the text-over, for instance, was almost immediately recognizable: a section from Speer's memoirs (also written in Spandau) discussing Germany's ball-bearing production (the section stressing that, if the allies had bombed the one remaining plant, the war could have been shortened by close to two years). Wilson may have been surprised by a German audience initially (an audience that interpreted rather than looking), but his learning curve was very fast.

Particularly interesting in this context is another facet of the European theater landscape that was alien to Wilson's prior U.S. experience in the theater or his international gallery and festival experience. This production purportedly marked the first time Wilson worked with that staple of the European stage, the dramaturge, who is both the intellectual and artistic director for the house: "I think they're [dramaturges] underestimated — in terms of my work anyway" (Stearns 119). As he explains:

> I learned so much about what I was doing and about the possibilities of what could be done. I've since learned to work very closely with dramaturges and now I think it's almost essential to have one because I'm not scholarly, I don't have a strong background in history or a lot of formal or classical education and, anyway, it's very helpful to have someone like that to talk to . . . . At the Schaubühne I worked with Peter Krumme, who was excellent . . . . he was there all the time and was directly involved with the actors and their interpretation. We worked as a team. (Stearns 115–116)

This statement is a nice clue to the way Wilson ended up working with the Schaubühne ensemble: Wilson did the piece, while Krumme dealt with the expectations of the European actors and audiences.

Accordingly, Krumme describes Wilson's work with the ensemble in two brief pages in the 1979 yearbook for *Theater heute* (84–85), which stress that the dramaturge and the actors were heavily involved in anchoring and interpreting what Wilson was opening and playing with (translation: they may have been working at cross-purposes). One actor, Otto Sander, was mentioned in virtually every review as integral to Wilson's game playing; he provided the "Brian" of the couple in love, various virtuoso stage "numbers" in the traditional sense (Wirsing 11), and a true Wilson ensemble member in the architectural sense. Otto Sander was the "found" resource for Wilson in this institutional context, as well as an anchor for the expectations of the ensemble and its customary audience.

The negotiation in which Wilson was involved was very complex. He was playing with actors in a love story and following the dramaturge. The audience was expecting a major statement about Nazism (as was in vogue for the avant garde at the time and still is). The German critics, however, were interested in analyzing Wilson's work as a cosmopolitan modernist triumph, much as their American colleagues did. Official votes in German theater circles did not fall out much better than the U.S. Pulitzer committee's had. In *Theater heute*, votes for a Critic's Choice award sponsored by the main stage journal of Germany came out tied for *DD&D* as best production of the year. Wirth, Wilson's in-house critic, was the chief positive voice, with a nonaffiliated critic (Iden) providing the tiebreaking vote against *DD&D* by calling it a "vision into nothingness." Iden understood the production in modernist terms and appreciated Wilson's work pattern: he spotted its multiple historical references and minimalist series, including the pictures out of the 1930s and 1940s that provided costuming, Jarret's music, the Speer photo, and the love story. But he found it "overproduced" (10) and a "word orgasm" (8) — a "retreat to pure enjoyment of the arranged" (9).

Another German critic, Rühle, felt that each scene was a number that didn't lead anywhere either for the house, for the actors, or for the audience. He successfully identified but decried the ethic behind Wilson's stage space; for him, it lacked the requisite seriousness for proper theater. Rühle blames this result on the Schaubühne (and thus on the politics of the German theater scene), which was trying too hard to seem avant garde, arty, or mannered. In fact, he may have been alluding to the Schaubühne's agenda rather than to Wilson's. Soon after *DD&D*, the ensemble moved into a new, customized theater designed to sponsor modernist directors' extreme productions. In doing so, it moved to a new level of state support and to being "legitimate" experimental theater.

The theater critics and the dramaturge figured out where to position Wilson, and Wilson figured out on some level what they wanted from him. Yet *DD&D* in performance remained a theater piece that defied the audience: it was neither a critique of Nazism nor the kind of experimental modernist theater for which the Schaubühne was famous. With critics' help, the audience could identify Wilson's main material as a set of found readymades about Hess and Spandau, and they learned to trace the roots of Wilson's set sketches to minimalist-modernist graphic conventions. What neither German critics nor German audiences mentioned was Wilson's unique approach to theater space, which was outside naturalism or ordinary reference conventions. The German public had a new splashy avant garde director to focus on and so underplayed the aesthetics issue.

Berlin public and critics alike also ignored another central fact about *DD&D*: that Wilson had constructed his theatrical space out of found materials dating from the years during and after the Second World War from

Germany *and* the United States. They simply did not see the piece's intercultural references or that Wilson's readymades about the war years — the years of "death, destruction" and the military-industrial complex — are from Europe (Speer) and the United States (Detroit). Moreover, they failed to consider that these readymades were not all derived from high political culture (the world of Speer and Spandau) but also from popular culture. Following Wilson's blend of two cultures is thus instructive in light of critics' decision that *DD&D* was an anti-Nazi play.

The introductory scene of *DD&D* is, to be sure, a reference to Hess and the Spandau wall. But many other scenes (particularly the backdrops) draw heavily on American commonplaces from the same epoch. Wilson's American materials are mainly from movies and television, choices that specifically foreground American-European clashes at the level of popular versus high culture. Even the scene titles confirm these cultural associations and the intercultural axis of the piece. Titles like "White Desert with a Black Hole" (a desert with saguaro cactus), for example, plays off the existence of Los Alamos and the atomic bomb project (for example, scene 16), as well as off Germany's long-term love affair with the American West, while others, like "The Wall," are specifically German references recognizable to the outside.

In fact, the pattern of the most obvious American references in *DD&D* as it was performed suggests that Wilson finally decided to confront his German audience with a specifically American set of challenges to their experience of the Second World War, a challenge that also confronts high and popular culture. Wilson might deny the systematicity of his cultural challenges to audience and critic, yet an overview of the American references to the Nazi context in *DD&D* would render such a claim improbable. That is, Wilson may have intended to thwart his overinterpreting German audiences not only by hiding behind a dramaturge but by offering them contemporaneous materials that they simply could not interpret — he forced them to experience the event by basing their new experience of that event on the almost completely unknown.

Many of the scenes contain explicitly U. S. materials to counter the German ones. After the Spandau introduction sequence, for example, scene 1 shows a Josef von Sternberg cinematic Nazi romancing a woman in blue jeans in a Louis Quinze interior; these figures are dressed in Hollywood studio-style exaggeration. Scene 2 is supposed to take place in a bus, but it looks more like a chauffeured limousine with an American society lady of the Audrey Hepburn type. Scene 3 is perhaps most interesting as an homage to the American movie musical since it quotes directly several of the most famous dance scenes in U. S. cinematic history. At the center of Wilson's scene, a chic dark woman stands on a foggy street while windblown newspapers float across the field of vision. When she turns, we see that she is dressed like the woman who introduces the famous "Lullaby of Broadway" in Busby Berkeley's *42nd Street* (Warner Brothers, 1933). This scene has one of the most distinctive cuts in cinematic history. A dark woman

(Ruby Keeler) is in a pinspot in an evening gown, smoking against a dark background. The camera pulls in to a close-up of just her face, which then inverts; the camera dissolves through that face into a fantasy sequence about a "Broadway baby." Wilson replicates this sequence with a pin spot on stage, shifting abruptly into a Gene Kelly quotation (replicating the famous scene in which he dances with a blowing newspaper that becomes a person). To be sure, behind this American visual quotation Wilson introduces a German political reference when a figure (identified by the audience as Hess) parachutes into the scene, just as Hess did into England. To conclude the scene, Wilson introduces a judgment — a set of mysterious European judges point at "Hess" with what look like *Star Wars* light sabers.

Filmic allusions proliferate and differentiate as *DD&D* progresses. Scene 5 quotes American science fiction cinema and television. A couple is dressed in Flash Gordon style. In front of them, an illuminated blob crawls across the stage, a direct takeoff on the "silicon monster" from an episode of the original *Star Trek* series. The pterodactyls which then appear reflect Wilson's ongoing dinosaur fetish, and they anticipate the "Death of the Dinosaurs" narrative that is the voice-over of scene 8. They are also the monsters that Flash Gordon fought in a typical episode of his serial and that science-fiction B movies endlessly dispatch as threats to the Western world. Scene 6 looks and is costumed like a Fellini film, another appropriate reference for the Fascist era (as is his *8 1/2*). The original English text (not recognizable in the German but reclaimed if one looks at the bilingual libretto in the program) uses "Here's looking at you" from *Casablanca*. And the mysterious continental man on the stage is twiddling the ball bearings from *The Caine Mutiny*, the famous cinematic twitch signaling oncoming madness.

Scene 7 has a piece drawn from a Palm Beach resort-type postcard reprinted in the program, showing look-alike ladies in Bermuda shorts, typical 1930s resortwear (187), followed by a huge set piece, a long dance by Brian (Otto Sander). No German critic has noticed that it is a characteristic Gene Kelly soft-shoe number (Sander doubled his style effectively), ending when Kelly "melted" into a rock on the sea (a nested quote about Wagnerian opera or about Richard Strauss's contemporaneous *Ariadne auf Naxos*?). Scene 8 is populated by Tweedle-Dee and Tweedle-Dum in their traditional striped beanies, while zeppelin-roadsters drive slowly through (behind a plump apparition who looks like a cross between Buster Keaton or Oliver Hardy and the Michelin Tire Man squatting like a baby in the foreground). The "Death of the Dinosaurs" voice-over is a backhanded reference to Detroit (when the big cars died) but also a reference to another famous film of the era. *Fantasia* (Disney, 1939) had a sequence on the death of the dinosaurs and also featured Leopold Stokowski conducting Bach's *Toccata and Fugue in D Minor* in Romantic genius style, a performance mimicked by Otto Sander, who conducts the voice-over text tape as if it were unheard music.

The backdrop of the ballroom scene opening act 2 (scene 9) has been widely identified as a quotation of Speer's "light-architecture" from the Nuremberg party rally. However, it may also be a quote from the ballroom scene of Lubitsch's *Great Waltz* (his version of *The Merry Widow*, with Maurice Chevalier as Danilo), particularly a landmark scene where the couples proceed between walls of mirrors. Hollywood thus meets Berlin on at least two levels.

Scene 10 retreats to "A Kitchen," but it is populated with an oversized Art Deco light bulb and an oversized cradle. Sander has another set piece dressed in sporting knickers; he tap-dances and "tends the baby" by rocking it in rhythm. This choreography is pure Fred Astaire to match the Kelly of the first act. (Astaire was noted for his ingenious use of props, like this baby cradle, in his numbers.)

The child's monologue voice-over of scene 11 reads a text about the three bears (and a child's book by E. H. Minarik is cited as a source in the program libretto). Scene 12's desert has a jeep occupied by a couple dressed as cowboys. In their 1950s television show, the ultimate show business cowboy couple, Roy Rogers and Dale Evans, had a sidekick with a similar jeep named Nellybelle. Is this a citation? Possibly, because their flashy clothes are rodeo-cowboy. Scene 13 inverts scene 5, a black to white, short to tall, man to woman minimalist reversal. Scene 14 shows chrome chaise lounges on the "American Rooftop," 1950s decor familiar from movies like *The Apartment*.

Pursuing the reversal theme with cultural references, scene 15 is a widely acknowledged homage to German opera. The "Magic Flute" summons a dragon, which is dispatched by an archetypal Bayreuth Siegfried, who then turns into Lohengrin as the light moves overhead and fades out as he swears on his upright sword in lieu of a cross. The following scene (scene 16) starts with desert race cars (the Bonneville Salt Flats?) and ends with the noise of an atom blast. Finally, in an acceleration of the scene-by-scene cultural reversals, the epilogue reintroduces "The Wall," in front of which the audience sees an old woman who may be Mrs. Hess. This scene is also constructed like a traditional vaudeville closing scene, in which the entire cast crosses the stage.

This is not a complete inventory of Wilson's visual citations based on U. S. popular culture, but it is enough to confirm that his sources include both Europe and America from the 1930s on. This series of references, however, did not emerge as part of either the critics' or the audience's experience of *DD&D*. The German audience present at one performance clearly did not recognize the American visual quotations (they didn't laugh at Kelly or Astaire, for instance). Keyed by the more obvious German references highlighted by the critics (especially the Speer ball bearings voice-over and the Spandau wall), the audience concentrated instead on the "serious political dimension" of Wilson's assemblage. The actors were not in a position to contradict these reactions since Wilson reminds us he couldn't understand them (a questionable claim) and tried to cut them off from audience reac-

tions. One critic felt that Wilson's collages "point to texts and contexts beyond the performance . . . . an intertextuality is brought forth" (Fischer-
Lichte, 152) but counted only German references in that intertextuality.

Wilson's assemblage, though, implies a larger cultural context. Yes, the
audience recognized main Nazi figures, but it didn't see that Wilson presented these characters as they appeared secondhand, through the media
(and largely from the American perspective). Wilson shows Hess, a thorn in
the Four Powers' sides, as one of the greatest media events of the war; his
Speer quotes come from "memoirs" designed by the architect for propa-
gandistic rehabilitation after the war. The one Nazi officer who appears
looks more like a cinema Nazi (or a Fellini or Wertmüller Nazi); even the
European judges who appear in scene 3 seem like costume extras from the
Nuremberg Trials. Beyond that, *DD&D*'s readymades are exclusively American: popular media (television, Disney characters, and Hollywood movies
and their particular "happy talk" version of the war years, orchestrated by
Busby Berkeley), popular culture (including fashionable resorts and advertising images, like Detroit car-dinosaurs), and the cultural icons of the era
(including emigrants like Stokowski and international stars like Astaire and
Kelly). This is, as Müller described, an explosion of all the impossibilities of
meaning that surrounded the war — from a largely U. S. point of view.

Yet *DD&D*'s audience and critics uniformly reduced the work to a single
explicit political dimension by ignoring the conflicting cultural references.
As a result, *DD&D* appeared to a German audience to be a "family narrative," as Müller decided, showing Hess and his wife as typical German victims of a terrible era. German critics thought the audience was supposed to
experience a mind-opening reinterpretation of its war experience (even if
that experience was as fragmentary as children's nightmares or Wilson's
images), a political gesture in a city that remained a scarred victim of that
war (Berlin). They overlooked his conscious intercutting of the essentially
unseen German war and the veneer of American culture, his placement of
politics within a social nexus, fueled by industrial money and packaged by
a Hollywood culture industry invigorated then by emigrant or refugee talent.

At this point, however, Wilson's claims about the isolation of his theatrical space seem particularly questionable since he cannot avoid the fact that
his chosen theatrical event plays out in a uniquely political environment,
even if those politics are not the political deeds of great men but part of the
fiber of everyday life — political experience as seen on the streets and
around the explicit politics of the war years, not in the history books.
Death, Destruction, and Detroit did not function as a theatrical event in an
isolated space for a German audience under the tutelage of critics stressing
politics and unfamiliar with American popular culture. The result was a
certain audience bemusement like that reported in many German state
theaters when subscribers are confronted with experimental theater — a result that Wilson anticipated when he wrote into the program a set of rules
for the consumption of *DD&D* quite literally, including the command that

they come and go at will (and they almost all left early, after three hours, to catch the last subway train). Yet this set of rules, combined with his earlier lack of reverence about the Schaubühne's professional actors, comes close to setting him on the side of the audience, in opposition to the authoritarianism of the avant-garde theater.

If the critics had been right about Wilson's work as politics, the audience would have had to question "where they were" in the war years and thereafter. Yet Wilson's theater is purportedly not designed to do something like tell Hess's story. So what kind of an event resulted when a set of imprecise bicultural historical references was touted as the premiere culture critique of the theater season?

First, the event took place in Berlin, which privileged the political references preferred by critics and by the German avant-garde theater public; that it was in a subsidized and progressive venue only reinforced such identifications. Yet in practice, Wilson reached his audience in much his intended way (nonnaturalistic, without outside reference) when he circumvented the critics by offering images that the audience could not decipher. Note, too, that *DD&D*'s German references would have been equally baffling to a U. S. audience not thoroughly familiar with Speer, Spandau, and the Second World War.

At the same time, the official publicity surrounding *DD&D* confirms Wilson's mastery of the implications of the theater culture in Berlin and the whole of Germany — his "learning" about dramaturges and his manipulation of conflicting public and professional evaluations of a publicly funded legitimate theater ensemble. As we have seen, Wilson packaged himself to U. S. critics as a postmodern critic of high-culture traditions; and the Berlin situation shows his willingness to allow German critics to construe his work politically. His success on two continents points to fundamental differences in U. S. and German cultures outside their institutional theaters as well.

Conclusion:
Two Cultures, One Theater

What Wilson achieved in Berlin is very much what he achieved in Paris and New York earlier and, since then, beyond those more elite venues. His great visual gifts are matched by his ability to challenge the master narratives of the legitimate theater in any context. He defines his theater practice by splitting critics from the audience and by catering to the independent horizons of expectation of each. Moreover, while not precisely pandering to audiences, he acknowledges them in ways that avant-garde theater all too often does not: he doesn't hesitate to amuse them rather than preaching, to catch their attention by acknowledging their tastes as often as he does those of the artistic elite.

Wilson's purpose in this choice seems to be a course of action derived from his experiences in the United States and abroad, but extremely original. Speaking as a European intellectual, Julia Kristeva and Philippe Sollers explain, in "Why the United States?," how art is marginalized in this country in a way that it is not in Europe. While art is largely public-sector in Europe (in state-financed theaters, for example), in the United States it relies on private-sector and corporate donors. This creates financial problems while also creating an ideological space for experimental diversity that does not exist in a more uniform European artistic climate (the authors thus ignore indirect financial manipulation by private donors). Kristeva notes that "it concerns a marginality that is also *polyvalent*: 'Aesthetic' experiments are more frequent and more varied than in Europe. There are many more enclaves of painting, music, dance, etc." (275). Moreover, European theaters purport most often to educate or challenge the audience, as "serious" art, while U. S. theaters offer performances to be consumed for many purposes (most often for entertainment, but also including serious theater). Wilson's challenge in Berlin reflects this dichotomy: that audience was too interested in interpreting, and so he befuddled it, while his average U. S. audience is interested in spectacle, innovation, or star collaborators as often as it is in serious art (all variations he can provide).

Kristeva identifies a second primary difference between audiences in Europe and America. Each audience relates to the word and to other symbolic gestures differently, an asymmetry fundamental for Wilson's work. Europeans are accustomed to a high literary culture, while Americans respond equally well (or perhaps better) to alternate languages of sound or color:

> Obviously, this numerical factor would be insignificant if one did not bear in mind the peculiar nature of these aesthetic practices. For they are *non-verbal*. The Americans today seem to me to excel in any research into gesture, colour and sound, which they pursue in great depth and scope and much more radically than is done in Europe. (275)

In the United States, then, Kristeva finds politics in the gesture, not in the word: "[T]he most radical practices are non-verbal" (276). Her description again transfers favorably to Wilson's work: it can be aesthetically radical in ways other than political ones. For this reason, Kristeva also concludes that "American literature is perhaps Cage, perhaps Bob Wilson . . . it is therefore something which opens up the word to the unspeakable, with all the risks of psychosis that this breakthrough implies" (276).

Wilson treated the Second World War as such an "unspeakable" in *DD&D*, just as he later would the existence of civil wars and unrest in Western cultures. If the horrors behind the words/signs emerge, Kristeva believes that the very fact of reference turns into systematized cultural psychosis. In this sense, Wilson's body of work reflects what may well be the cultural psychosis of the current theater on two continents: the insidious relations between critics, publicists, and the institutional theater (in any version of its institutionalization). Against their power, he sets a vision of popular culture, a vision expressed by visual citations (as he did in *DD&D*), use of popular tropes (for example, colonialism, Admiral Perry, and absolutism, as in *the Knee Plays*), or collaboration with celebrities (Byrne) or at visible venues (such as the Olympic Games).

Wilson is thus offering a different vision of what political theater ought to be. In the United States his critics stress his visuals, while theater directors have begun to appreciate his sense of spectacle; in Berlin his critics stressed his politics while dismissing the unique quality of his spectacle as a deep critique of representation, showing the limits on representation imposed by cultures on individual viewers. Yet his theater is not simply the visual spectacle that his U. S. critics assume as his total program, nor cultural politics, as Berlin critics assumed — both camps thereby underestimating him considerably. And his theater is postmodern, since it rests on a critique of the "metanarratives of culture" (two cultures) and on the "schizophrenia of late capitalism" identified by Jameson ("Politics"), Kristeva, and Sollers.

Tracing Wilson's work into two cultures whose institutional theaters are configured differently, however, teaches us one more thing about his theater: it is a critique of at least two dominant forms of contemporary theater, author theater and director's theater, because he has crafted a new role for a total theater professional. Wilson has moved beyond a simpler need to critique cultures and their politics while establishing his own point of view as a temporary master narrative for his audience. His work is indeed postdramatic in this sense, eschewing conventional forms of narrative theater and staging. This by no means implies that he has retreated to the visual, as his earliest critics were wont to assume, but rather that he has answered Kristeva's question "Why the United States?" for Western theater, at least. By tapping the power of the visual that Kristeva and Sollers identified and by adding to it his awareness of the interrelations of the roles of high-culture critics and popular audiences, Wilson has offered a vision of the future of the theater.

A German interview given on the occasion of Wilson's 1996 *Hamlet* monologue performances quotes Heiner Müller, who claimed that the theater is "a dialogue with the dead." Wilson's response as to why he chose to perform *Hamlet* unfolds this statement: "In all my works I see the Texas landscape in which I grew up. And in Hamlet's drama I rediscover my personal relationships, friends, lovers, family members. Hamlet reflects my life" ("Überall ist Texas" 13). Wilson's theater thus seeks to call the dead to life again as part of today's world rather than as convention, tradition, or authority; the incantation that can do that requires, however, a vision from more than one theatrical tradition. Moreover, that vision requires Wilson to accept the kind of plural reactions I have traced. When Umberto Eco asks him about how "the spectator is free to choose his own itinerary" in his "non-literary theater," for example, Wilson says, "I don't have the right" to be dissatisfied if they do so: "My responsibility as an artist is to create, not to interpret" (Wilson and Eco 89).

Wilson's work has thus moved toward a new vision of the role of theater in culture and of the artist in the theater, combining not only spectacle and the authority of various cultural traditions but also the active participation of the audience. His theater, his world of meaning, is non-naturalistic. It must be experienced, consumed, and construed by an audience that is willing to approach it as part of its life, with both a willingness to see in new ways (in which the U. S. audiences purportedly excel) and a verbal, historical, and critical intelligence that can reinterpret and defend its own experiences (as his Berlin audiences at least began to do in defying their critics and their theater system, or by walking out). No wonder, then, that Wilson now is sought after in various forms of the legitimate theater: he reclaims audiences by offering them the critical spectacles and cultural challenges now more familiar from popular culture.

Notes

[1] See Phinney's various articles for the history of *the CIVIL warS* and *the Knee Plays*. For academic discussions of Wilson, see two dissertations written on him, by Dietrich and Graff.

[2] See Rockwell, in Stearns (2d ed.) 23, for a description of the production explaining why New York's Metropolitan Opera had to cancel a planned performance in 1979.

[3] For the standard discussions of postmodernism, see Arac; Foster, *The Anti-Aesthetic*; Huyssen; Jameson, "Postmodernism"; Lyotard, *The Postmodern Condition*; and Ross.

[4] The best accounts of recent major productions are in Marranca and Dasgupta, eds., a special edition of the *Performing Arts Journal* offering "A Robert Wilson Retrospective" based on short contributions by many authors. The most visible of Wilson's recent stagings are Müller's *Hamletmachine* (1988); *Zauberflöte* (Paris, 1991); *Alceste* (Chicago, 1991, and Stuttgart, 1987); *Dr. Faustus Lights the Lights* (Frankfurt, 1991, and New York, 1992); *Parsifal* (Houston Grand Opera, 1992); *Danton's Tod* (Alley Theater, Houston, 1992); *Don Juan Ultima* (play; Madrid, 1992); *Black Rider* (Brooklyn Academy, 1993); *Madame Butterfly* (Paris Opera, 1994); Tom Wait's *Alice* (Brooklyn Academy, 1995); *Four Saints in Three Acts* (Houston Grand Opera, 1996); and a solo performance, *Hamlet: A Monologue* (New York, 1995).

[5] Posted as a wall text in the Laguna Gloria Art Museum exhibition of his "Drawings for the Stage," Austin, Texas, July 1986.

[6] See especially Stearns (2d ed.) 39 ff. for descriptions of Wilson's pattern manipulations; an interview in the introduction to the text for the German section of *the CIVIL warS* describes how he "found" its material and then built a pattern around it (41).

[7] When resources permit, he commissions scores. David Byrne has written for him, as has Philip Glass. In *DD&D*, Wilson used Keith Jarret's "Cologne Concert" as a centerpiece, supplemented with what I believe was the Stokowski score of *Fantasia*, the Disney film contemporaneous with the picture of Rudolf Hess he used to

open the performance and to set the diagonal "wall" image varied as the back-drops.

Section II:

History of Disciplines, Cultural Dislocations

5: An Alternate Stifter: Psychologist

The image of Adalbert Stifter in literary history is stodgy at best. In an epigram, Friedrich Hebbel called him one of the "poets of beetles and buttercups" (Fischer, *ASs Leben* 234–35). An Austrian bureaucrat of the educational establishment, Stifter was state school board supervisor for Upper Austria (the state around Linz), which exacerbated his image (see Schoenborn). Yet Stifter was also a very typical bourgeois victim of the post-Napoleonic disruptions in Austria. The aftermath of the Congress of Vienna forced Austria into a fixed political quiescence under the banner of Enlightenment thought, incorporating a new resigned, bitterly Romantic tone. Like many in his generation, Stifter hoped to support himself by writing, but 1848 disrupted these plans decisively, as it did for many in his generation (including Young Hegelian and Young German political activists).

Unlike his German contemporaries, Austrians like Stifter found themselves in small but nonetheless official positions within a cosmopolitan bureaucracy designed to reinforce a conservative European balance of power. As part of that bureaucracy, Stifter had a small voice to turn his typically Austrian notions about education and Enlightenment into policy. He thus was not confined to the opposition, as the typical German intellectual was. Stifter had access not only to the public forum of the popular press but also to the government.

Stifter's public role may not have satisfied his personal wishes, but he was nonetheless a successful (albeit reluctant) bureaucrat in the educational system, with a clear set of goals achieved through steady, conscientious work. Current literary criticism, however, overlooks Stifter's official career; at best, he is considered in his historical context, not as part of an explicit political environment (see Lachinger, Stillmark, and Swales). This essay will focus on Stifter's educational psychology as a product of the late Enlightenment, especially as it describes how individuals learn and change through time. His sources for psychology are probably Kant, Herder, and Johann Gottfried Herbart, whose textbook was approved by the University of Vienna. This educational psychology is echoed in Stifter's essays and reviews, but its implications for his fiction are less clear. A comparison of Stifter's psychology with his literary style calls general critical evaluation of Stifter's ontology into question by revealing his great skepticism about human ability to comprehend history.

The Question of Psychology and Education:
Kant, Herder, and Herbart

Stifter referred to the state-approved textbook for the University of Vienna when he requested permission to lecture (*Vermischte Schriften* [ed. Steffen] 376), which presumably was Herbart's work (Domandl, *ASs Lesebuch* 69 ff.). Indirect evidence supports Kant's and Herder's psychologies as his additional sources. Stifter read Kant in his younger days (Domandl, "Philosophische Tradition"); Herder has been more recently recognized as a source of Stifter's thought (see, for example, Neugebauer 98 ff. and Schäublin). Together, Herder, Kant, and Herbart represent a decisive turn in the development of nineteenth-century psychology. Their psychology synthesizes empiricism and idealism as the foundation for a modern, more relativistic model of mind, stressing the effects of culture and education.[1]

This tradition goes back to a relatively restricted number of texts. Herder integrated the physiology and psychology of sense perception into historicism, probably under the influence of La Mettrie and Albrecht von Haller, in the 1778 "Vom Erkennen und Empfinden der menschlichen Seele" ("On Cognition and Sensibility of the Human Soul," drafts back to 1774); in "Plastik" ("The Plastic Arts," reaching back in draft form to 1768); and, later, in his *Ideen zur Philosophie der Geschichte der Menschheit* (*Ideas on the Philosophy of the History of Mankind*, begun in 1784). His contemporary, Kant, also addressed psychology — in his *Anthropologie in pragmatischer Hinsicht* (*Anthropology from a Pragmatic Point of View*, in various drafts from 1772 to 1789). One of Kant's (somewhat dissenting) students, Johann Friedrich Herbart, took up one of the projects left after the *Anthropology*, the analysis of the mind's powers in processing the data of the world. His physiological-mathematical approach required ten years and two large volumes to delineate: the *Lehrbuch zur Psychologie* (*Textbook on Psychology*, from 1816 and heavily revised for an 1834) edition, and the *Psychologie als Wissenschaft* (*Psychology as Science*, 1824).

Herder's 1778 *On Cognition and Sensibility of the Human Soul* synthesizes the empiricist tradition of La Mettrie and Albrecht von Haller with Wolffian rationalism to explain the relation of body and mind in terms of nerve action. Stimuli (*Reiz*, Haller's word) from entities in the world transmit affects to the fibers of the organic being via nerves and muscles (which are virtually equated). Gradually, one group of muscle and nerve fibers becomes identified as an ego (*Ich*), a unity or unified entity driven by desire, love, or needs to move beyond its isolation. An ego acts as a center for organic reception, for pain and passion, and for contact with other entities, but the organism mediates between the individual's memory and the world. Herder's individual is thus more than an organism; it is also the center of a set of cognitions, stimuli processed into representations (178). While a being may be motivated at first by its reactions to the environment, it ultimately contributes to its own development through its life history; it is thus a constantly developing regional ontology, not merely a filter for incoming information. New inputs to a mind ("waves of sensation and feeling") from outside will affect the soul ("a *structure of nerves*," 185). Herder's individuals are thus historically contingent, subject to their individual development, and self-integrating through the imagination: "[Imagination] does not, however, consist only of images, but also of tones, words, signs, and sensations — often those for which language would have no name. . . . Out of all this, the soul weaves its raiment, its sensuous universe" (189).

Herder's individual can even be idiosyncratic (198), incorporating both an organism and pure mind to have an individual soul. Herder thus extends the idealist definition of mind toward the modern notion of psyche, including more than conscious or transcendental mind. This is a radical break from eighteenth-century psychology, stressing inner unity of process as the essence of mind (196). Again, though, the psyche becomes what it is through contact with the outside world. It is not born a particular way: its development depends not only on its experiences but even on the symbols available. Similarly, its knowledge cannot be a priori; it ties into the "sensing, loving and feeling" of the individual, dependent on a particular age and state. Like individuals, families and nations have thought styles particular to them because of the group's shared sensibility (*Denkart* [210]). Outmoded habits maintained by the group can affect (or retard) the forms of its thinking and feeling; even education can contribute to intellectual idiosyncrasy. Cultural inheritance thus crucially determines the newer members of a group, for reason, sensation, and language must all work together if thought and minds exist in commerce (218).

Kant may have disagreed with some particulars of Herder's work, yet his psychology takes over and extends its major tenets. Kant presented it in his *Anthropology from a Pragmatic Point of View*, a set of university lectures first delivered in the academic year 1772–73 and on and off until 1795–96 but only published in 1798, with a second edition in 1800.[2] Like Herder's work, Kant's psychology does not deal with first principles of mind, but rather with mind in the world, as an application of Transcendental Idealism or cognitive philosophy into the realm of the social sciences.

Kant's particular contribution to this tradition of psychology is his explanation of the cognitive capacity of man (*Erkenntnisvermögen*) as it relates to appetition and aversion (*Lust und Unlust*) and to volition (*Begehrungsvermögen*). He seeks to explain how the categories in the individual produce real, historical patterns of thought under the influence of experience and individual preference. Kant thus discusses not *general* knowledge, to which all beings have access (that is metaphysical [15]), but *utilitarian* knowledge, extending beyond the purview of the individual, supported by contact with the group and with the individual.

In general, the individual's path to knowledge leads through the three mental activities of attention, abstraction, and reflection (*attentio, abstratio,* and *reflexio* [27]). First one focuses on information acquired through sensory abilities (*Auffassungsvermögen*), then evolves patterns through differentiation (*Absonderungsvermögen*), and finally expands on the properties of these patterns through reflection on them (*Überlegungsvermögen*). In this way, sensuous intuition (the part affected by the outside world) is turned into internal knowledge. Yet, as this process continues and a mass of clear and distinct knowledge has been produced, this knowledge constitutes around a reference point, an "ego," assumed to be at the base of all decisions (31): Kant's model mediates between the activity of mind and the constituted historical knowledge that is the ego or self — again, virtually a modern psyche, although still tied to the primary mental agency of the categories.

However, higher-order knowledge and thought patterns distinctive of man in culture evolve; they stem from a reciprocal interaction of the senses and the world, anchored around the relative point of the individual ego. In this case, the senses constitute the horizon for extended interactions of world and mind and higher-order knowledge, on which cultural knowledge is based. Here the senses do not necessarily cause disorder, deception, or errors, as they were assumed to in the realm of the categories of pure mind. Instead, the senses connect the mind to the world, based on the history of an individual's experience, forming what is termed an "interior sense" (*sensus interior* [47]).

When sense input accumulates in the mind, other phenomena emerge: the individual ego and the identity of a cultural group in its thought patterns (representing psychological values and needs of the group as well as individuals [78 ff., 86 ff.]). In this way, Kant has adapted his model of the transcendental mind is adapted to accommodate mind in historical time. Those individual activities of mind may block development and keep an individual or an entire culture from achieving the intellectual growth commensurate with *Weltbürger* (citizens of the world, enlightened individuals). His model thus accommodates the variances arising from the contact of individual minds with unique historical environments.

As noted above, Kant's student Johann Friedrich Herbart took up the program left after the *Anthropology*, using a physiological-mathematical approach.[3] His immediate project was a redefinition of Kant's central terms, especially "representation," "sensation," and "appetition." He also reviewed traditional usages of other terms — sensibility, imagination, memory, understanding, reason, judgment, affects, appetition, and passions — to adapt these to the mathematics of nerve stimulation.

Yet in the midst of these expositions fall two assertions that distance Herbart from Kant. First, a mental system does not exist apart from the activity of human cognition; and second, the shape of the mind is affected by its activities (Herbart, *Lehrbuch* 302). Herbart believes that the capacities of mind exert pressure on each other in a cause-and-effect relationship of spiritual life or activity and the representations they produce; even so-called "pure reason," self-consciousness, and the pure apperception that constitutes inner sense are products of experience and practice (312–13). The mind is thus more than a taxonomy of categories; it exists in a dynamic tension between the interactions of data and representations. The mind thus *adapts* to the world, as well as the converse.

For Herbart, data enter through the outer senses into the inner senses, where they are classified as "series-forms" (*Reihenformen*). Such series-forms are preliminary organizational groups of received data, organized in terms either of their "characteristic secondary determinations" or their similarity (Herbart, *Lehrbuch* 324). After the mind sorts data into series-forms, it processes them into "logical forms," at which point conceptual work commences. Only at this point can judgments, intellectual intuition, and, finally, transcendental or abstract concepts like "thing," "substance," and "mutability" be formed. Such representations are, however, energies "in resistance to each other" (369). Once representations enter the cognitive structure of the mind, they make themselves felt by asserting their position within the mass of representations comprising the memory, experience, and logical knowledge of an individual; they may either facilitate the conceptual processing of further data or debilitate it, to cause a "degree of obscuring" (370).

Herbart thus construes representations not as points of information, as Kant tended to do, but as a dynamic system that must find various internal equilibria. A mass of representations settles into an equilibrium under dynamic tension, subject to shift, built of inhibitions and the interrelations of inhibiting energies of representations. If a new representation enters the system, old ones may be suppressed or fall beneath a certain energy threshold and be unnoticeable (372). Similarly, representations are habits for the mind, channeling energy as a "relief" for the mind; if a new representation exerts pressure on a great number of the extant ones, the whole "laws of movement of the spirit" will change (373). Herbart thus adds a depth-of-processing criterion for concepts, arguing that certain concepts are more durable or valid than others: each representation has not only an intellectual content but also a degree of energy that guarantees its memorability, its automatic superordination or subordination in the mass of other representation secured by the group (382). He also stresses the historical and individual relativity of thought, since each processing pattern is utterly distinctive.

Although the *Lehrbuch* would be in part superseded by the later *Psychologie als Wissenschaft* (*Psychology as Science*), Herbart does not significantly expand in the later book the basic model of the mind as an equilibrium of energies, his key contribution to the new paradigm. He outlines the rules for psychic energy in dynamic equilibrium, defining the ego as the center of all these perceptions. Where Kant discussed the representation system of the outside world as a function of the individual mind and the categories processing the data of sensations, Herbart works from a triad: ego, change or process, and object.

Herbart's psychology is also intended to be educational psychology: he stresses that institutions can enforce mental habits, which will ultimately mold minds. The individual is the center of experience, but history and community reinforce mental norms, creating inhibitions in the mind (*Psychologie* 2: 62). More important, the ego as a reference point is subject to a cultural history, and so the kind of "attention" (*Aufmerksamkeit*) that an individual mind pays is indicative of the individual's cultural values (2: 191). Herbart has thus evolved a very modern picture of the ego in the historical world — an ego that is only a point of reference and recollection, a system adapting to the sensations which impinge on its energetic equilibrium. Even the individual's worldview is a mental equilibrium, selected by the will on the basis of previous experience and affects. Herbart's work thus moves beyond that of Herder and Kant, but it does not essentially refute them.

Between Herder and Herbart, a model of the mind has been turned into a tool for education: while the capacity for thought is transcendental, the content of thought and each individual's psyche are relative and mutable, developing under the pressure of experience and historical-cultural inheritance. Stifter's pedagogy rests on this tradition. Domandl cites Stifter's request for a lecture series from 1848 to prove that Stifter knows what was going on in official psychology circles (primarily Herbart's work). Yet Domandl, like many historians of philosophy, assumes an antithesis between the Kant that Stifter favored and Herbart's work, which is not necessarily true in terms of the psychology paradigm just presented. True, their models of mind differ (Herbart's is more dynamic; Kant's, more static). Yet their pedagogical implications do not: each acknowledges that pragmatic, historical knowledge is culturally relative and that individual habit and experience affect quality of mind.

A stereotype about the Austrian intellectual climate helps to reinforce this false dichotomy between Kant and Herbart in Stifter's case. While Protestant, secular, or even anticlerical Enlightenment was taking root in Germany (culminating in Kant's work at the end of the eighteenth century), censorship and heavy clerical influence grew in Austria in the century after 1750. Leopold II, in a brief reign from 1790–92, sponsored an intellectual "catch-up" under the banner of "Illuminatism." After this moderate move to progressivism, Kant's name was still not mentioned publicly, perhaps in Habsburg deference to the Jesuits. But all evidence suggests that Austrian intellectuals remained in contact with philosophical trends from Germany (albeit often years late) and that Kant enjoyed great popularity, even after Leopold (see Lettner, Domandl). Stifter, then, began his bureaucratic career at a time when Kantianism was being reevaluated critically in Austria, as a late Counter-Reformation gesture.

The political realities of Catholic Austria would lead Austrian intellectuals to be more circumspect about the more overtly Protestant aspects of the Enlightenment (particularly the value of human agency in facilitating progress). That does not mean that its entire program for social improvement and change through education was cast out: just as Kant's and Herbart's psychologies are reconcilable, so, too, can other aspects of the Enlightenment be. If one assumes that Stifter was interested in Kant not as a model for absolute mind but as a pattern for education, then the purported gap between "official Herbartianism" and "Stifter's Kantianism" would be considerably lessened. Immersing Stifter in his intellectual-political climate can also shade the readings of his cosmology.

Perspectivism as Pedagogy

A Kantian-Herbartian bias about how individuals learn and apply knowledge extends through Stifter's essays. In the review of an 1857 art exhibition of the Oberderennsischer Kunstverein, for instance, Stifter strays from his more immediate purpose to discuss more generally why a painting may turn into a lifeless collection of objects. His conclusions echo Kant (or Schiller's adaptation of Kant), stressing a unity of form and content:

> [F]inally, [it is] the spiritual [geistige] idea . . . which raises the artwork as such. For that reason, mere reality in an artwork without an idea remains dry and empty, a mere idea without reality is without ground. The highest spiritual idea should dominate the artwork, buts its vehicle can only be the sensual in the artwork. ("Obderennsische Kunstausstellung [1857]" 114)

Ten years later, another review gives this a twist that puts Stifter beyond Schiller or Classicism, recognizing a sort of historical relativity in education and learning:

> From that already said, we can now explain the expressions common in art: realism, idealism, style. Realism (objectivity) is happily condemned straight away. But isn't God most real in His world? If art replicates [nachahmen] part of the world, it must present them as near to real as they can possibly be, that is, they must possess the highest realism . . . .
>
> Idealism is just that divine thing I explained above. If it is added to the greatest realism, the complete artwork results. Just as mere realism is a coarse burden, so, too, is pure idealism invisible mist or foolishness. J. Paul, in the Vorschule, says of such idealists: they paint ether in ether with ether. The idealists who disdain realism are usually those who cannot master it, and their idealism may be shaky, as well — it might rather be only hypersensitivity [Empfindelei]; for the high, healthy ideal is born at the same time as correct, healthy form. ("Ausstellung" 218–19)

This draws on Jean Paul as well as Schiller in a way typical for Stifter. Yet he sees that form-content constructs are historically relative and serve primarily psychological or epistemological functions, not ontological ones.

The form-content differentiation is, for Stifter, the fundamental problem in education. Even morality can stand under this differentiation. One acts for the benefit of the group, not for the individual, but there is no absolute morality: if there were, it would be only formal, lacking the realism that would tie it to time and space. As Kant would concur, the ultimate morality of nature is not revealed to humanity: moral laws, like natural laws, fit into human social situations and bring results that may be judged. The role of the pedagogue in this tradition is, then, not to prescribe moral law but to train individuals in the process of judgment — to teach how to correlate empirical data with received culturally biased concepts of morality, to teach sensitivity to a form and content balance in thought.

This educational purpose can also direct us to a new evaluation of Stifter's unique narrative style, which has received much attention of late in his handling of unreliable narrators. Stifter's essays, like his reviews, systematically train his readers in this style of interpretation, stressing the relativity and interdependence of the natural and moral worlds. His less familiar essays all carefully differentiate between empirical data and the interpretations, affects, or effects of this data. In "Die Sonnenfinsternis am 8. Juli 1842" ("The Solar Eclipse of 8 July 1842"), for example, Stifter describes the disparity between what one expected scientifically and what viewers actually felt:

> [W]hat is the most terrible storm in the face of this deathly still majesty? — it is noisy triviality. Lord Bryon's poem, "Darkness" [1816] occurred to me . . . but such majesty, or I'd prefer, nearness to God, appeared in these two minutes, that the heart could believe nothing else than that he must be somewhere. ("Sonnenfinsternis" 110)

We speak of God because we are trained to equate certain feelings with the sublime; this event happened "in proportion" (*rechtes Maß* ["Sonnenfinsternis" 111]) because the event lasted only two minutes, and so our assumptions are not seriously challenged.

Stifter describes a natural event from the point of view of an experiencer but clearly designates his reactions as appearance (*Erscheinung*); the observed "facts" refer to one's hearts and expectations, not necessarily ontological truth. Stifter closes the piece with two questions, the first relevant here. He asks if the laws of nature are "His shining mantle, that covers Him" ("sein glänzendes Kleid, das ihn [Gott] deckt" ["Sonnenfinsternis" 113]). But this is a question, not an assertion, something that the audience was to think about: we cannot know its answer, for, if He did indeed exist, this God would have to reveal himself to us. Stifter is not openly doubting the existence of God, but he is questioning his fellows' assumptions that a particular event is "the will of God": we see only the form of the event, not its context. On the other hand, if we provide a formal interpretation (such as a natural law), we ignore its full content (at the very least, its affective message).

Stifter's journalism contains other such examples, in which such speculation about the form and content of absolute truth is identified as personal and cultural habit. In his "Return after the Revolution" ("Rückkehr nach der Revolution") of 1849, he provides an example from the political realm, just as the "Solar Eclipse" was for natural science. He begins with what he says is the majority opinion: that the people were not ready for the revolution. More particularly, he calls current assumptions about "freedom" into question, identifying it as an abstraction that confuses people:

> If this opinion is correct, then, too, is the proposition that there is no absolute freedom, but only a freedom corresponding to the relative [state of] moral development then; it is also true that it is the holiest duty of the human race (that is, of its governments) to constantly expand this moral development and thus lead our people towards that freedom which they deserve at the highest pinnacle of their perfection. (*Vermischte Schriften* [ed. Steffen] 182)

The group fell into the error of abstract thinking: freedom is not accomplished by censorship or force but through the imposition of reasonable laws.

In the follow-up piece, "Die oktroyierte Verfassung" ("The Imposed Constitution," 1849), he again qualifies the concept of freedom in these terms. One should conceive of freedom not as an absence of restrictions (that would be an error of abstract form, an argument from the point of view of God) but as an affective truth achieving definition only in historical context (thus evaluating it from the empirical end):

> Humans have limits, namely the laws of nature . . . humans need for their existence a number of earthly things, which are coveted by the drives in them, which often emerge stormily and then are called *affects*. An affect is in itself egotistical; it only wants to appropriate its object to itself. Therefore, humans have reason, which says that all must exist in harmony and thus must curb their affects so that all can harmoniously pursue their reasonable goals — the greatest human perfection. (*Vermischte Schriften* [ed. Steffen] 185)

Unfortunately, such misjudgments can even mislead entire cultures, as they did the revolutionaries of 1848; however, actions can be judged as errors only in historical retrospect, as he states in "Die Zukunft des menschlichen Geschlechtes ("Future of the Human Race"; *Vermischte Schriften* [ed. Steffen] 212):

> Thus human learns from human, group from group, century from centuries, and the ideal of humanity gets ever richer and moves towards its boundary of perfection; we, the living, cannot even guess at how infinite it is, because, if we were to understand it, we would already have to possess it. ("Wirkungen der Schule [1849]/Effects of School"; *Vermischte Schriften* [ed. Steffen] 258)

Thus Stifter is attempting to teach the judgments appropriate to appearances, not ontological truth.

Other purportedly eternal values are also questioned. Typical for the late Enlightenment, for instance, is Stifter's close identification of "beautiful" with "moral." Yet even the "beautiful" and "moral" are clearly a relative judgment of reason, not of any eternal capacity: "The beautiful is also subjective to the degree that reason (the moral capacity) is capable, on the one hand, of development and strengthening, and, on the other, of decay and decline ("Die Poesie und ihre Wirkungen/Poetry and Its Effects"; *Vermischte Schriften* [ed. Steffen] 359). Reason is thus the "high referee of the Divine" (*hohe Schiedsrichterin des Göttlichen*; *Vermischte Schriften* [ed. Steffen] 368), the human cognitive power that designates or recognizes the divine — but only in empirical context.

The fact that reason can work to identify the moral and improve humanity is, moreover, a question of educational psychology: of building healthy cognitive habits. In a request for permission to give public lectures ("Beilage zu dem Gesuche um Bewilligung öffentlicher Vorträge über Ästhetik, 1847"), Stifter states that art can stimulate the higher powers, but morality (*Sittlichkeit*) emerges only in "the realization of objective humanity" ("Realisierung der objektiven Menschheit"; *Vermischte Schriften* [ed. Steffen] 377). Like moral concepts, art balances form and content as a cooperative venture that is historically bound to a particular group, corresponding to its psychological motivation.[4]

Stifter's essays clearly reflect the late Enlightenment psychology he inherited, stressing not absolute mind but culturally relative and group-supported mind. An individual's interpretation of an event will depend on historical experience of the individual, group tradition, psychological motivation, and historical contingency. What participants in an event see happen may not be what has "really" happened. Stifter's critics, however, largely ignore how this educational psychology may be represented in his fiction.

Stifter's "Gentle Law" as Educational Psychology

Critics reading Stifter as an Austrian Catholic easily conflate the ontological with the epistemological. To be sure, the political realities of Catholic Austria would lead Austrian intellectuals to be more circumspect about the more overtly Protestant aspects of the Enlightenment (for instance, the value of human agency in facilitating progress). Yet just as Kant's and Herbart's psychologies are reconcilable, so too can other aspects of the Enlightenment be. If one assumes that Stifter was interested in education, then Stifter's cosmology also is shaded differently than might be assumed.

For instance, when Stifter the author speaks of nature, he reflects his Kantianism (Schoenborn would say his reliance on Herder): the absolute constitution of nature is unknowable, but it is continually being interpreted. When, however, characters in the story speak about nature, they reflect their inherited cultural biases. Since his characters are usually Catholic and traditionally educated, they equate nature with the "Divine Order." This equation, however, is based on what Kant terms speculation and thus changes over time and between ethnic groups. When Stifter shows what his characters think, then, he is being a Kantian "realist," showing the prag-

matic consistency of what people believe (its epistemological value), and
not falling into an ontological trap. At the same time, Stifter preserves a
clear distance between his narrators and his characters. For instance, the
narrators tend not to refer to "God"; they prefer "the divine." In contrast,
those characters from pious social milieus express their fortunes in terms of
"God's plan."

The distance between the narrator and the characters has a Herbartian
pedagogical dimension for the reader. Generally, a tragedy happens or
threatens to happen when a character ignores Enlightenment dicta and
oversteps moderation (*Maß*, as in the "Vorrede" to *Bunte Steine* [*Many-
Colored Stones*]). But there is no guarantee that the characters, or even the
narrators, will see what moderation was violated. Stifter's frame narratives
usually place an event into a long historical perspective to show that short-
term effects of an event are often very different from long-term effects (see
Neugebauer). Through these juxtapositions, Stifter is implicitly questioning
how fate and history are interpreted by reason. Ultimately, this narrative
style functions as teaching parables fulfilling the desiderata of Herbart's
psychology: to train an individual into judgment by showing how to question historically interpreted conclusions.

This pedagogical purpose is commensurate with Kantian epistemology.
According to Herbart, human behavior is based on an equilibrium of concepts that the group deem useful, not on the unreachable absolute truth of
nature. Because Stifter's story has gaps in the narratives, the reader is forced
to take a position on how credible the story is, to judge if his or her own
personal equilibrium is adequate to the task Stifter gives it. If the narrator is
assumed to be in consort with is characters, then the story reinforces a belief in God, fate, and the divine as accessible to humankind — it is a bul-
wark against the general political and idealistic resignation of Stifter's Biedermeier era. If, however, the reader sees that the narrator is expressing
views that question the characters (as in the use of "the divine" rather than
"God"), then each work encompasses a lesson on how behavior and belief
interact relative to history and perspective. The narrator is not refuting the
characters, since he has no "better" or "truer" belief system than theirs; he
is, however, pointing to truths that neither position encompasses, that future generations may see as theirs.

If this is, indeed, Stifter's program, then he is far from being a late Clas-
sicist heir to Goethe's tradition of humanistic norms. Instead, he remains a
Kantian skeptic and Herbartian pedagogue even in his fiction, not only in
the essays. To bridge these contexts, we may consult the most famous of
Stifter's literary essays, his "Gentle Law," the 1852 "Vorrede" to the story
collection *Bunte Steine*. While conventionally read as Stifter's confession of
theism or pantheism (as an ontological statement), it also strongly reflects
the adaptive, relativistic educational psychology Stifter inherited from
Herder, Kant, and Herbart.

Stifter begins his essay by equating the quality of writings with the quality of the soul that produced them: "If something noble and good is in me,

it will in and of itself permeate my writings" ("Vorrede" 9). Art (like religion) is one of the most important products of mankind, a "speck of good to
contribute to the construction of the eternal" (9–10), but without any necessary direct correlation with the absolute constitution of reality (as Schiller
would have had it). This sounds like secular religious thinking, in which
each individual labors for the progressive Enlightenment of the group. But
then Stifter takes a decided turn toward empiricism, echoing the balance in
his other essays. The most infamous line of the essay contains a list of natu-
ralia Stifter considers great, including the movement of the air, butterflies,
and buttercups. To critics, these items constitute Stifter's focus and hand-
hold on a universe guaranteed by God. Generally overlooked is the sub-
ject-verb construction in the sentence: he *considers* these items great (*halte
ich für*); they represent his opinion, not necessarily the way the world is
constituted.

This statement is only his starting point for an investigation of the real
world, not the final resulting philosophy. He follows his statement with an
example describing the empirical method of science: a person learns that a
compass needle points north all over the earth. Repeated consultations with
a compass turn a person's observations into a principle; the process takes a
set of the "speck after speck" that science teaches us and actively assembles
the "mass of appearances" and the "field of the given" ("Vorrede" 11).
Through the ability to derive such general laws, humanity grows: individuals are moved to fear and pity by natural phenomena, but they become
more deeply moved through general laws to interact and attend to their
environment actively (12). Nonetheless, each individual is not working with
reality but only with a "field of givens," a field of phenomenal evidence.
Again, then, reality is epistemological, not ontological.

What Stifter actually calls the "gentle law" is thus not "praise the butterflies, for God is in them" but the Kantian dictum. Each individual must
work to learn, think, and deal with reality for the good of all (12), a project
facilitated by love (13). When we do so, we create an intellectual community: "then we feel raised in our humanity, we feel ourselves rendered general in our humanity, we feel the sublime as it sinks everywhere into our
souls, through which immeasurably great energies in time or space are
wrought together into a form-filled whole commensurate with reason" (14).
This is an Enlightenment apotheosis of reason for the group, but tempered
with thoroughgoing Kantianism. Note that Stifter constantly says "we *feel*,"
not "we learn" or "we know"; our physical habits find this to be an equilibrium, but our minds have not received divine revelation. Yet even when
we think we know something historically, we are only "seeing" an epic, a
story written in terms of historical justice (14).

Stifter is thus not explaining his "gentle law" ontologically; he is doing
so psychologically (and conservatively). The laws derived through empirical observation are not necessary or real, but we do assume they are, and
so we feel a certain way about them. In fact, general laws of nature are
historical, just as moral laws are (14). Despite their similar psychological

derivation, though, natural laws have a different status from moral laws: one rests on unknown natural processes, the other on human feeling. But all phenomenal evidence is necessarily historical: "Just as, in natural history, opinions about what is great have continually altered, so, too, has it been in the moral history of humanity" (15). For a purported theist, Stifter's analyses of culture end up sounding surprisingly like Nietzsche's, particularly when he says that particular cultures can be constituted on errors.

Generally, Stifter believes that cultures can err in two ways: stressing too much content (decadent cultures do that) or too much empty form (religions can fall into this trap [15]). Yet Stifter denies that this is a philosophy of culture or history: he is only indulging his "passion for collecting" (*Sammelgeist* [18]). In effect, Stifter is taking Kant's dictum to its logical conclusion in culture, while stressing the cognitive effects on historically sanctioned "knowledge" (that is, opinions) for the individual, as Herbart stressed.

If the placement of Stifter vis-à-vis the Enlightenment and psychology holds true, the problems with prevailing trends in criticism of Stifter's fiction become evident. Up through the early 1970s, people were looking for God in Stifter's landscapes: *Seelenlandschaften*, divine fate, a reality behind the world (see Seidler's three reports on scholarship; Belgum). From the early 1980s on, Stifter's relation to the Enlightenment began to be stressed, particularly with respect to his interpretations of revolution (he disapproves of revolution because it destroys the social contract). And most recently, focus has been on his narrators.[5]

Despite the amount of work done on Stifter, several of the stories still present problems, especially when one attempts to reconcile the political Stifter with the purported aesthete. We will turn briefly to five of these to indicate how Stifter the psychologist might have intended his work as education instead of as moral ideal or evidence of an unreliable narrator.

Some Newly-Told Tales

Stifter's historical novel *Witiko* (1865–67) is noted for its length and its deliberate (most would say deadly) narrative pace. It supposedly represents Stifter's concept of a historical epic, but that term has achieved no critical consensus about Stifter's own definition (see Neugebauer's discussion). Conventionally, the notion of "epic" refers to a narrative perspective stressing history or fate, implying patterns beyond the ken of the individuals involved. Yet a definition of *Witiko* is frustrated by this assumption since the bulk of the novel treats the mundane facts of ordinary life: discussions, homecomings, wanderings, preparations, or speeches, not historical or political events as such. In fact, Wiesmüller demonstrates that Stifter's editorial changes between drafts of the work were continuously in the direction of eliminating overt politics; Stifter worked progressively to remove the conventional data of political or national history from the foreground of the novel.

Many examples could support this odd weighting, but what should be a high political moment will illustrate Stifter's focus. Witiko's plea to be admitted to the bishop of Prague's assembly (as an observer for his master, Duke Sobéslaw) gets treated in great detail. It is basically a plea for a legal variance: every trivial moment in the ensuing discussion is recounted, given much more space than the actual political implications of the speech he delivers (book 1.3: "Es war ein großer Saal"). Similarly (in a *Henry V* gesture), the speeches Witiko delivers to his soldiers, stock utterances between leaders and men, are given pages, while the actual battles, sieges, or deaths are hardly mentioned. We are not shown councils of state deciding politics; we are shown the king rewarding followers and consolidating effective power on a personal level.

This is not traditional epic, because the spirit of history moving through the piece is refracted through a minor character, whose existence intersects the great only briefly, but significantly. Nonetheless, Witiko is not central to the historical event, although his history (his land grant and title) depend on it. From Stifter's point of view, he is following his program, teaching his readers the dichotomy between textbook history and history as it is experienced. By highlighting the "little things" and showing politics and history as the ordinary participant experiences them, Stifter contrasts explicitly how history feels with how it is interpreted in retrospect, when "great men" receive different faces and motivations.

The problem of history and fate as appearance instead of truth creates interpretive problems in other Stifter stories, as well. The 1842 *Abdias* is chief among them. The narrator's introduction refers to a "gay daisy chain of reason hang[ing] through the infinity of the universe" (238); he stresses that the ancients called the chain of events "fate" (*Fatum*), while we call it destiny (*Schicksal*). Typically, this statement is interpreted as introducing a story that concerns the fate of an individual. The mention of reason, however, opens an alternate interpretation: that it is a story about how people make sense of things that happen. The daisy chain is not fate's series of events, but the chain of human deductions, in which each succeeding generation "will find an ever greater, ever more magnificent store" of riches to be discovered in the material (238–39). Historical events are merely phenomenal data for minds to work with, hopefully with the intent of ultimately improving life for the community.

Abdias, though, is consistently interpreted ontologically, as "Stifter's definition of fate,"[6] or as Stifter's definition of how the world is put together. Taken instead as a product of the Enlightenment, the work may actually be a teaching parable, a koan, of great length. This story, like Stifter's essays, carefully upholds a distinction between interpreted reality and effective reality (between what is purportedly ontological and what actually happens). Abdias was a man of heart (Stifter's word for a character of particular balance). While he means well, he is clearly a flawed character throughout the story: he maintains two lives, one in the desert and one as a successful man of the world, but does not reconcile them.

This gap leads Stifter's readers to build a chain of insinuation about the man: the reader (led by the opinions of Abdias's neighbors) is led to think that his disfiguring smallpox is God's judgment about his wealth and pretension. These neighbors call this Abdias's fate, even though he only indirectly (at most) cause his settlement's demise. He dresses richly to overcome his ugliness, which, supposedly, shows covert wealth and leads the bey's men to sack the village. The neighbors accuse him of drawing the town to his destruction, even though he drove off the forces of the bey and pays them full compensation for anything he might have done, although he doesn't consider himself guilty. His neighbors expect him to avenge himself, yet instead, he flees to Europe, to an unfruitful, isolated valley, with his daughter.

His daughter Ditha proves to be blind, and Abdias again spends money to alleviate her misery, just as he did in his home for himself. Again, the public is brought to confuse the cause and effect in the situation. Just as the desert people attributed the cause of Abdias's disfigurement to his ostentatious show of wealth (it actually was a result), his European neighbors think that Ditha has been punished for her father's sins of miserliness. In truth, he works to stockpile money so that she will always be taken care of.

Stifter builds an explicit warning about too-hasty judgment (a misuse of reason) into the story. In a brief scene, Abdias assumes his dog has gone mad and shoots him; the dog was only alerting him to the loss of an expensive belt, protecting Abdias's cherished property as a dog should. (This technique of a narrative "aside" is also used in the "Flashback" chapter of *Indian Summer* (*Der Nachsommer*), recounting the tragedy of Risach that Drendorf is supposed to avoid.) A lightening bolt restores Ditha's sight, but a second bolt kills her much later: "The new marvel and punishment," the neighbors decide (341). However, the narrator cannot concur and so never ceases to assure the reader of Abdias's good heart. If Abdias erred, it was because he withdrew from the world and loved one thing too much. But his "error" has good results historically: the valley, presumed arid, has been proved arable, and it remains in the hands of one of his trading friends. Abdias made a mistake, but he has opened land for future use: how can that be divine retribution? Or is "fate" not Abdias's, but the valley — the landscape, not the people? The reader has no proof that what happened to Ditha is any more than an unfortunate accident. Unless the narrator is lying, the reader is almost forced to question the characters and to evaluate a set of events from a longer historical perspective, not out of their sense of "fate." Thus this "history" has thus been reduced to the product of human cognition; it is not "real" in an ontological sense.

Der Hagestolz (1844) is built around a similar gap between the interpreters in the story and the reader/narrator's long (but still relative) perspective. Superficially, Victor is caught between the "good mother," Ludmilla, and the "evil guardian-uncle," a dichotomy reinforced by its settings (a pleasant valley versus a dusty, decaying island cloister). Yet the plot runs counter to these expectations: the "good" mother set up a life script in which Victor could lose the woman he loves. Working behind the scenes and out of the public eye, the uncle corrects the situation: he has saved the patrimony that he purportedly stole so that the boy would get the future that his weak but kind father could not have secured. Victor will thus also get the love that the uncle did not get.

The reader, like Victor, is tempted to assume that the uncle's weird personality caused his isolation; but the inner story shows that Ludmilla may be "at fault," because she chose "the wrong man" — the uncle's life, too, is a result of circumstances beyond his immediate control. The uncle cannot remedy his own situation and save his own life, though he can save the island. Perhaps because of his lost love, he has devoted his life to returning the island to its original mountain vegetation, overcoming the artificial planting the monks brought with them.

These contrasts are setting up a paradox for the reader to uncover and meditate on: neither Ludmilla nor the uncle has children. The *Studien* version of this story ends with the parable of a fig tree, which purportedly is also eliminated from history (*ausgetilgt*). In actuality, however, the fig tree has many descendants; similarly, the odd family in this story has created a son by adoption and a new continuity of life. Stifter's story thus offers an alternate definition of family, one that emphasizes how appearances are deceiving. The uncle purportedly has no heart, but he held true for his whole life to his good-for-nothing brother, a woman, and her ungrateful stepson. From the Enlightenment question of head versus heart, or form versus content, these qualities are crucial, although not immediately evident to the audience.

Stifter has built an equivalent paradox into *Der Hochwald* (1841). The plot seems to hinge on the issue of passion: a hidden love may have led to the destruction of a castle hideaway. Yet the story also contrasts the personal and retrospective views of history that *Witiko* does. The frame narrative links the past and the present explicitly through a historical artifact, the ruins of Wittinghausen. The body of the story, however, presents phenomenological evidence, showing how each individual reacts differently to danger and a forest. The two sister heroines feel they are in a fairy tale. They are accompanied by Gregor, an old family retainer who acts like a forest spirit, and they assume they are protected magically, a belief reinforced by the tale of a magic hunter. Outsiders who do not believe in the forest's power interact with it improperly. Several people intrude on their seclusion and ultimately aid the tragedy. The elder sister's suitor, Ronald, plays the magic hunter to visit his beloved and, in doing so, reveals their location to the enemy. The marauding Swedes of the enemy army approach the forest because they want to sightsee a natural wonder, and that draws them to the castle that they otherwise would have missed. These people are assuming that the forest has the power to ward off evil or draw it toward them. Yet this is only human interpretation: the forest is actually all "virginal" (*jüngfraulich*; 318). As the introduction shows, it has its own web of family obligations and individual guilt in the botanical realm. The forest does not react to people; the narrator and the characters personify it and play out their fantasies about an essentially impassive entity, as stories within the story. These fantasies involve divine plans; the realities are a set of almost random chances that yield a catastrophe.

As in *Abdias*, the readers are not compelled to resolve the characters' varied points of view, but they can by no means read the story as a unified narrative. Unlike later realist prose (such as Theodor Storm's *Schimmelreiter*, 1888), the narrator cannot provide a rationale for the untoward occurrence. The tragedy of the *Hochwald* is explainable empirically although the participants persist in looking for the fantastic. Only the reader can resolve the narrator's paradoxical vision: is the forest gentle or evil? The historical truth is larger than any individual can guess; the reader is supposed to think about more than the characters see.

Finally, *Indian Summer* presents itself as an educational novel, or *Bildungsroman*, in a very different way. While critics like Geulen consider Stifter to be highlighting the act of narration in his work, another vista opens up if we take up the suggestion that Margaret Walter-Schneider picks up from Stifter: that the young couple Heinrich and Natalie are not the center of the novel ("Das Unzulängliche" 317). To be sure, the novel is structured around Heinrich's gradual introduction to progressively more complex facets of the natural and social world (Schoenborn 410–12). Yet unlike Goethe's *Wilhelm Meister*, *Indian Summer* is told as a first-person narrative: the reader sees the world not directly but through the eyes of a youth growing into manhood. Particularly in the early pages of the novel, that youth is educated into ways of seeing this world — and so is the reader. Heinrich's host Risach explains not only how to raise trees, make furniture, and run a household but also why each suggestion is optimal and how others may have disagreed with it. Moreover, the option of future change in such suggestions is always held forth as desirable. As does Goethe's, the book ends in the wedding that founds a new generation (against the background of the family that Risach and Mathilde founded by choice late in life rather than with their families). But an essential difference remains: the reader learns to read a world of work and companionship, as Heinrich does, and by the end of the book becomes interested in what that world *will be*, not what it is. The three families set themselves a contest to see who can improve their estates the most.

The final words of the book are "the pure family life that Risach was referring to has been founded, it will continue undiminished as our love and our hearts attest; I shall administer my property, shall be useful in other ways, and everything, including my scientific endeavors, has now gained significantly in clarity, solidity, and importance" (479). The reader has a sense of what skills and resources these people bring to the task (including resources of personality, ability, and property). To characterize this ending as closure is thus inadequate in almost every way, because each character is set up for a sequel, a next stage in his or her life. Moreover, only the end of the novel reveals the degree of social connection and prominence of the characters, since even Mathilde's last name is not cleared up explicitly until the engagement. The readers are thus in the position of seeing more than Heinrich, the hero-narrator: they make connections about the social and political worlds in which these families exist that he does not — about the relationships of servants and masters, princesses, barons, and the nouveaux riches, and about nature and nurture.

Contrary to the prevalent image of Stifter as a rural writer, *Indian Summer* and Heinrich's fate alternate between the city and the country, between nature and culture, and between past and future — and the reader learns to broaden his or her own vision and cherish both poles, even as Heinrich does. Just as Mathilde is based on the Fürstin Maria Anna zu Schwarzenberg, widow of Field Marshall Karl Philipp zu Schwarzenberg, supreme commander of joint forces conquering Napoleon at Leipzig (Schoenborn 327–28), the rules of the great houses in *Indian Summer* have the society and history of greater Austria as their shadows; their Upper Austria is inextricably linked to the unnamed Vienna and to the world beyond it. The young couple founds its future on family but must go out into the world in order to nourish a younger generation with new soil in its own Indian summer; the reader has been systematically (re)educated by following Heinrich from the domestic interiors of his childhood up to the threshold of his future engagement with the larger world. Family is the cornerstone of the future but not the entire one, unless the whole world be part of it. Stifter has thus inverted the domestic values of the rising bourgeoisie, even while being more domestic than they; women and men must all reach beyond themselves to choose and make their families actively. This most politically conservative of novelists thus offers a convincing argument for change and teaches his readers about how such change fulfills rather than challenges family and tradition.

As these too brief examples suggest, reading Stifter as an educational psychologist seriously calls into question his reputation as the deistic poet of nature. The narrators in each of these stories are doing the best they can, but they are by no means omniscient in the traditional sense. Thus they are not "in charge" of the narrative for the reader, nor is their word to be taken absolutely as the interpretation of the stories' events. The costs, threats, and causes the characters and narrators identify exist only as customary assumptions stemming from human tradition, not any absolute truths. Even in the historical panorama of *Der Hochwald*, the narrator is just playing out all his childhood fantasies about the forest. Virtually any conclusions may be called into question through the effects of time and distance, and the gaps in the narration force this questioning on the reader. As in *Der Hagestolz*, the narrator leads the reader into a "who's good, and who's bad" puzzle that he does not resolve successfully himself. Similarly, the frame of *Abdias* explicitly tries to force the reader to realize that histories aren't logical, that perceived reality is based on "the last unreason of being" ("die letzte Unvernunft des Seins"; 238); "wasted lives" change as the perspective on the events in Abdias's life change, from the desert, to Europe, to future generations.

To realize that the narrator is there to be undercut does not change the interpretations of the inner story materials.[7] What does change decisively is the assessment of the significances of the stories: the effect Stifter hopes to have on his readers. The gaps in perceived truth that Stifter's narration reveals show that "reality" is much less comprehensible than characters assume; people guide their lives through these "reasonable assumptions," but that does not make them ontologically true nor render them proper examples for later generations with other needs and traditions.

Conclusions:
The Pragmatic Enlightenment

Stifter's unreliable narrators directly reflect Herbart's educational psychology and reduce history to a question of cognition. According to this, each individual must learn actively, through cognitive processing, not through example. Each individual mind must mesh new data with its extant conceptual mass; and its learned material must reach a new stable state for its results, a new ego conception. Each individual assesses the world only phenomenologically since the absolute constitution of the world is unknowable. Stifter's work thus educates individual minds; it does not explain the world in a religious or ontological sense but presents epistemological paradoxes, a manifestation of the gap between how things are presumed to be in reality and other data that are not accounted for in those presumptions.

Stifter's is thus a realism based on cognitive philosophy, far away from that of later generations. When Storm, in *Der Schimmelreiter* (1888), shows how superstition plays a role in men's actions, his narrator represents a larger historical perspective and is presumed to report correctly on what ultimately is important about an event. But Stifter's future generations may err; his narrators are marked as unreliable, not like Storm's "manuscript in a bottle" tactic that grants the reported material some authenticity. Stifter's characters err, and so do his narrators: they, like the readers, need to *rethink* history instead of merely *uncovering* it, as the German realists must. For Stifter, then, "realism" is a question of understanding, not only finding; not only the material of thought but the very ground for understanding has been rendered problematic. Stifter does not understand the world, but he feels that all history is worth rethinking, whether it be personal details (*Witiko, Der Hagestolz*, or *Indian Summer*), great events (*Der Hochwald*), or moments when historical consequences arise from pure chance (*Abdias*). The result of that rethinking, though, is decisively *not* a statement about reality. Stifter's work stresses the relativity of epistemology and the necessity of inculcating strong habits of mind into individuals so that they can improve their lots and those of their fellow humans. Stifter's goal in writing is, then, ultimately pedagogical instead of ontological: he is not discussing history as an absolute but only as one of many relative products of human cognition.

The narrative paradox on which Stifter bases the reader's education is distinctive of an Austrian literature tradition (especially in the plays of Raimund and Nestroy, the form of which was replicated by Brecht to achieve his alienation effects in the theater). It is, moreover, not a product of the "Classicism" myth in Germany: German Classicists (like Schiller and Goethe) still felt empowered to give visions of the absolute ideals that should be embodied in human history — they felt that, through art, visions of an ideal future could be implanted in humankind. In contrast, and as a result of his focus on educational psychology instead of on construction of an absolute reality or history, Stifter knew that such visions represent at best relative ideals that will be rethought by the next generation. He chose to educate minds in the relativity of thought, to question rather than reinforce what any tradition from the past had decided was important. History and fate are thus much less than the power of the human mind, the true topic of Stifter's writings.

Notes

[1]For a detailed treatment of this psychology, see Katherine Arens, *Structures of Knowing*. For a discussion of the relation of Herder's and Kant's work, see Arens, "Kant, Herder, and Psychology." J. G. Herder was probably the stimulus who turned Kant toward a consideration of history. For accounts of Herder's work, see Clark and Broce. For classic accounts of the development of psychology in Germany and Austria, see Boring, Ellenberger, and Doerner.

[2]Citations in the presents discussion have been modified from M. J. Gregor's English translation of Immanuel Kant, *Anthropology from a Pragmatic Point of View*, on the basis of Karl Vorländer's German edition of Immanuel Kant, *Anthropologie in pragmatischer Hinsicht* .

[3]Herbart, who enjoyed a renaissance in American educational psychology around the turn of the century (with a concomitant flood of book-length discussions of his work and its applications), remains a little discussed figure today. The *Text-Book in Psychology* was translated as part of this renaissance by Margaret K. Smith. David Leary agrees with the present discussion that Herbart's program derives from Kant's while still placing Herbart in the Idealist tradition, following Leibniz and Wolff.

[4]This is echoed in one of the copious quotations from Wilhelm von Humboldt that Stifter included in the *Lesebuch zur Förderung humaner Bildung*:

> Humans feel a need to verify the great ideas in them (and which they find expressed in nature) in the small circle of their existence, and often, even when they believe they are following motivations drawn from everyday life, they are actually following this secret trait. Human nature is in deepest ground absolutely much nobler than it appears on the surface. (308–9)

[5]On social contract, see especially Neugebauer, Plumpe, and Lachinger, Stillmark, and Swales. On narrators, see Begemann, Lorey, Petterson, Piechotta, Rogan, Schiffermüller, Walter-Schneider, and Whitinger.

[6]See, for example, Neugebauer: "dieses Modell der nach zwei Seiten gerichteten Kräfte der Geschichte" (33).

[7]See, for example, in Lachinger, Stillmark, and Swales on *Abdias* for a recent, typical interpretation; see Neubauer for the social implications and background of Stifter's situation.

6: Schnitzler's Characterology: Science and Cultural Practice

In Vienna at the end of the nineteenth century, the scientific community was in the middle of a fundamental redefinition of its terms, addressing questions of individual mental development, personal wellness, and personality.[1] In the city's formidable and pervasive medical school and hospital system,[2] doctors and therapists had inherited diagnostic practices focusing on the inherited wellness or frailty of constitutions, on a "therapeutic nihilism" resting on a belief in nature's ability to help the human body and mind heal. Yet at the same time, newly arising (and well publicized) therapeutic models like Freud's and Breuer's *Studies in Hysteria* countered by suggesting that mental and physical wellness could be redefined as mental phenomena in terms of an individual's ability to function and shape a life history.

Hidden under debates about therapeutic practices, however, was what we have come to acknowledge today as a more central debate in the biological sciences: Darwinism versus Lamarckianism. The more conservative reading of the question assumed that the individual is determined through biological inheritance; the more liberal, that environmental influences affected the development of both the individual and the species. As is familiar, this debate was reflected both in medical diagnostics and in social legislation of the period. The conservative social Darwinist believed that the place of the individual in society was determined at birth; the liberal (perhaps a socialist) held that it could be altered through education and cultural influence, thus improving succeeding generations. In political circles, this debate remained active in Austria at least from the turn of the century to its absorption into the racism and pan-Germanism of the Third Reich.[3]

The more familiar work in medical diagnostics in Vienna was complemented by a contemporaneous explosion in philosophical physiology throughout the German-speaking world.[4] A group of physiologists and physicists took up psychological projects as they tried to devise experiments that could determine thresholds of normal function for the sense organs, and thus the thresholds to the kind of knowledge that could be synthesized using sense data.[5] Wilhelm Wundt and Hermann Helmholtz, whose laboratories in Leipzig and Berlin lasted well into this century, determined limits beyond which sense organs would not perceive stimuli such as variations in lights and tones. In Prague and later in Vienna, Ernst Mach expanded this idea of an observer's limits to explore how they would affect the validity of scientific experiments. He believed the physical world, and thus all science, to be ultimately limited by our senses, inherited language, and conceptual tools. With later psychologists like William James, these scholars constituted a psychology that focused on normal development and wellness — on the interactions between mind, body, and physical environment.

In the nineteenth century, then, two parallel trends in psychology were developing in Germany and Austria. One became institutionalized in the medical schools, particularly at Vienna, with its stress on physical self-healing; it focused on the diagnostics of illness through physical symptoms. The other, stressing normal mental and physical functions, became associated with physiology, physics, and educational psychology. A disjunction thus separated cognitive theory, laboratory research, and practical diagnostics and therapy. "Illness" and its diagnosis stressed the primacy of the physical; "wellness" stressed normal function and learning, which at that time placed mind over body as prime determinant.

Particularly in Vienna, with its extended medical community, such debates also found popular forms. One of these is the argument about "characterology," which the following discussion will trace, using two texts from the popular science of the era. One is by a successful physician in general practice who was also a playwright, the other by a failed philosopher who nonetheless wrote a dissertation acceptable to both physiologists and philosophers of his day. Physician Arthur Schnitzler's *The Mind in Words and Actions* (*Der Geist im Wort und der Geist in der Tat*, 1927) discusses character and human behavior patterns; philosopher Otto Weininger's *Sex and Character* (*Geschlecht und Charakter*, first published in 1903) is an adaptation of his dissertation, an infamous proto-Nazi discussion of racism.

All differences aside, both authors share assumptions common to the dominant biological/psychological debates of the day. Yet since these texts were designed to be popular, their "characterology" also allows us to see what unstated but widely accepted assumptions about the minds of individuals were at play in Vienna in 1900. As we shall see, they tie popular ideologies to institutionalized medical practice in a way that highlights various continuities between Austria at the turn of the century and later developments in Europe, including the Third Reich and the later East Bloc.

Schnitzler's Anthropology: Character as Predisposition

Schnitzler (1862–1931) was a member of the upper-middle class and the often, but not exclusively, Jewish intellectual circles so prominent in Viennese culture under the Empire.[6] Through the coffee-house society of the city, Schnitzler remained in almost daily commerce with scientists such as Otto Brahm (whose *Tierleben* remained a standard in zoology) and Freud, financiers such as the Wittgenstein family, musicians, and publicists. His position and contacts thus make Schnitzler's work a plausible norm for the continuing intellectual interests of the first quarter of this century — for the way that science would be perceived outside the narrow circle of professional scientists.

His slim volume *The Mind in Words and Actions* is intended for a popular audience.[7] Bound into the text is a set of four diagrams labeled "Spirit in the Word" and "Spirit in Deeds." The book itself is divided into an unmarked preface, a chapter on each of the two major topics, and "An Intermediary Chapter on Aptitudes [Giftedness] and States of the Soul." The preface explains the subject matter of the book as how innate character types are revealed in an individual's words and deeds: "insofar as mind can manifest itself, primarily by means of actions" (5). Schnitzler thus represents an essentially conservative point of view, the belief that an individual is determined by inheritance.

Schnitzler intended this book to be an *anthropology* of human character, or a *characterology*: a study of the types of human spirit observable in the world. Such an approach signals more than a psychological or even a psychoanalytical analysis as we know it today, for Schnitzler bases his work on a picture of the total person in culture. In what he called the "Intermediary Chapter," Schnitzler outlines his model of the total personality: "[It is] the innate, uniform, unchangeable prototype . . . determined by his predispositions, aptitudes (general and specific), *Seelenzustände* (fluid traits, states, and moods), and, to a lesser degree, by external appearance and physical properties" (43–44). Each warrants a brief separate treatment since Schnitzler's redefinitions underscore his anthropological portrait.

An individual's *spiritual constitution* has, first of all, its "innate, integral, and immutable" qualities (9). These are innate predispositions of character, not the later character "types" that emerge not only from innate character, but also from the person's profession and activities. These individual's predispositions represent a nucleus, "core," or "prototype" that will condition the total personality (9). The predispositions are, therefore, the deepest layer of personality, corresponding to the body's major structural elements, its gifts, and its prevailing moods (32). Roughly, an individual can be predisposed either towards the *word* or to *action*, which will lead him or her eventually to develop a personality of a particular positive or negative type.

Schnitzler finds it unlikely that any layer of personality will be localized in a specific area of the brain or in any particular bodily secretions. Nonetheless, inheritance will determine an individual's essential personality: "the innate, uniform, and unchangeable mentality . . . that, in rare cases, reveals itself only in historical retrospect" (53–54). The predispositions are thus also not necessarily immediately evident from behaviors.

The character types resulting from these innate predispositions are, moreover, divided into "positive" and "negative" variants, shown on the horizontal axes in Schnitzler's diagrams, and into analogous variants, shown on the vertical axes. Yet character types cannot transmute into one another, as the diagrams seem to indicate, even through their relative positions are important to a diagnostician. In daily activities, for example, a negative type will be easily confounded with its positive variants. A "reporter" with an innate negative affect and tendency to fragment facts can be confused with a journalist or writer, who tends to form continuities, tell coherent stories. The negative type lives for today, without a sense of time; the positive lives without a sense of space but for the continuity of time. Similarly, the positive type is assimilated into the group but lonely; the negative is isolated but companionable (15). Seemingly inactive, the former concentrates on the long view, and produces without worrying about momentary effects. Conversely, the latter worries about the moment, not the bigger picture; someone of this type is active without really achieving.

The type and countertype are ultimately difficult to differentiate since each consciously or unconsciously adopts some of the modes of expression and ways of life of their negative countertypes, and since the resulting character of each will also be influenced by the person's gifts, moods, and physical properties. The observer of either type will, in the last resort, be able to distinguish them only after observing their motivations over a period of time and by checking them against the secondary circumstances that surround them (20). Moreover, the types do not necessarily correspond to professions but rather to an individual's inborn interface with reality (52). Still, Schnitzler decides that "great" personalities must be positive types, while "significant" ones are negative. Implicitly, too, he is equating strength of innate character with a healthy mind — while acknowledging that there is more than one "type" of character or behavior that can be identified as normal and healthy.

Less immutable than innate character disposition, but contributing to the personality that an individual develops, are what Schnitzler calls aptitudes and moods. Gifts or aptitudes refer to the scope of a character type, not to its attributes, and so reflect an individual's intellectual broadness and acuity. Aptitudes may naturally, although not necessarily, show an affinity with certain predispositions, so terminology often overlaps. For example, specific aptitudes characterize the poet, the musician, the journalist, and the politician. They are a person's skills, what she or he does well. Like predispositions, aptitudes are inborn; but while predispositions are fixed, aptitudes can be improved or allowed to deteriorate but are not necessarily developed (35).

More fleeting than aptitudes, moods or "states of the soul" are the most transitory or mutable elements of individual personality — elements that change easily when one is physically ill, for instance. In order of ascending mutability and importance for the appearance of personality, they include what Schnitzler calls character traits, spiritual characteristics, fluid states, and moods proper. "Character traits" can be influenced from within and without, even changed at will. "Fluid states" alter in intensity and duration; they can even disappear completely. "Spiritual characteristics" (such as enthusiasm, bravery and cowardice) may emerge alternately. Moreover, any character trait may correlate with aptitudes and predispositions: what one is and what one does well may also be reflected in the mood of a moment. "Dilettantism," for example, is a fundamental character type, a description of a certain type of intellectual talent, and a mood that can overcome one at a particular moment: "an artist of a certain aristocratic inner style of life, a playfully disposed intellect who is less interested in the perfection of a work than in the enjoyment of creativity or play per se" (41). From this perspective, poets are more easily dilettantes than are literati, who tend (as "continualists" in fundamental dispositions) to finish things. The negative variant of dilettantism is "feuilletonism" — an individual's tendency toward satirical journalism.

Schnitzler's picture of an individual's total personality thus involves a determination of predispositions, aptitudes, and moods. In this, his model diverges fairly sharply from the more familiar Freudian model of character, which rests on a tripartite division of the mind into id (unconscious drives), ego (conscious personality), and superego (internalized prohibitions and traditions). Where Freud draws a picture of how an individual's nature becomes a personality when it enters culture, Schnitzler's definition of character more closely resembles the assumptions of social Darwinism since they acknowledge that individuals are born as recognizable social types.

Schnitzler's individual is defined as an interplay between permanent and mutable forces, determined by mutable, acquired characteristics as well as immutable, inherited ones. Schnitzler is, to be sure, not interested in inheritance per se, but his sketches connect human character with behavior patterns in social and ethical environments. If he were to address an individual's state of mental wellness or illness, he would have to do so by referring to biological predispositions and aptitudes, not simply to moods or to environmental factors. Because individuals' predispositions are innate, he could not assume that essential changes can take place in individual character. However, individuals' moods and fluid states could be corrected, possibly with some minor long-term effects on their character traits. That is, they can become better, but not different, variants of what they already inherently are. And in contrast to Freud's vision, Schnitzler believes that they are already predisposed to certain social positions, not simply developing into social contexts.

In this sense, Schnitzler's characterology argues at the same time a liberal and a conservative view of individuals in society. It is liberal in acknowledging a plurality of social types: all individuals' characters will correlate with different patterns of behavior and with different skills under environmental pressures. Yet it is still conservative, since some part of each individual is immutable, and not necessarily in ways that society would recognize as positive: characters can be prone to disengagement, to a lack of closure, or to too simple explanations offered in the spirit of drawing continua. Ultimately, however, Schnitzler is conservative in much the way that Freud is: in both views, society is locked into certain patterns based on individual physical inheritance (albeit as "character types" in Schnitzler's work rather than as "drives"). Yet Schnitzler's society is a considerably more social and more diverse place than is Freud's. They are part of the same worldview but not identical.

A third contemporary, Otto Weininger, offers yet another variant of this vision of human character and society. His contribution, however, moves as far to the conservative end of the model as Schnitzler moved to a pluralistic, liberal one.

Weininger's *Sex and Character*: Character and Biology

Like Schnitzler, Otto Weininger (1880–1903) was an educational product of turn-of-the-century Vienna, immersed in the intellectual and scientific conflicts of the day. His book *Sex and Character: An Investigation of Principles* is infamous even today. Originally written as a dissertation, it was expanded in 1903 to become a popular success, running to almost thirty editions by 1940. The basic material may have been stolen from Freud (some contend that Freud's patient Hermann Swoboda showed or discussed an unpublished manuscript with Weininger).[8] Today the book is seen as scientific bunk. At the time, however, it played a significant role as an interface between the medical and popular communities, especially as the general populace's introduction to scientific racism.

Part of Weininger's popular success was perhaps due to the aura of genius he acquired after his suicide at age twenty-three because of depression. Like the many other suicides of his age, he became identified with the spirit of a generation whose aims were not fulfilled, nor even fulfillable within the context of a restrictive society. But another part of his appeal lay in his ability to offer simple versions of the day's major debates about character: in his oversimplified logic, all human types are composed of male and female sides, which influence their characters and behaviors. This clear, if false, generalization was supported by "proofs" he drew from credible sources: from his dissertation advisor, Friedrich Jodl, a respected member of the University of Vienna's philosophy section; from medical trends of the day, yet without explicitly mentioning Freud, who had been publishing for ten years (lending tacit support to the assumption that he stole material); from popular characterology, especially from Paul Möbius (1854–1906), who wrote *Über den physiologischen Schwachsinn des Weibes* (1901); and from a physiology resembling that of Wilhelm Wundt's famous Leipzig laboratory (see Boring). Such a collection of sources almost automatically looked credible, especially to an audience that was conditioned by its art and music to believe the doctrine of the feminine principle as the passive, and the masculine as the active element in humans.

And the social message that was attached to Weininger's biology of human character was gaining in popularity in imperial Europe as well. Those persons or races with a preponderance of either principle or "protoplasm" in their makeup were classified as innately active or passive. The active were innovative and strong; the passive were receptive and weak. And those who were born weak deserved special treatment. Women were to be protected. Sexual deviance began to be viewed as an organic imbalance.[9] Weininger thus easily sounded plausible at the end of a century that set up ethnographic museums with models of physiological types and that enumerated the physical characteristics of the "criminal type." However, from the perspective of the twentieth century, such a volume instantly suggests Nazi eugenics and racial programs.

Weininger follows the nineteenth-century pattern of experimental psychologists (particularly Wundt and Fechner) to evolve his approach to character. In the fifth chapter of the first part of his volume, "Characterology and Morphology" (60), he begins by asserting a correspondence between an individual's physical and psychic characteristics: "psychic types . . . are mediated in spiritual terms, as well as in physical ones" (60). His "psychology of individual differences" (61) traces how psychological behavior is organically conditioned. However, these psychic types are also conditioned by biological sex, as an individual type oscillates between masculine and feminine poles, as a kind of periodic function in sexuality (echoing the work of Freud's friend Wilhelm Fliess without attribution [61]). Thus the pure man and the pure woman are fictions — the degree of mixing in any individual can be determined partially through morphological characteristics.[10] Moreover, the degree to which an individual has specific characteristics of either sex will determine the degree to which he or she will be drawn to the opposite type (65).

By starting with gendered physical types as determining of psychological type, Weininger redefines psychology. He implicitly discards the study of sense impressions or feelings — the work of Helmholtz and Fechner, James and Avenarius — offering a new science beyond biology or physiology. This science is a characterology based on "the concept of a constant, unified essential being"; it does not consider the individual to be a product of his experiences: "the character is not something poised behind the thinking and feeling of an individual, but rather something that reveals itself in *every* thought and every feeling of that individual" (98). His characterology thus aims to study the permanent in the temporary stages of each individual; it studies essences, not the differences between individuals. This essence is not metaphysical — it is not the "soul" but rather an unchanging foundation within each individual that conditions differences that emerge in history. Weininger thus agrees with Schnitzler in tracing both a permanent substrate and changes in historical inheritance.

Weininger believes that what distinguishes men and women is their different experience of sexuality (part 2, chapter 2), a variant that ultimately also differentiates male and female consciousness (part 2, chapter 3). Their biological differences yield different social roles. Despite shared experiences, the male thinks in more clearly articulated units than the female does (120–21). The woman must therefore rely on the man to clarify the "Henides" (raw idea units) into discrete, usable concepts. Here Weininger's work correlates with Schnitzler's quite directly since both correlate clarity in thought with "Giftedness and Genius" (the title of chapter 4). In Weininger's version, talents are inborn, and they are not necessarily accompanied by genius, or marked by high degrees of clarity in thought. Only a person of genius, a person with a scope of character, experiences intense cycles in his basic constitution and possesses the ability to communicate them. Moreover, since they are inborn, talents are inheritable, while genius is not (it correlates with everyday function, not with innate physical endowments). The genius is also characterized by an almost universal ability to remember experiential, but not necessarily learned, data (140–41).

Weininger correlates ability very tightly with biological inheritance. Where he exceeds Schnitzler's model, however, is in the idea of basic types of inheritance. Where Schnitzler believed there was a palette of character types that correlated with possible social and intellectual types, Weininger considers biological sex endowment determining. For example, Weininger believes that the notion of genius is inherently incompatible with the female, who is inherently passive (139). In a similar vein, men possess a memory for universal categories of information, while women only remember their drive for procreation and the moments in society that aid it (153). As a consequence, he, like Freud, believes that memories are the key to the individual: "What a person never forgets, and what he cannot remember — these make most possible the uncovering of his essential being, his character" (153). Yet Weininger believes that there are only two fundamental types of remembering (one more abstract [male] and one more biologically concrete [female]), a restriction on biological-social typing that Schnitzler would not have accepted and that Freud would have felt was an undervaluing of the individuality of experience.

Thus for Weininger, biology and biography may become part of psychology in a manner different from Freud's. In both systems, however, consciousness will show both subjectivity and objectivity, a "will to value" (Weininger 167). For Weininger as for Schnitzler, though, genius is found in the man whose consciousness transcends time (168). The genius's activities clarify the past and give it a form for others to receive. This is a normative evaluation of successful personalities much stricter than Freud's or Schnitzler's. Quality and scope of mental function are inborn to a greater degree than Schnitzler would have allowed; individuality is even more biologically restricted than in Freud's concept. Weininger feels that an additional mark of a significant person is that he makes history, just as the creative scientist does (172). His image of the woman, in contrast, paints the image of a person not even interested in herself — she not only lacks a history but also a psychology since her gender has not been self-aware or self-reflexive enough to create women psychologists (182) or any causal, continuous picture of women in history. Weininger's women and men are thus both largely immune to the environmental conditioning stressed by Freud; they are biologically conditioned, and so their wellness or illness will be as well.

The strongest possible personality, in Weininger's terms, is the genius — a male. He is characterized by his sense of the whole, which enables him to filter experiential data on a large scale to form a coherent worldview (213). While the normal individual has a restricted world within him, the genius has the "living macrocosm in himself" (212). Yet no matter the scope of his personality, all that the person feels of the world or of himself grows out of his constitution (226). Each individual's physical constitution is an anchor for his communication and coherency, the center of a united picture of the sensible (190 ff.). Growing out of that physical constitution, personality is the central event of consciousness. Moreover, the core of our *Weltanschauung* is influenced by this "ego-event" (211). For Weininger, the first thing one knows is that one exists; a sense of self or of the soul will therefore precede all world experience (209–11). One's sense of time and the world grows within that personality structure. Weininger is thus a modified solipsist, stressing the primacy of ego over environment.

Because of this model of the relationships between physical constitution and consciousness, Weininger sees two sciences of mind as necessary, where Freud and other contemporaries like Ernst Mach assumed one would suffice. For Weininger, characterology must stand next to psychology proper: it is the science of innate constitution, standing next to a psychology conceived as the science of experience (205). With this observation, Weininger also asserts the priority of characterology over psychology as the science modeling the workings of the mind, just as Freud asserted the priority of his psychoanalysis over psychiatry as therapeutic disciplines. Until the characterology of an individual is determined, his or her psychology cannot be evaluated without imposing false values (262–63).

This picture of characterology is still considerably more restrictive than Schnitzler's, despite superficial similarities. For Weininger, the crucial differentiation grounding all personalities is that between the passive and the active, the female and the male. While man's personality encompasses a coherent vision of the universe, woman (or the female type, such as the Jew or homosexual) sees only an aggregate — a compendium of impressions that cannot be gathered by that individual into a coherent worldview (269). Moving clearly toward the racist and sexist stereotyping for which he is remembered, Weininger finishes his book by equating the woman and the Jew as personalities linked in worldviews, in cultures of narrow bestial consciousness. He uses his science to justify racism and sexism.

Weininger's *Sex and Character* is not exhausted by this exposition, but even this brief discussion shows that he, like Schnitzler, relies on a modified Darwinian point of view, assuming that inheritance determines the individual. While Schnitzler's text embraces a greater social diversity than Weininger's, both men clearly privilege biological inheritance whereas more famous contemporaries like Freud were moving toward a vision of human adaptability in sciences and history. What are the larger implications of these correspondences within the scope of the scientific and popular scientific establishments of the day?

Characterology and the Audience

At first glance, the audience for the two texts seems to be fundamentally different. Schnitzler's volume is unpretentious, with no claims to completeness. Weininger's text, in contrast, intends to offer an encompassing theory of character, supported by half the acknowledged experts in philosophy, physiology, and psychology, while refuting the other half. Yet the two texts do correspond in their underlying models of the human spirit despite their respective appeals to more popular and more technical audiences.

Each presupposes a fixed, deepest level to the human spirit: Schnitzler calls it the "spiritual constitution" (*Geistesverfassung*), the predisposition to act, speak, or otherwise deal with experience; Weininger terms it "character," a pregiven mixture of male and female cellular matter, which predisposes all other facets of personality. An intermediate level of the human spirit exists for both thinkers, variously called "talent," "genius," or "giftedness" — terms that refer to the scope and style of activity of which the individual is capable. This factor is not necessarily connected to the innate constitution but is partially inborn as well. Rather, it indicates the ease or scope of the individual's mental functions. The most superficial layer of the individual is the personality (the fluid states, for Schnitzler) or what is experienced (experiential data filtered through character, according to Weininger). Only that superficial layer of the person is conditioned not by his or her essential constitution but by the environment.

If the two books share this model, they then point to a possible continuity between characterology as a popular science and other sciences of the day. First and foremost, the underlying model of these books would correlate with a very specific model of how medical diagnoses and therapy of mental illness are to be conducted. Mental illnesses that manifest themselves as dissolution of personality (not affecting "inherent character") would not necessarily be considered serious since the patient's fundamental constitution would, in most cases, be intact despite moods or transitory fluctuations. Deep therapy would not be crucial; a cure would involve reestablishing an individual's healthy relationship to stimuli of the moment. Using assumptions like these, a physician or scientist accepting this characterology would also almost automatically be taking a position in the conflict between Darwinism and Lamarckianism as philosophies of science.

Our current stereotypes of these positions by no means reflect the subtleties of the debate within the scientific community of the time. By the middle of the nineteenth century, Lamarckianism (maintaining that acquired characteristics can be transmitted to the offspring of individuals whose survival has modified their basic structure) was being adapted from its original scientific context and turned into popular science, just as the Darwinian position (stressing the primacy of genetic inheritance) was emerging with its strong proponents and opponents in the British scientific establishment.[11] These two positions also conditioned two basic approaches to the question of what determines the existence of the individual, a conflict that had to be latent in a scientific community like that of Vienna, which was focused on neurology, surgery, and medical therapy. At the same time, the popular science of the day was taking positions with regard to this conflict in various "popular-scientific lectures" (for example, Mach's), and in popular science books, such as those under consideration here. Acceptance of characterology, then, meant taking a position more in favor of Darwinism than of Lamarckianism.

However, that debate was not carried on publicly in these terms but rather reflected only the base positions of "heredity" versus "environmental adaptation."[12] Yet this is not surprising, given that biological research in the Monarchy virtually had to be aligned with the medical establishment and human biology. In contrast, biologists in England were confronting geological evidence of past biological evolution as an outgrowth of their Empire's growing industrial interests.[13] Biologists in Russia focused on the questions of inheritance and conditioning brought up by Mendel and Pavlov.

Stuck in a largely medical framework, then, the Viennese biologists may have been insulated from international attempts to reconcile the questions of adaptation and inheritance. It was left to physicists such as Mach and philosopher-psychologists such as Franz Brentano to take over the questions of environment and adaptation into their sphere in their closer focus on psychophysics as an outgrowth of physiology, leaving genetic questions behind (see Johnston). Given this map of research focuses, the question of inheritance was left tacitly on the side of a vague Darwinism, in the hands of the medical school. In this model for therapeutics, which was necessarily conservative about physical types, the young of a species would be seen as essentially continuous in character with their parents; changes in thought or behavior would result from successful survival adaptations.

From this perspective, the scientific vanguard would be seen as more interested in adaptation, as was Schnitzler. Two parallel cases of intellectuals whose influence remained significant well into the twentieth century support this assumption. Ernst Mach shunted the question of inheritance away from strict biological conditioning and onto patterns of conceptualization reinforced by cultural inheritance. Freud argued for change in personality as well when he applied a similar model in psychological therapy. But the fact that the question of inheritance versus environmental conditioning was in some ways not actively engaged in Vienna because it was hidden behind disciplinary boundaries does not mean that it had less inflammatory potential there than elsewhere in the world. When Vienna's scientific community interacted with the rest of the world, however, they were forced to deal with it. Perhaps the biggest scandal arising from this ill-focused ideological conflict was the case of an exact contemporary of Schnitzler and Weininger: the experimental biologist Paul Kammerer in Vienna.

The Case of the Midwife Toad, by Arthur Koestler, describes the case of a largely forgotten hallmark of biological research on environmental conditioning.[14] Kammerer, a musician turned biologist, became in 1903 a member of the "Biologische Versuchsanstalt" in Vienna. This was one of the first environmentally controlled breeding laboratories in the world, consisting of an aquarium and terrarium; it offered biologists the chance to work with live animals rather than with the laboratory preparations that were the norm for zoology then. Over twenty years, Kammerer compiled an unparalleled record in the breeding and observation of amphibians (especially salamanders and toads), specializing in forced breeding and survival conditions.

Yet just before the First World War, Kammerer's work, which had been appearing in major journals almost as long as he had been working at the institute, was questioned in Great Britain. The reason was his purported Lamarckianism: he claimed to have found that when he altered their breeding or general living conditions, certain amphibians could change their essential types ("blind" animals could regenerate eyes; progeny could alter protective coloration; reproductive patterns could switch between land-based and amphibious subspecies). Because the British establishment was committed to Darwinism by that point, Kammerer was attacked for allegedly falsifying specimens to prove his point; he responded as a Viennese, not conditioned by a half century of conflict on the issue, by merely pointing out that no one had replicated his experiments (partial attempts failed because other scientists were not able to replicate his breeding strategies, for reasons as simple as the sheer quantity of specimens he kept alive). Moreover, he had photographic evidence (severely questioned by outsiders) documenting specimens that could not be killed, if the breeding was to be continued, or that had been lost in the war. Ultimately, he committed suicide, just before he was to go to Russia to set up a new experimental laboratory at the Pavlov Institute (Koestler 35). His struggles to maintain international credibility and to support his income during and after the First World War had worn him out.

The details of the case, as well as the veracity of the various scientific claims made in it, are still a matter of debate, but the present discussion of Schnitzler and Weininger suggests a clear underlying cause for it: although not formulated in those terms, Kammerer's message would have supported a Lamarckian viewpoint, while the scientific establishment in Britain and on the continent was then committed to Darwinism. He had therefore provoked a reaction that he might not have anticipated on the basis of his experiences in Vienna, where his type of work in zoology or species biology was not perceived to be in the mainstream of the Empire's scientific reputation. A second historical factor for Kammerer's late reception may also have come into play after the First World War: because of its Marxist conception of history, Russia between the wars committed itself to a modified Lamarckianism, which said, in the narrowest sense, that the economic and social environments determine the individual. The commitment would be continued beyond both world wars as a necessary correlate to the Socialist message derived from Marxism-Leninism. The East Bloc was founded on the premise that changing socioeconomic conditions will change individuals and society (see Cocks).

Weininger and Schnitzler clearly stand in an opposing tradition. Rudimentary Darwinists, they believe the individual is determined *by biological inheritance*, although they define this inheritance with marginal differences. If they represent the scientific mainstream rather than the vanguard, as I am arguing here, we have an additional avenue by means of which we can understand popular and scientific opposition to Freud since his studies concentrated on mental disease and behavior or behavior modification *as a product of the environment.*[15] The basic popularity of a text such as Weininger's for the first half of the century in the West argues for general public acceptance of a conservative view on character, which correlates with the comparative unpopularity in Vienna of Freud's work (demonstrated in his late professorship, heated debates with the medical establishment, and the like).

Weininger's and Schnitzler's successes seem to indicate that the public, like the medical community in Austria before the Second World War, assumed an essentially Darwinist view of man. Both the public and the scientific establishment held a conservative view of human potential, which supported the continuation of class structure on the grounds of inheritance. These assumptions would not only alienate the international scientific community (as in the case of Kammerer) but would also oppose the adherents of "Red Vienna" and the Socialist International, who believed in educated workers for general social progress with a cumulative positive effect on society.

Case Studies in Characterology

There is not only a scientific and popular scientific reception of the Darwinian-Lamarckian debate around character but also a more popular one focusing on how human behavior is perceived and evaluated. It is therefore instructive to follow the conservative vision of character that has been drawn into the literature of the period, since Schnitzler was a popular author as well as practicing physician and since his work is considered to represent the typical attitudes of the Viennese middles classes. Schnitzler's stories and plays may be said to present cases of his contemporaries' odd or constrained behavior in ways designed to be "diagnosed" by their audiences. However, the diagnoses reached by an audience that believed in inheritance may not be those that are most comfortable today. These stories are earlier than his work on characterology, but they support the line of development in medical therapeutics that I am arguing here.

Schnitzler's short story "Leutnant Gustl" (1900) presents the inner life of a middle-class army officer in perpetual fear of losing his "honor" as an officer, one who is living on unfulfilled promises of an allowance from a rich uncle. His hypertrophied sense of honor leads him to assume insults at a concert when a baker, a member of a class that is not capable of satisfying honor in duels (*nicht satisfaktionsfähig*), bumps into him. This puts him in a dilemma: he already has a duel scheduled for the next day. Puzzling all night, he is saved by an act of God: the baker dies of natural causes during the night, and no one in military society will ever learn of the officer's shame.

The modern reader tends to assume that this piece exemplifies the psychological stress placed on the individual by a restrictive society, and thus critiques its social and political institutions. Schnitzler's contemporaneous reader, however, could easily provide a different diagnosis of Gustl's problem. They could consider the innate disposition of Gustl in the characterological terms outlined above. Gustl's social and family positions are indirectly, but clearly marked in the story. Gustl has a rich uncle whom he expects to support him (but who will probably not) — an uncle with an estate (probably in Hungary, since the servants didn't speak German). His mother is the mainstay of the family, while his father disapproves of him; his sister is in the "Sängerverein," the city-wide public choir, while he himself hasn't ever been to the opera; he has a twenty-eight-year-old unmarried sister; he himself is twenty-three or twenty-four, and he was scared of the dark in the woods as a child.

To the audience of 1900, believers in the power of inheritance, this life story adds up to a very different critique at the base of Schnitzler's story. It was a given for the nonmilitary audience that the army's honor code was harsh — the story of an army with excessively high standards would not have raised the hackles it did. But there is a second story here, one about Gustl's past as it rendered him a priori unfit for military service. In this frame, Gustl is a lower-middle-class person who cannot cope with his position and its attendant responsibilities; this is a more social Darwinist reading, in tune with those from Gerhart Hauptmann's *Vor Sonnenaufgang* (1889) or *Die Weber* (1892). Gustl is from the provinces, from Graz, where old army officers go to retire on the meager pensions for the career officers of low rank and no family. From the point of view of the Viennese, he could well be of suspect lineage, possibly even partially non-Germanic — a member of a questionable element in the Empire's structure.

The diagnosis of "Leutnant Gustl" by its original audience in Vienna could thus differ considerably from that of the modern audience. When he gets caught by his own interpretation of the honor code, the middle-class Viennese would see a confirmation of their class prejudices instead of castigation of society's moral system. This "Gustl" of questionable lineage is not necessarily a victim of society by their standards — he has risen to his position on the strength of his personality, demonstrated by his knowledge of the officer's code. However, he has risen higher than most of his family, and despite what must be innate characterological deficiencies, which might damage the corps in the long run: he is of a lower class than most officers, of lesser inherited talents and gifts, and so, in a certain sense, his plight is almost comic rather than tragic.

The critique of the military in this reading is much more damaging than it first seems today. The Viennese audience may well be asking why "people like that" are allowed to be officers. When the military establishment got upset about "Leutnant Gustl" and took Schnitzler's commission, it was indeed reacting to an insult against its institutions. However, that insult was not necessarily directed against the honor code. The problem with the military in the story can easily be seen as a characterological one: the establishment was clearly promoting too many of "those people" to the middle ranks, from the middle-class perspective. After all, anyone who had never been to the opera would of course have problems dealing with bakers and other tradesmen. From this perspective, Schnitzler may not have been calling the military establishment itself too harsh; he was countering its official policy of ethnic diversity and somewhat open access and suggesting that some officers didn't deserve the respect due an army that should recruit and promote better candidates than Gustl.

A one-act play by Schnitzler (also 1900) offers another text to which his contemporaneous audience may have reacted differently than we assume today. The family in *Das Haus Delorme* (*The House of Delorme*) is second-generation French, trying to live up to a purported noble background in Vienna.[16] The play parodies the manners and morals of the nouveaux riches: one son, Charles, looks to marry an heiress; a daughter, Mathilde, supports herself on the stage while looking for a permanent patron. The son courts a girl who is acceptable, even though she is Jewish — until he finds out that her family has gone broke; Mathilde throws over a baron for a mysterious "Herr Franz," a handsome young man who appears to worship her; the mother speaks with a pronounced French accent and cultivates the family legend; the father appears to be seeking recompense from the French government for lands lost over a half-century before (in the uprisings of the 1830s, we assume).

This is all humorous enough, but the final scene contains a particular punch for the character-sensitive audience of 1900. Near the end of the play, Father Delorme shows up for the first time, and the audience discovers that he has actually been in an insane asylum, not pressing claims to the French government. After he starts threatening Herr Franz with a gun, Herr Franz reacts for the audience — he begins to cry, as he realizes that the supposed high spirits of his beloved may be hereditary insanity. Today many would see the play as damning social climbers; in 1900 the audience would see that apparent social climbing (at best a personality flaw, thus not of deep consequence) as a genetic disposition. The "characterology" of Schnitzler's characters would necessarily focus on their innate constitutions. Again, family inheritance, not social mores, is highlighted, and successful personalities of potentially bad characterological stock are accidents waiting to happen.[17]

In the original context of the play, then, mainstream scientific and popular assumptions about character would lead audiences to very different judgments about the health and suitability of particular individuals. If read as just suggested, Schnitzler's literature is clearly aimed at the same mainstream middle-class audience that his characterology and Weininger's were. This set of assumptions about characterology that we have been exploring in literature would become more acute when tested by history. If we move back to the issues of therapeutics with which we began, additional significances for the paradigm emerge.

Institutional Consequences of Characterology: Some Conclusions

No matter what artists and intellectuals may have thought of the turn-of-the century's Socialist program to improve humanity or Freud's work to improve the individual functioning in society, the educated middle class who bought Weininger's book and lionized Schnitzler likely sought confirmation for the point of view represented in the popular texts: that people were predetermined by their birth.

Historical forces would make these assumptions comfortable to the middle-class conservative position. Ethnic polarization had increased in the Empire after the 1867 Compromise with Hungary, which forced the Slavs into Hungarian rather than Viennese control and increased German-Austrians' sense of ethnic embattlement. The socialism that had characterized Red Vienna and its social programs became ever more closely identified with the International and with revolutionary communism instead of social welfare — a leftward shift that easily led to a conservative reaction. In a phenomenon of lesser scope but greater long-term significance, Freud and his work moved out of the university and the sphere of its medical establishment to form an independent organization — out of the Vienna Medical Society and into its own Psychoanalytic Circle, from which it went more easily into exile.

To be sure, all these shifts have other causes. However, a look at first-generation Freudian psychoanalysis and its split from the medical establishment shows how scientific assumptions about inherited illness resonated even within Freud's own circle, perhaps as contributing causes to conflicts that have been interpreted largely as personal. Freud's breach with C. G. Jung, for instance, is easily illuminated from a characterological perspective. Paul Roazen, among others, has acknowledged that "Jung was far more prone to cite phylogenetic interpretations than was Freud himself, though after their encounter Freud seems to have adopted some of Jung's method of approach" (261). Freud concluded that it was a methodological error "to seize on a phylogenetic explanation before the ontogenetic possibilities have been exhausted" (quoted in Roazen 261), even though certain "primordial phantasies" may be a product of some type of inheritance. By 1914 Freud complained that "the investigation of individuals [by Jung] was pushed into the background and replaced by conclusions based on evidence derived from anthropological research" (quoted in Roazen 270).

Such statements clearly indicate that Freud was more eager to investigate the individual adapting to environment and history than typological group inheritance.

Statements from the time when Jung was a fellow traveler of the Nazis in the 1930s confirm his more tacit reliance on biological (not only cultural) inheritance. In a critique of Freud, he wrote, "The Jews have this peculiarity in common with women; being physically weaker, they have to aim at the chinks in the armor of their adversary" and "The 'Aryan' unconscious has a higher potential than the Jewish" (quoted in Roazen 291). Both his statements obscure the difference between physical and cultural inheritance, stressing inheritance as primary. Even Jung's postwar observations stress inheritance over environmental conditioning. In 1951, describing his deposition while director of the International Medical Society for Psychotherapy in favor of Göring and his ultimately unsuccessful attempts to shelter colleagues from the Nazis, Jung states: "I was a black sheep on account of my Wotan essay which only a complete ass can misunderstand as a pro-Nazi sentiment. I have never changed my views about the Nazis, nor have I ever been an anti-Semite; but I am convinced of the psychological differences between Jew and Gentile as between French and English and so on" (quoted in Roazen 293). He has not clarified whether those differences are characterological in Weininger's terms or in Freud's — that is, whether they are inherited or learned. Reception of Freud and Jung may therefore parallel a shift in the scientific values of the ages concerned. To accept Freud, the audience needed to focus on the adaptability of the individual, rejecting the assumptions of innate type favored by Freud's Viennese audience; to accept Jung, one could still support the innate characteristics of racial types — and the Nazis. Just as *The Case of the Midwife Toad* suggests that Lamarckian ideology caused Kammerer's debacle, the exclusion of psychotherapy from the Reich thus does not rest solely on the fact that the *psychoanalytic* community was predominantly Jewish (today's popular explanation).

Conflict between the variants of Darwinism and Lamarckianism under discussion here also directly influenced other organizational aspects of medical practice that grew out of the Viennese medical community. The variant Darwinist position of Weininger and Schnitzler automatically corresponded to institutional practice that continued entrenched power structures; if social changes were to occur, nature, not governmental intervention, would facilitate them. In contrast, work such as Freud's and Kammerer's suggested strongly that interventionist agencies could modify behavior, maybe to the end of an acquired change in the individuals concerned.

In this context, while the Soviets have traditionally used asylums to rid themselves of political enemies, the Nazis did not (Cocks 12). On the basis of the popular Lamarckian position outlined here, the Soviets could construe an asylum as an aid to the individual — as behavioral modification that would contribute to the long-term development of a healthier group.

In contrast, the Darwinist position affiliated with the Austrian Empire would not admit of this solution. Later the Nazis, as covert Darwinists, would stress the continuity of genetic material in similar ways, making the therapeutic approach of an asylum inadmissible. Once officially deviant elements (homosexuals and people with various hereditary illnesses) were removed from the gene pool of the country, any other psychic illnesses would necessarily be considered transitory; they would reside not in individuals' fundamental constitutions, but in the "fluid states" of personality. Illnesses could thus be treated successfully without extreme therapeutic means because the underlying genetic constitution of individuals was sound, needing no modification. In contrast to the Nazi position, mental illness could be styled by the Soviets as undermining the progressive health of the nation in the short run. Acquired characteristics could be transmitted, but they were treatable within the individual's behavior, not as a gene-pool problem.

Deep-level treatment, such as the Soviets later purportedly suggested to modify the group over the long term, was unnecessary, even impossible. The deputy director of the Göring Institute, Johannes Schultz, thus could describe the purview of the psychotherapist's job as "advice, discussion, instruction, enlightenment, encouragement, reassurance, hardening, exercise, and prohibition" (74). This is a far cry from Freud's attempt to eliminate the short-circuiting characterizing repressions and neuroses. Schultz's range of activities constitutes topical therapy only. It assumes that the deep health and cognitive functioning of the individual are not impaired. This was "kleine" psychotherapy within the Nazi institution — a leveling of minor interactional difficulties among individuals. This is to be distinguished from the "grosse" psychotherapy practiced by medical doctors, which dealt with medical psychology and emphasized drug and physical therapy. Interventionist medicine, it relied on a fixed relation between the body and character, with the body primary. Schultz did also acknowledge "core neuroses," which required the treatment of the whole character, as a type of depth psychotherapy — they were charactergenetic, tied to the fundamental constitution, not to accumulated experience (75). Popular support for psychotherapy in the Third Reich, therefore, came from the natural-health movement and from the military-industrial sector, which was interested in "healthy," normative behavior in its soldiers and workers.

This reflects the core of the racial hygiene notion, as Walter Cimbal noted in 1934: "A ground rule for all of these [psychotherapeutic] situations is that the psychological drilling machine [seelische Bohrmaschine] which had been formulated in the psychoanalytic method must be avoided" (quoted in Cocks 94). Again the Darwinian prohibition against alterations of inheritance has emerged. Cocks identifies this prohibition as "founded on the old nineteenth-century psychiatric notion of the untouchable psyche, which charged that any attempt 'to reduce the psyche to its humble and primitive elements' was, at best, irreverent" (96). That is, the psyche was considered by Nazis to be whole and inborn, not "assembled" out of experiences.

Ulfried Geuter's *Die Professionalisierung der deutschen Psychologie im Nationalsozialismus* (*The Professionalization of German Psychology Under National Socialism*, 1984) adds a further note to this discussion. Geuter documents the pressure on universities to produce the military and industrial psychologists who could serve the war effort. In the 1920s, the academic conflicts in psychology focused on the relation of psychology to philosophy. This was particularly important because many universities did not have independent psychology departments, so many "psychology professors" were actually professors of "epistemology, cognition, and psychology" (in philosophy departments), of "education and psychology" (in teacher-training institutes), or of "physiology and psychology" (in medical institutes). World depression and war did not allow many departments to open in Germany, but psychology chairs were added to existent universities. In further expansion spurred by this ideology, courses were added to virtually all universities' curricula that would allow students to certify as psychological therapists in the sense that was used in the Göring Institute. As noted earlier, the dominant medical ideology that I identified in Vienna just after the turn of the century was gradually becoming institutionalized throughout German-language culture, precluding to an even greater degree those psychologists who tried to stress acquired instead of innate physical wellness of patients.

The concept of characterology indicates that the models for anthropology, mind, and human behavior of the period in question do not conform to prevailing assumptions about human behavior characterizing Western thought in the latter part of the twentieth century. The contemporary Western world defines personality in terms of individual potential. According to the messages of popular psychology, particularly in America, the individual is under control of the individual will. In contrast, the Central European world of the turn of the century operated in terms of a physical anthropology. Maintaining a perspective firmly established by 1800, the individual in 1900 was still seen as a biologically determined being to a much greater extent than is assumed today. Concomitantly, *personality* now has a different role: today, the successful personality is a self-created work of art — the person is made through work, money, and/or determination. These popular variants of psychotherapy all stress wellness.

Within the context of the characterology of the turn of the century, however, that concept of individualism cannot be applied without serious modification. The successful personality of 1900 would result from inheritance, breeding, or cosmic accident. The personality type — artist, wordsmith, man of action, or passive person — would be set essentially at birth, by sex.[18] On top of that, a set of gifts or talents could be refined through practice or deteriorate through misuse. Basically, however, they remain part and parcel of the way in which that individual will interface with the world, as an innate style of living and facility for life. The personality in the narrow sense, the face a person presents to the world around him, is influenced through the organism's experience of and response to the immediate environment. Inheritance from the lower classes would produce a personality that could be burnished somewhat, but that would be innately crude when forced to reveal itself.

Our long trip from medicine through literature and back thus suggests an important omission in the evaluations of the cultural-historical milieu of the turn of the century in Austria. Perhaps because the assumptions involved were so ubiquitous at the time, post-Second-World-War interpreters of the period (either in history of medicine, literature, sociology, or history) have tended to bracket the issue of Darwinian anthropology and its conceptions of personality, personal responsibility, and the possibilities for change in society. The essays of Weininger and Schnitzler provide indices for assessing continuities in the concept of character between the two world wars, at least in areas of investigation reflecting medical practice.

A largely covert scientific paradigm had emerged into a full-blown scientific argument only after 1900. The paradigm, however, can be traced as an ideology conditioning later institutional developments and medical practice. The resulting conflicts persisted well into the twentieth century and influenced the medical community's preferences for a wellness therapy under the Third Reich. A question remains, however: to what degree should historians systematically account for this paradigm as a set of covert requirements governing the form and content of scientific work and the public success or failure of scientific institutions?

Notes

[1] This interest was reflected specifically in the development of social policy in the last days of the Empire, as part of the Social International; see Carl E. Schorske, *Fin de slècle Vienna* (especially the chapter entitled "Politics in a New Key"). For information on Socialist Vienna from the turn of the century through the First Republic, see in addition John W. Boyer, *Political Radicalism in Late Imperial Vienna*; Anson Rabinbach, *The Crisis of Austrian Socialism*; and *Austro-Marxism*, translated and edited by Tom Bottomore and Patrick Goode.

[2] The definitive treatment of the state of medicine in the Austro-Hungarian Monarchy is Erna Lesky, *The Vienna Medical School of the Nineteenth Century*.

[3] For information on development of the Austrian Nazi Party as distinct from that of Germany, especially its organization since the turn of the century, see Bruce F. Pauley, *Hitler and the Forgotten Nazis*.

[4] Three influential texts exemplify a host of others that taught the diagnosing physician how to evaluate physical symptoms in correlation with the mind. Franz Gall's *The Functions of the Brain* (completed 1825), the basis for the science of phrenology, assumed a one-to-one correlation between a faculty of the mind and an organ. Physical development would thus reveal mental development. A genius, for example, would have large cranial bumps above the overused area of the brain. In contrast, "illness," indicated by odd behaviors, led a physician to search for physi-

cal abnormalities or hypertrophy of the brain. In the extreme case, physical type could predict illness. Later in the century, the psychiatrist Wilhelm Griesinger offered another version of the mind-body tie when he published a textbook that was to be a standard for several decades (and that was known by Freud): *Pathology and Therapy of Psychic Illnesses* (1845). In it he fused psychology with neurology and anatomy, systematically cataloguing mental illness as correlations between physical causes (not only in the brain) and resulting behavioral symptoms. Still later, Emil Kraepelin published his *Compendium* of psychiatry that was based on a systematic exposition of how physical symptoms indicated various mental diseases (1883; 6th ed. 1899). Using tables, charts, and case studies, Kraepelin outlined diagnostic approaches to and prognoses for psychiatric illnesses on the basis of how mental habits were affecting patients' bodies and behaviors.

[5]This section relies on materials from several sources, as expanded in Katherine Arens, *The Structures of Knowing*. See also Gregory Zilboorg, with George W. Henry, *A History of Medical Psychology*; Robert M. Young, *Mind, Brain and Adaptation in the Nineteenth Century*; Dieter Wyss, *Psychoanalytic Schools from the Beginning to the Present*; W. Griesinger, *Mental Pathology and Therapeutics*; and Henri F. Ellenberger, *The Discovery of the Unconscious*.

[6]For an overview of the interrelations of the artistic and general intellectual situations of the era, see Carl Schorske, *Fin de siècle Vienna*. For background information on the cultural policies of the era, see William M. Johnston, *The Austrian Mind*, 265 ff.

[7]The volume was issued by S. Fischer in Berlin. Which audience this was is not clear today since the book is not mentioned in the Schnitzler literature. Fischer was, however, a visible publishing house, and 1927 saw the first through third printings. Despite the position of Fischer in the German book market, Weiss's introduction to the English translations of the text indicates that the original edition of the work had been small and that many, perhaps most, copies extant in Germany and Austria were destroyed in the Nazi book burnings. Schnitzler was denounced for his suggestive material and for his race (viii).

[8]Johnston devotes a section to Weininger in *The Austrian Mind* (158–62), which serves as the basis for the biographical information used here. The definitive treatment of Weininger's work and influence is Jacques Le Rider, *Der Fall Otto Weininger*. An essay compilation in English indicating the scope and impact of Weininger's work in many fields is Nancy A. Harrowitz and Barbara Hyams, eds., *Jews and Gender*.

[9]See Georg Markus, *Der Fall Redl*, on a military traitor just after the turn of the century, especially 90 ff. on the homosexual regulations to which officers were subject.

[10]After establishing the possibility of a correspondence between mental and physical types, Weininger provides an interesting succeeding chapter, "Die emanzipierten Frauen,"which anticipates his eventual racial calumnies. These he includes under the rubric of intermediate sexual forms, since their drive for emancipation is a byproduct of the proportion of "M" in them (the male protoplasm [76]): "The greatest, the only enemy of the emancipation of women is woman" (89). Psychologically speaking, a person must be at base either male or female type (94); eventually, Weininger equates "female" with "Jewish" as well as "passive."

[11]For the fullest accounts of the evolution of Darwinism and evolutionary theory, see the various accounts by Peter J. Bowler, especially: *Evolution*, which contains

an exemplary account of Lamarckianism in chapter 4; *The Eclipse of Darwinism*; and *The Non-Darwinian Revolution*.

[12]Freud's contact with Darwinian theory has been convincingly documented by Wilhelm W. Hennecker in *Vor Freud*.

[13]An exemplary account of how English biology and geology were mutually influencing is Martin J. S. Rudwick, *The Great Devonian Controversy*.

[14]Another reason suggested for the debacle of Kammerer's English lecture tour is that English Darwinists were interested in discrediting Kammerer as a scientist affirmed to the last by Russian Lamarckians.

[15]Follow-ups on Freud's cases indicate that some of the most spectacular cures reported were actually short-lived because he overlooked the physical side of mental diseases — his patients turned up in sanitariums later in life. From the point of view of today's medical psychology, some of these patients may have had problems requiring organic therapy. For example, Frau Emmy, diagnosed by Freud as a hysteric, probably was actually a victim of Tourette's Syndrome. See E. M. Thornton, *The Freudian Fallacy*, 155 ff.

[16]*Das Haus Delorme* (performed 1900) was published only posthumously. Note that the surname Delorme may be a reference to the fictional poet, Joseph Delorme, created by Charles-Augustin Sainte-Beuve for his *Vie, Poésies et Pensées de Joseph Delorme* (1829). Here, Sainte-Beuve transforms his own life into that of a Werther-like late Romantic hero who welcomes death because of the meaninglessness of the universe. See, for example, Richard M. Chadbourne, *Charles-Augustin Sainte-Beuve*.

[17]Active consideration of the scientific paradigm in which a text's audience participates can have ramifications for more than just literature, as another reference to Freud can clarify. From the point of view of the 1900 audience, not only popular works such as Schnitzler's novellas and plays but also examples in more scientific work, such as that of Freud, were written to conform to their standard, middle-class expectations and prohibitions. For instance, the assumption of a Darwinian point of view in the audience would explain why Freud changed the identification of the seducer in the Katharina case from the father to the uncle; that would have sounded less offensive, less disruptive of the audience's harmless image of the family: Freud's cases were written for a Darwin-conditioned audience who would assume that the female was indeed innately different from the male and so would tend to "be hysterical" without seemingly serious cause in her life — as the audiences of Schnitzler did seem to expect in the case of *Das Haus Delorme*. Only in later editions of the *Studies on Hysteria* did Freud add a footnote explaining that discretion had caused him to alter his evidence and blame the uncle instead of the father.

For an overview of recent work placing Schnitzler into social-historical contexts in different ways than is done here, see also Horst Thomé, "Sozialgeschichtliche Perspektiven."

[18]There is some evidence that the question of innate types may be arising again. Following up on the work of Cesare Lombroso, who was noted for describing the "criminal type" in biological terms, a recent book discusses predispositions towards criminality: see James Q. Wilson and Richard Hernstein, *Crime and Human Nature*; and Nancy A. Harrowitz, *Antisemitism, Misogyny, and the Logic of Cultural Difference*.

7: Grillparzer's *Fiddler:*
The Space of Class Consciousness

Franz Grillparzer's *Der arme Spielmann* (*The Poor Fiddler*) is a novella that is generally considered one of the masterpieces of German prose. But beyond that general accord, virtually everything about the novella and its reception is problematic. One of only two prose works produced by a writer known principally as a playwright, it was begun in 1831, completed in 1842, but not published until 1847, in an almanac dated 1848 (Bair 301–2). That publication happened in Hungary (in Pest); it was included in the *Iris: Deutsche Almanach für 1848*, published by Gustav Heckenast, who is remembered today principally as Adalbert Stifter's publisher. Appearing out of the way and basically swept from public view by the political situation of 1848, it received practically no notice until it was reprinted in 1871 in the *Deutscher Novellenschatz* by Paul Heyse, the writer and editor responsible for codifying the aesthetics of German realist prose by establishing his multivolume set of the classics of the genre. Yet it was only published in volume 5 of the series (Cowen 9).

That late emergence as a realist novella meant that *Der arme Spielmann* was received and evaluated by norms thirty years younger than those at play in its original cultural and political milieus. Grillparzer had realized from the first that the piece was destined for misunderstanding, as an 1846 letter to Count Mailáth, the editor of that volume of the *Iris* documents:[1]

> That the story planned for *Iris* has pleased you makes me unusually happy, and I only wish that the same would be the case for the public. But because there's nothing in it about German unity, the German fleet, or German world power, and because our compatriot in it has none of that energy that has befallen the nation overnight, I only expect very little acclaim. But since the thing is written, let it be printed. (quoted in Cowen 13)

Written in the Austrian Empire, it was received in the nascent German one; written in the political climate of the *Vormärz* of Metternich's Europe (in the Restoration or Biedermeier), it was evaluated by a generation of post-1848 readers who were leery of politics.

Even aesthetically it seemed out of date to that later generation. Its overt Catholicism was particularly at odds with the more scientific bent of realism.[2] It "lacks the necessary bourgeois optimism" (Cowen 17) and aesthetic balance characteristic of the German version of realism (especially of "poetic realism"). The novella's narrator does not allow the reader to identify with him comfortably (he is unsympathetic or a cynic caught in the class structure), and its hero, the Fiddler, seems less a representative of any class than simply incompetent to participate adequately at any social level: "That there is something in these opening pages to which we instinctively react negatively seems clear" (Ellis 33). Even the title is not entirely clear, as translations reveal. A 1965 translation calls it the "Poor Musician," and a 1967 one, the "Poor Fiddler." However, the term "Spielmann" is closer to "entertainer" and could actually be a reference to the narrator, who is himself a playwright (Bernd, "From Neglect to Controversy" 7).

To explain certain of these purported failings, a number of critics have taken the novella and its narrator as being autobiographical since it plays in the milieu of the civil service: Grillparzer, born in 1791, was employed by the state as *Archivdirektor* from 1813 to 1856 (Swales 67; see also Politzer and Thompson). The plot incorporated an actual flood of Vienna's Leopoldstadt on the night of the 1 March 1830 and the following day, as well as images from the 1830 July Revolution in France (Seeba, "Ich habe keine Geschichte" 216), and a good representation of Viennese dialect. In this sense, it nominally fulfills Grillparzer's goal of making history "concretely visible," albeit in romanticized form. Critics also believe that the novella foreshadows Grillparzer's eventual turn away from the theater, when he himself was rejected by an audience who did not appreciate his play *Weh dem, der lügt.*[3]

An equal number of critics have concluded that that same narrator is not actually Grillparzer, although like him in some ways (Browning 50, 54), a claim that justifies more strictly formalistic or aesthetic approaches to the novella. Seen this way, the novella uses two characters to demonstrate a split between inner and outer man, between the abstract world of art and the concrete world (Swales 67). Or perhaps the narrator's irony masks his fear of the masses, as the flood scene demonstrates (Swales 69–70). According to some, the novella stresses class barriers and lost love: "Barbara would have fit better with the honest Court Councilor's son and in the Viennese hat shop than she did with the crude butcher from the provinces" (Hunter-Lougheed 87). To others, it offers a parable about the limits of the real and ideal, staged in a kind of Baroque world theater, in the novella's frame (Reeve 95). Framed in this way, the novella has been read as a parable of compromised social ideals (Roe 133 ff.) and the "Josephine gradualism" of the Habsburg system (Wittkowski). Yet another group see in it a distinct image of historical causality (Thanner) and of the role of the social outsider (Porter 178) or misfit (Cook). Thus it is a "mythologizing of Austrian history" (Seeba, "Ich habe keine Geschichte" 206), stressing the tragedy of the bourgeois in the historical moment of the Biedermeier (Seeba, "Ich habe keine Geschichte" 210). Its clear religious references have also led it to be considered as a biblical parable (with Jakob seeking a father's blessing [Mahlendorf 114]), or as a religious allegory for the church calendar (with multiple narrative embeddings [Porter 184]), since it opens on 24–25 July, on the saint's day of James the Elder, the apostle (Wittkowski 159). It incorporates visions of what time means (Birrell); of the meaning of music in the era or for Grillparzer (Fetzer, Lindsey, Levin, Mullan, Yates); or of the poet in the carnival of life (Ritter). Such readings limit considerations of the work to its aesthetics, which has contributed to its marginalization within realism, and they can proliferate almost endlessly.

Its reception thus has, as Grillparzer predicted, remained problematic, to say the least. In John Irving's *The World According to Garp*, Jenny Garp echoes many critics when she calls it "Trash . . . Simplistic. Maudlin. Cream Puff" (Irving 46). Dutifully, her son T. S. Garp prefers Dostoyevsky as his own role-model. Small wonder that *Der arme Spielmann* had the distinction in 1983 of becoming the object of a moratorium on interpretations.[4]

The reading that follows will break this moratorium on the story in order to address *Der arme Spielmann* in a way not heretofore done: by addressing the use of space in it. Because of their stubborn insistence on inserting the novella into the canon of poetic realist prose, critics have not noted how space stages the action of the novella in almost theatrical ways. All the main figures (and particularly Barbara) relate to spaces both inside and outside the city, as these spaces reflect the unstable social relationships in Vienna of the *Vormärz*. Following these spaces allows me to shift the emphasis from Jakob, the failed artist, toward the moral and economic issues around which the novella revolves, and to the character who best represents them, Barbara. I will argue that she is the center of the story since she is the only one of the novella's main characters who enters it bearing a name, not just a profession. Moreover, she is given the task of naming the fiddler for the reader: Barbara calls him "Jakob," whereas the narrator-playwright only refers to him as "the old fellow" (*der Alte*) or "my Original."

As the fiddler moves downward through society, Barbara's upward mobility reflects the shifting landscape of a Vienna in social change; her life conveys the meaning of the city for individuals' lives, the greater historical changes in class and rhythms of life that both the narrator and Jakob miss. Barbara's rise toward the bourgeoisie moves through a distinct series of interior and exterior spaces that offer the reader mute testimonial to Vienna's social struggles for control over just these kinds of spaces. Her life's pattern is testified to more clearly by silent stage sets exposed to the reader's eyes than by the novella's explicit tale as voiced by Jakob or the playwright-narrator. While the figures in the story believe that they have disposition over their lives and thus offer explanations, plans, and hopes, the spaces they inhabit consistently mirror (and often betray) the limits imposed by their social station and actual options. Whether the reader sees these characters indoors or outdoors, in generous or cramped quarters, acquiring a dwelling or relinquishing it, owning a room or subdividing it, looking out windows or into interior courtyards — these uses of space have their own metaphoric function in the novella, independent of the narrator's voice that earlier critics have preferred to follow; they call into question the choices made by the tale's three main characters. As I shall trace below, the spaces of the city of Vienna reveal characters' social status and the dilemmas of their class stations more clearly than words do.

Grillparzer's permission to publish specifically points to this social and political content for the tale; his main occupation as a playwright makes probable his investment in telling a story through spatial relations as well as in words. Conceived in 1830, it is a work begun in an era when civil unrest was stalking Paris. By the time it was published in 1847, civil unrest was shadowing Vienna itself and its populace. While the novella's opening and closing sections or scenes are set against historical events that the fiddler and the playwright share with the underclasses of Vienna, the novella is actually telling two tales: the foregrounded story of the fiddler's "peculiarities" as he fails to live up to the norms of larger Viennese culture and the more questionable success of Barbara. The map of Vienna's interior and exterior spaces offered here, however, mutely testifies to the existence of a third story, untold by either of the other voices, about the tensions between classes of humanity in the city. On this map, Grillparzer stages the story of the successful Barbara and the failed Jakob as a piece of a larger tableau vivant, interwoven into a subtle but unmistakable social critique — offering discomfiting messages that might, if voiced, otherwise have led to censorship.

From this perspective, then, the nameless narrator is less the storyteller than the reader's point of view inserted into the story as an observer, one who may (or may not) learn to understand what lies underneath the pathos he prefers to see in others' lives; he believes himself to possess knowledge of his fiddler, but he himself may be the *Spielmann* doing a solo turn, the entertainer turned entertainment for a reading audience who sees more broadly than he does. In this way, Grillparzer has constructed a novella with more than one layer of truth in it: he shows the truth of the bourgeoisie and the would-be bourgeoisie, each in its own integrity, yet also how those clash in the space of a city that is a group organism, a civic space of interdependency between the bourgeoisie and the "working people" of Vienna.

First Act, Introduction:
The City Map, The Lay of the Land

In the sense introduced by Henri Lefebvre in *The Production of Space*, Grillparzer starts his novel by *producing space*. That is, he begins to tell the story by describing the space in which it will occur, not simply as a stage set but rather more like the space of a chessboard, as space articulated in terms of and dominated by a particular social hegemony.

The space that opens the story is the space of the "common people," a flood of humanity exercising its right to celebrate. The occasion is the celebration of a church's anniversary, held each year according to the lunar calendar and organized to celebrate the traditional "working people":[5]

> In Vienna every year, the Sunday after the full moon in the month of July, together with the day that follows it, is a true public

festival, if ever a festival had deserved that name. The people attend it and give it themselves, and if the better classes turn up there, they can only do so in their capacity as members of the general public. There is no opportunity for distinction; at least, up until a few years ago there wasn't any.

On these days, the Brigittenau celebrates the consecration of its church, together with people from the Augarten, Leopoldstadt, and the Prater, in an unbroken line of pleasure. The working people count their good days between one such church festival and the next one . . . . The differences between classes has disappeared; citizens and soldiers share in the mass movement. The crush grows at the city gates. (146)

This real space exists in the city of Vienna, and here Grillparzer introduces it almost as a tourist guide. The tourist (the narrator-playwright) offers us a glimpse of Vienna's local history, of the suburbs outside the city walls (not yet torn down to create the *Ringstrasse*, as discussed by Carl Schorske in *Fin de siècle Vienna*). The "common folk" live in the Brigittenau, a town named after a real church. Brigittenau was founded in 1645 but did not become part of the official city administration until 1850, when it, Zwischenbrücken, and Leopoldstadt were formed into the "II. Bezirk" (now the XX. district [Koutek 283]). That other district will play in the story, as well: it is also named after a church (dedicated to Kaiser Leopold I), and it is the real location of the "Gärtnergasse" in which the fictional fiddler lives,[6] and of the castle named the "Augarten," which was thrown open to the people by Josef II (Koutek 31). At the time of the story, these three districts were outside the city's official jurisdiction (and outside its gates), each its own small town with a different character.[7]

One must not forget, however, that such "real" space is constructed: its images reflect stereotypes about the people who occupy them and about the meaning of their histories. In this sense, this "natural" mixing of the people on cyclical time (the time of the seasons, nature, and the church) is anything but natural. Grillparzer's use of "people" explicitly contrasts workers with the "citizens and soldiers" who are part of official Vienna; this mix happens outside the gates of official Vienna, when, "until recently, there were no grounds" to divide them — an allusion to civil unrest.

The Viennese citizens who enter this space must cross the Danube over a bridge into a world that obviates their control of organized space. When they cross, they cross a Rubicon that reduces their security about their positions and power: they enter into this swollen mass of people at the masses' tolerance. This mass has power paralleling that of nature and acknowledges no betters:

Finally victorious here as well, two torrents converge, the old Danube and the swollen wave of people, crossing under and over each other, the Danube following its old stream bed, the torrent of people, released from the confinement of the bridges, a broad, wild lake, pouring

out into a flood that covers everything. A new arrival would find the
signs worrisome. But it is only a riot of joy, pleasure unbridled. (146)

This image of the power of the people, of their utter dominance, alludes to
the construction of real city space. Not only was official Vienna walled off
from this area, but the Danube itself had not yet been regulated, as it
would be later in the century when it was dammed to control the yearly
floods that devastated Vienna. One of these river floods will close the narrative — but so will another kind of human flood, as we shall see.

Contrary to the way the story's space marks itself out for the eye, the
narrator now intrudes another kind of social division into this space. He
straight forwardly analogizes the power of nature and the people, but
nonetheless he has noticed what he feels are "worrisome signs." Worrisome
to whom? "*But* it is *only* a riot of joy," the narrator reassures himself. He
nonetheless reveals the possible source of that sense of threat: he sees the
basket chaises (*Korbwagen*) that will take to the festival those whom he
considers the people, "those who really celebrate this festival of consecration: the children of servitude and labor" (146). These basket chaises, however, do not really belong in this rural space; their occupants (the middle,
possibly rural, class?) must forge an uneasy pact with those on foot: don't
run anyone over, and don't be run over. Although the narrator shows the
"mass of people" flowing like a river, even as the masses get denser, social
differences try to emerge into this space, to claim parts of it.

The vehicles are keys to the social differences within the rising tide of
egalitarian humanity that the narrator-playwright ignores: "A few of the better classes' rigs are already mixing in the often unbroken chain," "single
horse- and coach-atoms" (147). And while folk wisdom has it that riding is
better than walking, the reader can see that that is not the case here since
one can pierce the crowd only on foot. Hemmed in by the little chaises, the
"Holsteiner Rappe," a thoroughbred carriage horse, rears up, threatening
the women and children in the lesser vehicles (147). And the "fiacres," the
drivers of the two-horsed carriages-for-hire familiar from pictures of Vienna's inner city, realize that they are caught in unprofitable traffic ("[since]
the stubborn standstill is really only an unnoticed inching forwards"), losing
income and tempers: "Arguments, shouts, coachmen mutually attacking
each other's honor, now and then a stroke of the whip" (147). This mob is
considerably less than faceless, anything but a flood. Instead, it offers the
reader telling vignettes characterizing class relationships in Vienna: servants
consider themselves a different class from workers; coachmen have a strict
hierarchy; the lust for pleasure is paralleled by a lust for money.

Act 1, Scene 1:
The Observant but Unseeing Narrator

The narrator, however, does not see these crucial differentiations. He believes himself to be part of a flood, the release of which is heralded by a

cry of "Land!" as the "new world" comes into view (actually, the open fields in the town where the festival will be held). This narrator sees the festival grounds in literary terms, as a kind of *locus amoenus*, offering the promise of "wine, women, and song," a "pays de cocagne," "Eldorado," or "Schlaraffenland" that will last only two days, and then disappear, "like a midsummer night's dream, remaining only in memory and, in any case, in hope" (147). The Shakespeare reference, however, plays into the construct-edness of the space that a reader familiar with the theater of Grillparzer's day would recognize: in *Midsummer Night's Dream*, the "upper classes" (the fairies Titania and Oberon and their courts) amuse themselves (albeit benevolently) at the cost of the lower, who inhabit this piece of nature, not rule it.[8] This panoply of "little people" lives here, outside the city walls; the city people leave the safety of those walls to join them, but their coaches may even become the instruments of destruction in this alternate world. The narrator's literary references remove his vision from the real people he purports to be seeking; the reader sees different dangers from those he sees.

That initial passage thus is crucial to establish the narrator's point of view within the frame of the story and to undercut his authority since he sees a dream instead of the carefully constructed social reality that Grill-parzer enables the reader to see. More significant to undercutting his point of view is the fact that the narrator stays nameless, a tourist from the city, a writer who is simply looking for material outside the confines of the city walls, outside the city hierarchy. He understands the people only in the terms he brings with him, as a faceless audience, not in themselves:

> I do not easily forsake attending this festival. As a passionate lover of humankind, especially of the people . . . I, as a dramatic poet, always find the unreserved eruption of an overfilled theater ten times more interesting, yes more educational, than the rationalizing judgment of a literary matador, crippled in body and soul, and swelled up like a spi-der from the blood sucked out of authors; . . . [it is] a real festival of the soul . . . a pilgrimage, an act of devotion. (147–48)

Proclaiming himself a Plutarch who leaves his books to read real faces in-stead (148), the narrator actually sets himself up to patronize the people he proclaims to love because he does not see how social spaces construct human differences: "one cannot understand the prominent if one pene-trated the obscure . . . in the young maid lie the embryos of the Juliets, the Didos, and the Medeas" (148). In his vision, maids are mythical creatures whose real stories do not suffice for his poetic imagination.

Poetically, that may well be true, but such a statement is a false note in the tableaux spreading before him outside the walls of Vienna. As he exited the city walls, the narrator had first imagined these people as a mass flood. Now he has reverted to being in a utopia (to being *nowhere* [*outopos*] as well as in his preferred pleasant place [*eutopos*]), when he proclaims them spiritual equals of heroic cast. Significantly, that utopia told to the reader is in the narrator's past: to paint himself into that picture of the people, he must turn to his poetic memory to relate how, two years earlier, he had joined this festival outside the walls. As a pedestrian (148), he "had commended himself to the procession of the masses" (149). On his way through the crowds pushing out through the city gates into the open, he saw a group of musicians standing along the side of the road. These individuals could not be part of the *Volksfest* because they "weren't up to the competition" (149): a blind harp player (a stock Viennese folk character), with "repulsively frozen eyes"; an invalid, a lame boy playing a waltz on the violin; and finally the eponymous hero of the story. "Finally — and he drew my whole attention to himself — an old man of easily seventy years, in a threadbare but not unclean Molton overcoat, with a countenance smiling to itself, applauding itself" (149).

What sets this figure apart from the others characterizes the narrator as much as it does the musician himself. This set of stock Viennese types are not real people but liminal characters created by the economics of the festival. These are not simply streetside musicians down on their luck; they are beggars who are using the pretense of music to draw attention to themselves. Not unlike the beggars' guild in Brecht's *Threepenny Opera*, they are the unemployed and the unemployable, trading on their misery for Christian charity (and careful to station themselves where their music cannot be heard over the din of the passing crowd). They are not part of the working-poor group of musicians, of whom there were legions in Vienna; they, like the archetypal Viennese blind harpist or *Natursänger*, were on the fringes of professional musicianship, no matter their talent. While the Viennese reader know that, the narrator does not seem to realize that these unfortunates are not "real" members of a well-known sociological type, the suburban Viennese musician.[9]

The narrator is unconsciously falling back into habits bred inside the city when he does not recognize who these roadside musician-beggars are. When he finally manages to notice one as an individual, it is the one who is marked by icons of the urban middle class: he notices a laughing fiddler dressed in threadbare but clean middle-class clothing, scraping a split violin, marking time by twitching. This fiddler seems transfixed when he plays — he is not working the audience but instead seems entranced, "coming to himself out of a long absence" (150). Where the others are playing by heart, the fiddler has set up a music stand with sheet music on it, to play unmusical music ("a disconnected series of tones without tempo or melody" [149]). And just as the crowd is reaching its peak, the fiddler utters some Latin words ("correctly intoned," the narrator notes [150]) and sets off home "in the opposite direction, as someone returning home" (150). Visually and behaviorally, the fiddler does not belong among the common people of Vienna (as beggar or street musician), just as the playwright does not.

The narrator has found himself "an original" who is not one of the common people he purports to have sought by going outside the city walls.

The narrator confesses to his "anthropological craving" and is caught by a voyeuristic urge to follow his new specimen: "The man had thus enjoyed a more careful upbringing, had acquired skills, and now — a beggar-musician! I trembled for curiosity about the sense of it all" (150). This description decisively marks the narrator as interested in the fiddler's fate as a member of the middle class; his fate is interesting not because he is poor (as so many other Viennese workers were) but because he is poor and middle-class ("a more careful upbringing") yet languishing in the midst of the people.

In a real sense, the fiddler is indeed an anthropological subject out of "his native habitat," outside of the city. And there is a paradox: the fiddler has positioned himself to play for money but does not do so: he is quite literally on the side of the road to anywhere. Significantly, the narrator's mood is ruined when that odd individual gets lost in the real crowd outside the walls: "The adventure I'd missed robbed me of my pleasure in the festival" (150). The narrator's preference for the individuality of the bourgeoisie is clearly highlighted: he has ceased to look for potential Didos once he has found his lost bourgeois musician, and he leaves the "new land" of the festival fields to return to the city (or rather, to the nearer suburbs with a more urban environment).

The narrator and the fiddler have their first confrontation in a narrow back street, where a group of boys taunts the fiddler by trying to get him to play a waltz. The fiddler claims that he was doing precisely that already and that it's their fault if they don't have the ears to recognize it: "They don't want to dance" (151). Spatially as well as musically, he has moved onto a back street, off the main track. The fiddler does not realize what he has done, preferring to believe that the people (*Volk*) just are not able to hear his music, that he is different from them. The fiddler and the narrator have thus both struck false notes in their commitment to "the people." They are not in tune with the crowds (one literally, one figuratively), and they uphold false fronts by removing themselves from active confrontation with the masses.

Act 1, Scene 2:
The Unobservant but Visionary Protagonist

In this back-alley discussion (almost literally), the reader hears a tale that almost parodies an ordered, bourgeois life in music yet entrances the playwright-narrator, who will later find tragedy in it. The narrator inquires why the fiddler has left his post on the road at precisely the moment when he could earn the most money. The fiddler finds the suggestion distasteful: "I . . . don't consider it proper to tempt others through music and song into such repulsive lapses" (152). When offered a silver piece, the fiddler tries to emphasize his distance from the narrator: he insists that the coin be thrown into his hat — he will not take it in his hand, despite his evident pleasure in having made money (151). This gesture, however, shows the reader how far he is from the "musicians" on the open road that he had left. The children had not understood his music; the mass of people haven't paid him in proper form, the way the narrator finally did. However, he had left them all behind to go home since "the evening belongs to me and to my poor art" (152). He claims independence, just as he claims to know real music.

The fiddler's domestic world (as yet unseen) is far removed from the masses, as he believes must be the case for real musicians. He is scrupulous in maintaining that isolation. At night he claims to play independently: "I believe it's called 'fantasizing' in the music books" (152). Just as the narrator had claimed to be a true lover of the common man but felt threatened when he was among such people, the musician claims to be a "real musician" because he presents the music of the masters, not the stuff the rest of the street musicians play:

> I prove my veneration of the long-departed masters and composers who are honored for their rank and honors, I please myself with the pleasant hope that the gift given me so graciously should not remain uncompensated, by ennobling the taste and heart of the listeners who are in any case troubled from so many sides and led astray. (153)

This is his own world, under his control, embodying his own ethic: he practices three hours every morning, goes off midday to earn money, "and the evening belongs to me and to the dear Lord" (153). The fiddler falls silent, which embarrasses the narrator: the fiddler must be ashamed to reveal his "secret life." The almost paranoiac sense of isolation in the scene narrows even further when the narrator asks permission to visit and the fiddler cautions him to send a message so he doesn't disturb anything "improperly" (152). The narrator and the fiddler are thus *Doppelgänger* in their relationship to the wide world: each claims to influence it but actually lacks true engagement with it. Each is only too happy to pull back into the back streets of the quiet parts of town, away from the *Volksfest* and from any input that would disturb their preferred fantasy worlds.

That the fiddler acts out of pride of workmanship in this way drives the narrator to an equal act of spatial self-isolation. He withdraws to a quiet beer garden at an inn (a *Schannigarten*); it is empty because of the festival, with idle waiters standing around. This description (the garden is empty *except* for the waiters) demonstrates that the narrator's consciousness is equally cut off from the working classes as the fiddler was. He feels that his day has been ruined and that he has even lost his connection to the festival because he had followed "his original" home: "I had, as I said, lost my liking for staying at the festival any longer this day. I therefore turned towards home, setting out on my way to Leopoldstadt" (154). Full night has fallen, and he decides to seek out the fiddler — to become a voyeur out of the darkness. Note, too, that his probable home, the Leopoldstadt, was a crowded, almost urban district — the one to which Freud's family moved

when it migrated from the provinces, a kind of last stop before one pene-
trates the city walls.

The narrator has forgotten the fiddler's house number, but he has no
problem once he finds the street. The fiddler is a known neighborhood
noisemaker: "The old fellow is scratching away again . . . and is disturbing
decent people in their night's rest" (154). Listening in the dark street, he is
amazed to see how bad the music is. He finally manages to figure out what
the fiddler is playing: first single tones, then simple intervals, and stretching
or repeating tones whose sounds please him — there is no melody, and it
all sounds poor, in his artistic assessment: "And that's what the old man
called 'fantasizing'! . . . only for the player, not also for the listener" (155).
The neighbors yell at him to stop and to close the window. That sends the
narrator home, "fantasizing to myself, in my head, disturbing no one" (155).
The metaphors of isolation in space proliferate: dark streets, windows
closed, disembodied voices rejecting each other because the fiddler does
not respect the space of decent folks who need sleep to work.

This is the close of the first act, temporally, just as the isolation of darkness and night has closed it spatially. The day of the festival is over, leaving
the narrator to find not the people, as he had claimed in memory, but a fiddler cast off by the bourgeoisie and closed off from "decent folks." The two
mirror-image characters both literally run against the tide of common humanity in the streets of Vienna. Each claims to be an artist who wants to
play for or to people, yet each uses aspects of his art to isolate himself from
real experience of the world: the narrator thinks the common folk are hidden Didos and Medeas, while the fiddler thinks only "the masters" and not
common waltzes constitute "real" music. And the narrator's justification for
not immediately visiting the fiddler is eerily like the fiddler's own justification for leaving his post at the side of the main road: he had to do
"something higher in the first hours of the day" and so simply listened at
windows (155).

The two have day-and-night versions of the same value systems in their
heads — systems that do not match those of the people and that exclude
them both physically and psychologically. They set their schedules, draw
lines between themselves and the masses, and look down on those masses
for lack of artistic sensibility.

Second Act: Failings of the Middle Class

The second act of the story of the two nameless men is taken up after a
gap in time. The festival is lost from sight; the reader is expected now to
enter domestic interiors for the next series of key events. When impatience
gets the better of the narrator, he returns to the fiddler's house to startle its
owner, the "gardener's wife," and enter his room. Thus the second act of
the story has moved out of the common space of the city and into domestic
interiors.

Grillparzer again marks his tale through a telling metaphor of interior space that underscores the degree of the fiddler's willed isolation from the mass of Viennese humanity. The fiddler shares a loft with two apprentices, a garret that has been decorated with flowerpots (although, he assures the narrator, he has his own bed).[10] However, he does not really live with the apprentices, since he has literally marked off his space by drawing a chalk mark on the floorboards that he calls "this equator of a world in miniature" (156). This division from the working classes represents his psychological space as well: in his own world, with his own bed, the fiddler refuses the narrator's renewed offer of money since he is not working for it on the streets as he believes he is supposed to. When he draws the equator across his floor and his life, the fiddler rejects not only the apprentices but also his normal social equal.

Just as the space outside the city walls was the key to the first section of the story (the narrator's mental space), this garret's interior space is the key to the ideology of the fiddler's world. The narrator walks in on the fiddler standing in front of a small window, on his side of the room's symbolic equator:[11]

> A while spent listening finally allowed me to discover the thread through this labyrinth, the method in his madness. The old fellow was enjoying the playing. But his idea of the matter broke it down into only two issues: euphony and dissonance; the former made him happy (even ecstatic), while the latter (even if grounded in established harmony) he avoided whenever possible. Instead of placing emphases in a piece of music according to its sense and rhythm, he accentuated euphonic notes and intervals, and lengthened them for the ear — yes, he didn't even hesitate to repeat them at will . . . It almost got too much for me. (156–57)

The fiddler is next to the window, but he is not looking out of it: he has withdrawn completely from any perception of space and has engrossed himself in listening, to such a point that the narrator has to drop his hat to interrupt this flood of tones that has swept him away.

The "method in his madness" is revealed in the fiddler's sudden metamorphosis into a bourgeois host who tries in vain to get some fruit from his landlady to serve his guest. He notes that his two roommates (two journeymen) don't respect the line (although he does, in a typical one-sided gesture [157]); their possessions, their mess, threaten to flood into his space. This world of artificial equators is the stage on which the fiddler's story is told, a bourgeois world as isolated from the reality of working Viennese as it could possibly be and as isolated from "true art" as the playwright assumes the fiddler to be.

Yet the fiddler does not see how artificial his physical and psychological environment is since he only relates to the others in his world aurally (just as the narrator had related visually and metaphorically): the journeymen wake him up at night when they come in from carousing, and he disturbs them in the morning with his music (remember, however, that the fiddler had ignored his neighbors down the street). When asked about his use of Latin, about his past, the fiddler denies that he has a story. But he finally realizes that he has one: "Ah, yes! In that sense, yes, then all sorts of things have happened; nothing special, but all sorts of things. Maybe I would like to tell myself that story again" (158). He simply feels he "wants to talk nonsense" (159) when he starts telling his life story.

The fiddler is even further displaced than the narrator had originally assumed. He is from the *haute bourgeoisie*, probably from a higher class than the narrator is from, judging by the latter's reaction. This poor fiddler is one of three sons of a famous (but still unnamed) *Hofrat* (court councilor), who in the second half of the previous century "had exercised prodigious influence under the modest title of Bureau Chief, influence almost like that of a minister" (158–59). This startles the narrator: "That influential, powerful man, his father?" (159). He who had seemed lesser is greater by birth.

The story held within the fiddler's garret world is a story of limits imposed by the *haute bourgeoisie*. The fiddler describes his progressive inability to fit into the spaces of the world, from childhood on:

> My father was proud and severe. My brothers were enough for him. He said I had a slow head; and I was slow . . . . if I remember rightly, I would probably have been able to learn all manner of things, if they had only granted me the time and order [for it]. (159)

The fiddler's obsession with the aural began early and is marked by Grillparzer as a prime cause of his dislocation, part of an inborn one-sidedness. As a child, the fiddler could learn things only by repeating them straight through; if he were interrupted (if anything intruded into his mental space), he would have to start over again (this almost sounds like some forms of mental retardation). Consequently, he could not keep up with an ordinary curriculum: "New things were supposed to be inserted into the place that the old had not yet vacated, and I began to get obstinate" (159). He failed his school exams when he was disturbed, forgot a word of a Horace verse, and then could not pick up the passage again, not even when the words were whispered to him. The father responded badly but predictably: "*Ce gueux*, he chided me — which I wasn't then, but am now. Parents prophesy when they speak!" (160). After that, his father talked to him only through the servants and took him out of school despite his best efforts to make up the Latin verses by replacing through hard work what he didn't have in ability. His aural singularity is the precipitating cause of his being thrust out of the central spaces making up the map of the bourgeois world for the male: school and business leadership.

The fiddler-to-be begins an odyssey through other such nonplaces. First his father threatened to give him to a trade, which could not have been done since that would have been a space outside his inherited class: "I didn't dare to say how happy that would have made me. I would only too happily have run a lathe or set type. But he would not have permitted it, out of pride" (159). The fiddler's father tried then to put him into an accounting office, but "figures were never my strong point" (160). The fiddler himself rejected the suggestion of entering the military: "Shedding blood and maiming as a profession, as a job. No! No! No!" (160). Finally he entered the world of the working bourgeoisie at the very bottom (the world of Bob Cratchit or Bartleby the Scrivener). He was set to be a copyist, which he loved, but at which he did not excel either: "I was diligent, but too timid. An incorrect punctuation mark, a word left out in the original (even if it could be provided by context) — they made my hours bitter" (161). Because he couldn't decide on such corrections, he got the reputation of being negligent even though he tortured himself about his work. He worked there for a couple of years without salary, as his father promoted others over him — he stayed at the bottom of his class, remaining there only through influence.

At the same time, he was spatially confined to class margins as well: he was banished to live in the back rooms of the house with the servants, isolated from the rest of the household. As his brothers left home, he was even physically forced out of that small refuge when the house's kitchen was closed to save money. He was sent out into the world, and his meals were paid for in a local inn. This was, however, not a release from the confined spaces of his class: he was under orders from his father to be home a half-hour after the office closed — to sit there in the dark. This fiddler has thus been consigned to spaces outside the pale of his class, family, and would-be profession.

However closed and limited this world had become, its identity as a Viennese city space is nonetheless crucial. Large houses in the city, like the one Grillparzer assigned to this family, have interior courtyards with trees, onto which the windows of the private rooms of the house open (or several houses sharing the same *Hof*). These courtyards are conventionally identified as the "green lungs of Vienna," and they serve this function as a stage set for the next stage in the fiddler's life. One evening he hears a voice singing out of a neighboring *Hof* as he sits next to one of these typical courtyard windows. This voice pierces the isolated space of his life, even though he preferred music without words (162). That song gets him interested in music again, and he finds his old violin hanging on the wall (he had hated it, and a servant had presumably been using it since he had discarded it): "Now, when I drew the bow over the strings, Lord, it was as if God's finger had touched me. The tones penetrated my innermost being, and emerged again from inside" (162). A window had opened into his physical and mental space.

Yet the fiddler's new space was still constrained in a timeless realm, away from the real life of the city, away from some kinds of "real" music: "Thus I could not play just any piece, I could simply play. . . . Musicians play Wolfgang Amadeus Mozart and Sebastian Bach, but no one plays the dear Lord" (162–63). And just as the novella's narrator was looking for characters from literature when he looked at the masses, the fiddler as-

serted that his personal music consisted of series of notes "like a hope fulfilled" (163), a building out of the hand of God, without mortar. He could
not play conventional music correctly because he didn't have the sheet music for the songs he heard.

The singer herself eventually crossed the courtyard, into his limited field
of vision to the outside. He recognized her as the "the general-store daughter" who sold lunch to workers in his office.[12] She was not pretty, but she
was sturdy, although too small and of nondescript coloring, with "cat eyes"
and pockmarks (164). They met formally when she became the butt of an
office practical joke. As recompense, she asked for some paper to use as
wrapping; he could not steal the office stock, so he brought her some from
home. He asked for the notes to her song, which made her realize that he
was the one "who has been scratching on the violin that way" (165) and
caused her to regret her earlier anger. She has thus been in both of the fiddler's narrow worlds, albeit on their margins.

In these spaces of his world, their interactions are clearly marked as
being class-based, given her limited access to them. The girl had learned
the song by ear and knew that the words were for sale on every corner. He
was astounded but ultimately not impressed: "I was astounded about her
natural genius; uneducated people like this often have absolutely the most
talent. But that is not the proper thing, the real art" (166). Similarly, when
he wants to kiss her, he does so "although she was only a poor girl" (166).
In this bourgeois space, she is a lower-class alien who could not read music and who thought one bought the words to songs.

But the window had decisively opened into the fiddler's narrow world.
The fiddler had to embark on an excursion, to go out into the city, when
he wanted to collect the paper copy of the song she had promised to have
the *Peterskirche* organist write down for him (167). His breakout is psychological and spatial: he had to practice for three weeks behind closed
windows until he dared to sneak out of the house at night, leaving his hat
behind as he hoped to leave his bourgeois identity: "I took heart and one
evening left my room (this time, too, without my hat), went down the
stairs, and strode firmly through the narrow street up to the general store"
(167–68).

This excursion into the city, outside the walls of his family house, does
not console him. When the fiddler gets near her store, he begins to shake.
When he actually enters the store, he sees her sorting peas and talking to
the clerk — he registers her visually, not just aurally. The owner (her father) thinks he is trying to steal something because he was skulking about
so badly, but then he introduces himself, saying that he has come to see
her. His position as the *Hofratssohn* overcomes her father's suspicions
about his hatlessness since he is "a gentleman from the office" (169). The
fiddler has broken into what had been a blank space on his mental map;
he has conquered a new inside space (that belonging to the lower-middle
classes) by virtue of his class position if not because of his own finances.

Barbara's father introduces the two properly at that point, and a new game is set into motion in that space where two classes have come together:

> Many changes have happened to me in life, but none so sudden as that which came over the man's whole being with these words. . . . whose entire face had lit up. "Would Your Grace like to make Himself comfortable?" . . . "Do you perhaps sing, like my daughter does, or perhaps in a totally different way, according to the notes, like art?" (169)

The class difference is constantly at play in these interior domestic games: the still nameless fiddler can purportedly teach the storekeeper's daughter "real" music simply because he is upper-class, although the girl can actually sing well. This space is not inviolable since the class that owns it cannot control it. When the storekeeper tries to keep the fiddler there and hide him from family servants, he fails (170).

The consequences of the fiddler's violation of the spatial cordon his father had placed around him are decisive: he is banished completely from his father's house, and she is banished from the office (and from her income). Predictably, the storekeeper shuns him later, when they meet on the street. When the fiddler is banished, however, he acquires a name when she bids him farewell: Jakob. As he is alienated from the confines of his birth sphere, Barbara will also move out of hers. He has lost his family name and gained his own; she has lost her income and thus her place in her family business as well.

Since the narrator had been looking for classical heroines, the reader of this tale can now see a set of references that he does not. Once they are thrust out of the interior spaces in which they had done business and hoped to gain or retain bourgeois respectability, Barbara and Jakob will play out the fates of the Christian martyrs after whom they are named, not the plots of classical tragedy. In church legend, St. Barbara was kept under custody by her father but still contrived to be converted to Christianity. Her father denounced her to the authorities, and she was beheaded. As she died, her soul was borne to heaven, and her father was killed by a lightening bolt (Farmer 28). Grillparzer's Barbara is being sold to an improper suitor by her father as well. She will not marry the fiddler but rather a butcher, and then she will have to leave the city.

Barbara is the one who will identify the fiddler's martyrdom by naming him: he is Jakob, which is an alternate name for St. James, the apostle who was in the Garden of Gethsemane with Jesus. His feast day is July 25; his story opened when the narrator went to the festival on the evening of July 24 (Wittkowski 159). In one version of his saint's story, James was martyred for preaching the Gospel in Spain; he was known as the patron for pilgrims (Farmer 207–8); he was the first apostle martyr for the Christian faith he preached. "Jakob" is, however, not only a single reference: his story also offers undeniable overtones of the tale of Jacob and Esau, the favored but scorned son, or a more political one, about James Stewart the Catholic pretender.

By the end of Grillparzer's novella, both named characters will indeed be martyrs: he for his faith and she for hers. But the rest of this second act, still played out in the domestic interiors and connecting alleys of Vienna, must define what each one actually has faith in. Their martyrdoms are not as simple as they look initially but conform closely to the physical and psychological limits of the class-bound spaces they inhabit; they are class-oriented fates.

After he was forced out of his father's house into an inn, Jakob's fortunes changed ironically: one of his brothers died and the other was brought up on libel charges.[13] The result was that the *Hofrat*'s enemies were able to bring him down; he broke down in court and died shortly thereafter (171). As his family fell apart, the fiddler was sent a black suit through a messenger, but he missed his father's funeral because he fell into a fever: "I hope to meet him again someday in a place where we are judged by our intentions, and not according to our works" (171). This religious rhetoric marks Jakob as religious but also as bourgeois: he has the best intents but will in his future be judged by readers in terms of his works in the world.

Unfortunately, the world that will judge Jakob is the world of business, not the kind of protected domestic interiors to which he had been confined or the back streets to which he had been banished. He must emerge onto public streets. At first, not only Barbara and her father but also his father's chief clerk all pay attention to him because they wish to use his money: "[T]hey said I was now a rich man and didn't have to worry about anyone else any more" (172). They were trying to remove him from the world abstractly by taking over his money for him, just as his father had taken over his career choice. Barbara again opens a window onto this new closed world, this time literally. She whispers out a window to Jakob, warning him against such partnerships (especially with her own father): "Don't trust just anyone; they mean ill for you" (172). He ends up by going into a copy business with his father's chief clerk, and with Barbara ignoring him. But Jakob persists in returning to the store; eventually Barbara begins to talk to him now and then.

Her father thought such interactions heralded a resumption of his possible matchmaking between his daughter and Jakob's money, but Barbara begins to enter into her personal martyrdom by professing her own faith in personal strength rather than money and position:

> No one would deny that you have an honest disposition, but you are weak, always concentrating on peripheral things, to the point where you would hardly be able to stand up for your own affairs. In this case it is the duty and responsibility of friends and acquaintances to take that into account so that you are not harmed. (177)

Yet her martyrdom will come anyway when her father's faith in money pre-
vails in her life, as in the saint's tale. Her father's business is failing, and so
he plans to change it into a bar, which will put her out of a job
(presumably, because bars have a higher profit margin than groceries, especially with pretty waitresses — the environment 'that Barbara refused to
work in). She will therefore be thrown out of her father's small business
world, just as Jakob had been thrown out by his father. So she makes
Jakob another offer that could keep the two of them in the city, in the kind
of business interiors that are familiar to both of them:

> But if you trust me and like being near me, then buy the milliner's
> shop that's for sale next door. I understand the trade, and you would
> not lack the proper return on your money that a citizen would expect.
> You yourself would also acquire a decent job, dealing with billing and
> correspondence. (177)

In this gesture she attempts to reconcile her faith with her father's: she
wants to make a capable man out of Jakob. She will not be a martyr to
money in terms set by her father (to cut out Jakob), but she will remold
that faith into one of her own. She wants a strong man, or at least a good
one, who will understand what it means to be "proper." However, that
good man will also put business in order and raise both of them to middle-
class lives and moral standards through hard work and self-application.

But her plan to build a milliner's shop as a bourgeois space of asylum is
doomed to fail: Barbara finds out too late about Jakob's deal with the clerk,
and she remembers that the clerk's name was in the paper as a bankrupt
fraud (178). Jakob can find no trace of his investment, so they cannot build
a life together. Predictably, there are spatial consequences as well, as her
father ejects the ruined Jakob from his shop: "We don't give handouts here"
(178). Barbara stood to the side of this scene with her eyes averted, looking
downcast (179), and stamped her foot to shoo him off, which startled
Jakob: "I well understood the old man, selfish as he was, but the girl . . ."
(180). Days later, she turns up to return his laundry to him. She calls him
weak, but at the same time she uses his proper name for the first time:
"And yet I am sorry for you . . . God be with you, Jakob" (181). She can
bless him since she is a martyr.

A few days later Barbara's martyrdom has been set into motion and her
removal from Vienna planned: she's getting married to a young butcher in
a neighboring town — to a man with an honest trade. Jakob misevaluates
her situation, using bourgeois ideas about domestic bliss: "a blissful sensation came over me. That she now was free of all worry, mistress in her
own house, and no longer needed to bear worry and misery . . ." (182).
Misassessing her situation, he feels she has married into an honest trade, so
he will do the same. He will use the last shreds of his inheritance for musical training so that he can earn his bread honestly as a musician, "not
ashamed" (183).

Because of his family misfortune, Jakob has been removed beyond the walls of the center of Vienna to the marginal garret where the narrator has found him. Barbara has been removed from the city as well, to a distant suburb and a marriage made for money and her need for social respectability. If Grillparzer's characters are indeed martyrs, they are so because they have sacrificed themselves to these notions of respectability, notions that are really class-based and money-driven.

Both are martyrs to the values of the middle class that identifies virtue with a particular kind of success. Barbara cannot marry Jakob because he is unsuited to earning a living: "poor but honest" has little draw for a woman who understands what it is to be poor *and* to be subject to dishonest people. Jakob, having been protected by his father's money and cursed by the position he is supposed to uphold, is led first into a trade that he cannot perform but that is sufficiently "white collar" to satisfy his family's idea of position. When he is forced into his own space by the dissolution of that family and its money, he creates his own musical "fantasy," making the music to which Barbara had converted him into his new faith — into a distinctly romantic, bourgeois concept of what music means and what a musician should do to be "proper." Near the end of this story, the narrator finally gets the missing story. Years after her marriage, before the narrator met Jakob, Barbara returned to Vienna as the mother of two children (the elder of whom was named Jakob) and wife of a successful master butcher — a prosperous woman who has gotten fat. At that point, she called Jakob to her house to give her son violin lessons, and has since watched over him indirectly as she would have another child. Their two worlds remain entwined into the narrator's time on the basis of a covert financial arrangement: she is probably keeping Jakob alive by her makework.

The tragedy for both players is spatial and silent, as Grillparzer draws it. They do not die as their martyrdoms set in, but they are "dead to the world" of Vienna — closed out, pushed to the margins, removed from their original social spaces. However, they are not necessarily unhappy — or they do not realize that they are unhappy: Barbara has found a business she can build with her abilities, and Jakob engages in a profession that he believes he enjoys, as the narrator confirmed when he was first seen. Grillparzer has kept his two stories intact: the narrator's tale of success and failure and the spatial isolation that characterizes both.

Note, too, that Grillparzer's first act offered the parallels between the fiddler and the playwright-narrator as two parallel bourgeois artists who meet in the open fields and remove themselves to the isolation of night and marginal domestic interiors. This second act began within the city walls of Vienna (at the heart of domestic interiors and their commercial basis), but it culminates in a dual expulsion when two parallel saint-martyrs are forced into the suburbs and neighboring towns, into the social backwaters that do not appreciate Jakob's music and that will make Barbara fat.

The third act will bring these two mirroring pairs into contact at least half a year after the narrator heard Jakob's story and years after the two had been "expelled" from Vienna. This third act will bring the city and the suburbs, nature and culture, and the poorer and richer classes of Vienna into the active conflict that all three major characters have avoided for years.

Third Act and Denouement: The Flood and Its Consequences

The third act of the story, like the second act, takes place after a time delay and a spatial derangement. The narrator had gotten involved in the tangle of his own life, forgotten the fiddler in his garret, and gone on a trip. Then the outside world crashes in on Vienna, and the narrator is shocked into recalling him. In the spring of the next year, the breaking ice jams up in the Danube and catastrophically floods parts of the city. With this act of nature (a true flood), Jakob, Barbara, and the narrator are reunited onto a single stage for the reader. The deep pasts of Barbara and Jakob are brought out of the nostalgic fairy tale of memory and into direct confrontation with the narrator's present, closing the spatial circle on the three characters.

The narrator attempts to think seriously about the flood, but again he reveals his lack of engagement with its reality. He simply does not understand what a flood implies for the inhabitants of the part of the city just outside the walls, the near suburbs in which he had played tourist the fall before: "There seemed to be no worry for the old man's life — after all, he did live high up under the roof, while Death picked its too-frequent victims from among the inhabitants of the ground floor" (183). The narrator again has mythologized the dwellers on the ground floors as "victims of Death," an archetypal metaphor that distances him from the reality of their pain and from the realities of the city map that cause the disaster. And rewriting the true script of a natural disaster, the narrator feels Jakob is quite literally above all that.

Then, presumably driven again by his "anthropological craving," the narrator goes to visit the flooded districts and sees but does not see these poorest of flood victims: their corpses are poised grotesquely in death, clutching bars on their ground-floor windows where they could not escape from the rising water. Like the garret window in the first act and the back-street windows that Barbara opened for Jakob in the second, another set of windows characterizes this third act. Just as those earlier windows did not really lead Jakob outward psychologically, this third set of windows offers the reader Grillparzer's mute vision of windows as physical nonexits. Grillparzer draws these windows not as ways out but as views into the realities of lives of people who do not have control over their own destinies. As he descends into the lower city outside the walls and into the flood, the narrator does not empathize with the misery of the baroque scene that spreads itself before him, equivalent in its horrific vision to the plague columns ubiquitous in Austria and southern Germany, tributes to past martyrs, to souls transfigured through suffering. This narrator is interested only in the official Vienna from inside the city walls, the world that keeps tracks of statistics and civil order in the abstract, not in the individual poor people involved: "[L]acking were both time and the proper officials to undertake the legal certification of so many deaths" (184). He has staved off any possible flood of emotions, just as he removed himself from the first act's flood of humanity.

Instead of confronting the lower classes' destinies, the narrator again flees public space, just as he had retreated to a more private garden restaurant in his earlier encounter with the people. Again he turns voyeur, trying to pursue the final threads of the fiddler's story. He traces down Barbara's house and talks to the maid: "Yes, our poor old fellow! He's making music with the dear angels now . . ." (184). He learns how the musician had saved things (and possibly people, although it is not clear which ones) from the rising water but then had gone back into the waters one time more than he had strength for. He rescued the butcher's money and papers out of a cabinet in the flooded apartment, but the exertion left him vulnerable to catching cold. He died, and "the Mistress," "die Frau Fleischermeisterin," is burying him. If Jakob's name designates him a martyr for his religion, what that religion is is money and papers, not people.

Again, however, the maid's eyewitness report from the perspective of the suburban streets shows the reader more than the narrator himself understands. The maid refers to Jakob as if he were one of the family and to the family as if it were decisively middle-class. Barbara is "the Mistress" and is rich enough to wear a black dress, have a maid, and pay for a proper funeral. She is clearly a neighborhood leader, the kind of middle-class success who understands that she will be judged precisely by her works and not necessarily by her intents (as Jakob had hoped to be).

The narrator cannot deal with less overt aspects of her reality. Consequently, this voyeur commits a faux pas that again reveals his focus on the middle class instead of the mass of people he purports to value. When he sees Barbara for the first time during the funeral, he evaluates her looks, remembering how Jakob saw her but not anything of her deeds: "It almost seemed as if she never had been beautiful" (185). He sees only the kind of middle-class normalcy that she has achieved in her life, nothing deeper. The narrator does not see the darker side of her bargain, the side that Grillparzer signals to the reader when he follows the narrator up the stairs into Barbara's apartment — to the final, interior space of the novella.

The final scene of this tragedy's third act, a kind of postlude, is the narrator's attempt to buy Jakob's violin; it leads to one final spatial characterization of their respective worlds. The narrator's final move is into a totally confined space — into an apartment that is characterized not by windows but by a crucifix, a violin, and a mirror hanging on the only wall described. The crucifix and the violin are aligned symmetrically around that mirror, framing it just as they frame the illusions of Barbara's new neighborhood prominence:

> A few days later — it was a Sunday — driven by my psychological cu-
> riosity, I went to the butcher's apartment, under the pretense of want-
> ing to acquire the old man's violin as a souvenir. I found the family as-
> sembled without remaining traces of any special impressions. But the
> violin hung next to the mirror, arranged in a kind of symmetry on the
> wall, across from a crucifix. (186)

The husband would have sold the violin, but Barbara won't let him. Saying that they didn't need the bit of money, she locks it in a drawer and turns away with "with a flood" of tears flowing down her cheeks. Because dinner comes at that moment, the narrator has to leave to allow the family to sit down: "My last glance found the woman. She had turned around, and the tears were streaming down her cheeks" (186). The story that started with a flood of humanity thus ends with a flood of human feeling. Barbara has achieved the middle-class standards to which she had aspired when she offered to be Jakob's partner in a milliner's shop. Yet she mourns him, as she probably mourns for herself.

As represented by the mirror, her beauty (or lack thereof) becomes the centerpiece of that icon wall without a window (the centerpiece of the tale within the tale that has unfolded itself to the outside); there is no view outside this apartment in this representation but only her ability to look at herself, not at the world. Yet Barbara "never had been beautiful" to the narrator's eyes. He prefers to ignore the fact that, without beauty, she has had to take care of herself and offer her intelligence as a substitute contribution to a partnership or dowry for a marriage. Because she was not beautiful, she had lost her place in her father's tavern — she would not attract clients with her looks. Her life, should she look in her mirror (or in society's), is framed by the two tokens of bourgeois respectability in her era: religious virtue and the respectability of art. And to achieve this, she has left the streets of Vienna's suburbs behind her to enter rooms with no notable windows and to remain there, elevated above the sufferings on ground floors, as the neighborhood's icon to local respectability.

The ending of this novella has traditionally been taken as a hagiography of Jakob, but one must resolve the story with strict reference to its use of space, especially since Barbara's mirror, not Jakob's violin, is at the center of her wall shrine. This final space represents the kind of power that Barbara has acquired through her marriage and her work. In this final scene, the narrator has replicated his earlier journey from the flood of people into the domestic interiors of the bourgeoisie. In his first journey, he found the fiddler; in this second one, he finds the fiddle hung on a wall, juxtaposed with a crucifix, the relics of martyrdom. The playwright does not, however, see that the mirror is at the center of this tableau — Barbara is beneath his notice, to a certain degree.

This final scene, as Yates confirms, is like a theatrical tableau (195), one with a certain devotional tone (82). But the silent space of the city emerges here again as crucial. While transfixed with the tragedy of the fiddler as it plays out in the domestic interior of Barbara's apartment, the narrator has overlooked the tragedy of the flood in the Leopoldstadt, out on the streets. The *Volksfest* of the first scene of the novella also merges with the fiddler's funeral — an ironic echo of the mass of common folk who have become the subjects of autopsies rather than pious elegies. The funeral guests from the neighborhood wear black, which the narrator construes as their mourning for Jakob, "our old fellow," rather than referring to what must be other losses beyond him in the streets. Ultimately, that narrator fits in no-where because he has seen nothing of significance. He is even thrown out of Barbara's house. He never has a name; he is never reliably engaged with others. The closing tableau thus directly ironizes the introduction, but the narrator refuses to see that. The "real people" of Vienna are not merely participants in festivals, they have their own life-and-death struggles. Their tragedies do not make them Didos but allow them instead to figure in mute tableaux of death and destruction.

Remember, however, that Grillparzer uses the figure of that unseeing, foolish narrator to spring the spatial frame of the story open: the narrator goes out into the street (and presumably toward home) only after the story ends, after a final glance back into the apartment at the crying Barbara. The spatial resolution of that final tableau shows the importance that Grillparzer gives to Barbara, the only character with the power of putting an outsider under the protection of her household ("our" old fellow). Barbara had first entered the story in its spatial center, in the interior courtyard of Jakob's father's house. The final tableau places her in the center of her own domestic interior, as the center of a vision encompassing Grillparzer's stunning critique of his characters. Barbara has recreated for herself the kind of domestic interior from which Jakob came; she has earned a place at the head of a household, as "die Madame" who is known for her good works. She has climbed the economic ladder that allows the lower classes to move into their own walls and perhaps even into the walls of Vienna. Those who had failed to follow Barbara into the *belle étage*, into a proper upstairs apartment, remain below the stairs; they were the ones trapped behind barred windows by the rising flood.

Barbara's diligence has insulated her family from natural floods, but her power is fictitious: she cannot protect the fiddler, who sacrifices himself to salvage the trappings of her life. The final tableau thus also suggests that she may realize the errors of her way: she doesn't need the bit of money offered for the violin, and her family may not have needed the papers that Jakob sacrificed himself for. She has locked the violin into a drawer, into yet a smaller space, just as she must lock her heart away when her husband calls her back to the table. Jakob's life had been dedicated to music and to the control of the hours of his life; Barbara's, to the establishment of her control over her domestic tranquillity, despite her lack of beauty. Yet the reader sees (and the narrator does not) that both martyrs have sacrificed themselves on the altar of bourgeois values, to values that could not protect them: to the purity of domesticity, control of self, and domestic isolation from the turmoil of the world.

The story ends with the narrator in a doorway, looking *inward* into Barbara's claustrophobic room, seeing her tears (186). The first image in the novella thus balances the last: it is a dialectic, offering the reader a view inward on Barbara that the narrator sees but does not understand, just as he had not understood the stream of people as he had looked outward beyond the city walls. The story that started on the feast of St. James (Jakob) ends up with Jakob's relics being closed into a drawer; the story that started out by leaving the city walls over the river reaches into the domestic interior of a materialistic woman who mourns an impractical dreamer as saint. The narrator has erred when he believes her and her family to be untouched by any special impressions (186).

What the narrator cannot see, but Grillparzer signals to the reader by her placement in this final tableau, is that Barbara is the fulcrum of both male characters' stories. This woman has moved into the walls that the narrator has pretended to escape: out of the country into the store, then into the courtyard, and finally into a room with a drawer at its heart. In this sense, she has closed her own metaphoric circle in the floods, just as the narrator has — from humanity (general) to humanity (her own) — and has drowned in the flood of her own making, taking Jakob with her. The narrator's "original" has become *her* "poor old fellow."

Yet the bourgeois security she chose (her ability to control walls and keep out floods) has led to two deaths: Jakob's physical death and her own spiritual one, signaled by that final flood of human tears. Each has become a saint, but each has won that status at the cost of isolation and by living up to domestic, artistic, hierarchical pretensions — to the values of the bourgeoisie, a class that glorifies sole custody of space, individual artistry ("beautiful" music between the musician and God, outside the group), and the innate capability of those who make money. This is the martyrdom of the ugly woman in bourgeois society known from so much nineteenth-century literature, the martyrdom of domestic interiors and patriarchal families. Jakob died for his faith, for a choice that he made, just as Barbara's soul may have died for hers. Yet the great mass of humanity in the city is simply crushed against the bars by the flood of history — these people have no choice, and the powers in official Vienna are interested only in their death certificates, not in the meanings of their deaths (the kinds of meanings that make Jakob the fool into a martyr). The middle classes achieve their isolation at this human cost: abstract values cloud their visions of real human tragedies.

In this doubled fate of domestic interiors, therefore, Grillparzer's narrator's look inward signals a mute critique of the rising bourgeoisie (albeit a sympathetic one). The narrator's interpretation of the final tableau demonstrates his personal belief in the tragedy of the middle class, a class under

financial stress, which can easily be martyred by circumstance, as he believes Jakob to have been. His vision is, however, limited since he is the
playwright who believed that Didos were hidden in chambermaids, though
he was not paying attention to them. Grillparzer, in contrast, shows that the
bourgeois that Barbara and Jakob represent may prefer to look into mirrors
rather than out of windows; they are destined for martyrdom because they
have pulled themselves out of the great flood of life, the natural cycles of
birth, death, and work in the streets of the city.[14]

The narrator's blindness is confirmed by the details of the closing tableau that he has overlooked but that Grillparzer underscores for the reader.
A nameless maid is serving dinner; the master of the house, the master-
butcher, loudly starts saying grace to crowd his wife's scene out of his consciousness and to shove the narrator out the door of the apartment. That
narrator leaves, giving the "proper" greeting. The children chime in on the
prayer "piercingly" (*gellend*). Barbara's tears are unanswered, the narrator
notices them, but the story ends with no indication that he understands
them as anything other than tears for a departed friend.

Conclusion: Vision out of Season

Missing from the narrator's final vision is what always had been missing: his
ability to see outside the walls. Yet for the reader, the narrator's initial fears
about a "flood of threatening humanity" from the start of the novella must
recede in light of the two floods that close it. In terms of the visual balance
of the story, Grillparzer is inviting his readers to compare the Danube flood
that victimized the poor with the flood of tears from a woman whose
choices condemned at least one of these poor to die in the rising waters.
Behind these images of floods, Grillparzer is offering an unvoiced assessment of a social threat to "the decent folks" of Vienna: walls — creating
spaces without windows, windows with bars, courtyards that don't face the
street, and differentiations between apartments below stairs, in garrets, and
in the *belle étage*. The enemy of life in this story is precisely such social
space that isolates, traps, removes individuals from each other while fostering the illusions that their lives are under their control and that they are
bettering themselves. Such illusions killed Jakob, broke Barbara's heart, and
seduced the narrator into believing that his anthropological specimens are
living the tragedies of fate rather than scripts of their own writing.

Grillparzer chose to resurrect and publish a story in 1847 that he had
begun in 1830. These are two significant years in the annals of history
documenting the rise of the bourgeoisie in Europe, and they are noted to
be times of civil unrest. By 1848, however, Barbara's world had triumphed,
as the popular dramas of both Raimund and Nestroy also document. The
Volksfest outside the city walls from 1830 had become part of the nostalgic
vision of *Altwien*, of the Vienna of the Biedermeier, the "good old days"

when the little people had a chance in the city. Money and financial speculation was driving humanity out of the city walls.

By 1848 Grillparzer was also driven behind his own walls, out of the theater that had been his second home for years because *Weh dem, der lügt* failed in 1838 before a public that no longer saw the humor in confrontations between the Germans and the barbarians. This withdrawal is often attributed to Grillparzer's sense that he was aging. Yet he did not stop writing when he withdrew from the theater: in his desk drawer at his death in 1872 there were masterpieces of the status of *Libussa* and *Ein Bruderzwist in Habsburg*, major plays taking on the issues of legitimacy of rule and limits on traditional authority — issues touched in a lighter vein in *Weh dem*. These plays are mature works, by no means aged or withdrawn.

Der arme Spielmann was taken up by Grillparzer twice in times of social unrest. The reasons for both its abandonment and its completion may lie in the vision of politics that it offers. In 1831 Metternich's Europe was at its contested peak, the world privileging the aristocracy and the old order against the protests of a younger generation that included critical voices such as Heinrich Heine. But if the dual reading I am proposing here is correct, Grillparzer has by no means written a story privileging that younger generation of bourgeois, to which the narrator would have belonged. Jakob's father was clearly a member of the old order ("with virtually the power of a minister"), but he was nonetheless bourgeois — affiliating with the order that censored and spied. By 1848, that old order was finished in its post-1815 form — Metternich himself would be run out of Vienna in 1848 and Habsburg hegemony saved by a thread when the throne was vacated in favor of the young Franz Joseph. Historically, these events are taken to be the first triumph of the bourgeoisie.

But the way *Der arme Spielmann* is resolved by no means shows approval of the behavior of this new moneyed bourgeoisie (the class that would have been Grillparzer's principal audience). Grillparzer understands both the playwright and the fiddler of his story, but the way his story is resolved belies any attempt to assume that he is nostalgic about or approving of their world.[15] The playwright is blind to the people; Jakob is deaf to what they say or believe (as when he believes Barbara must be happy in her marriage); Barbara has been martyred to this world, the one of her father, the one that the playwright esteems and that has ruined Jakob.

It is Barbara who calls the fiddler "poor" as well as having named him — her maid reports that Jakob is "our poor old man." It is Barbara who gets the final scene, the sense of which the narrator cannot see and which Jakob is no longer alive to notice. What is Grillparzer showing us? A woman who had been one of the ordinary working people, who has pulled herself out of their midst, and who may be regretting that choice — a choice that she thought would guarantee her security but that still left her dearest friend vulnerable to floods.

If *Der arme Spielmann* is Barbara's story, then Grillparzer's political critique of the bourgeoisie of 1847 is devastating. The poor folk in his story will always be subject to the floods of the world, but they will be safe as long as they are all together, on foot, as they were in the Brigittenau (the meadow of St. Bridget, Celtic saint and missionary to the heathens of Ireland). When, however, they acquire horses, they become instruments of each others' destruction; when Barbara gets her own walls, she begins to run the lives of others, just as the old rich had — she has led Jakob to just as certain a death as his own father did through negligence.

Those who control spaces as places of inclusion or exclusion control lives: this is the message of Grillparzer's story, a plea for a healthier space for the class consciousness of Vienna. If Barbara is meant to represent nostalgia, it is a nostalgia for a return to the values of simple humanity and popular justice that Barbara too had forsaken. This is a call for a return to a world in which walls do not designate the powerful — a very unpopular message for 1848, which, as Grillparzer knew, was more interested in world power and control than in its heart and the simple lives of common people.

In this sense, then, Grillparzer's novella is his testimony to the bankruptcy of the bourgeois civic values of all three of his main characters — victims of a class that was eating its own children under the banners of respectability, art, and religion. Barbara has won the battle of saving her family (who "bray" their prayers) from the flood at the cost of her own soul. In her, Grillparzer showed what he could not state to a public that refused to hear: the cost of that surrender of life and heart to the abstract values of a class that does not look through windows. He shows the tragedy of a martyrdom for any abstract cause that divides people from each other and so brings them to ruin in overrunning their humanity. From this perspective, the novella cannot be read as "poetic realism" because it rejects the abstractions of bourgeois values while highlighting the real and random forces that inexorably change people's lives.

Grillparzer's novella thus documents the emptiness of a class that believes itself to be on the rise — a critique as biting as Thomas Mann would offer fifty years later in *Buddenbrooks*, decrying the complicity of money, art, and status that was purporting to lead the nation but actually was bringing it to its ruin by ignoring the true politics of the city, the fostering of its agora rather than its walls.

Notes

[1] All translations are by the present author. I have not used either of the two existing translations of the novella because of important differences in nuance. Page citations thus refer to the German edition.

[2] See Cowen, especially 14 ff., for the history of this sad and warped reception, especially in the context of realism. Perhaps the worst review ever (an anonymous one appearing in an 1858 issue of *Europa* in Leipzig) is characterized by a distinctive anti-Austrianism. It starts out by saying that the story is characterized by "a certain hypochondriac narrowness of heart" as well as offering freshness and a

true-to-life flavor not usually expected from "the greyed Romantics of Austria." However, then the story deteriorates, when readers encounter a "spiritually and physically bent, half-simple old man" that represents a "poetic celebration of those cretins that are to be found in such great numbers in some of Austria's regions" ("Es ist eine poetische Feier jener Kretinen, die in einzelnen Landschaften Österreichs so zahlreich zu finden sind"; quoted in Grillparzer, *Apparat* 73).

[3]Critics like Moritz Saphir attacked the play for setting excessively high standards for the audience, expecting them to weigh the truth of official culture (Politzer 269).

[4]Hinrich C. Seeba declared it in his "Franz Grillparzer." Originally in German, the moratorium reads, "This story should be granted a rest period until substantive and overarching questions arise from a changed historical situation, framed within a new constellation of interests" (401).

[5]Note too that the actual festival fell into abeyance between the time Grillparzer started his novella and the time he finished it.

[6]Now Gärtnerstraße (Koutek 33).

[7]For further information, see the material provided in the 1930 edition of Franz Grillparzer's *Prosaschriften 1*, especially 327 ff., which traces in great detail the genesis of the story in real events and places; and the *Apparat zu den dramatischen Plänen und Bruchstücken und zu den Prosaschriften*, which documents the early reception of the work, including statements about its realistic depiction of the city.

[8]And this nature is constructed differently from that in Kleist's *Erdbeben zu Chili*, which plays off egalitarian, natural space against the socially stratified spaces of church and jail.

[9]For a description of the low-end musician's career in the Viennese suburbs of the 1830s and 1840s, see Karl Ziak, *Des Heiligen Römischen Reiches größtes Wirtshaus*, which describes the *Natursänger* and *Harfenisten* out of contemporary chronicles.

[10]This detail sounds comical but again simply attests to the sociological realism of the piece. By mid-century, Vienna was known for a particular class of renter called *Bettgeher* who quite literally rented one shift in a bed and perhaps a drawer in someone else's apartment. This was the direct result of rent inflation and scarity of housing.

[11]Note, too, how similar this garret is to those in Spitzweg paintings, which can be seen as glorifying or critiquing the life of "little people" like the fiddler.

[12]A *Greisler-* or *Kolonialwarenladen* is a corner general store.

[13]"He [the first brother] had to pay for an ill-considered bet with his life. He had to swim across the Danube, overheated from riding as he was — it was deep in Hungary. The elder, most beloved brother was brought in front of a provincial court" (171).

[14]And note that the narrator will not find his Dido to make a play: he left the festival and has trouble seeing Barbara in the beauty of her soul since he is more interested in Jakob.

[15]See Roe, chapter 5, for his succinct discussion of how critics have grounded such identifications.

8: Christo and Judy Chicago: Gender, Art, and Culture

In the mid-1990s, two well-known modern artists reemerged into the public eye after periods of comparative invisibility, each now familiar from interviews, exemplary documentation volumes, and the kind of media exposure that most artists only dream of.

Judy Chicago's "Holocaust Project" opened in 1993 in Chicago as the culmination of eight years' work. A 7,000 square-foot installation with sixteen major works in various media (painting, manipulated photography, stained glass, and tapestry), this traveling exhibit began to tour the United States as Chicago's testimony to the Holocaust. This exhibit is a major media event, well publicized and documented; it is intended to stimulate discussion and ancillary events as much as it is to be seen in its own right. While she was working on this project, Chicago's media exposure had been considerably more limited. Most mentions of her work focused around her attempts to house her monumental project of almost two decades earlier, "The Dinner Party," a celebration of the history of intellectual woman, in the form of a huge triangular table set with symbolic table runners and place settings. In 1990 her attempts to donate "The Dinner Party" to the University of the District of Columbia had fallen victim to the public debate about pornography and the arts.[1]

An equally prominent media event happened in summer 1995 in Berlin when Christo's "Wrapped Reichstag" project came to fruition after over twenty years of planning and negotiation, which began in 1971. The international media enjoyed the spectacle of the Berlin parliament building standing sheathed in shimmering gray cloth, an event blocked for decades by political circumstances that had shifted dramatically with the fall of the Berlin Wall.[2] The political discussion Christo had originally planned to elicit was almost drowned in a circus of tourism. Still, Christo's project signaled his reemergence as clearly as Chicago's "Holocaust Project" had hers. He needed this kind of favorable exposure. When Christo's "Umbrellas" were unfurled in Japan and California in 1991 (huge yellow and green umbrellas, dotting the rolling hills of two sites), storm winds caught individual umbrellas and lofted them; they killed one person in each locale, which brought the project to an early end.[3]

These two artists' long and extremely public series of large-scale art projects make them ideal case studies to explain how modern artists use their positions in culture to craft their careers. They are parallel cases in that the artists are approximately the same age, offer works of parallel scale that are only conditionally destined for art museums, and were trained in the heyday of the modernist art aesthetic in the 1960s. Judy Chicago was an avowed feminist at the time of her "Dinner Party" in the mid-1970s (and has been since); since the time when he did the main planning for the "Wrapped Reichstag" in the 1970s, Christo has been known as a maker of ephemeral events. Nonetheless, both intended their projects as political interventions, and both have developed projects that are widely and variously critiqued from the right and the left. Yet they differ, since Christo was trained in Bulgaria and came to his earliest prominence in Europe before he worked in the United States, while Chicago tried for the New York and Los Angeles gallery scenes directly. And most critically, they differ in national position, gender, and genre and thus in their access to (or exclusion from) the domain of art norms and patronage.

In the discussion that follows, I am going to trace how these two artists represent themselves to their audiences, in order to show how each conceives of the role of an artist who wishes to execute projects that stimulate public discussion and require the participation of more than the professional art community to be implemented. This essay will thus approach art as a cultural practice by addressing two artists' strategies of group work and career management instead of comparing artworks or thematics. This approach to the phenomenon of modern art through its practice rather than its products circumvents persistent problems of aesthetics. Is china painting art, or can wrapping buildings be? Are Chicago's violent birth images sensationalism or correlates to previously unsymbolized female experience? Is Christo's focus on legalistic permitting processes political criticism or a media gambit?

Whether or not they are practicing traditional "high art," the artists to be discussed below espouse a belief that large-scale or public art has psychological, political, and aesthetic consequences for their cultures that smaller-scale work cannot (if only in that large works require a corporate purchaser instead of an individual patron). Instead of treating art as a product (the work), moreover, both Chicago and Christo stress the work as process (happening, experience, or interaction).[4] Despite the very different nature of their works of art, however, these two artists have chosen parallel alignments toward the art establishment, their audience, and the public quality of their works. At some point, though, the issue of gender enters these careers. Certain of their thematics are facilely characterizable as male (law) or female (birth); certain materials, too easily attributable to the social situation of males or females (males learn to use tools and so sculpt; females learn to sew, so they adapt more easily to textile arts). Yet the similarities in their practices may ultimately be more indicative of their cultural positioning than their genders.

To explore art as a potentially gendered practice, the following discussion draws on the artists' "official" autobiographical and biographical statements to see how they present themselves and their projects to a public. The documentation surrounding "The Dinner Party" and the "Wrapped Reichstag" is the most public and the broadest of all these artists' projects, and the two projects are contemporary in conception (if not in realization). In consequence, they will be the focus of the discussions that follow. The goals of this comparison are to uncover the practice of modern artists who are aware of their locations in culture, to show what parts of that practice are susceptible to being gender-coded, and, in turn, to discover how gender identity plays into other kinds of cultural practice.

The Artists: Sociology and Gender

What links these two artists most prominently is the fact of their emergence in the 1970s. As the sociology of knowledge would predict, the dominant culture influences these artists' development: Christo's and Chicago's biographical statements frame their careers according to the familiar gender stereotypes of the 1970s. Most immediately obvious is that, despite gender asymmetry in their careers, both artists portray themselves as outsiders to U.S. culture.

Using almost classic feminist rhetoric, Judy Chicago's autobiography, *Through the Flower*, stresses the alienation between her life and her art. In art school in the 1960s, Chicago felt her work was validated when it matched men's art, not on its own terms. Even her attempts at "female forms" were rejected by juries explicitly because of their claims to femaleness (34). Her alienation was reinforced by traditional patterns of women's education: she was not prepared for technical and crafts enterprises since she did not know how to use tools (which slowed her work initially [33]). More serious for her career, she had only male archetypes to copy from for images and lifestyle (35). She was also caught in the macho world of modern minimalist art of the 1960s, which stressed high-tech happenings like fireworks, auto spray painting, and acrylics, together with a new "chic" gallery culture (39). Her education, her work, and her career projections were thus under continual pressure from male norms. One of her first reactions to this triple alienation was a shift of career and work patterns: to assert gender equality with her male peers, she took on large-scale sculpture (a branch of art stressing technology [43]). By 1965 male aggressivity versus female passiveness emerged as explicit themes in her work (63). She thus felt she had created a place for a female artist in the terms established by the male art community. In 1969 Chicago began to confront her alienation more publicly in a series of paintings called "Pasadena Lifesavers," exhibited with the following entrance sign: "*Judy Gerowitz* hereby divests herself of all names imposed upon her through male social dominance and freely chooses her own name *Judy Chicago*" (63). She had earlier claimed a public position for herself as a female artist; with this act (or with its announcement), she claimed a woman's consciousness as she reassumed her voice through painting, her preferred genre.

Chicago's name change ushered in a career somewhat apart from the male art establishment even though she still worked primarily as a painter.

She taught a woman's art class at Fresno and encountered what would emerge for her as the central problem in woman's art: poor self-image and weak personal identity of the potential artist, exacerbated by society's reluctance to push women (72, 74). For example, she found that no one had ever asked her students' opinions, the expression of which should be crucial to "art-making" (Chicago's term). She and Mimi (Miriam) Shapiro, a somewhat older woman painter, started a Feminist Art Program to encourage experimentation with any media, and tool use. In 1971 it was moved back to Los Angeles under the sponsorship of Cal Arts, where she again fought for women's art and social space (including training in using proper tools and the right of women to dispose of their own time [97]). These actions underscore Chicago's idea that access to and support from the public sphere are crucial to the artist's consciousness, and they document her growing interest in art as a process rather than simply a product destined for a museum.

A series of projects tested such artistic access. In 1971 and 1972 Chicago's group did the "Womanhouse," an abandoned house "redecorated" before it was razed. Images of woman's domestic bondage emerged, notably the "Sheet Closet" holding a woman intercut with the sheets and the "Nurturant Kitchen" decorated with pink breasts (105–7). A series of accompanying performances stressed consciousness-raising about the woman as social product. After *Womanhouse*, Chicago's 1972 "Through the Flower" lithographs furthered her rediscovery of painting. By 1973 she opened Womenspace, a woman's gallery.

Encouraged by Anaïs Nin, Chicago also began to read women's biographies and research women's histories as documentation of a suppressed tradition (132). Ultimately, this research led Chicago to her great project, the "Dinner Party," which took 1974 to 1979 to create, "five years of [Chicago's] life" (Chicago, *Dinner Party* 8). The work and its two volumes of documentation uncovered and valorized women's craft, women's history, and women's art simultaneously. Chicago's research team found "lost" women of history, who would then be celebrated in the thirty-nine settings of the table. The settings themselves emphasized women's crafts: china painting for the plates and needlework of all kinds for the runners. From 1980 to 1985 another group project extended Chicago's commitment to women's art and crafts: the "Birth Project," stressing icons and images for woman's experience — the icons that the male-dominated tradition of art lacked. These two projects remain today prime testimonials to the rhetoric of women's art in the 1970s and early 1980s.

The narratives in the documentation volumes are drawn in close parallel with the women's movement through the late 1960s and 1970s. Chicago's evolution began with her alienation from her womanhood through the influence of the art community; thereafter, until she found woman's art, she was alienated psychologically as well. Chicago's women's art projects overcame her personal resistance to women's traditions to a degree, but not the alienation of the woman artist and women's arts from the arts community. "The Dinner Party" failed to be accommodated by art institutions — Chicago recovered the female artist but not necessarily female art, she asserts. This is, then, the story of an individual female who overcame the restrictions of her culture and who hopes to move her compatriots in the same direction.

This narrative strategy makes it easy for the reader to assume that the gap between the arts community and the artist's self-concept is a product of gender stereotypes in the culture. Yet when we turn to Christo's biography, many of the same tropes of alienation occur: they seem to be part of the way the modern art community defined itself during the 1960s, not attributable just to gender roles in the era. It is instructive at this point to see how Christo tells the story of his alienation from the traditional art community as a variant of Chicago's story.

He was born Christo Javacheff in Bulgaria in 1935, son of a fairly well-to-do chemical manufacturer and a Macedonian general secretary of the Academy of Fine Arts in Sofia (Cullen and Volz 29). His mother cooperated with his desire to become an artist. She told him "fairy tales" about Mayakowski, El Lissitzki, and Tatlin, stressing especially the open-air pieces that celebrated the October Revolution (40,000 M^2 of canvas painted by Nathan Altman), and their manifestos that said that artists should go paint the town (literally). He thus learned early the notion of large-scale revolutionary art intended to influence the masses as well as the idea of the artist as visionary, which is endemic to modern art in the West. So nurtured, Christo started painting at age 6. From 1952 to 1956 he attended the academy, studying economics and political science along with technology, theory, and art history (Cullen and Volz 30). His art education was, then, as good or better than Chicago's, but he enjoyed a degree of parental and public support that Chicago had not had. It is interesting that his role model was female, his artist-mother — the role model that Chicago sought but did not find in Mimi Shapiro.

As a citizen of a socialist country, Christo was thoroughly sensitized to the relation of art and the social sphere through some unusual practical experience. In summers, art students were sent out to beautify Bulgaria so that Western visitors seeing the country from the Orient Express would get a good image of it (as long as they stayed on the train). They taught farmers to present their tractors and yards properly: "We placed machines dynamically. We told the farmers to put their threshers very visibly on small hills — like on a pedestal. . . . one also convinced factory workers to stack industrial waste so that it could be shown publicly" (Cullen and Volz 31).

Christo thus learned early that exhibition and presentation were crucial to art making; this education helped him find his place in the West. In fall 1956 he visited Prague, experiencing works by Klee and Miro in the midst of the uprising. In January 1957 he fled to Vienna with a "student visa" arranged through personal connections. He then moved to Geneva, where he made a living doing portraits. In March 1958 he moved to Paris and did more portraits. There Christo fell in with the young French modernists, although was not among them in their "New Realism" manifesto of 27 October 1960 (his own work was considered "too subjective" [Cullen and Volz 33]). In Paris, Christo found his own voice (his distinctive projects) when he wrapped his first objects: bottles, boxes, and the like, since he could not afford expensive materials. He also received his first public validation when an Italian artist bought a wrapped tin can in 1959 (Cullen and Volz 33).

In documentary volumes, Christo's reactions to this displacement are rarely recorded. His personality disappears into his work, into a series of notable "packings." In Cologne in 1961 his "Dockside Packages — Temporary Monuments" packed heavy industrial goods; simultaneously, Galerie Haro Lauhaus showed two packed grand pianos, a Renault 4, a torso, and a wall of scavenged oil barrels. After the Berlin Wall was erected on 13 August 1961, Christo showed his sense of political timeliness (and media savvy) when he put up an "Iron Curtain — Wall of Oil Drums" back in Paris, a four-meter-high pile closing the rue Visconti on the Left Bank. In 1962 in Paris, he packed a woman. In February 1964 he went to New York for nine months, but he returned to Europe with many plans. He came back to New York in 1968: unfortunately, the New York authorities wouldn't let him build an oil-drum wall in the street as part of a DADA exhibit for the Museum of Modern Art (he got consolation space inside the museum and huge publicity for the rejection). He went back to Kassel to pack air (a 280-foot-high sausage) and finally to wrap his first building: the Kunsthalle in Bern — another "Temporary Monument." In 1969 the city of Chicago showed that it was up to the challenge: Christo packed the Museum of Contemporary Art, a project deemed a success because "Christo has done more than any other artist to make people think about art" (Cullen and Volz 39). In the same year he also did "Wrapped Coast — Little Bay (Sydney, Australia) — One Million Square Feet." From 1970 to 1972 he planned and realized the "Valley Curtain" in Colorado (an orange wall of fabric), followed most notably by "Running Fence, Sonoma and Marin Counties, California" in 1976. His "Wrapped Walkways, Loose Part, Kansas City, Missouri" appeared in golden yellow in 1978; and "Surrounded Islands," in pink, was realized in 1980–81.

The idea for the "Wrapped Reichstag" (the House of Parliament for pre-Second-World-War Germany) goes back to 1971. Christo's most intense planning for the project in the mid-1970s is simultaneous with his period of active wrapping and quick responses to publicity opportunities. Over time, it became clear that the "Reichstag" would materialize only when certain federal chancellors were out of office (the earliest possible date was 1991), given the legal impasses involved (Crockett and Samuels). Christo was up to the challenge of waiting, though, since it had taken from 1975 to 1985 to get permission and work out the "Pont Neuf Wrapped" in Paris. In between these projects, Christo did pyramids of oil drums in Abu Dhabi, giant gates in New York (1980), and a joint Japan-California project (1991) of giant landscape umbrellas (theirs were blue, ours yellow [Crockett and Samuels]). Ultimately the fall of the Berlin Wall in 1989 opened those crucial political discussions for the "Reichstag" project in another way but hindered the project's realization until Germany's new political boundaries were more or less regularized, after the four-power occupation of the city was lifted.

In speaking of the challenges involved in realizing his projects, Christo stresses not his persona or artistic program but his cultural locus, albeit in a slightly different way than Chicago did. Where she described the cultural challenges to her opportunities and her thematics, Christo consistently describes the technical and legal problems inherent in the dominant social structures that any large-scale work (not necessarily artwork) must overcome. Chicago stresses the artist; Christo focuses on the event. Yet he or his interlocutors also consistently stress the alienation of his artistic practice from the dominant culture. For example, because he is a Bulgarian, when Christo attempts to gain right-of-way or access permits, he often becomes an "enemy alien" in the eyes of the ruling powers, a political alien from the dominant culture of the United States if not a gendered one. The "Running Fence" and "Reichstag" projects evoked typically suspicious questions: Was he trying to mess up the California landscape? Or was he (perhaps as an East Bloc plant) single-handedly attempting to violate the Four-Power Agreement establishing the occupation of Berlin (Lotringer 253)?

Both artists thus understand the role of alienation from U. S. culture and how to integrate that alienation as part of their self-images. A 1970s feminist would easily assume that Christo was initially not as alienated from certain segments of the art community as Judy Chicago felt herself to be. Yet he was able to evoke a public role as a sociopolitical alien who sought the "rights" of art in public spaces. Christo, as a refugee, understands the value of political alienation in his self-representations as well as Chicago does:

> The *Reichstag* is definitely a very dramatic project. It is almost like a return to the site [*sic*] of the crime. I escaped from an Eastern European country, and I have never been back to Eastern Europe. I don't like to go back there, except that I will go back to East Germany for my project. I was a refugee from 1957 until 1973 . . . for 17 or 16 years without a passport, with only refugee papers. (Crockett and Samuels)

Both artists thus clearly trade on their respective statuses as aliens to the dominant U.S. culture.

Chicago and Christo are differentiated by gender and educational backgrounds, but their backgrounds both fulfill common sociological criteria that predict career choices (Tuchman 176). Christo is the son of an artist, and a political refugee; Chicago comes from a middle-class, possibly even upper-middle-class, Jewish background, characterized generally by a certain degree of political marginalization (which allows its members some freedom in career choice). Yet despite their outsider roles, both artists nonetheless possessed the credentials required for entrance into the artistic hierarchy: art school and practical gallery exposure (which Chicago asserts that she, as a female, acquired the hard way).

Different readers would take these two stories of marginalization differently. Feminists would highlight the pressures of Chicago's middle-class background, which tends to be conservative in its support of values that maintain its position within the social hierarchy (Tuchman 190–92). A parallel myth is quietly implied in 1970s documentation to make Christo a victim of politics who may be victimized again in the West, where he is just trying to make the democratic process work for him. The two artists thus ultimately share traits that position them similarly in the art discourses of their age: they are partially at odds with the art establishment of their day, they suffer sociopolitical alienation that impinges on their art production, and they had to negotiate differences between the art traditions in which they were raised and those in which they chose to produce art.

The *quality* of each artist's psychological alienation is thus clearly tied to gender bias, but the *fact* of that alienation does not seem to be since other variables underlie their narratives and self-concepts as alienated artists. Parallel myths makes both artists' careers plausible. Chicago's "typical" female life history turned her interest to women's art; Christo's leap from socialism to capitalism made him concentrate on the role of art in public spaces. These two artists are "male" and "female" only in conjunction with other sociological narratives of marginality from the 1970s. Alien, outsider, loss of self: these themes are used by both artists in the 1970s and early 1980s to describe their positions as artists vis-à-vis a modern art community and public sphere in the United States. These themes will alter a bit in the 1990s but remain parallel. Christo and Chicago thus share very similar perceptions about what being an artist in the West means and what images they need to project.

Funding and Art: Locus of the Work

While they share their sense of public image making (and, as we shall see, their concept of art funding), Chicago and Christo nonetheless define the life of their works very differently. The power that each gained by purveying a plausible artistic persona to the public (and the power to exploit media opportunities with their works) is used very differently by each when it comes down to defining what their art is (not just its themes). Again the question of gender enters the comparison, but at a comparatively late phase in each career.

Christo defines his artworks as "temporary monuments" that cause public art events that he finances, not as permanent art objects. His ideal artwork is short-lived, but not the process that ultimately produced it. The "Wrapped Reichstag," quadrupling the usual time for a Christo project, ran over twenty-four years from first planning to realization. As the time scale of his projects grew, Christo acknowledged how art planning and art financing were interconnected. Until 1968 and the "5600 Cubic Meters Package" of air done for Kassel, West Germany, Christo worked within a traditional financial framework: the artist buys (or finds) materials, composes, and sells (mainly through galleries), aided by occasional small grants from purchasers or patrons. At Kassel, the scale of Christo's work required a change of tactics. The Kassel package was guaranteed only $3000 by the "documenta 4" exhibition sponsors. Yet to execute it, Christo had to find $54,000 himself to pay the design engineers. The materials firm Hoechst sold him the balloon nylon at cost, but much of the labor in the piece was no longer Christo's to contribute (Cullen and Volz 37). This disparity between "payment" and costs grew. "Wrapped Coast" was commissioned for only $3,000 from its sponsors but ran to $120,000 (Christo commissioned specially woven materials so as not to damage the land as solid plastic would [Cullen and Volz 39]). The "Reichstag" cost millions over the initial estimates.

Christo's finances clearly moved him out of the legal purview of what either galleries, museums, or private donors would expect to cover. "Valley Curtain" and "Running Fence," for instance, required environmental impact statements and biological inventories as well as security bonds for damages, clean-up, security and traffic directors, and construction workers. Moreover, a work included costs for design and materials firms. For his fabric curtain projects, for example, Christo needed wholly new types of anchors and materials to accommodate wind effects on huge sheets of materials and secure them on varying terrains while allowing the unfurling to be accomplished in very short stretches of time. In the case of the "Running Fence," lawyers' costs to acquire rights-of-way added substantially to the project total of $3.25 million (Cullen and Volz 53).

Christo shifted the burden of financing onto his own shoulders. He sold or marketed parts of the project prior to the realization of the whole yet maintained rights to that whole. The "Curtain" was prefinanced by sales of sketches, drawings, and models to about sixty customers (half individuals, half galleries or museums, and mostly in Europe [Cullen and Volz 44]). The "Running Fence" got galleries and private customers to purchase at least $20,000 worth of work each (a special rate for a minimum purchase [Cullen and Volz 48]). These purchasers, however, had not acquired the project itself, which stayed in Christo's hands. Christo is open about these strategies, which give him unusual control and put certain critiques out of play.

Ultimately, the art becomes money. Despite these price tags, Christo got very popular when the state of California figured out it had made about $7 million from tourism around the "Running Fence" project. In one way or another, 9.5 million people participated, numerous part-time and full-time construction jobs were created, and landowners got the materials used as compensation for the rights-of-way (Cullen 99). Miami almost immediately invited a Christo project of any sort and got the "Surrounded Islands." Whatever Christo was doing (art?), civil authorities would lose not one cent. For instance, a typical Christo "extra" incentive for a project was a huge trash clean-up on the islands, reclaiming them from under trash Miami could not afford to move. Christo also backs his claims with money up-front to preempt or silence objections. Approximately $3.25 million rested in a bank under the name of the "Wrapped Reichstag" project in the late 1970s, waiting for the moment; technical requirements caused him to plow more money into it during the realization (the final costs were estimated at $10 million). Christo projects are thus exemplary capitalist enterprises: cash up-front and value gained for value given, either in kind (art sales) or exchange value (tourism dollars or a city clean-up for those not interested in "artistic merits"). He presents himself not only as a designer but as a public implementer: all funds and bonds are taken care of in advance, documentation is offered in exquisite form, and he beats his deadlines. Whatever galleries say, his projects speak with money, and Christo controls them.

Christo thus frames his works two ways: financially and artistically, with the financial tied into the legal and the artistic tied into the personal-psychological. Christo gauges the artistic "length" of his projects psychologically, encompassing anticipation, problem solving, and memories, especially the semimystical tales of "how wonderful it was." Their lives as documentary exhibits in museums about the true art event are also explicitly secondary. This removal of the artwork from the control of the art establishment is crucial, for Christo wants the public to carry the project; he focuses more on the process than the product, in part to undercut eventual gallery or museum control of the work. Within this concept, Christo engages in consciousness raising of a particularly political sort: he overcomes preconceptions about art through public support (and he is identified as a '60s artist for this today). His "art" is found in the experience of participation; his temporary monuments live as monumental memories for the public.

Yet Christo's handling of the projects also stress how they rely on publicity. He must, for example, always push the limits of what has been tried publicly. While the city of Chicago still had to waive zoning ordinances when he wrapped the Museum of Contemporary Art, any later Christo museum projects virtually came with feasibility guarantees since he had become too famous — almost a cultural icon himself. Yet when the "Reichstag" was suggested to him, he was already saying, "I don't do buildings anymore." However, the East-West political dynamics of the "Reichstag" project offered a new dimension since he would be working against the governments of two Germanys and four occupying powers, a particularly politicized act not tried before and sure to be covered in the press.

Christo's narratives about his artworks thus stem from a curious but ingenious compromise about their status. He has involved both traditional gallery patronage and the general public while limiting his personal transformation into a cultural icon; as an event, he retains a certain degree of freedom not vouchsafed a media personality-artist (like Warhol). Galleries may acquire his sketches, models, and photographic documentation, but not a completed work, so his work cannot be used as a "standard" against which others' achievements may be measured. Christo has relocated the work of art into the public sphere while maintaining the artist's authority over its finances (a rare achievement), its sociopolitical locus, and its "aesthetic constitution." And so, by the time the Reichstag was wrapped, he was even willing to market calendars, day-planners, and postcards to supplement the limited-edition folios of prints (Christo and Jeanne-Claude, *Wrapped Reichstag* 96).

Judy Chicago follows many of the same rules for financing that Christo exploited, reflecting a parallel consciousness of the "gallery game" of the 1960s and 1970s. Yet the ramifications are not the same. Chicago's "Dinner Party," like Christo's projects, was purportedly prefinanced with capital from sales of her own work. However, where he sold the plans for a project, involving the art consumer, she sold *other* paintings, keeping the large projects isolated. Chicago stopped and applied for federal grants, getting only one National Endowment for the Arts small grant of $2,000 (Chicago, *Dinner Party* 40). Her second solution was fundraising by public speaking — selling herself as part of the project; her third, again selling paintings not related to the project (245–47). By the time of "The Birth Project," however, Chicago adopted the tactic of pre-selling drawings that Christo uses, relying on the project to sell itself and disengaging her person from the finances.

Unfortunately, Chicago's fund-raising is not finished because of her concept of an artwork: for her, a work must be permanent and integral. The holding company for the work, Through The Flower, Inc., is still trying to raise the money for a permanent installation of "The Dinner Party" at a museum in a geodesic dome, a special wing designed to accommodate the piece's size. In an attempt to circumvent such problems, Chicago designed "The Birth Project" with smaller and larger pieces for two reasons: first, so that a museum would not be required to stage or maintain a huge single project; and second, so that smaller groups of craftswomen could work in homes instead of a workshop. Nonetheless, costs for "The Birth Project" still escalated beyond original estimates since Chicago emphasized durability in the materials, backings, and mountings for exhibition and simple transport. Nonetheless, the financial burden escalates for potential museum-homes with the custodial care of works that are irreplaceable and that suffer in handling.

Several facts about Chicago's fund-raising reveal much about her definitions of art. First, it does not exploit many traditional art-funding sources in America today, while the artists claims to be stressing the public and legal domains as her project. It seems, for instance, that she has not played to the galleries to the degree she could have. Yet this decision has largely eliminated her from public funding, without creating an alternate funding base; money for art tends to be funneled through art museums and institutions with traditions of fund-raising and public participation, or to visible projects with their own dynamics. Moreover, she has seemingly not gone to Europe for money, as Christo has. There more public money is earmarked for the self-proclaimed avant garde than in America, both through corporations and public coffers — "different" approaches to establishment art often become *causes célèbres*. Christo started using that narrative and then rejected it; Chicago remains steadfastly a U.S. project manager, probably because her references are much more culture-bound than his.

A second financial narrative is at play here as well since both projects relied heavily on volunteer labor, paying only for technical expertises not available in the volunteer pool (or creating a paid position when a volunteer position turned into a full-time job, by anyone's definition). Yet the question of payment for this labor came up, especially in the "Birth Project" (113). Chicago replied that you just couldn't pay for experimental craftwork — the work was emerging in a situation where no budget was possible. Too much work, for example, was "reverse stitched" (torn out) or rejected after hours' experimentation led to a piece that was simply not coming out to Chicago's standards. Christo's volunteers had much more predictable roles (such as "unfurling crew," which lasted no longer than a day).

Chicago's other justification for this financial structure was her focus on exhibition and outreach, on trying to get around the art establishment to the public, as Christo did: "My idea is to extend the 'democratization' of art (which is what I've been involved in for some time) so that it not only allows more people to participate in the art-making process, but also brings work to communities that would not ordinarily have access to high-quality art, particularly art from a woman's point of view" (Chicago, *Birth Project* 142). Chicago thus associates "democratization" with sharing financial responsibilities, not only with public access, as Christo does. She intends that the work challenge individuals and small groups (viewers and art makers), but she does not question traditional notions of ownership, control of artistic property, and legality. The documentation volumes, rather than the works, extend the process of consciousness raising into the more general public. We do not see the work: in their original circulation, "The Dinner Party" was exhibited once in San Francisco and once in Houston. "The Birth Project" needs money to continue storing, shipping, and maintaining the pieces (Chicago spends $13,000 a month in its final phases [*Birth Project* 154, 166, 220]).

Chicago and Christo thus place their large-scale artwork in very different public dynamics, while each asserts the connection of art and public over the involvement of galleries. Fiscal exigencies seem to surprise Chicago: she bemoans the present lack of a woman's support system to curate for the projects, and she wonders why the artist must take responsibility for this (*Birth Project* 223). Like Chicago, Christo sees that public involvement is the key to successful projects, yet he is not surprised to find out that he can't do it alone on the scale he wishes. Christo does not expect the public either to generate large parts of the work or to maintain it: each work is designed to be temporary, and even museums do not need to plan long-term high participation since they retain only drawings and small models. Chicago, in contrast, wants permanent recognition from museums for her projects, and on a major scale. She thus conflates her responsibility for the piece with its public dimension: such public support is her guarantee of the work's importance as an object.

Both artists therefore rely on public cocreation as an active part of their art. Christo plans the audience reaction as the guarantee of a work's later life; Chicago evaluates the work as an art object in order to secure artistic vision for a later audience. Yet these two narratives about "aesthetics" also mask very distinctive cultural control practices. From a feminist point of view, Chicago's assertion of position is a well-founded narrative: she demands the kind of public-sphere and official recognition so long denied to women. Again, however, this is a psychological explanation reflecting her personal preferences, not necessarily her access to the public sphere as an artist or her socialization. Unfortunately, the fact that Chicago has not turned to alternate funding strategies does not indicate that she is not aware of them — her education and previous gallery successes indicate that she does know where the money in the art world is, just as Christo does. Nonetheless, Chicago has been unwilling to compromise the gallery and museum notion of art to guarantee her funding, while Christo has been willing (if not eager) to turn his artwork into a commercial commodity. A sociological commonplace may be in effect here, a byproduct of gender: outsiders interpret a dominant culture conservatively once they gain admittance to it.

Two very different notions of the role of the artwork thus result from two similarly positioned artistic consciousnesses. Christo clearly accepts the modern art work as consumer product, even a transitory one. In contrast, Chicago supports the myth of the artist creator as a modern studio artist. Again, this may be conditioned by her female-outsider role: she wishes to include more people in the art establishment, not realign or redefine it, as Christo may have done. The two artists thus share a desire to rewrite cultures but in different ways.

Where Does Art Happen?
The Aesthetic Question

While Chicago and Christo purportedly share an ideal of public art and its educational function, where they differ most significantly is in their control of an aesthetic program (not simply of the artwork). Each artist's "group project" requires many hands in an act of cocreation. Yet Chicago's works are tied to her in a way that Christo's minimalist pieces can never be.

Christo subcontracts materials he cannot build; Chicago insists on learning new technologies so that she can control their adaptation. Christo lets engineers design his windproof anchors (and insures himself against design failures, as in the "Valley Curtain"); Chicago learns the rudiments of how to fire outsize china plates and assess fabric durability, working slowly instead of letting others supervise. Her control has thus been more absolute than his in the aesthetic sphere.

Christo chooses colors and textures and sets his specifications, then turn details over to engineers. If the project is not functioning, details are adjusted in consultation with the design firm — Christo does not attempt to learn technology for artistic effect, but relies on his consultants. In this, he is more industrial designer, instigating and coordinating a project, than artist-creator, controlling all its phases directly. In contrast, Chicago imposes her design and color standards on the fabric and clay arts in all phases, from planning to production. The china plates for "The Dinner Party," for instance, ended up being fired by others more skilled than Chicago but painted at least in part by herself. Moreover, in both of her group projects, she was clearly trying to replicate her signature blending of colors through needlework. In part, this was to guarantee "unity of the work" for these complicated pieces, but this nonetheless reflects her own standard for artistic quality. Chicago demands her personal stamp on the work, while Christo does not adjust his results to suit preconceived notions and so lets the work evolve more freely, even though his technical standards are as high as hers. In *Through the Flower*, Chicago even shows ambivalence about such "help" from the public: because she "needed to learn self-reliance," she kept the actual artwork in her hands. She also measured a project's costs in terms of her own production (how long it would take her and how much of "her work" in painting she would sacrifice). In consequence, she assumed almost total responsibility for the work's completion, even though she was not the major source of the labor going into it.

These two artists thus answer the question "Where does art happen?" by practicing their art in two very different ways.

Answer A: Audience as Art

As already noted, Christo's definition of the artwork stresses a project dynamics rather than the integrity of an artist's personality or aesthetics. In consequence, each work is an engineering masterpiece of great individuality, but its "artistic" characteristics are openly derived from engineering standards and pragmatics, not only aesthetic planning (for example, the colors of the "Wrapped Coast" and "Valley Curtain" were influenced by the synthetic materials that uniquely fit the sites' environmental requirements). Except for the workers who participate in the actual unfurlings as short-term volunteers, Christo's labor pool is generally paid and so may treat the whole thing as a business arrangement instead of an art project (as an occasional newspaper review indicates). Even documentation, such as the documentary film on the "Running Fence," is designed principally as a biography of the *project's* struggles, not the artist's, although Christo's role is not underplayed.

In fact, in the average project documentation text, Christo positions himself as a relative authority on a project rather than an individual artistic consciousness: he is someone a reporter can catch for an ephemeral interview
or who will show up in court on the day the permit process is going to be
argued. Christo thus displaces any aesthetic conflict about the work away
from being a dispute about his person, transforming it into questions about
the relationship between the work and its site or the legal restrictions on
that site. In his preferred narrative strategy, a work is designed "properly"
when a consensus is reached about the project's realization, usually among
Christo, a site owner or municipality, and a technical team. After that, any
aesthetic debates are often displaced by "more mundane" legal, financial, or
environmental battles. The "Running Fence" documentation volume, for instance, speaks of the project's "internal dynamics" (*Eigendynamik*), referring to a series of legal and personal confrontations preceding its realization. The work does not *ride* on this consensus; it *is* that dynamic
consensus: "Reality exists only in the mind of the people, it doesn't exist on
its own. I need to have that reality hold in the minds of people" (Crockett
and Samuels). The reception of the work is thus guaranteed the minute the
work is conceived, permitted, and executed; it is successful and complete
because it has been achieved, not simply for the way it looks.

Christo has thus split the artist-work-audience dynamic to put the artist
on the line in the planning, and less in the work. The art-quality of a work
is argued as part of several planning discourses and usually among the least
obvious of them. Since no one knows how a "wrapped coast" should look,
"traditional aesthetic criteria" or precedents cannot be used against it.
Moreover, some of the audience are precommitted to approve the project,
no matter how it comes out, because they have been involved in the planning — the artist is sharing risk. As Christo describes this process, each
work has a "software" period (the planning and permissions stage) and a
"hardware" period. The hardware phase is the actual construction, but, as
he explains,

> The software period is very creative, it is extremely artistic. It is very
> much like a writer or a poet in the way that there is no recipe, there is
> no precedent or book to create the right chemistry for things to work,
> or things to overcome. Blame yourself for the failure, listen to advice
> and be humble. What we are doing in that software period, we are
> creating a participatory public. Unlike normal work which is exhibited
> in a museum or a garden, people like it or dislike it, then go away. We
> sensitize the area and we create anticipation. We create a public who
> fantasizes. Many of them think how awful the things will look and try
> to stop us. They go to the hearings, they write letters, and make state-
> ments. And some of the people, many of the people try to help us.
> They say how beautiful it will look. But none of them *know* how it will
> look, not even myself. In the same way, creating that anticipatory pub-
> lic creates some kind of anticipation, some kind of energy, which is an
> essential part of the perception of the work. It is the visualizing, it is

how the people try to see or dream how the things will look. All that is impossible to have if you don't go through that process; you don't suddenly create this all by magic. You do not have an advertising company to round it all up. There is no way to do it, if you do not go one by one, and spend the time. (Crockett and Samuels)

Christo thus defines the artist as someone who manufactures public consensus *out of public opinion*. This is an important disclaimer: as an artist, Christo may stand at the head of a project, but not *above* the public. Without the public dynamic, the project will not exist, no matter what Christo thinks. Christo's art does not pretend to conform to standards that exist outside or above the public (not even in terms of a "refinement" of those public norms); his projects catalyze something in the public's mind, even if only its wildest fantasies. Despite his emphasis on a public dynamic, Christo does not credit creative individuals on his team, although the documentation clearly names participants (lawyers, design firms, and so on). He does not credit the individual workers directly: they name themselves gladly and proudly once a project has been realized.

Perhaps even more crucial to the definition of a Christo "artwork" is the fact that the work is not around long-term to have its artistic qualities second-guessed by experts. Its image remain behind in a set of drawings or photographs to stimulate the memories of those who saw it. Public reaction is thus credited next to (not in opposition to) Christo's own reactions to a piece. A typical media report on a Christo project will contain a person-on-the-street reaction such as "I didn't think I'd like it, but . . ." Aesthetics is what works for the viewer, and the first-hand viewer will always have authority over later commentators. Later museum exhibits and documentation will always be fragments: one anchor and five feet of fabric from the "Running Fence" may show it was made, but they will never exhaust it. Christo has thus removed his works from control of the art world, or rather, he has equalized the art world's access to them with that of the public. The projects are not intended to become exclusive icons of high culture, because tens of thousands of "ordinary people" have a more authentic experience of the work than museumgoers have.

Answer B: Art Is for the Art-Maker

The authority for and judgment of aesthetic quality are much more complicated for Chicago's audience and workers. Womanhouse taught Chicago her first lessons in public interface. Women workers had problems accepting women as authority figures in executing the project (Chicago, *Through the Flower* 108), while the male audience felt threatened (116). Their asymmetrical reactions affected funding as well. The largest contributions Chicago received were about $5,000, which indicates that they were not coming out of the corporate (male) purse. The "quality" of this feminist art project was also judged by these reactions: that's not art (that is, I don't like

it; it makes me nervous). Male reactions also easily mutated into general
antiwoman arguments turned against the "pseudo-artwork." The formal art
community did no better. Chicago shocked her audiences, as the avant
garde should, but she could not be evaluated as a proper artist-*auteur* if
she used volunteer labor and relinquished solo control of the project
(Chicago, *Birth Project* 6–7).

Chicago's understanding of audience reaction shows that she considered the artwork an object to be consumed by a public, and (as gradually
becomes obvious) in something like a museum setting. Chicago's descriptions of her workers emphasize her largely tacit definition of art as a museum-quality object. When she first discovered the world of china painters
that helped her conceive "The Dinner Party," she was amazed at how many
people were at their show and how poorly they exhibited (Chicago, *Dinner Party* 9). She thus began the project with an aesthetic judgment: Chicago evaluating a crafts show with the "eye of an artist." Even her description of art-making contained a quality judgment. Chicago felt china painters
"squandered their talents" with decorative projects reflecting woman's psychological dependencies (11). Some of this aesthetic judgment is projection:
Chicago feared a long-term project of this nature, enmeshed in simultaneous education, consciousness-raising, and the women's sphere instead of
the art world (29). If she had failed, she would have harbored feelings of
resentment that women didn't support her in either project (Chicago, *Birth
Project* 57).

If Chicago's idea of art was secure, the people she needed to realize it
often became the problem, whether they were workers or audience. For instance, men were integrated into the centralized studio of the first project
only with difficulty (Chicago, *Dinner Party* 34). In the 1980s, a few hardy
male souls, mainly husbands, happily worked with the "Birth Project." Chicago repeatedly tells her readers that she has to be the project's energy
source (36). Many of her workers agree that they had "no idea what professional work was" (Chicago, *Birth Project* 16). Such stresses caused by her
workers' consciousness-raising did not change Chicago's definition of the
art project, however. Instead, she systematically trained her workers to realize the artist's vision in the artist's terms.

What is significant, however, is that Chicago perceived the small-group
dynamics that were required for her "museum-quality art" as an onus
(Chicago, *Birth Project* 60). She accepted this onus by focusing on the
process of working, not on the work product. However, Chicago evaluated
her worker's pieces in terms of their "returns" as usable (that is, museum-
quality) art, a standard she achieved for fewer than half the pieces she
"gave out" (30). Adherence to such norms set the stage for authority conflicts when the designer and the needleworkers saw differently. Chicago
did try to accept the needleworkers' assessments about textures and technical possibilities, but she retained the determining vote, which often resulted
in group "ego struggles" that led to tears (88).

The letters of one worker, Pippa Davies of New Zealand, explain the dynamic Chicago typically set up around her essentially normative definition of art. Davies wrote Chicago: "Your letter has made me realize how very important it is to me that some of my ideas be incorporated into the piece. I know that the concept and the design are Judy's and that she is a major artist. But I am more than a pair of hands pushing a needle; this is a major undertaking for me, and I need a share in its interpretation from paper to fabric" (95). In Chicago's response letter, she validates the technique or idea that Davies was suggesting and congratulates her for sticking up for her work.

Despite cases like that of Davies, Chicago did not confront the conflict between workers' personal empowerment and the norms of "museum-quality" art. Chicago did not empower these women to extend designs or to design pendant works that might be included in the show. She only gave them their voices in the documentation, more or less as "servants of the work" (in "The Dinner Party," headed by group leaders called "runner mistresses"). Chicago bore the burden of this tacit choice by bridging over its inherent contradictions, building a support system for her workers: a newsletter, voluminous personal letters and phone calls, and "love packets" with documentation the women could keep and show their friends (Chicago, *Birth Project* 103). She recognized that the women were dealing with their fear of her and of professionalism as well as their self-conceptions in taking on such a large volunteer project (105). Sally Babson, the eventual technical supervisor of the project (in charge of stretching, bordering, and mounting to gallery standards), realized she was self-subverting by not acknowledging that finishing standards were possible: "I don't want to be organized! I don't even want to learn to be organized. Will it help? Will it *really really* help me become more — or better — or a different person?" (133). Chicago summarized that it was "very difficult for [Babson] to face the solitary task of becoming a professional and that she, like many of the needleworkers, had trouble working alone" (132). One woman went home and reported to her husband what she considered a surprising fact: Chicago had stressed that they needed to be active in the organizational structure of their work, to cocreate actively. The husband responded, "Welcome to the real world" (155).

Eventually Chicago told the story of her situation in social terms, not questioning the authority of her aesthetic decisions. She realized she was dealing with "middle-class women" used to a loving atmosphere, not challenge (134). Nonetheless, she concluded that these women needed to learn to structure their lives to structure work: "I am faced with the fact that most women seem totally confused about what power means" (148) and "[that they] find it hard to take responsibility" (155). She asserted that she would not work this way again, coping with other women's sense of isolation and their willingness to accept choices forced on them in order for them to escape individual responsibility (149). Ultimately, then, Chicago refused to

question her notion of museum-quality art — she bows to this social narrative, framed in that society's terms.

Chicago clearly claimed "esthetic authority" (her term, referring to the
art standard), while she denied asserting personal authority — a choice reflecting her knowledge of what the 1970s female market would bear, since
"authority" was often equated with male dominance, not shared work
(168). Yet she still had arguments about "whose job it was" to make the
piece work as needlework and as art (169), and she felt she was not always
successful in communicating the aesthetic norms for the piece (especially
her concept of "blending") to the workers so that they could take active responsibility for upholding them. Joyce Gilbert confirmed her frustration and
said Chicago exploded when she thought there were no "plans for the future of the piece" — when planning norms for high art were violated (170).

The background to such an argument also lies very much in the rhetoric of the 1970s feminist movement. It took Chicago herself a long time to
say that standards are not male or arbitrary per se (164). The artistic
"learning to see" was not arbitrary but a part of professional art and teach-
able to some degree (166–67). However, at the same time she was questioning the validity of technique as gendered, Chicago did not question the
origin of her concept of the artwork. Were there alternatives to "museum-
quality" art that may have validated women's sense of organization and
process? And why must the work be validated in a museum — aren't her
magnificent documentation volumes enough recognition for the artwork?
By the end of the "Birth Project," Chicago felt the work was finally taking
precedence over consciousness-raising: she had left to go paint on many
occasions where everything was becoming "her fault," and she made the
workers solve their own problems (218).

The consciousness-raising that happened to the women in the projects
also applied to Chicago, as she tells her own story and realizes how time-
bound it is. She finally acknowledges that there were social roles tied up
with aesthetic norms: "I then faced the struggle of accommodating myself
to a studio environment that was very different from what I thought a serious artist's space should be. Reared on modernist ideas of the isolated artist, I felt uncomfortable working with so many strangers . . . This challenged my internalized beliefs that I really was too difficult to be around"
(Chicago, *Dinner Party* 248). Chicago herself may not have been too difficult to be around, but her definition of the work of art may have been —
an issue she really did not confront head-on.

Chicago's women learned her lessons well: they knew they learned
honesty and responsibility about work habits, and they discovered how to
take care of themselves as social beings and how to solve problems
(Chicago, *Dinner Party* 221–22). They rediscovered missing role models in
serious women in art history (237). They also learned to validate their female perceptions and experience as "constructive input" to art (232). A real
surprise to many was that a lack of formal training in art was not a sufficient excuse for noninvolvement (229). Chicago's workers learned the in-

stitutional tricks that kept women in their places, but it is questionable if they learned about art in any other sense than museum art — they learned the dominant socialization of the art institution.

The question of the socialization of the art-making process and the artist reveals a very real asymmetry between Christo's and Chicago's definitions of art. Christo defined art to accommodate both the piece and the workers. When something didn't work in Christo's project, the piece went back to the design engineers to be redone. Errors were to be expected, and professionals should be able to fix them. Christo's personal position was never in question: he had a position of authority and a clear chain of command about the production of the work, so he accepted change in the project.

Chicago did not have the luxury of a trained staff among her workers or the ability to draw on extant authority hierarchies. She needed to build her organization of women from the ground up, not buy it, as she could do more easily for the "Holocaust Project" a decade later. By the end of the "Birth Project," however, Chicago's team functioned professionally. Unfortunately, this may not be attributable directly to the project: these needle-workers may be a younger generation of women, interested in urban homesteading instead of china painting and altar cloth societies (key resources for the "Dinner Party"). Chicago believed that she was facilitating women's art. Yet from another perspective, she was actually propagating male hierarchy and authority in the work's status, even when she championed women's art themes, materials, and organizational "weaknesses." She taught her workers how to achieve success within a male hierarchy and how to find their voices within that hierarchy, but she did not identify the tacit power structures her work encompassed. For Chicago, the artwork controls the personal dynamics between worker and artist, and acts as the source of power and authority in the production and reception of the artwork (Witzling).

These two definitions of the artwork as aesthetic object reflect two different (and probably highly gendered) reactions to the sociological situation of art in the United States. Christo's definition of art as audience reaction is utterly consistent with his avoidance of the art establishment and a successful tactic through which to maintain his personal control of the works; it thus represents a challenge to the art establishment because it redefines how the artist behaves, but it does not necessarily affect any other establishments. Chicago's reliance on a concept of museum-quality art, in contrast, is aesthetically more conservative but much more of a challenge to both the art establishment and the public: she is demanding a change in the concept of art itself, and hence of the society using that concept.

Some Conclusions:
Art, Artists, Gender

These two artists' concepts of their roles and their artworks clearly rest on a shared perception of the roles for art and the practices expected of artists in the United States. Chicago and Christo agree on the marginalization of the artist and on the problems associated with funding, while choosing different thematics and aesthetics — that is, while choosing different ways to interact with the public in affirming their respective art.

Chicago's aesthetic agenda is aimed at social change, at using her work and her image as an artist to reframe the value of women's experience in the art world. Her work thus points to what may still be the real crux of woman's problems in art: internalized self-image problems in females, exacerbated by the kind of organizational powerlessness sanctioned in the dominant culture of the 1970s and early 1980s (if not beyond). However, at the same time, she is writing her critique of that society into gendered terms that may not be entirely appropriate, although these terms offer extremely plausible narratives to the contemporaneous public. For example, Chicago's difficulties with the projects may stem as much from class differentials among her workers as they do from gender socialization, no matter her claims. "The Dinner Party" was particularly middle-class in its stitchers, while "The Birth Project" acquired at least a few upper-middle-class, college-educated workers (including some grown-up hippies, the last replacements for workers in the traditional stitchery crafts, which are dying arts in the younger generations). Both organizational behavior and the willingness to violate social taboos vary between these two groups. Chicago's greatest problems stemmed less from her woman's imagery in the public sphere than from the behavioral norms she imposed on the women producing and consuming those images: the middle class always holds most tenaciously to social taboos. Christo had many fewer aesthetic problems in this sense simply because he wasn't trying to make any of his audiences acknowledge art; he was just trying to stage his project, whether it was considered genius or a sideshow.

This blindness to class also may have impacted Chicago's fund-raising: elites tend to be the fund-raisers in projects (Tuchman 186–87). To join Chicago, a woman had to promise a significant number of work hours, which favored the participation of in-home females with few outside interests but enough education to react to her offer of a prestige project. In a similarly middle-class placement of her activity, Chicago never developed a traditional "ladies' auxiliary" for her women's art project — there were no t-shirts, scarves, bake sales, or balls. In the feminist sensibility of the time, such was unthinkable, and so Chicago excluded an area of public organization in which elite women traditionally excel. In contrast, Christo played elite and popular culture against each other more actively. He unabashedly sells to galleries (mainly in Europe) to set up art for the American masses. In excluding such money from her projects, Chicago is embracing the artist-outsider myth much more firmly than Christo does. In her version, she is doubly alienated, as artist and woman, whereas Christo is alienated only as a Bulgarian in a capitalist country (not as an artist — he simply doesn't use the term).

Despite these differences, however, Christo and Chicago share an awareness of the gap between art for the public and art in museums. However, Christo's documentation belongs in a museum, not the project itself: his art is supposed to aid ordinary people in reconceptualizing the everyday world. In contrast, Chicago brings the museum to people who have never seen "good" art before (and she extends this work in her "Holocaust Project"). She does not challenge the existence of museums (traditionally, where validation and power rest). Instead, she wishes to inject women's concerns and craft techniques into the high canon of art (museum- quality art) and art history. Chicago thus accommodates women by adding a dimension to the museum-quality debate; Christo reorganizes the entire debate about museums to upset their control over him. Feminists from the 1970s would say that he appropriates his freedom to do so more easily than Chicago ever could, simply because he is male. Yet the sociology behind their choices is at least as important as other gender factors (for a parallel discussion, see particularly the critique of Evelyn Fox Keller's notions of gender bias in science offered by Kelly Oliver). That is, the asymmetry in Christo's and Chicago's willingness to manipulate the system rather than changing it may be based on their gender-specific internalized (or introjected, following Julia Kristeva and Jacques Lacan) notions of their cultural power. In consequence, when they tell the stories of their roles as artists and of their works, each is inserting his or her practice into a social framework under the cover of an aesthetic argument.

For instance, the reader is easily led to believe that Chicago found "psychologically damaged womanhood" when she had organizational problems, and that her finished works met and meet with resistance from dominant patriarchal culture.[5] She tells a doubled tale of the dominant power structures of her society, as she sees them (and in ways reflecting what Luce Irigaray called "This Sex Which Is Not One"), showing how her works reenact the kind of alienation from the dominant society that she as an artist also felt. Christo agrees that dominant societies alienate individuals (a lesson he learned early, in the East Bloc), but he refuses to reenact that domination, even if only in the name of countering it. Instead he robs the dominant culture of its power over him by eschewing its words: he is doing projects for the people, not art for the galleries. Chicago is thus trying to rewrite society's stories about art for her audience, while Christo offers his audience (not himself) an opportunity to write their own narratives about art (or anything else). Christo's project exploits the dominant culture through manipulation of its discourses, hoping to change it through innuendo; Chicago's art sustains a direct challenge both to that culture and to the institutional authority rejecting it.

What we see in their narratives, however, is that each artist is stretching to assert an artistic identity and to claim the social authority in that identity. As Kristeva explains: "An ego, wounded to the point of annulment, barricaded and untouchable, cowers somewhere, nowhere, at no other place than the one that cannot be found . . . . phantoms, ghosts, 'false cards': a stream of spurious egos and for that very reason spurious objects, seeming egos that confront undesirable objects" (47). Such an ego is doing more than reacting personally (neurotically) to society; it is also pointing to social *abjection*, to those areas that a dominant society has declared beyond the limits of expressibility — in an area that could fundamentally decenter the dominant power relations of society. The cases of Christo and Chicago point clearly to several of these moments of abjection in U.S. society and play out in their practice as artists.

One of these areas of social abjection in the United States of the 1970s and 1980s is the issue of gender. Christo does not evoke gender roles explicitly, but he is clearly aware of them. It is significant that the original plans for the "Wrapped Reichstag" had his name, but when the project came to realization in 1995, he and his wife (and long-term collaborator) Jeanne-Claude got equal billing in the press and on documentation volumes. There has been no particular comment on this publicly; it is as if a long-known secret had finally been acknowledged. This low-key announcement of a modern artist's collaboration with a female is typical of Christo's approach to his art since he consistently frames the artwork as event rather than focusing on the artist's creativity or on the artistic qualities or caliber of the work. Yet his acknowledgment of Jeanne-Claude in 1995 thus tells us something about how the modern art scene has changed: it will now tolerate collaboration, and collaboration with a female — two "abjects" of the modern art scene of the 1960s and 1970s, which still relied on marketing the artist as genius (and hence as unique) and all too often still defined that genius as male (Nochlin). However, what that naming of names implies is still not entirely clear to us as readers: is Christo acknowledging that the art world will tolerate females, or that the public will? What is clear is that his stance vis-à-vis the gender of artistic production is part of his general resistance to the institutional constraints of his culture. He is quite happy with staging a successful event like the "Reichstag," even if the media remember it primarily as a tourist event. And public events in the 1990s (in the U.S. and in the European West) can fairly easily accommodate a female presence in a way they could not in the 1970s, particularly if she is billed as something closer to "comanager" of the project than as cocreator.

Chicago's recent reactions to and manipulation of that same art market by use of gender point to a similar shift in her perceptions of the public and art worlds. Her 1970s projects were narrated as thwarted by what she saw as opposition to the female in modern art and by masculinist prejudices in the art market — antipathies not necessarily shared by the general public (especially the female public), which often liked (or at least sup-

ported) the works decried by the professionals. She thus posited a rift between the public reception of a work and that of the art world, as did
Christo did, but with a significant difference. She clearly hoped that public
reaction would force an equivalent reaction from the "official art world,"
which it did not do. That world intersects with too many other official
worlds, and so, for example, her 1990 hope of housing "The Dinner Party"
fell victim to the same wave of public fiscal and moral conservatism that
fueled the Mapplethorpe debacle (see Strand and Lippard).

Such experiences clearly affected Chicago's self-promotion strategies.
Her 1993 "Holocaust Project," for instance, was envisioned as an independent exhibition designed to tour for at least two years, one that could be
booked by museums but also by other cultural institutions, even of more
moderate size, or by anyone else interested in the Holocaust, a visible interest in U. S. society today. The typical booking made it into an event as
well, usually surrounded by lecture series and her personal appearances; it
was even booked into spaces outside the official walls of museums. In
Austin, Texas, for instance, it was booked under the auspices of the Laguna
Gloria Art Museum and various arts auxiliaries of that museum, the city,
and the state; but it was staged in empty commercial space in a downtown
bank building as a "satellite campus" for the museum. Chicago has thus
learned the value of reaching her public by going directly to it, circum-
venting to a degree the narrowest spheres of the art world — the new institutional and financial lesson about patronage in the 1990s that Christo
and his "Wrapped Reichstag" calendars also reflect.

A review of Chicago's 1996 expansion of her autobiography, *Beyond the
Flower*, points to a second issue hidden in the comparison of these two
modern artists:

> Ms. Chicago's insistence on injecting herself into her art's meaning, as if
> it couldn't mean anything without her anecdotes, her thoughts, her nar-
> ration, annoys. And yet, clearly, she can't help it. . . . One senses that
> the woman she really is interested in, the one who most wishes she
> could have helped up, was her own younger self. (Schillinger 21)

Schillinger stresses that a number of women artists have come to prominence in the twenty years since "The Dinner Party" first shocked its audience and that Chicago's newest projects suffer from an "excess of explanation and justification" that undercut the power of her art. These assessments
refer to "The Holocaust Project" as well, which Schillinger feels is undercut
by the wall texts that critics hated.

Yet Chicago believes she is as "misunderstood as . . . ever" (Schillinger
21). If one looks at the "Holocaust Project," however, several other factors
come into play about its reception. Most evidently, the images she uses run
against many of the dominant explanations of the Holocaust as a unique
event in history. The centerpiece work is "Rainbow Shabat," a stained-glass
window depicting ten guests of various ethnicities at a Seder meal given by
a traditional Jewish family; many images juxtapose the inhumanity of the

Holocaust with other moments in modern genocide. Each of the ethnicities represented is, however, somewhat stereotyped (especially by headgear — the Arab is wearing a head cloth; the Chinese male wears a Mao cap). Chicago has to accompany each image with a text about what it is supposed to do: a reader's guide to the work's impact. In this, she is again trying to rewrite central discourses of modern U. S. culture, using what seem to be vaguely 1960s visions of a shared humanity. No wonder that reactions were not uniformly positive, since she is pushing her audience instead of accommodating the last fifty years of history on which their identities are built. One should note that, in contrast with this extreme political rhetoric, Christo did not publicize the politics around the "Reichstag" in his final realization of the project, no matter how prominent those politics were earlier in the documentation. It is thus not only gender that figures into the artistic politics of these two artists but, as noted earlier, Chicago's more overt desire to rewrite the dominant political scene.

The question of authorship of the "Holocaust Project" puts another spin on Chicago's politics. A number of the project's pieces are "manipulated photographs": her "husband-photographer" (the term is from the project handout leaflet) Donald Woodman took them on the couple's trip to European concentration camps and Jewish cemeteries, and then she worked with them in various ways (from air-brush painting and silk screening to dissection). But the results are billed as *her* project, even when the wall-texts acknowledge acts of cocreation. Where Christo "suddenly" acquired a coworker (who, by implication, had been working with him for twenty years), Chicago, "the descendant of twenty-three generations of rabbis," offers "a fiercely personal record of her quest to imagine the unimaginable" (leaflet text), even though she and Woodman set out together.

These comparisons point all too easily to what might be called Chicago's relatively neurotic approach to self-aggrandizement, as Schillinger was suggesting. But this choice also speaks to another abjection of U. S. culture. Both artists are having an easier time now than they had twenty years earlier, even though their press may not be much better than it was in the 1970s; many critics still say "it's not art" to both. And the audiences have become more tolerant of public females — Chicago can manage funding with museums (even if peripherally) more easily to run her own show, and Christo can market Jeanne-Claude along with himself. Chicago and Christo have each overcome the image of 1970s female socialization that had left her to struggle, him to elide his coworker. Yet Chicago is still maintaining the politics of gender in her role as an artist if not in her artworks. Now she has abandoned her claims to "high art" in favor of seeking "to engage viewers and communities [in] enlightened dialogue that can contribute to a transformation of consciousness" (leaflet text). She still treats art as responding to the ethical/moral norms of culture and so conceives of her own practice as related to her person, whereas Christo continues to frame his artworks as technical challenges (legal, engineering, crowd-control, ecology, or preservation), just as he did in his earliest works. Chicago seeks to bring her personal view of history to an audience, accompanying images with words; Christo takes an experience to an audience, letting them write it into history in their terms, not his.

The asymmetry in these positions may be as attributable to the two artists' respective positions within national cultures as it is due to gender or class issues from the art community. Following models for feminist empowerment familiar from the 1960s and 1970s United States, Chicago still tries to insert her point of view into official history, speaking from her authority as a female and the descendent of rabbis, even as she is less fixated on inserting her art into official institutions. From this perspective, even her early experiments created artworks that inserted women into history and into art history (including herself); she created images that reflect less a feminist aesthetics than the images that her audience in the 1970s and 1980s would have expected from a "woman artist" with a specific political agenda. Chicago's early projects were feminist in the same way that her current one is anti-genocide: they confront an audience (male and female) with uncomfortable images that question the authority of the dominant culture. They are thus utterly bound to the culture of that ideology. The "Holocaust Project," no less than the earlier "Dinner Party" and "Birth Project," thus is conceived with a paradox at its heart: an artist attempts to intervene in history aesthetically (rather than just documenting it) yet by manipulating images drawn from the dominant culture and by justifying her intervention through an appended narrative explaining her point of view. Again in contrast, Christo offers even less text about his projects now than he did twenty years earlier.

Following these two artists from their years of struggle to their visibility today thus shows us a harrowing message about gender in U. S. culture today. Chicago and Jeanne-Claude, as women artists, can now be accepted more easily by the audience, and to a degree by public institutions, and they are accepted as speakers for more than women's issues. Chicago can be a public individual who is woman, Jew, social critic — a plurality of roles whereas she earlier had access principally to one. And Jeanne-Claude can appear as part of an equal team of private individuals staging public events. But Chicago and Christo also share a vision of the public that is doggedly bourgeois if not still patriarchal: their world still opposes public and art institutions, "official" and "public" culture. And concomitantly, an elite critic in the *New York Times Book Review* (Schillinger) can call Chicago's approach to public consciousness-raising outdated, but her work is reaching out further than it ever had before in terms of topic. Yet while she is offering critiques of world politics, she still does so by stressing her authority as a female, not just as an artist.

Although Christo's world seems almost gender-free (or gender-neutral), his self-representation also confirms the essential continuity of gendered consciousness over the last twenty years. On two continents, Christo has worked to avoid official history at all points and has interacted only with museums and galleries on his terms. He has not solicited granting agencies.

One might say that his Bulgarian past left him with a permanent skepticism toward official narratives of any sort or that his exile status left him without the kind of cultural base to work against that Chicago clearly had in the United States. In the 1970s, for "Running Fence" as for the original "Reichstag," Christo's projects aimed at audience consciousness-raising about the natural and created landscapes and about the legal and social restrictions placed on experience; those spaces were not seen as gendered in his planning — although they did not allow for his wife's collaboration to be credited, probably for various reason beyond simply the gender/art stereotypes of the era. But the wide publicity for his projects on two continents indicates one further twist on the role of women in the United States. While reports in both Europe and the U. S. media about the "Wrapped Reichstag" credit Christo and Jeanne-Claude equally today, as they credited Christo alone earlier, that female presence is achieved in different contexts. European reports still stress these artists' political engagement, as they did twenty years ago. U. S. media reports have, in contrast, begun to stress their art as event — and U. S. publicity events gain good press when women participate, while politics are less tolerant of their presence. Western culture has become more tolerant of women's presence, but official U. S. culture may be less tolerant of women's authority — which may explain the harsh reviews of Chicago's "Holocaust Project" in another way.

Following two artists through twenty years and two continents thus also allows us to trace aspects of the gender debate in U. S. society, showing how gender has been revalued as part of social practices and expectations — as part of the narratives through which a culture organizes its perceptions of reality and the lives interwoven with it.

Notes

[1] In brief, anonymous paragraphs, *Art in America* 78 (December 1990): 37, reports on the donation being called off, with further details provided by *ARTnews* 89, no. 10 (December 1990): 61–62. John Strand noted that the work was being referred to as "3-D Pornography," and Lucy R. Lippard provided the final postmortem, stressing that "media sensationalism" and the attitude of Congress were responsible for the debacle.

[2] Christo's "Wrapped Reichstag" project fared better in postreunification Germany. Stephen Kinzer, in the *New York Times*, reported on his renewed attempts to realize the project (7 January 1994) and then on various political attempts to block it (15 and 18 January 1994). Finally, on 25 February 1994, the German Parliament voted 292–223 to give the project a go-ahead (reported in the *New York Times* on 26 February 1994). It was unfurled in summer 1995.

[3] See the exemplary report in *Newsweek*, 21 October 1991: 70, and the reports on the deaths in the *New York Times,* 28 October and 1 November 1991.

[4] See the article by Calvin Tomkins on Max Neuhaus for a typical discussion of the dynamics between a public work of art and the artist, in this case working with sound.

[5] Participants' reports on Chicago's projects differ in ways typical of the gendered stereotypes of the day. One of the "Dinner Party" potters, Ken Gilliam, summarized: "I think men operate in such a way that they avoid coming into contact with not knowing something, particularly when it's connected to oneself. Admitting my weakness and vulnerability, remaining open to input and criticism about my ability to operate with other people — this is what I've had the most difficulty with" (quoted in Chicago, *Dinner Party* 224). Gilliam is speaking about himself almost in the third person, and he evaluates his performance without articulating a specific reaction, which is a typical male pattern of speech. He was in the project as an expert potter (bringing to it an expertise that Chicago could not find in a woman, in this case) yet has caught the project's "consciousness-raising": he pinpoints one power discourse he had trouble with and learned to articulate what men do not articulate traditionally.

Leonard Skuro, another potter, also casts the notion of sharing of work differently than the women, at the same time valorizing it in a way Chicago could not — he almost expresses her ideal better than she does. In the design process, he realized that he was seeing the "Dinner Party" plates as shapes while Chicago was seeing images, which led them to work very closely, especially on the three-dimensional plates. But he would express this work as if it were task-based: "Judy would do the curves because she had the patience. I would do undercuts and the flat areas because I could make the flat areas very flat. Judy's areas were dependent on my areas, and my areas were dependent on Judy's. Nothing looks good unless what is next to it looks good" (225).

In describing their work on the plates, the female potters and painters would interface their feelings with their technical descriptions in a more personal way, talking about their "preconceived notions" (Judye Keyes [226]) or the personal risks they had to take (e.g., the china painter Sharon Kagan [227]).

Conclusion: Pushing the Margins

We are today in what Russell Jacoby calls the "age of academe." Prominent academic feuds generate major media coverage, from the debate at Stanford about multiculturalism (see Vobejda), through the activities of the National Association of Scholars, to the case of Paul de Man. In the media, humanists are depicted as being involved in arcane battles, as, for example, when Yale University got media space in the mid-1980s as the new literary-critical think tank of American academia (as in Campbell, J. Hillis Miller, and Lehman) and again in the mid-1990s in its unionization battles with teaching assistants (Eakin). What critics see as central seems marginal at best to reporters and the general public alike.

Despite such bad press, these critics have not really acknowledged the public's right to a road map for these newly created academic margins. There have been rare attempts to explain or justify what professors do and why that might be good for the general public (such as *Criticism in the University*, by Gerald Graff and Reginald Gibbons). In even rarer cases, academics have believed they are speaking for the needs of the culture at large, as in the case of two familiar titles: Alan Bloom's *Closing of the American Mind* and E. D. Hirsch's *Cultural Literacy* (the latter alluded to in the introduction to this volume. Both, however, believe in their right to set the agenda for the reading practices of the more general public. Bloom wants the classics taught as a "common heritage" so that today's students will have contact with the great minds of the past. Hirsch more modestly asserts that contact with the culture of the parents is contingent on familiarity with a body of names and concepts that have become part of the public mind. Both critics are arguing for kinds of continuity within the institutionalized cultural heritage of the dominant culture; in consequence, they assume their authority over that culture's tradition of reading.

As the public press testifies, these assumptions have erected a wall between these academic critics and their purported public. The "cultural heritage" they tout is a creation of a particular historical moment (albeit a long moment), and by asserting its continued immutable validity, critics are in many ways ignoring the possibility that that history has changed — or that the dominant culture that created their institutions has. Current evidence suggests that such a shift is now in process. Graff's *Professing Literature*, a brilliant internal history of the profession of English, shows how departments have always altered their shapes as social-historical desiderata turned into institutional-internal problems in turf management. And today, The *Chronicle of Higher Education* regularly reports on the graying of the professoriat that itself signals an imminent generational shift.

Inside the academy, a subgenre of new books has emerged that purport to teach academics and their students how to deal with historical change in their institutions (for example, DeNeef et al.'s *The Academic's Handbook* and Rosovsky's *The University: An Owner's Manual*). But in general, such texts concentrate on improving the institutional systems as they stand, in more or less their present historical incarnations. Paul A. Bové's *Intellectuals in Power* suggests the dark side of such engaged professionalism hiding behind its historical walls: "[As I planned the book] it became more and more striking how resistant most traditional humanistic and belletristic forms of literary critical or theoretical activity are to admitting any involvement of criticism or theory with specific forms of power, politics, desire, or interest" (ix).

Literature departments have, to be sure, accepted the truth that their activities are tied into the norms of the dominant culture. The fact is documented in internecine wars about how departments should incorporate into their traditional canons what heretofore have been identified as the margins. However, accepting the margins into the institution supporting the center (the dominant culture) simply acknowledges how cultural centers are involved with power, politics, desire, and interest. Such an absorption does not necessarily allow for an open dialogue between the margins and the center of the culture but may only add compartments behind the institutional walls. And so the public press has justifiably reacted to the essential rudeness and condescension of this position, often by telling embarrassing anecdotes about how far removed professorial debates are from the "real concerns" of society (most notably, in the last few years, aimed at high-dollar institutions like Stanley Fish and the "Fish Tank" at Duke University) or about the "politically correct" liberals who are purportedly undermining the credibility of American education by teaching politics instead of traditional wisdom. Academic criticism has thus been gracious enough to invite others into its institutions, but it still treats the more general culture with a rudeness based on its assertion of authority, facilitated by denying that its authority is historically connected to the dominant centers of their shared culture (or to past versions of those centers).

Today's critics have been preserving the culture (and its "approved" opposition) within the academic traditions; they have, in contrast, largely ignored the historical and cultural imperatives that have formed the current states of both their academy and the culture(s) outside it. As the studies contained in the present volume have tacitly argued, it is not culture that must be tested by the critics (assessed for its "truth" value or its utility as "high" or "popular" culture). I would rather argue that critics and their institutions must be tested by that culture, in an active dynamic rather than as a pass-fail test aimed at admission.

Professional academic criticism at this historical moment has largely failed to subject itself to these crucial tests, even while it appears to have adapted to many of the new cultural imperatives in the U. S. context. To clarify why these failures are particularly pernicious, I need to turn to several recent fallacies about the purported changes in academic criticism to show how they do not answer adequately to the challenge of cultural-historical change.

Fallacy 1: Reclaiming "Critical Interpretation" as Applicable to Culture Means That the Critic Reads Culture Critically

The preponderance of debates about academic criticism's role in critiquing the limitations of dominant culture reflects a crisis in today's academic culture, which since the 1970s has theorized about changes in reading practice in order (purportedly) to subvert the authority of older schools of criticism and their hegemony over today's readers. In retrospect, however, countering theory with new theory merely shifts balances within the academy — it has left the nonprofessional reader in a deauthorized margin, even as it has pulled "professional criticism" or literary theory into the limelight.

When W. J. T. Mitchell introduces his book *Against Theory*, for example, he presents "theory" (schools of literary criticism) by formulating a series of oppositions between "theory" and "nontheory" (here somewhat excerpted):

THEORY IS	THEORY IS NOT
reflection	immediate perception
fundamental principles	surface phenomena
models, schemes, systems	things in themselves
. . .	. . .
speculations	traditional wisdom

(6)

Mitchell thus places theory "at the beginning or end of thought, providing first principles from which hypotheses, laws, and methods may be deduced, or summarizing, encoding, and schematizing practice in a general account. It is unhappy with the middle realm of history, practical conduct, and business as usual" (7). Mitchell clearly hopes make interpretation "pragmatic," which he defines as dealing with textual meaning and intention in order to establish critical conversations. Still, understanding texts is something under the direction of abstract principles.

From the perspective of the present volume, however, even such progressive suggestions as Mitchell's purport to redefine the act of criticism as an act of reading. However, he still leaves the act of reading subject to the test of professional readers (as a "critical conversation" or interpretations). Mitchell is not alone in calling "pragmatic" what is essentially a move to preserve the domain of the professional critic (reader) in the form it has enjoyed essentially since the Second World War. The Modern Language Association is, for example, heavily invested in producing a series of volumes called *New Approaches to Teaching*, which deals with various of the classics. These volumes aid critic-teachers in integrating new cultural perspectives into the classroom to make humanities more relevant to a new generation of students.

However, such solutions, like Mitchell's, are actually suggestions for critic-teachers to incorporate new types of display behavior into the academy's acceptable canon of authorized readings. Even the "new readings" they are suggesting are new *professional* readings, new readings accepted into the departments behind the wall of the academy. They are new readings for old critics adapting to new moments in cultural history; readings that purport to derive from historical change but do not necessarily participate in general culture.

Newer "metavolumes" from the theory debate take other tacks on the issue, with essentially the same result. Barbara Herrnstein Smith speaks not against theory but of *Contingencies of Value*, as her book's title makes clear. She addresses theorists as agents of valuation within a society, involved in varying social economies of sign and subjecthood (see particularly 173 to the end). She posits that the theorist's activity is contingent on the various contexts in which it is enacted, especially with respect to the critic's individual political position. Smith thus tries to make the theorist into a new humanist who can acknowledge that critical activity is relative to history, "continuously changing, irreducibly various, and multiply configurable" (183). In these diagnoses, she stresses how the critic-theorist transacts the value systems of the culture in which the activity is conducted; she does not, however, suggest that these strategies of reading should serve anyone but the critics or those who join them within the academy.

These critics clearly acknowledge the power of their positions within the academy as a function of their service to cultural ends. In this vein, an essay by Jacques Derrida, "Sendoffs," is exemplary. Derrida reports to the French government about the teaching of philosophy, stressing how a philosophical system or theoretical program from a particular academic discipline is tied to a "destination or goal" (10). For his France, this goal is realized within the locus of an institution and is overtly tied to a desired student outcome and a set of pedagogical practices (41). Through this institution and its practices, a theory "inscribes itself" within the field of history, and in instincts, society, and economy. A theory about appropriate readings will, in essence, establish itself as a discipline within an institution by enacting the evaluation standards and sanctions that are tied up with the

historical moments that initiated it; it will also confer on students the rewards that a particular culture distributes through that institution and its
ideology. In Derrida's view, then, a discipline and its underlying theory represent the formalization of a set of cultural values, administered by professionals and guaranteed by the institutions that are empowered to distribute
the rewards earmarked for that purpose by the general culture.

Derrida's essay is only one among a legion that acknowledge the power
of critics within institutions, as administrators of cultural values. Jonathan
Arac and Barbara Johnson, in *Consequences of Theory*, have no difficulty in
locating a large number of discussions about the professionalization of theory. And others (for instance, Bruce Robbins and Cornel West in that volume) observe that theory is institutionalized to justify critics' roles as
"oppositional intellectuals," upholding values to oppose human suffering
and aid self-realization. With this extension, "theory" has today become
clearly identified with a political agenda, to be administered from within the
academy for the benefit of the culture as a whole; the critic becomes the
ultimate engaged intellectual, able to articulate cultural values in particular
ways.

Unfortunately, all these positions rest on a central self-delusion: that critics' readings can be the equivalents of critical reading of culture — a rude
assumption that places the academy in an absolute position of authority
over culture. However, the opposite situation is more probable, given the
state of the modern university: the academic critic is not in authority over
culture; he is in authority because of it. When critics change, they do so not
only to lead culture but to maintain the kind of authority that they may lose
when history changes culture.

Academic criticism is not, to be sure, hermetically sealed off from culture and history. The models for reading culture that the academic critic
uses do, indeed, arise out of historical contexts: an example is the common
assertion that both Freudianism and Marxism arose out of the tensions of
bourgeois European culture. Moreover, these models can be critical of that
culture. But when the academic critic assumes such a critical stance (even
an oppositional one), he or she is assuming a critical position that is part of
that culture and is enacting part of that culture's self-image. Such a critic is
not the *other* to that culture but is only enacting one relation of margin to
center encompassed within it. That enactment can yield a critic's reading
within culture, but not necessarily a critical reading of that culture.

Hidden behind such a critic's reading, however, is the question of why
the culture that institutionalizes the critic's job tolerates this particular strategy of criticism. In other words, it is a fallacy to assume that the "critic" institutionalized within a dominant culture (or even one purportedly at its
margins) is actually being critical of that culture; purported margins that are
incorporated onto the official playing field of their culture may be nondo-
minant, but they are not true margins. "Oppositions" are part of extant
structures. In contrast, Roger Caillois notes that there is another kind of
margin within the established sciences: those "facts" that institutionalized

scientists prefer to call "anomalies" in order that these facts cannot be seen as *systems*, as parts of reality that need to be accounted for in their theories (13). From Caillois's perspective, then, one should rather say that the true margin of a culture is not one that is factored into it officially but one that does not exist in its optics.

These margins are the ones that the studies collected in the chapters of this book are intended to speak from, margins that fall outside the "normal" disciplinary fields, as I explained in the introduction. Yet these margins may well be safely within the optics of general culture (which easily asks why, for instance, John Irving would write a novel "like that") while not necessarily within those of official science or criticism. What I am discussing here I prefer to call *critical* readings of culture rather than *critics'* readings. They often violate official critical perspectives and tend to undercut the performance of a critic's power as institutionalized. For this reason, critical readings of culture often come from nonauthorized perspectives, be they willfully assumed by a critic engaged in self-critique of his or her critical practice or as accidental eruptions from outside the academy. The point of a critical reading in this sense is to enable *any* reader, not just an institutionally authorized one, to pursue an understanding (a reading) of culture by systematically working through a text as it stands in dialogue with a moment in cultural history (present or past). Where the point of a critic's interpretation is often the reenactment of official culture's values, then, a critical reading of culture tries to reopen a dialogue between a text and the various historical forms of culture with which it can be in dialogue (only *one* of which is academic criticism).

The introduction to this volume has already alluded to this shift in expressing the dichotomy between "reading culture" and "the critics' text." To assume an identity between a critic's critique and a critical reading of culture is perhaps the primary fallacy of today's literary criticism since particularly academic critics are part of that culture — "loyal opposition," delegated to producing performances ("interpretations," "readings") that reveal the constitution of that culture's elite and its past values. This power is perhaps insidious. Ensconcing a (somewhat) loyal opposition within an institution of culture is, in many ways, the strategic game of a cultural elite — an elite that the academic critic is empowered to be in conversation with. Still, we must remember that even the academic critic turned "oppositional intellectual" rarely can claim to be a true voice from the margin. The critic is speaking for the institutionalized (if alternative) values of the dominant culture, attempting to assert a kind of dominance over the general culture outside that institution, not necessarily speaking from that more general culture or about it.

To this point, I have tried to debunk the fallacy of assuming a necessary priority of the critic over culture and to question the possibility of a professional critic's being a voice to criticize general culture. Now, however, I must turn more directly to the issue of power: to address the fallacy about the critic as an empowered individual, to ask whether the critic's power transfers to contexts outside the institution.

Fallacy 2: The Power of the Academic Critic Is a Power in Culture

As we have seen, institutionalized criticism has power because its professionals prescribe procedures, choosing some and discarding others, in order to exemplify the cultural values for which they stand. These critical professionals thus have clear roles inside their academics, inside their cultures. But an additional question begins to intrude itself here: do those professionals have *any* predictable roles outside those institutions (or even outside their specific academic disciplines)? Are critics strong readers outside their academic institutions, and, if so, what kind of readers?

A version of this question was posed two centuries ago by Immanuel Kant in "What is Enlightenment?" when he differentiated between public and private uses of reason. In his sense, a critic within an academy is exercising a private use of reason since he is fulfilling a contract made with society by taking on the job of criticism, *as that job is defined by the culture* (which includes, in this case, being a specialist in the texts valued by the culture).

If Kant had asked what the public use of such a critic's reason would be, he would have looked for that critic to act as a member of the general public, to critique that job and its historical contingencies, not just the context in which the job was being exercised — even if that operated against the form of the job the critic had contracted to do. In this framing, definitions of the job of the critic negotiated from the inside (such as what Mitchell and the MLA have done in that vein) cannot qualify as a public use of reason since they do not allow the open public to question its relationship with that critic, as we have seen, or require the critic to justify his or her job description to the public in this time of general historical unrest. Today's critics have been questioning their power vis-à-vis other critics, but not other kinds of critical readers — not vis-à-vis the possible culture of readers in the historical era.

In fact, a growing number of scholar-historians today seriously question the assumption that critic-theorists are speaking to a public or to shifting public needs at all. Terry Eagleton's *The Function of Criticism* speaks more openly than some, but in a familiar tone: "The argument of this book is that criticism today lacks all substantive social function. It is either part of the public relations branch of the literary industry, or a matter wholly internal to the academies" (7). In Eagleton's vision, this was not always the case, nor need it continue to be that way. But he points up an important fact about the relation of the academy to society, one ignored by those who assume the transfer of power between theory (the academic's private sphere) and the public sphere: as bourgeois society develops, definitions of the public and the private spheres shift, as do their relationships (117).

Eagleton argues that, in the eighteenth century, for example, politics, social and moral judgments, and aesthetics used to be part of public sphere discussion, while education and formation of character used to be considered part of the private sphere. Therefore, in this account, "culture" was defined apart from education: "The role of 'culture' is to generate new forms of subjectivity by a ceaseless mediation between two dimensions of social life — the family and political society — which have now been defined as distinct" (116). Education, in contrast, focused on filling group needs in political society. In the terms I am using here, this would mean that issues like aesthetics were not simply in the hands of a professional elite — they were public in Kant's sense. In contrast, education was a private issue — not just a domestic issue, as we would assume today, but (again in Kant's sense) part of each individual's contract with that society.

Eagleton contends that, in the course of last two centuries, this private sphere has gradually turned public. Where culture had been seen as the medium through which individuals were to negotiate their basis for introducing personal concerns into the public sphere (and hence aligned with novelty and individuality), it later became public (and tacitly aligned with education and other activities that are the responsibility of the group), serving as a support of the dominant order, an arbiter of "standards." The post-eighteenth-century critic thus became a voice who was supposed to arbitrate for the state, not innovate against it: "Modern criticism was born of a struggle against the absolutist state; unless its future is now defined as a struggle against the bourgeois state, it might have no future at all" (124). Here Eagleton describes this shift in order to define the necessity of an "oppositional intellectual," echoing West's proposal. He sees the critic as responsible for marketing a product in the public sphere through the institutions of that public sphere, but not necessarily to support it, as it has done since that eighteenth-century shift.

From the perspective introduced here, however, Eagleton has made a fundamental error: he has confused a critical function in society with the job of the critic. As we are arguing here, his analysis merely shows that, after the eighteenth century, criticism was delegated to a specific professional rather than to the group as a whole. When this happened, "criticism" developed two faces where it had earlier had only one. Again returning to Kant's dichotomy, I would prefer to say that Eagleton is arguing for reclaiming the general, public duty of all members of a society to assume as far as possible the role of oppositional intellectuals — to assume a critical function within the group, a function that cannot, *by definition*, be satisfied by the professional critic. It is unclear, from Kant's perspective, that the professional critic could ever be an oppositional intellectual in that critical sense because the profession of critic remains a private contract with the culture as a whole.

And I would concomitantly argue that the "critical function" to which I refer here can best be conceptualized today as the responsibility of each member of a society to "read culture," to contribute their individual sense of history and values to building a comprehensible, if not a shared, vision of the culture to which historical accident and understanding have brought the group. In other words, the power of the critic should never be intended to be the power of criticism within general culture. The critic can become publicly critical, but not necessarily about academic criticism and definitely not in order to supplant the group's authority over the critic's job.

I am thus suggesting that the job of criticism that has been discussed for the last two decades is simply the wrong issue within discussions of U. S. academic institutions. Today we need to rethink not the job of the critic but rather individual entitlement and the necessity for each individual to exercise critical functions. As Jean-François Lyotard defined in a report submitted to the Conseil des Universités of the government of Quebec (*The Postmodern Condition*, 1979), the process of knowing (generating and exchanging knowledge) in which a culture engages has changed fundamentally (and in a way different from how Eagleton had described it). Whereas education previously had been defined as affecting an individual (*Bildung*), Lyotard contends that the process of knowing has itself been changed: knowledge no longer adheres to people (or, hence, to the private sphere, as Eagleton defined it), it is a medium of exchange (4).

In the terms used in the present discussion, this would imply that the critic no longer exercises authority because of his or her ability to know; instead, critical authority stems from the constraints of institutions — from the culture's consensus about where authority lies. As Lyotard notes, then, this means that the institutions are actually guardians of knowledge, not of any particular individual doing a job within that institution. Knowledge is now defined and legitimized through the constraints of institutions (17). In his account, these institutions do not acquire their power to legitimize simply because a particular individual has actually seen their successes and has (metaphorically speaking) voted for their existence.

Instead, an institution accrues its power by establishing its myth of power, success, and legitimation — the *narrative* of its existence: "Thus the narratives allow the society in which they are told, on the one hand, to define its criteria of competence and, on the other, to evaluate according to those criteria what is performed or can be performed within it" (20). Each such narrative identifies a culture's heroes of knowing, defines competence, and demonstrates how the institution's validating criteria are to be applied — it creates a "narrative fiction" that legitimizes knowledge functionally rather than as attached to any single individual. Individuals do occupy roles in these narratives; they enact them, but they are not the source of their power. The narratives create belief systems within groups, which then yield power.

Lyotard agrees about what limits critics within an institution's particular narratives. Each narrative's efficacy creates or subverts the power of any individual within its system. Following the terms laid down in the system, a "community of equals" (here, we would say, a group of professionals organized into a discipline) form a consensus about what they consider valid knowledge to make a basis for their collective power (48). Such a community trains students in the acceptable institutionalized language game, perpetuating their values across history (43). Eventually, when research funding is established (after professional standards yield surplus value instead of only fulfilling momentary cultural needs), "science becomes a force of production, in other words, a moment in the circulation of capital" (45). The narrative thus forces a "commodification of knowledge." Because institutions work this way, universities play a role that education in the eighteenth century did not: they are not intended to purvey life values (a private-sphere activity) but instead to train students in public-sphere skills (48). Restated in Kant's terms: the university employs experts (each on private contracts) to train students in those skills that purportedly support the good of the group. The university educates individuals in a set of skills that have been put up to public debate and then institutionalized because those skills create "surplus value" for the group as a whole.

If this detachment of the critic's job from the critical function has, in fact, occurred in the way I have just described, the consequences for the academic critic are severe. Eagleton was worried that academic criticism has become divorced from the public sphere; Lyotard posits instead that academic specialists have actually lost their autonomy since they are training students in skills defined by the public sphere (particularly the liberal elite, the university's traditional public [50]). If, as Eagleton hoped, there is a new role for the academic in this situation, it cannot be that of the "critical intellectual" (at least not as a professional) since teaching critical skills and enacting criticism are not necessarily parallel activities.

Lyotard also hopes that the teaching skills and enacting criticism can be brought close together, but he persists in identifying the institution as severely restricting his hopes: the existence of professionalization narratives within socially approved institutions means that humanist-scholars will be deluding themselves if they equate opposition from within the constraints of a public institution with freedom. For these critics in institutional employment, oppositional ideas will still emerge only in relation to the power of their sponsoring institutions (even if not the sponsoring ideologies). To be truly oppositional, Lyotard's preferred kind of humanist (his redefinition of the oppositional intellectual) must strive to present forms of knowledge from outside the consensus without using its formalizations. By assuming what he calls "the postmodern stance," his "postmodern humanists" attempt to present the unpresentable, the "future anterior" from the outside of these institutionalized language or narrative constraints (81) — counterfactuals and anomalies, not merely oppositions structured into the dominant consensus.

Again, Lyotard is arguing that culture needs the kind of public critical function that I have been describing to this point. But others support his contention that the odds are very small that this critical function can be exercised by an individual who is a professional critic, a critic with a job in the academy. Samuel Weber's *Institution and Interpretation* underscores how seriously institutionalized games can restrict individuals; Lyotard's hope is probably vain. Weber, like Lyotard, believes that the purpose of institutions is to establish a discourse community and the definitions of knowledge. However,

> the definition of meaningful thought as the establishment of fixed habits becomes self-defeating: internally, because it produces a kind of automatism that eliminates the self-control it is designed to achieve, and externally, because such fixed habits become, by virtue of their very fixity and hence inflexibility, incapable of dealing with changing and infinitely variable circumstances. (14)

Such habits of thought prescribe the "limits of professionalism" within an individual's knowledge (18) and ultimately constitute the "culture of professionalism" (25).

Weber posits this professional culture as a particular detriment to an academic critic's self-liberation: it trains individuals in a set of learned behaviors and calculated responses that correlate with social needs defined as having inherent "values" for the society (27). The professionals involved use these habits and their implied values to define rank and privilege: when they do so, they identify themselves through "the calculability of *competence*" instead of through competition or conflict (31). Academic habits thus automatically limit social struggle. Like Lyotard's narratives, Weber's habits turn the critic into a tool valorizing the established order and his own place in it. This criticism also acquires an "aggressive humility" vis-à-vis the text when it legislates "good readings" from improper ones that distort culture's dominant sense of order (38). More important, as different critical orders emerge, they diffuse their conflicts among each other within the institution, even further away from the outside public sphere. As a consequence, that conflict cannot be turned against the institution from outside, for insider discourse has usurped all positions of power (43).

Eagleton, Lyotard, and Weber clearly share a concern about the relation of academic knowledge (particularly humanistic or critical knowledge) to the public sphere. They warn us of the encapsulation of the academic in an internal discourse that eschews connection with the public sphere: a particular academic may, as an individual, address the public sphere, but the institutional disciplines tend not to — a result that Kant predicted two centuries ago. More important for my present discussion is an anomaly shared by all three of these scholars: each still believes that professional critics should have impact on the more general public, an impact beyond their job as critics, as mediators of cultural values (approved or oppositional). And this, they would tacitly agree, would aid the "crisis in education" seen by the popular media.

At this point, however, it is again useful to return to Kant's differentiation and to Lyotard's warning that the individual is not the unit of knowledge. If both analyses are considered together, the academic critic can be seen as stuck in an institutional framework designed by the dominant culture for its aims. Moreover, this framework cannot be overcome by individuals, as Weber would have hoped it could: to change the framework would require an alteration in the public consensus that designed the institution and the values that it was designed to uphold.

What all these discussions have avoided is the realization that the job of academic critics now needs to be redefined for the future, for it is not the job they describe or prescribe as desirable. If Eagleton is correct in his description of what happened to the role of the critic in the Enlightenment, then that critic can now be redefined as part of the public sphere's dominant consensus institutionally but of the private sphere in terms of its educational values. I am arguing here that the job of the academic critic has to this point been to represent aspects of the dominant public consensus, even its dissenting aspects. I am also arguing in Kant's terms to stress that a "critical function" as he would have defined it cannot be claimed by these academic critics in more than a limited fashion.

At the same time, however, Eagleton is probably correct in assuming that the culture that has redefined the critics' job by creating the educational institutions has abdicated its ability to self-critique those critics. Today's academic critics actually have been empowered and institutionalized to validate the values supported b the consensus of the dominant culture; they assume, in contrast, that critics can assume the power to generate cultural values rather than simply validate them.

The critics' individual power within the academy does not, however, mean that they can legislate outside that institution. The critics' culture has no responsibility to listen to a "new" set of values originating outside of the academy. Culture institutionalized a set of critics to uphold a set of values and to train the next generation. Historical needs, however, have changed since such institutions were defined after the Second World War, but the dominant culture has not yet engaged with its official critics either to negotiate new values or to redefine the role of critic. And today's academic critics of culture remain authorized only to create values within the institution, no matter what they may choose to believe, unless that set of necessary redefinitions is undertaken in negotiation with the culture that created the jobs. Criticism from within must engage with culture on the outside to redefine its job and its institutional purview. That is simply not being done today.

From this perspective, the critics' voices that I have been quoting above are indeed documents of a crisis in public education. Their solutions, however, rely strongly on the strengths of the Enlightenment model of what social consensus is and what the dominant culture is supposed to represent. What they have not realized is that today's crisis in public consensus is less a discussion about particular sets of values (although these are the terms in which debates rage) than it is a question of authority: what should be the responsibility of private individuals in the public sphere before they delegate the administration of their chosen values to any institution (educational or otherwise)? The educational institutions that presently exist in the United States were designed to administer elite versions of dominant cultural values, to disseminate what a past culture considered important: awareness of "great works" representing its cherished values. More recently, that consensus (the one that generated "the Western canon") has been called into question as the historical forces supporting it have altered. But academic institutions have not been reshaped; they have responded by becoming representatives of what they themselves have defined as "new public values," not by any deeper act of self-criticism.

In one sense, then, I am arguing that, if Eagleton, Lyotard, and Weber are correct in their analyses as I have presented them above, today's critic has been "upholding traditional cultural values," even when arguing for including new voices in the present cultural canons. But historically, we are at the moment when the whole public consensus that defines narratives of dominant culture and their institutions needs redefining. All the aspects of critique need to be renegotiated: the critical function, the power of cultural critique, and the nature of cultural values. And to do so within the constraints of existing institutional structures (even by adding "new majors") is simply retrenching an existing power base. That kind of emendation may still describe academic critics' most cherished self-definition, but it is not the act of a critic acting publicly in Kant's sense; it is the act of a critic who believes that he or she can speak for that culture, even when the public consensus that institutionalized the critic has altered in fundamental ways. It constitutes an act of academic rudeness — an abuse of the power that was given that critic by a culture, enacted against a culture that has begun to withdraw its consent.

In these harsh terms, the critic cannot be an engaged intellectual as a professional critic when he or she reads in the terms established by the institutions supporting criticism. His or her authority about cultural values extends only as far outside the boundaries of those institutions as the dominant cultural consensus (not necessarily the dominant culture — the two may not be identical) allows it to. No matter how unclear the situation of cultural values is presently, however, the academic critic still has another aspect of his or her role available, one that has not been explored in the present debate on cultural values: the academic critic as an empowered educator rather than an empowered representative of dominant culture.

This role, critical educator instead of critic, will be the subject of the final section of this discussion.

Reading Culture: Acts of Reading, as Contracts in Public Context

What I have been addressing to this point is how the role of academic critic has been wrongly defined in the present culture wars. Yet it is still possible to salvage the job of critic if we can redefine both what an academic critic does as a private individual (what kind of contract critics should be seen as engaging in when acting professionally) and what kinds of critical public communication all readers (not just professional ones) should be encouraged to engage in. Taken together, these desiderata also mean that institutions need to be rethought.

In the introduction to the present volume, I argue that the true act of cultural critique is a critical reading of culture, not a critic's performance within the academy. The essays contained in this book demonstrate how a critical reading of culture must be primarily subject to the authority of history, not to an institutionalized reading strategy. In other words, critical readings of culture should be the purview of the "public uses of reason," not of the critic doing a job as a private person, but as a delegate of that public. If the critical function I have been seeking is redefined as a critical reading of texts in cultural-historical contexts, then its reliance on institutional authority becomes of lesser importance.

The introduction also argues that critics doing their jobs are performing or reenacting the values of their academic disciplines or cultures. Now I would like to argue that a critical cultural reading more closely corresponds to a true "public use of reason" in Kant's sense. And, as I have tried to exemplify with the notion of a critic speaking from the margins, a critical reading of cultural texts must look less to authority and power (look less to profiting from the authority of that culture) and more to the act of critique as an analysis of the strategies of empowerment and disempowerment available at a particular historical moment. To say it more simply: a critical act of "reading culture" should be redefined as a focus on *the act of reading as it is implicated in a historical state of culture* in order to reclaim critical potential within the culture of readers meeting their own new and present needs, not from readings ensconced as valuable by a dominant (past) culture.

In the essays above, I have attempted to recreate possible acts of reading within representative cultural nexes. By so doing, I have, to be sure, "proved" in academic terms that I am a valid critic (although working from the margins lowers the likelihood of their general success). But I have also tried to open new arbitrations of cultural values: to invite debates about how texts spoke in their own contexts and about how we prefer to interpret that speech today because of our historical position. That is, I have asked not only about the meaning of texts in cultural context but also about the powers that have established, valorized or marginalized these meanings (including my own when I choose to set a marginalized perspective against a dominant, established reading).

By redefining criticism as an act of reading, I am also necessarily redefining the function of the university as an institution of knowledge. As we have seen, the present university structure reflects a culture's dominant ideology. Within that structure, the critic (as humanist) arbitrates the culture's values. Unfortunately, that arbitration is subject to the general historical lag for which institutions have been renowned (at least since Nietzsche's *Anti-Christ*), since the values arbitrated are often those of the past.

In moments when history seems continuous, students profit from learning these values: they become "certified" representatives of the values of the dominant culture supporting a particular institution. At moments of clear historical and cultural change, however, the profit in learning values that have been called into question is considerably less clear. Today, for example, this questioning lies near the core of the present debates about the validity of "the canon" and the inclusion of heretofore noncanonical voices into that value structure. To deny, however, that such profit (social power, distinction, cultural capital) is intended or accrued is nonsensical. Or that the teacher of the values bringing that profit is profiting from his or her engagement in the institutions of the culture.

How can this cycle of profitmongering be adapted? I would suggest by moving the critical function to be exercised within culture into the center of both institutional and cultural interest rather than cultural values themselves — by focusing on the act of reading rather than the readings themselves as the proper purview of academic professionalization. That is, I believe it will be more productive for professional critics to redefine themselves not as guardians of knowledge or cultural values (oppositional or otherwise) but rather as expert readers — as articulate mediators between various loci in cultures (separated by time, space, ethnicity, or any other classifications favored by a particular moment in history). The "postmodern humanist" or "engaged intellectual" must now focus on the strategies through which knowledge and power are produced rather than on the knowledge itself.

In 1918, in *The Higher Learning in America*, Thorstein Veblen articulated one version of what I am speaking about: he rejected what could be termed a redefinition of the humanistic disciplines as purveying "skills" to students. In his opinion, if the humanities purvey skills, they are in danger of being considered commodities subject to a market economy rather than vales in themselves. Moreover, as commodities, they lack free space and so cannot serve innovative inquiry. But Veblen's definition of skills is narrower than I am suggesting here and closer to the activities described by Weber above: in Veblen's expositions, skills are conceived by academic guilds mainly to uphold professionals' ability to arbitrate quality.

Contrary to Veblen's assumption, skills are not only activities subject to perfection through practice but also valued activities *on or with the objects of culture, in historical space*. I have attempted to argue here that skills do indeed attach themselves to professionals in the present but that the materials, patterns, and rationales defining these skills are attached to historical legacies and to cultural centers and margins created by the power of public consensus (only secondarily by the institutions). Most likely because he was writing when the notion of dominant culture was acceptable, Veblen did not consider that each skill might tie to a different historical site, power structure, and cultural value structure — that a professional might demonstrate a skill within one institutional (cultural) context, but the student might consume (learn) and apply that skill within another.

I thus argue here that institutionalized academic disciplines need to redefine themselves as sets of critical skills for their own survival, and in precisely the direction that Veblen feared. Critics must acknowledge that the values they represent are products of particular sets of professional or expert skills exercised in different cultural-historical environments. As professionals, their role is to show how such values are derived and substantiated — to enact demonstration behaviors, as they are presently doing. Yet to become critical intellectuals (public individuals, in roles beyond their professional and private ones), they must exploit the other part of their job: they must teach critical readings of values, to teach not only values themselves and how they are constructed but also why (for what social or personal profits). Such critical teacher-intellectuals will thus also have as their goal not only the replication of their professional skills but teaching their students their skills as strategies of self-definition and self-empowerment in ways that allow them to be exported into other institutional, historical, or cultural contexts as well. Skills support cultural authority in more than one context.

To diffuse some objections in advance, let me draw an example outside the academic community to restate the point. The making of fine musical instruments may serve. Instrument making is a highly refined skill (or set of skills) that must be very responsive to market pressures — the amount of handwork necessary to the production cannot be reduced significantly, so the relation of time to materials cannot be cut. However, historical knowledge of the profession's development is crucial, especially when the market for sounds or available materials changes. Italian violin makers produced varnishes that made the wood sound in ways not available today; this explains the claim to fame of the Stradivarius violins and violas. Historically, however, these varnishes did other things: they also made instruments respond to dampness in very predictable patterns, and they made usable certain grades of wood not considered acceptable today. In analyzing such a situation, critical readings of moments in cultural history enhance the knowledge represented in the skill — no single set of instrument-making skills can ever universally define the norm of "the best violin," which is a judgment established only as a consensus within a particular culture. Moreover, any instrument-making skills may also be turned to serve other purposes: a skilled instrument maker can easily find other things to make if his culture no longer requires violins (to be sure, these other things may not pay as well if they are not of as high status, but they can still be useful).

The same analysis, in my view, must apply to the "skills" purveyed by university disciplines and their academic professionals as critics engage with the culture to define our common institutional frameworks: no matter which profession they stem from, academic skills have developed over time in response to varying real needs and cultural consensuses. Students thus need to know the historical canon of skills, but not as norms that apply to-day without further validation or alterations. The example of instrument making just used can thus be replicated in almost every field. Each skill has multiple historical meanings, not just to replicate the canon of cultural values in which it is used. Contrary to Veblen's objections, then, "teaching skills" requires a specialist historical knowledge apart from the virtuosity that the business market may foster.

A Morality Fable: Disciplines in the New University

Clearly, both critics and the various consensuses within culture must remain active in redefining their institutions. "Academic-theorists" cannot isolate themselves as an individual guild but need to work in full knowledge of their cultural-historical positions. And as an institution, the university has a unique role in preserving a historical depth of information, practices, and specialist skills (not necessarily values) kept as resources to be tapped at need or interest. In this framing, professionalization need not always be equated with authority but may perhaps also be associated with facilitation — the professional need not dominate or regulate meanings, but perhaps articulate, identify, or circulate them to other markets, especially those outside the narrow professionalization.

This by no means implies that the university in its new form must simply cater to needs of the dominant culture or that "teaching" will become more important than "research" (or the contrary). Instead, as the post-Enlightenment public consensus shifts, the university must be seen in new ways, as having two faces: as a site that teaches culture in sets of private contracts between cultures, professionals, and students and as a site that enacts a kind of cultural guardianship in those historical moments when a group consensus threatens to take too narrow a view and to ignore lessons and skills of the past (its public contract). Academic "free inquiry" is, as we have shown, free only within the constraints of a particular culture. "Teaching" can potentially do more than advocate the values of a dominant culture: it can also purvey and assess skills as possible agents in reforming or supporting cultural consensuses. Similarly, scholars do not exist in and of themselves; their skills have different values within culture and because of it. Yet what emerges as academic knowledge is contingent on its context, on the "fit" of its research projects, past and present, into social-historical contexts — on what skills are put to use in what contexts.

To empower its professional practitioners to become purveyors of this new empowerment for critical engagement, each particular discipline must define its "fit" in this mediation between knowledge and world (as Eagleton suggests that the profession of criticism has not in the last two hundred years). Professional "knowledge" must thus be reconceived as a reading of facts according to the strategic values of a culture; teaching this knowledge to students means to teach not only an approved assemblage of such facts (a disciplinary canon) but also the strategies and skills that guide that reading (the relations of power and cultural capital in which that disciplinary canon functions). Canons are not simply values; they are also ways of knowing that have been designated as valuable by particular cultures. In this vision, the changing of canons will not only imply the possible loss of the values of an old dominant culture; it may also mean changing the cognitive style of that culture and privileging different interest groups within it.

Such a redefinition of canons as cognitive styles has a historical parallel. "Rhetoric" used to be a discipline in which students practiced a certain limited repertory of "figures" — public and private speech genres that exemplified the communicative needs of an individual within his or her speech community. Today the notion of rhetoric has been flattened to mean "writing across the disciplines" and "rhetorical organization," largely discarding this discipline's earlier goal of teaching an individual to have a public voice that can be heard by the group and exert influence. Why? The discipline of rhetoric has not also redefined itself as a repository of strategies for addressing the public and for the skills needed by professional *who will evolve new ones in new situations*. Seen in this more active sense, the traditional profession of "rhetoric" surrendered its adaptability to new cultural missions when it surrendered "mass communications" to media departments. These new electronic public speaking venues may not seem to need traditional rhetorical figures like "exhortations" and "laudations" since these figures evolved as authoritative and effective in different historical contexts. Yet what has supplanted them? And how do any new inventions in communication relate to traditional rhetorical figures?

The case of rhetoric is exemplary for how a discipline can shift (not always in most beneficial ways). It evolved originally when a historical situation yielded a set of cultural norms, which subsequently turned into a discipline that needed to be taught to the upholders of that culture. This need to teach yielded "departments" and "specialists," who were later subjected to various alterations in professionals' cultural authority in consequence of historical shifts. What had at first been seen as cultural problem solving in context was given to an institution to disseminate; that institution (professional rhetoricians) preserved the forms of the solution while surrendering the contexts of the problems to other disciplines. Rhetoric as classically institutionalized detached from active cultural history sometime in the nineteenth century, and it is only now seeking a new kind of attachment — perhaps to avoid its total eradication from the active archive of cultural knowledge.

My hypothetical rhetoricians are simply reenacting what too many academics have done and what the literary professions today need to consider so that they too will not fall prey to the threat of being reorganized out of the active institutional community. Many forms of humanistic knowledge have been declared dead by the media and "in danger of perishing" by education critics. When they have not fled from acknowledgment of this danger in situations like this, too many literary and cultural critics have simply turned nostalgic, tried to stem the tide, or turned inward, either to create a cohort or students who identify themselves as antiquarians rather than as educators or to circle the wagons against historical change, guarded by fellow professionals, by a group of like-speaking individuals who will protect each other against such philistines. They prefer to arbitrate their own importance rather than change it or their links to the group outside the academy — they do not wish to reread their own cultural text critically.

But as I have been arguing, such deferrals cannot be the case in times of shifting cultural-historical norms. As Kenneth Burke's *A Rhetoric of Motives* phrases it, the practice of any author (and, by implication, that of any reader who seeks to produce a text of meaning if not exactly a book) is tied to the real world: "The fact that an activity is capable of reduction to intrinsic, autonomous principles does not argue that it is free from identification with other orders of motivation intrinsic to it" (27).[1] And this position may accommodate the artifacts of culture even better than the academic critic's may. For instance, in *Unbequeme Literatur*, Jost Hermand describes disquieting literature as works that are "disquieting, because they don't just simply accept the contradictions of their time, but rather search for the possibility of a 'third way'" (14–15). These books often are forgotten, or they fall on deaf ears because they do not reflect the prevailing taste of their ages (which itself is often many years behind the accepted avant garde). They are not always "great" or "good" books, but they attempt some reaction to their environment that was basically unessayed before their emergence. In the strictest sense, they are historically relevant but ineffectual in their moment.

The essays in *Austria and Other Margins: Reading Culture* have tried to act as a small repertoire of "disquieting criticism" in Hermand's sense. Each provides a critical reading of culture without asserting the privilege of any particular school of criticism over any text but rather based on the primacy of the text's position vis-à-vis a reader in context. Moreover, the volume as a whole has sought to be "readerly" rather than "writerly" (in Roland Barthes's sense), to be accessible to readers from the common culture rather than primarily to other critic-writers. That is, it conforms to the reader's sense of basic logic and historical knowledge, simply foregrounding details in a consciously shared discourse. It therefore has not tried to shock or estrange the reader, as the innovative, writerly critic often must to assert his academic prestige.

This book has concomitantly attempted to redefine the act of criticism as an act of critical reading (not merely as a kind of random academic pluralism of the kind that Armstrong, for example, describes — as a contract existing not just among experts but between professional critics and the culture that supports it, as a contract among readers. To accept this redefinition of criticism is thus to redefine not only the job of the critic but also the position of professional scholarship vis-à-vis the dominant culture and the relation of disciplines within the university to each other. A dual mastery is required to be a fluent critical reader. At one level, there are basic tools and skills that must be mastered to insure some independent mastery for a reader: data from a culture, information in discipline-specific use contexts, and prevalent logics. Beyond that, a reader must master the impact and significance of these tools, data, and logics; each must ask about a reading, "what's going on here, and *what is its impact*, both inside and outside of the professions?"

"Reading culture" from the margins thus is the central project for today's academic institutions: not adding margins to the old geographic and disciplinary centers but using margins to redefine the centers of cultural authority. Only in this way can we turn critics back into experts who learn from new dominant and marginal cultures and who teach the skills of critical reading rather than representing or displaying values evolved by old authorities. Only in this way can "postmodern humanists" reclaim a vital function within the increasingly commodified public vision of the new university.

Note

[1]Unfortunately, even Burke's critic seems to be hiding within the academy, behind an order of organization that guarantees the ultimate intelligibility and value of a literary work and its readings (c.f. Brombert and Lindenberger for similar attempts to reposition the critic, yet not fundamentally challenge the role). Academic policy debates are more easily controlled than cultural commentary. And even the more politically-sensitive criticism practiced by more engaged critics like Toril Moi and Frederic Jameson, one that "shows a great willingness to jump over the wall that separates intramural from extramural praxis," still must, as David Kaufmann summarizes, "defer the dream [of a mediation between theory and praxis] while anchoring it firmly in the literary academy" (526).

Bibliography

Abbott, Scott H. "Günter Grass' *Hundejahre*: A Realistic Novel About Myth." *German Quarterly* 55, no. 2 (March 1982): 212–20.

Adams, Jeffrey, ed. *Mörike's Muses: Critical Essays on Eduard Mörike.* Columbia, SC: Camden House, 1990.

Amann, Klaus. *Der Anschluß österreichischer Schriftsteller an das Dritte Reich: Institutionelle und bewußtseinsgeschichtliche Aspekte.* Frankfurt/M: Athenäum, 1988.

Anderson, Benedict. *Imagined Communities: Reflections on the Origin and Spread of Nationalism.* Rev. ed. London: Verso, 1991.

Angress, Ruth K. "Der eingerichtete Mensch: Innendekor bei Adalbert Stifter." *Germanisch-Romanische Monatsschrift* 67 (N. F. 36), no. 1 (1986): 32–47.

Arac, Jonathan, ed. *Postmodernism and Politics.* Theory and History of Literature 28. Minneapolis: U of Minnesota, 1986.

———. and Barbara Johnson, eds. *Consequences of Theory: Selected Papers from the English Institute, 1987–1988.* New Series 14. Baltimore: Johns Hopkins UP, 1991.

Arens, Katherine. *Structures of Knowing: Psychologies of the Nineteenth Century.* Boston Studies in the Philosophy of Science 113. Dordrecht and Boston: Reidel, 1989.

———. "Kant, Herder, and Psychology." In Wulf Koepke, ed. *Johann Gottfried Herder: Academic Disciplines and the Pursuit of Knowledge.* Columbia, SC: Camden House, 1996 (forthcoming).

Arker, Dieter. *Nichts ist vorbei, alles kommt wieder: Untersuchungen zu Günter Grass' "Blechtrommel."* Heidelberg: Carl Winter, 1989.

Armstrong, Paul B. "The Conflict of Interpretations and the Limits of Pluralism." *PMLA* 98, no. 3 (May 1983): 341–52.

Ashcroft, Bill, Gareth Griffiths, and Helen Tiffin, eds. *The Post-Colonial Studies Reader.* London: Routledge, 1995.

Bachem, Michael. *Heimito von Doderer.* Boston: Twayne, 1981.

———. "Irony, Satiric Irony, and the Grotesque in the Works of Heimito von Doderer." *Colloquia Germanica* 18, no. 3 (1985): 264–70.

Bahr, Ehrhard. "Geld und Liebe im *Armen Spielmann*: Versuch einer sozioliterarischen Interpretation." In Clifford Albrecht Bernd, ed., *Grillparzer's "Der arme Spielmann."* 300–310.

Bandet, J.-L. "Les chiffres de la solitude." *Etudes Germaniques* 40, no. 3 (July-September 1985): 271–80.

Barker, Andrew E. "Heimito von Doderer and National Socialism." *German Life and Letters* 41, no. 2 (January 1988): 145–58.

———. "Heimito von Doderer's 'Indirekter Weg.'" *Forum for Modern Language Studies* 18, no. 4 (October 1982): 289–98.

———. "'Kammern der Befängnis' — An Aspect of Thought and Image in the Work of Heimito von Doderer." *Modern Austrian Literature* 14, no. 1–2 (1981): 25–43.

Barthes, Roland. *S/Z: An Essay*. Trans. Richard Miller. New York: Hill and Wang, 1974.

Bartmann, Christoph. "Der totale Konservative: Über Heimito von Doderer." *Merkur* 40, no. 11 (November 1986): 989–96.

Begemann, Christian. *Die Welt der Zeichen: Stifter-Lektüren*. Stuttgart: J. B. Metzler, 1995.

Belgum, Kirsten L. "High Historicism and Narrative Restoration: The Seamless Interior of Adalbert Stifter's *Nachsommer*." *Germanic Review* 67, no. 1 (Winter 1992): 15–25.

Bernd, Clifford Albrecht. "From Neglect to Controversy: Introducing a Volume of Criticism on *Der arme Spielmann*." In Bernd, ed., *Grillparzer's "Der arme Spielmann*." 1–8.

———. ed. *Grillparzer's "Der arme Spielmann": New Directions in Criticism*. Studies in German Literature, Linguistics, and Culture 25. Columbia, SC: Camden House, 1988.

Bernheimer, Charles, and Claire Kahane, eds. *In Dora's Case: Freud-Hysteria-Feminism*. New York: Columbia UP, 1985.

Bertram, Ernst. *Studien zu Adalbert Stifters Novellentechnik*. Schriften der Literaturhistorischen Gesellschaft Bonn 3. Ed. Berthold Litzmann. Dortmund: Verlag Friedrich Wilhelm Ruhfus, 1907.

Beutin, Wolfgang, ed. *Literatur und Psychoanalyse: Ansätze zu einer psychoanalytischen Textinterpretation*. Munich: Nymphenburger Verlagshandlung, 1972.

Bhabha, Homi K. *The Location of Culture*. London: Routledge, 1994.

Birrell, Gordon. "Time, Timelessness, and Music in Grillparzer's *Spielmann*." In Clifford Albrecht Bernd, ed. *Grillparzer's "Der arme Spielmann*." 233–53.

Blackall, Eric A. *Adalbert Stifter: A Critical Study*. Cambridge: Cambridge UP, 1948.

Bloch, Peter André. "Perspektive und Dimension," *Etudes Germaniques* 40, no. 3 (July-September 1985): 281–96.

Bloom, Allan. *The Closing of the American Mind: How Higher Education Has Failed Democracy and Impoverished the Souls of Today's Students*. New York: Simon & Schuster, 1987.

Bloom, Harold. *The Western Canon: The Books and School of the Ages*. New York: Harcourt Brace Jovanovich, 1994.

Bohning, Elizabeth E. "The Lure of the Little in Grillparzer, Stifter and Wald-müller." In Herbert Lederer and Maria Luise Caputo-Mayr, eds. *Österreich in amerikanischer Sicht: Das Österreichbild im amerikanischen Schulunterricht,* 2. New York: Austrian Institute, 1981. 10–18.

Bolton, Jürgen. "Heimat im Aufwind: Anmerkungen zur Sozialgeschichte eines Bedeutungswandels." In Hans-Georg Pott, ed. *Literatur und Provinz.* 23–38.

Borchmeyer, Dieter. "Stifters *Nachsommer:* Eine restaurative Utopie?" *Poetica* 12 (1980): 59–82.

Boring, Edwin G. *A History of Experimental Psychology.* 2d ed. New York: Appleton-Century-Crofts, 1950.

Bottomore, Tom, and Patrick Goode, trans. and eds. *Austro-Marxism.* Oxford: Clarendon, 1978.

Bourdieu, Pierre. *Language and Symbolic Power.* Ed. John B. Thompson. Trans. Geno Raymond and Matthew Adamson. Cambridge, MA: Harvard UP, 1991.

Bové, Paul A. *Intellectuals in Power: A Genealogy of Critical Humanism.* New York: Columbia UP, 1986.

Bowler, Peter J. *The Eclipse of Darwinism: Anti-Darwinian Evolution Theories in the Decades around 1900.* Baltimore: Johns Hopkins UP, 1983.

——. *Evolution: The History of an Idea.* Rev. ed. Berkeley: U of California, 1989.

——. *The Non-Darwinian Revolution: Reinterpreting a Historical Myth.* Baltimore: Johns Hopkins UP, 1988.

Boyer, John W. *Political Radicalism in Late Imperial Vienna: Origins of the Christian Social Movement, 1848–1897.* Chicago: U of Chicago, 1981.

Brecht, Stefan. *The Original Theatre of the City of New York, From the Mid-60s to the Mid-70s: Book 1, The Theatre of Visions: Robert Wilson.* Frankfurt/M: Suhrkamp, 1978.

Broce, Gerald. "Herder and Ethnography." *Journal of the History of the Behavioral Sciences* 22 (April 1986): 150–70.

Brombert, Victor. "Mediating the Work: Or, The Legitimate Aims of Criticism" (MLA Presidential Address 1989). *PMLA* 105, no. 3 (May 1990): 391–97.

Browning, Robert M. "Language and the Fall from Grace in Grillparzer's *Spielmann.*" In Clifford Albrecht Bernd, ed. *Grillparzer's "Der arme Spielmann."* 47–65.

Burke, Kenneth. *A Grammar of Motives.* New York: Prentice-Hall, 1945.

——. *A Rhetoric of Motives.* New York: Prentice-Hall, 1950.

Caillois, Roger. *The Mask of Medusa.* Trans. George Ordish. New York: Clarkson N. Potter, 1964.

Campbell, Colin. "The Tyranny of the Yale Critics (Jacques Derrida, Harold Bloom, Geoffrey H. Hartmann, and J. Hillis Miller)." *New York Times,* 9 February 1986: VI, 20.

Campbell, Karen, J. "Toward a Truer Mimesis: Stifter's *Turmalin,*" *German Quarterly* 57, no. 4 (Fall 1984): 576–89.

Carr, Francis. *Constanze and Mozart*. London: John Murry, 1984.

Cepl-Kaufmann, Gertrud. "Verlust oder poetische Rettung?: Zum Begriff Heimat in Günter Grass' Danziger Trilogie." In Hans-Georg Pott, ed. *Literatur und Provinz*, 61–83.

——. *Günter Grass: Eine Analyse des Gesamtwerkes unter dem Aspekt von Literatur und Politik*. Kronberg/Ts.: Scriptor Verlag, 1975.

Certeau, Michel de. *Heterologies: Discourse on the Other*. Trans. Brian Massumi. Minneapolis: U of Minnesota, 1986.

——. *The Writing of History*. Trans. Tom Conley. New York: Columbia UP, 1988.

Chadbourne, Richard M. *Charles-Augustin Sainte-Beuve*. Boston: Twayne, 1977.

Chicago, Judy. *The Birth Project*. Garden City, NY: Doubleday, 1985.

——. *The Dinner Party: A Symbol of Our Heritage*. Garden City, NY: Doubleday/Anchor, 1979.

——. with Susan Hill. *Embroidering Our Heritage: The Dinner Party Needlework*. Garden City, NY: Doubleday/Anchor, 1980.

——. with photography by Donald Woodman. *Holocaust Project: From Darkness into Light*. New York: Penguin, 1993.

——. *Through the Flower: My Struggle as a Woman Artist*. Garden City, NY: Doubleday/Anchor, 1977 Expanded ed. published as *Beyond the Flower*. New York: Viking, 1996.

Christo and Wiener Secession. *Christo — The Running Fence: Zeichnungen, Collagen, Modelle, Technische Dokumente und Film (9.2–11.3. 1979)*. Vienna: Wiener Secession, 1979.

Christo and Jeanne-Claude. *Wrapped Reichstag, Berlin, 1971–1995: The Project Book*. Cologne: Benedikt Taschen Verlag, 1995.

Cimaz, Pierre. "Unheil und Ordnung in Stifters *Die Pechbrenner*," *Etudes Germaniques* 40, no. 3 (July-September 1985): 374–86.

Clark, Robert T., Jr. *Herder: His Life and Thought*. Berkeley: U of California, 1955.

Cocks, Geoffrey. *Psychotherapy in the Third Reich: The Göring Institute*. Oxford: Oxford UP, 1985.

Cook, Roger F. "Relocating the Author: A New Perspective on the Narrator in *Der arme Spielmann*." In Clifford Albrecht Bernd, ed. *Grillparzer's "Der arme Spielmann*." 322–36.

Cowen, Roy C. "The History of a Neglected Masterpiece: *Der arme Spielmann*." In Clifford Albrecht Bernd, ed. *Grillparzer's "Der arme Spielmann*." 9–26.

Crockett, Tobey, and Ainlay Samuels. "Christo [Interview]." *Splash*, October 1988: unpaginated.

Cullen, Michael S., and Wolfgang Volz, eds. *Christo: Der Reichstag*. Frankfurt/M: Suhrkamp, 1984.

DeNeef, A. Leigh, ed. "Rereadings in the Freudian Field." *South Atlantic Quarterly* 88, no. 4 (Fall 1989), special issue.

DeNeef, A. Leigh, and Crauford D. Goodwin, eds. *The Academic's Handbook.* 2d ed. Durham, NC: Duke UP, 1995.

DeNeef, A. Leigh, Crauford D. Goodwin, and Ellen Stern McCrate, eds. *The Academic's Handbook.* Durham, NC: Duke UP, 1988.

Derrida, Jacques. "Freud and the Scene of Writing," *Writing and Difference.* Chicago: U of Chicago, 1978. 196–231

——. *Of Grammatology.* Baltimore: Johns Hopkins UP, 1976.

——. "Sendoffs." *Yale French Studies* 77 (1990): 7–43; special issue, *Reading the Archive: On Texts and Institutions.* Eds. E. S. Burt, and Janie Vanpée.

Dietrich, Dawn Yvette. *Archetypical Dreams: The Quantum Theater of Robert Wilson.* Diss. U of Michigan, 1993.

Doane, Janice, and Devon Hodges. "Women and the Word According to Garp," In Doane and Hodges, *Nostalgia and Sexual Difference: The Resistance to Contemporary Feminism.* New York and London: Methuen, 1987. 63–76.

Doderer, Heimito von. "Auszüge aus dem letzten Tagebuch." *Das Pult* 5, no. 3 (1973): 5–8.

——. *Die Dämonen: Nach der Chronik des Sektionsrates Geyrenhoff.* Munich: Biederstein, 1956. *The Demons.* Trans. Richard and Clara Winston. New York: Alfred A. Knopf, 1961; rpt. Los Angeles: Sun & Moon Press, 1993.

——. *Das Dodererbuch: Eine Auswahl aus seinem Werk.* Ed. Karl Heinz Kramberg. Munich: Biederstein, 1976.

——. *Meine neunzehn Lebensläufe und neun andere Geschichten.* Munich: Biederstein, 1966.

——. "Sexualität und totaler Staat." *Wiederkehr der Drachen: Aufsätze, Traktate, Reden.* Ed. Wendelin Schmidt-Dengler. Munich: Biederstein, 1970. 275–98.

——. *Die Strudelhofstiege.* Munich: Biederstein, 1951.

——. *Tangenten: Tagebuch eines Schriftstellers*, 1940–1950. Munich: Biederstein, 1964.

Doerksen, Victor G. *Eduard Mörike.* Wege der Forschung 446. Darmstadt: Wissenschaftliche Buchgesellschaft, 1975.

Doerner, Klaus. *Madmen and the Bourgeoisie: A Social History of Insanity and Psychiatry.* Oxford: Basil Blackwell, 1981.

Domandl, Sepp. *Adalbert Stifters Lesebuch und die geistigen Strömungen zur Jahrhundertmitte.* Linz: Adalbert Stifter-Institut des Landes Oberösterreich, 1976.

——. "Die Idee des Schicksals bei Adalbert Stifter: Urphänomen oder Gegenstand der spekulativen Vernunft, *VASILO* 20, no. 3–4 (1971): 81–99.

——. "Die philosophische Tradition von Adalbert Stifters 'Sanftem Gesetz.'" *VASILO* 21, no. 3–4 (1972): 79–103.

Dostoyevsky, Fyodor. *The Devils [The Possessed]*. Trans. David Magarshack. Baltimore, MD: Penguin Books, 1953.

Durzak, Manfred, ed. *Zu Günter Grass: Geschichte auf dem poetischen Prüfstand*. Stuttgart: Ernst Klett, 1985.

Düsing, Wolfgang. *Erinnerung und Identität: Untersuchungen zu einem Erzählproblem bei Musil, Döblin und Doderer*. Munich: Wilhelm Fink, 1982.

Eagleton, Terry. *The Function of Criticism: From* The Spectator *to Post-Structuralism*. New York: Verso, 1984.

Eakin, Emily. "Walking the Line." *LinguaFranca* 6, no. 3 (March-April 1996): 52–60.

Eichner, Hans. "Heimito von Doderer, die Politik und die Juden." In Donald G. Daviau, ed. *Austrian Writers and the* Anschluß: *Understanding the Past, Overcoming the Past*. Riverside, CA: Ariadne Press, 1991. 224–33.

Eisenmeier, Eduard. *Adalbert Stifter Bibliographie*. Linz: Oberösterreichischer Landesverlag, 1964.

Eissler, K. R. *Talent and Genius: The Fictitious Case of Tausk contra Freud*. New York: Grove Press, 1971.

Ellenberger, Henri F. *The Discovery of the Unconscious: The History and Evolution of Dynamic Psychiatry*. New York: Basic Books, 1970.

Ellis, John M. "The Narrator and his Values in *Der arme Spielmann*." In Clifford Albrecht Bernd, ed. *Grillparzer's "Der arme Spielmann."* 27–44.

Enzensberger, Hans Magnus. *The Consciousness Industry: On Literature, Politics and the Media*. Ed. Michael Roloff. New York: Continuum/Seabury, 1974.

Epstein, Joseph. "Why John Irving Is So Popular." *Commentary* 73, no. 6 (June 1982): 59–63.

Evans, R. J. W. *The Making of the Habsburg Monarchy 1550–1700*. Oxford: Clarendon, 1979.

Faber, Marion. "Wolfgang Hildesheimer's *Mozart* as Meta-Biography." *Biography* 3 (1980): 202–8.

Farmer, David Hugh. *The Oxford Dictionary of Saints*. Oxford: Clarendon, 1978.

Fetzer, John Francis. "Jakob: Guardian of the Musical Threshold." In Clifford Albrecht Bernd, ed. *Grillparzer's "Der arme Spielmann."* 254–72.

Fischer, Kurt Gerhard, ed. *Adalbert Stifters Leben und Werk in Briefen und Dokumenten*. Frankfurt/M: Insel Verlag, 1962.

———. "Entwicklung und Bildung in Adalbert Stifters Dichten und Denken." *VASILO* 33, no. 1–2 (1984): 53–60.

Fischer-Lichte, Erika. "The Quest for Meaning." *Stanford Literature Review* 3, no. 1 (Spring 1986): 137–55.

Foster, Hal. "(Post)Modern Polemics." *New German Critique* 33 (Fall 1984): 67–78.

———. ed. *The Anti-Aesthetic: Essays on Postmodern Culture*. Port Townsend, WA: Bay Press, 1983.

Foucault, Michel. *Language, Counter-Memory, Practice: Selected Essays and Interviews*. Ed. Donald F. Bouchard. Ithaca, NY: Cornell UP, 1977.

———. *Madness and Civilization: A History of Insanity in the Age of Reason*. New York: Vintage/Pantheon, 1973.

———. *The Order of Things: An Archaeology of the Human Sciences*. New York: Pantheon, 1970.

———. *Power/Knowledge: Selected Interviews and Other Writings, 1972–1977*. New York: Pantheon, 1980.

"Franz Kafka meets Rudolf Heß (Gespräch)." *Spiegel* 10 (2 March 1987): 204–14.

Frizen, Werner. "*Die Blechtrommel*: Oskar Matzeraths Erzählkunst." *Études Germaniques* 42, no. 1 (January-March 1987): 25–46.

———. "Zur Entstehungsgeschichte von Günter Grass' Roman *Die Blechtrommel*." *Monatshefte* 79, no. 2 (Summer 1987): 210–22.

Geulen, Eva. *Worthörig wider Willen: Darstellungsproblematik und Sprachreflexion in der Prosa A. Stifters*. Munich: Iudicium, 1992.

Geuter, Ulfried. *Die Professionalisierung der deutschen Psychologie im Nationalsozialismus*. Frankfurt/M: Suhrkamp, 1984.

Gianakaris, C[onstantine] J[ohn]. *Peter Shaffer*. New York: St. Martin's, 1992.

———. ed. *Peter Shaffer: A Casebook*. New York: Garland, 1991.

Gibaldi, Joseph, ed. *Introduction to Scholarship in Modern Languages and Literatures*. New York: Modern Language Association, 1981; 2d ed., 1992.

Gillespie, Gerald. "Space and Time Seen Through Stifter's Telescope." *German Quarterly* 37 (1964): 120–30.

Gorceix, Paul. "Ernst von Feuchtersleben et Adalbert Stifter," *Études Germaniques* 40, no. 3 (July-September 1985): 400–412.

Görtz, Franz Josef, ed. *"Die Blechtrommel": Attraktion und Ärgernis*. Darmstadt and Neuwied: Luchterhand, 1984.

Graff, Bernd. *Das Geheimnis der Oberfläche: Der Raum der Postmoderne und die Bühnenkunst Robert Wilsons*. Tübingen: Niemeyer, 1994.

Graff, Gerald. *Professing Literature: An Institutional History*. Chicago: U of Chicago, 1987.

——— and Reginald Gibbons, eds. *Criticism in the University*. TriQuarterly Series on Criticism and Culture 1. Evanston, IL: Northwestern UP, 1985.

Graham, Olive, producer. "Robert Wilson: Avant-Garde Artist (An Interview)." Produced by the UT Center for Telecommunications, University of Texas at Austin. Aired as *Forum* 34 on various dates in 1987; originated in 1986.

Grass, Günter. *Cat and Mouse*. Trans. Ralph Manheim. New York: Harcourt Brace & World, 1963.

———. *Dog Years*. Trans. Ralph Manheim. New York: Fawcett, 1966.

———. *The Flounder*. Trans. Ralph Manheim. New York: Harcourt Brace Jovanovich, 1978.

———. *Headbirths*. Trans. Ralph Manheim. New York: Harcourt Brace Jovanovich, 1982.

———. *The Rat*. Trans. Ralph Manheim. San Diego: Harcourt Brace Jovanovich, 1987.

———. *The Tin Drum*. Trans. Ralph Manheim. New York: Pantheon, 1962.

Grass, Günter, Hansjürgen Rosenbauer, and Ulrich Wickert. "Trommler und Schnecke. Ein Fernsehgespräch" (Westdeutscher Rundfunk, 2 May 1984). In Franz Josef Görtz, ed. *Günter Grass: Auskunft für Leser*. Darmstadt and Neuwied: Luchterhand, 1984. 31–47.

Greenblatt, Stephen, and Giles Gunn, eds. *Redrawing the Boundaries: The Transformation of English and American Literary Studies*. New York: Modern Language Association, 1992.

Griesinger, Wilhelm. *Mental Pathology and Therapeutics*. New York: William Wood, 1882.

Grillparzer, Franz. *Apparat zu den dramatischen Plänen und Bruchstücken und zu den Prosaschriften*. *Sämtliche Werke, Erste Abteilung* 22. Ed. August Sauer and Reinhold Backmann. Vienna: Anton Schroll, 1944.

———. *Der arme Spielmann: Erzählung. Sämtliche Werke*, 3: *Ausgewählte Briefe, Gespräche, Berichte*. Eds. Peter Frank and Karl Pörnbacher. Munich: Carl Hanser, 1964.

———. *The Poor Musician*. Trans. J. F. Hargraves and J. G. Cumming. In Jeffrey L Sammons, ed. *German Novella of Realism I*. German Library 37. New York: Continuum, 1989.

———. *Prosaschriften 1. Sämtliche Werke, Erste Abteilung* 13. Ed. August Sauer and Reinhold Backmann. Vienna: Anton Schroll, 1930.

Grossberg, Lawrence, Cary Nelson, and Paula A. Treichler, eds. *Cultural Studies*. London and New York: Routledge, 1992.

Guidry, Glenn A. "Theoretical Reflections in the Ideological and Social Implications of Mythic Form in Grass' *Die Blechtrommel*." *Monatshefte* 83, no. 2 (Summer 1991): 127–46.

Gump, Margaret. *Adalbert Stifter*. New York: Twayne, 1974.

Hamburger, Käte. *Die Logik der Dichtung*. Stuttgart: Ernst Klett Verlag, 1957.

Hannemann, Bruno. "Heimito von Doderer." In Donald G. Daviau, ed. *Major Figures of Modern Austrian Literature*. Riverside, CA: Ariadne Press, 1988.

Harrowitz, Nancy A. *Antisemitism, Misogyny, and the Logic of Cultural Difference: Cesare Lombroso and Matilde Serao*. Lincoln: U of Nebraska, 1994.

———. and Barbara Hyams, eds. *Jews and Gender: Responses to Otto Weininger*. Philadelphia: Temple UP, 1995.

Harter, Carol C., and James R. Thompson. *John Irving*. Boston: Twayne, 1986.

Härtling, Peter, et al. *Dichter und Richter: Die Gruppe 47 und die deutsche Nachkriegsliteratur*. Akademie-Katalog 151. Berlin: Akademie der Künste, 1988.

Helmetag, Charles H. "The Gentle Law in Adalbert Stifter's *Der Hagestolz*." *Modern Language Studies* 16, no. 3 (Summer 1986): 183–88.

Hennecker, Wilhelm W. *Vor Freud: Philosophiegeschichtliche Voraussetzungen der Psychoanalyse*. Munich, Hamden, Vienna: Philosophia Verlag, 1991.

Herbart, Johann Friedrich, *Lehrbuch zur Psychologie. Sämtliche Werk* 4. Ed. Karl Kehrbach and Otto Flügel. Aalen: Scientia Verlag, *Text-Book in Psychology*. Trans. Margaret K. Smith. New York: Appleton, 1891; rpt. Washington: University Publications of America, 1977.

———. *Psychologie als Wissenschaft neu gegründet auf Erfahrung: Erster synthetischer Theil, Sämtliche Werke* 5; *Zweiter analytischer Theil, Sämtliche Werke* 6. Ed. Karl Kehrbach and Otto Flügel. Aalen: Scientia Verlag, 1964.

Herder, Johann Gottfried von. *Ideen zur Philosophie der Geschichte der Menschheit: Erster und zweiter Teil* (1784–85). *Herders Sämmtliche Werk* 13. Ed. Bernhard Suphan. Berlin: Weidmannsche Buchhandlung, 1887.

———. "Vom Erkennen und Empfinden der menschlichen Seele: Bemerkungen und Träume (1778)." In *Herders Sämmtliche Werke* 8. Ed. Bernhard Suphan. Berlin: Weidmannsche Buchhandlung, 1892. 165–333.

———. "Plastik: Einige Wahrnehmungen über Form und Gestalt aus Pygmalions bildendem Traume (1778)." In *Herders Sämmtliche Werke* 8. Ed. Bernhard Suphan. Berlin: Weidmannsche Buchhandlung, 1892. 1–163.

Hermand, Jost. *Die literarische Formenwelt des Biedermeiers*. Giessen: Wilhelm Schmitz Verlag, 1958.

———. *Unbequeme Literatur: Eine Beispielreihe*. Literatur und Geschichte: Eine Schriftenreihe, 3. Heidelberg: Lothar Stiehm, 1971.

Hertling, Gunter H. "Adalbert Stifter und die Tiere." *Etudes Germaniques* 40, no. 3 (July-September 1985): 387–99.

———. "Der Mensch und 'seine' Tiere: Versäumte Symbiose, versäumte Bildung. Zu A. Stifters *Abdias*." *Modern Austrian Literature* 18, no. 1 (1985): 1–26.

Hesson, Elizabeth C. "Bibliography of Secondary Material on Heimito von Doderer." *Modern Austrian Literature* 19, no. 2 (1986): 47–60.

———. *Twentieth Century Odyssey: A Study of Heimito von Doderer's "Die Dämonen."* Columbia, SC: Camden House, 1982.

Hildesheimer, Wolfgang. *Mozart*. Frankfurt/M: Suhrkamp, 1979; New York: Farrar, Straus, & Giroux, 1982; Noonday Press, 1991.

Hill, Jane Bowers. "John Irving's Aesthetics of Accessibility: Setting Free the Novel." *South Carolina Review* 16, no. 1 (Fall 1983): 38–44.

Hinterhäuser, Hans. "Heimito von Doderer und *Die Strudelhofstiege*." In Wolfgang Bandhauer and Robert Tanzmeister, eds. *Romanistik Integrativ: Festschrift für Wolfgang Pollak*. Wiener romanistische Arbeiten 13. Vienna: Wilhelm Braumüller, 1985. 205–11.

Hirsch, E. D., Jr. *Cultural Literacy: What Every American Needs to Know*. Boston: Houghton Mifflin, 1987.

Hobsbawm, Eric, and Terence Ranger, eds. *The Invention of Tradition.* Cambridge: Cambridge UP, 1983.

Höller, Hans. "Die sozialgeschichtliche Bedeutung der ästhetischen Wahrnehmung bei A. Stifter." *Wirkendes Wort* 4 (July–August 1982): 255–67.

———. "Thomas Bernhard und Adalbert Stifter: Die Radikalisierung der Isolation und Todesfixierung von Stifters *Hagestolz.*" In Alfred Pitteratscher and Johann Lachinger, eds. *Literarisches Kolloquium Linz '84: Thomas Bernhard.* Linz: Oberösterreichischer Landesverlag, 1985. 29–41.

Hollington, Michael. *Günter Grass: The Writer in a Pluralist Society.* London: Marion Boyars, 1980.

hooks, bell. *Feminist Theory: From Margin to Center.* Boston: South End Press, 1984.

Horowitz, Michael. "Heimito von Doderer — Versuch einer Biographie." In Michael Horowitz, ed. *Begegnungen mit Heimito von Doderer.* 131–88.

———. ed. *Begegnung mit Heimito von Doderer.* Vienna: Amalthea, 1983.

Huber, Werner, and Hubert Zapf. "On the Structure of Peter Shaffer's *Amadeus.*" *Modern Drama* 27, no. 3 (September 1984): 299–313.

Hunter-Lougheed, Rosemarie. "Adalbert Stifter: *Brigitta* (1844–47)." In Paul Michael Lützeler, ed. *Romane und Erzählungen zwischen Romantik und Realismus: Neue Interpretation.*" Stuttgart: Reclam, 1983. 354–85.

———. "Das Thema der Liebe im *Armen Spielmann.*" In Clifford Albrecht Bernd, ed. *Grillparzer's "Der arme Spielmann."* 79–92.

———. "Wald, Haus und Wasser, Moos und Schmetterling." *VASILO* 24, no. 1–2 (1975): 23–36.

Huyssen, Andreas. "Mapping the Postmodern." *New German Critique* 33 (Fall 1984): 5–52.

Iden, Peter. "Death of a Thief: Ein Nachruf anläßlich Robert Wilsons *DD&D.*" *Theater heute* 4 (April 1979): 15–16.

Iehl, Dominique. "Réalité et pénurie dans l'œuvre littéraire et picturale de Stifter." *Études Germaniques* 40, no. 3 (July–September 1985): 297–310.

Irigaray, Luce. *This Sex Which Is Not One.* Trans. Catherine Porter and Carolyn Burke. Ithaca, NY: Cornell UP, 1985.

Irmscher, Hans Dietrich. *Adalbert Stifter: Wirklichkeitserfahrung und gegenständliche Darstellung.* Munich: Wilhelm Fink Verlag, 1971.

Irving, John. *The Cider House Rules: A Novel.* New York: Morrow, 1985.

———. "Garp's Dismissal of *The Poor Fiddler.*" In Clifford Albrecht Bernd, ed. *Grillparzer's "Der arme Spielmann."* 45–46.

———. "Günter Grass: King of the Toy Merchants" [Review of *Headbirths*]. In Patrick O'Neill, ed. *Critical Essays on Günter Grass.* 61–68. Rpt., *Trying to Save Piggy Sneed.* 397–412.

———. *The Hotel New Hampshire.* New York: E. P. Dutton, 1981.

——. "Humans Are a Violent Species — We Always Have Been" [A Conversation with John Irving, conducted by Alvin P. Sanoff]. *U. S. News & World Report*, 26 October 1981: 70–71.

——. "Is Celebrity Good for You?" *Newsweek*, 18 October 1982: 68.

——. "The Narrative Voice." In Allen Wier and Don Hendrie, Jr., eds. *Voicelust: Eight Contemporary Fiction Writers on Style*. Lincoln: U of Nebraska, 1985. 87–92.

——. "Porn and the Novelist: Freedom to Read" [section 2 of a 5-part article of that title]. *Current* no. 290 (February 1987): 27–28.

——. *A Prayer for Owen Meany: A Novel*. New York: William Morrow 1989.

——. *Setting Free the Bears*. New York: Random House, 1968.

——. *A Son of the Circus*. New York: Random House, 1994.

——. *Trying to Save Piggy Sneed*. New York: Arcade, 1996.

——. *The World According to Garp*. New York: E. P. Dutton, 1978; London: Corgi, 1982.

Ivask, Ivor. "A Bio-Bibliography of Heimito von Doderer." *Books Abroad* 42, no. 3 (Summer 1968): 380–84.

——. "Introducing the Symposium: A Winter with Heimito." *Books Abroad* 42, no. 3 (Summer 1968): 343–48.

——. ed. "An International Symposium in Memory of Heimito von Doderer (1896–1966)." *Books Abroad: An International Literary Quarterly* 42, no. 3 (Summer 1968); special issue.

Jacoby, Russell. *The Last Intellectuals: American Culture in the Age of Academe*. New York: Basic Books, 1987.

Jahnke, Walter, and Klaus Lindemann. *Günter Grass, "Die Blechtrommel": Acht Kapitel zur Erschließung des Romans*. Modellanalysen Literatur. Paderborn: Ferdinand Schöningh, 1993.

Jameson, Frederic. "The Politics of Theory: Ideological Positions in the Post-modernism Debate." *New German Critique* 33 (Fall 1984): 53–65.

——. "Postmodernism, or the Cultural Logic of Late Capitalism." *New Left Review* 146 (July-August 1984): 53–92.

Jauss, Hans-Robert. "Literary History as a Challenge to Literary Theory." In *Toward an Aesthetic of Reception*. Trans. Timothy Bahti. Minneapolis: U of Minnesota, 1982. 3–45.

Jehle, Volker, ed. *Wolfgang Hildesheimer*. Suhrkamp Taschenbuch Materialien. Frankfurt/M: 1989.

Johnston, William M. *The Austrian Mind: An Intellectual and Social History, 1848–1938*. Berkeley: U of California, 1972.

Jones, Daniel A. "Peter Shaffer's Continued Quest for God in *Amadeus*." *Comparative Drama* 21, no. 2 (Summer 1987): 145–55.

Jones, David L. "Heimito von Doderer and Man's 'Existential Fear.'" *Papers on Language and Literature* 20, no. 2 (Spring 1984): 205–17.

Kaiser, Gerhard. "Der Dichter als Prophet in Stifters *Haidedorf*." In *Wanderer und Idylle: Goethe und die Phänomenologie der Natur in der deutschen Dichtung von Geßner bis Gottfried Keller.* Göttingen: Vandenhoeck & Ruprecht, 1977. 240–57.

Kant, Immanuel. *Anthropologie in pragmatischer Hinsicht.* 7th ed. Hamburg: Felix Meiner, 1980. *Anthropology from a Pragmatic Point of View* . Trans. M. J. Gregor. The Hague: Nijhoff, 1974.

Kanter, Rosabeth Moss. "Women and the Structures of Organizations: Explorations in Theory and Behavior." In Marcia Millman and Rosabeth Moss Kanter, eds. *Another Voice.* 34–74.

Kaufmann, David. "The Profession of Theory." *PMLA* 105, no. 3 (May 1990): 519–30.

Kazin, Alfred. "God's Own Little Squirt: A Prayer for Owen Meany." *New York Times Book Review*, 12 March 1989: 1, 30–31.

Keele, Alan Frank. "' . . .Through a (Dark) Glass Clearly': Magic Spectacles and the Motif of the Mimetic Mantic in Postwar German Literature from Borchert to Grass." *Germanic Review* 57, no. 2 (Spring 1982): 49–59.

——. *Understanding Günter Grass.* Columbia: U of South Carolina, 1988.

Kelleher, Maureen. "Interview mit Robert Wilson: Während des Stückes aufs Klo." *TIP* 4 (1979): 36–37.

Keller, Evelyn Fox. *Reflections on Gender and Science.* New Haven: Yale UP, 1985.

——. "The Gender-Science System: Response to Kelly Oliver." *Hypatia* 3, no. 3 (Winter 1989): 149–52.

Keller, Thomas. *Die Schrift in Stifters "Nachsommer": Buchstäblichkeit und Bildlichkeit des Romantextes.* Cologne and Vienna: Böhlau, 1982.

Klein, Dennis A. *Peter Shaffer.* Rev. ed. New York: Twayne, 1993.

Koestler, Arthur. *The Case of the Midwife Toad.* New York: Vintage, 1971.

Koutek, Eduard. *Wien: Straßen, Gassen und Plätze erzählen Geschichte.* Vienna: Verlag H. Kapri, 1977.

Kramberg, Karl Heinz. "Nachwort des Herausgebers." In Heimito von Doderer. *Das Doderer-Buch: Eine Auswahl aus seinem Werk.* 389–402.

Krispyn, Egbert. "The Resonant Past in Austrian Literature." In Herbert Lederer and Maria Luise Caputo-Mayr, eds. *Österreich in amerikanischer Sicht: Das Österreichbild im amerikanischen Schulunterricht, 2.* New York: Austrian Institute, 1981. 34–39.

Kristeva, Julia. *Powers of Horror: An Essay on Abjection.* Trans. Leon S. Roudiez. New York: Columbia UP, 1982.

——. and Philippe Sollers. "Why the United States?" In Toril Moi, ed. *The Kristeva Reader.* New York: Columbia UP, 1986. 272–91.

Kröll, Friedhelm. *Die "Gruppe 47": Soziale Lage und gesellschaftliches Bewußtsein literarischer Intelligenz in der Bundesrepublik.* Stuttgart: J. B. Metzler, 1977.

Krumme, Peter. "Passe-partout: Robert Wilsons Bühne in 'Death Destruction & Detroit.'" In Peter von Becker and Henning Rischbieter, eds. *Theater 1979: Jahrbuch der Zeitschrift "Theater Heute."* Seelze: Friedrich Verlag, 1979. 84–87.

Kucher, Gabriele. *Thomas Mann und Heimito von Doderer: Mythos und Geschichte — Auflösung als Zusammenfassung im modernen Roman.* Nuremberg: Hans Carl, 1981.

Lacan, Jacques. *Écrits: A Selection.* Trans. Alan Sheridan. New York: W. W. Norton, 1977.

Lachinger, Johann, and Regina Pintar. "Adalbert-Stifter-Bibliographie." *VASILO* 39, no. 3–4 (1990): 41–86.

Lachinger, Johann, Alexander Stillmark, and Martin Swales, eds. *Adalbert Stifter Heute: Londoner Symposium 1983.* Linz: Adalbert Stifter Institut des Landes Oberösterreich and Oberösterreichischer Landesverlag, 1985.

Lawson, Richard H. *Günter Grass.* New York: Fredrick Ungar, 1985.

Leary, David E. *The Reconstruction of Psychology in Germany, 1780–1850* . Diss. U of Chicago, 1977.

——. "The Psychological Development of the Conception of Psychology in Germany, 1780–1850," *Journal of the History of the Behavioral Sciences* 14 (1978): 113–21.

——. "Immanuel Kant and the Development of Modern Psychology." In Mitchell G. Ash and William R. Woodward, eds. *The Problematic Science.* New York: Praeger, 1982.

——. "German Idealism and the Development of Psychology in the Nineteenth Century." *Journal of the History of Philosophy* 18, no. 3 (July 1980): 299–317.

Lefebvre, Henri. *The Production of Space.* Trans. Donald Nicholson-Smith. Oxford: Blackwell, 1991.

Lehman, David. "Yale's Insomniac Genius (Harold Bloom)." *Newsweek* 108 (18 August 1986): 56–57.

Lehmann, Hans-Thies. "Robert Wilson, Szenograph." *Merkur: Deutsche Zeitschrift für europäisches Denken* 39, no. 7 (July 1985): 554–63.

Le Rider, Jacques. *Der Fall Otto Weininger: Wurzeln des Antifeminismus und Antisemitismus.* 2d rev. and exp. ed. Vienna: Löcker, 1985.

——. "Heimito von Doderer und Otto Weininger." In Pierre Grappin and Jean-Pierre Christophe, eds. *L'Actualité de Doderer: Actes du colloque international tenu à Metz (Novembre 1984).* Metz: Didier-Erudition, 1986. 37–45.

——. "Variations sur le Theme de l'*Anschluß*, de Robert Musil à Heimito von Doderer." *Austriaca* 26 (March 1988): 101–6.

Lesky, Erna. *The Vienna Medical School of the Nineteenth Century.* Baltimore: Johns Hopkins UP, 1976.

Lettner, Gerda. *Das Rückzugsgefecht der Aufklärung in Wien 1790–1792.* Frankfurt/M and New York: Campus, 1988.

Levin, David J. "The Tone of Truth? Music as Counter-Discourse in *Der arme Spielmann.*" In Clifford Albrecht Bernd, ed. *Grillparzer's "Der arme Spielmann."* 287–299.

Lewis, Lionel S. *Scaling the Ivory Tower: Merit and Its Limits in Academic Careers.* Baltimore: Johns Hopkins UP, 1975.

Lieberson, Jonathan. "Lovely to Look At: *the CIVIL warS.*" *New York Review of Books* 11 (April 1985): 18–21.

Lindenberger, Herbert. "Introduction. Ideology and Innocence: On the Politics of Critical Language." *PMLA* 105, no. 3 (May 1990): 398–408.

Lindsey, Barbara. "Music in *Der arme Spielmann* with Special Consideration to the Elements of the Sacred and Profane." In Clifford Albrecht Bernd, ed. *Grillparzer's "Der arme Spielmann."* 273–86.

Lipman, Samuel. "*Einstein*'s Long March to Brooklyn." *New Criterion* 3, no. 6 (February 1985): 15–24.

Lippard, Lucy R. "The Dinner Party." *Art in America* 79 (December 1991): 39.

Lorenz, Dagmar C. G. "Stifters Frauen." *Colloquia Germanica* 15, no. 4 (1982): 305–20.

Lorey, Christoph. "'Alles ist so schön, daß es fast zu schön ist': Die sozialkritischen Motive in Adalbert Stifters Roman *Der Nachsommer.*" *German Quarterly* 66, no. 4 (Fall 1993): 477–89.

Lotringer, Sylvère. "Christo: Die Geschichte verpacken." In *New Yorker Gespräche.* Trans. from French by Kornelia Gantze and Babs Petersen. Berlin: Merve Verlag, 1983. 245–61.

———. "Bob Wilson: Es gibt eine Sprache, die universell ist." In *New Yorker Gespräche.* Trans. from French by Kornelia Gantze and Babs Petersen. Berlin: Merve Verlag, 1983. 37–48.

Lunding, Erik. "Forschungsbericht: Probleme und Ergebnisse der Stifterforschung 1945–1954." *Euphorion* 3, no. 49 (1955): 203–44.

Lyotard, Jean-François. *The Differend: Phrases in Dispute.* Trans. Georges Van Den Abbeele. Theory and History of Literature 46. Minneapolis: U of Minnesota, 1988.

———. *The Postmodern Condition: A Report on Knowledge.* Trans. Geoff Bennington and Brian Massumi. Foreword by Frederic Jameson. Theory and History of Literature 10. Minneapolis: U of Minnesota, 1984.

Magris, Claudio. "Doderers erste Wirklichkeit." *Literatur und Kritik* 114 (May 1977): 209–26.

Mahlendorf, Ursula. "*The Poor Fiddler*: The Terror of Rejection." In Clifford Albrecht Bernd, ed. *Grillparzer's "Der arme Spielmann."* 111–132.

———. "Stifters Absage an die Kunst." In Gerhart Hoffmeister, ed. *Goethezeit: Studien zur Erkenntnis und Rezeption Goethes und seiner Zeitgenossen, Festschrift für Stuart Atkins.* Bern and Munich: Francke Verlag, 1981. 369–83.

Märchenspiel, Theatertraum, Kunstmausoleum (*DD&D II*)." *Spiegel* 10 (2 March 1987): 202–8.

Märki, Peter. *Adalbert Stifter, Narrheit und Erzählstruktur.* Europäische Hochschulschriften, series 1, no. 262. Bern: Peter Lang, 1979.

Märkisch, Anneliese. *Das Problem des Schicksals bei Adalbert Stifter.* Germanische Studien, Heft 233. Ed. Walther Hofststetter, 1941. Rpt. Nendeln/Liechtenstein: Kraus Reprint, 1969.

Markus, Georg. *Der Fall Redl.* Vienna: Amalthea, 1984.

Marranca, Bonnie. "Robert Wilson: A Letter for Queen Victoria (1976)." In Marranca, ed. and intro. *The Theater of Images.* New York: Drama Book Specialists, 1977.

——. and Gautam Dasgupta, eds. "A Robert Wilson Retrospective." *Performing Arts Journal: 43* 15, no. 1 (January 1993).

Matt, Peter von. *Literaturwissenschaft und Psychoanalyse: Eine Einführung.* Freiburg: Verlag Rombach, 1972.

Matussek, Matthias. "Stars in der Manege: Über "The Forest" von Robert Wilson and David Byrne in Berlin." *Spiegel* 43 (24 October 1988): 252, 255.

McCaffrey, Larry. "An Interview with John Irving." Tom LeClair and Larry McCaffrey. *Anything Can Happen: Interviews with Contemporary Novelists.* Urbana: U of Illinois, 1983. 176–98. Orig. published in *Contemporary Literature* 23, no. 1 (Winter 1982): 1–18.

McElroy, Bernard. "Lunatic, Child, Artist, Hero: Grass's Oskar as a Way of Seeing." *Forum for Modern Language Studies* 22, no. 4 (October 1986): 308–22.

McInnes, Malcolm. "Doderer versus Hausmeister." *German Life and Letters* 41, no. 2 (January 1988): 131–44.

——. "Österreich — Österreicher — Am Österreichischsten: Heimito von Doderer and Austria." *Colloquia Germanica* 18, no. 1 (1985): 18–39.

——. "Wordplay in the Works of Heimito von Doderer." *Forum for Modern Language Studies* 23, no. 1 (January 1987): 66–78.

McLaughlin, Jeff. "The Robert Wilson Experience . . . ." *Boston Globe,* 9 March 1986: 57, 60.

McVeigh, Joseph. *Kontinuität und Vergangenheitsbewältigung in der österreichischen Literatur nach 1945.* Vienna: Wilhelm Braumüller, 1988.

Meier, Albert. "Diskretes Erzählen: Über den Zusammenhang von Dichtung, Wissenschaft und Didaktik in A. Stifters Erzählung *Brigitta.*" Aurora: *Jahrbuch der Eichendorff-Gesellschaft* 44 (1984): 213–23.

"Mein Vater, der Schelm, der mich gessen hat." *Spiegel* 4 (23 January 1984): 159 and 162.

Mews, Siegfried, ed. *"The Fisherman and His Wife": Günter Grass's 'The Flounder' in Critical Perspective.* New York: AMS Press, 1983.

——. "From Admiration to Confrontation: Günter Grass and The United States." *U of Dayton Review* 17, no. 3 (Winter 1985–86): 3–13.

Miller, Gabriel. *John Irving*. New York: Frederick Ungar, 1982.

Miller, J. Hillis. "How Deconstruction Works." *New York Times*, 9 February 1986: 25.

Millman, Marcia, and Rosabeth Moss Kanter, eds. *Another Voice: Feminist Perspectives on Social Life and Social Science*. Garden City, NY: Doubleday/Anchor, 1975.

Mitchell, W. J. T., ed. *Against Theory: Literary Studies and the New Pragmatism*. Chicago: U of Chicago, 1985.

Mörike, Eduard. *Mozart auf der Reise nach Prag*. Stuttgart: Reclam, 1970.

Mouton, Janice. "Gnomes, Fairy-Tale Heroes, and Oskar Matzerath." *Germanic Review* 56, no. 1 (Winter 1981): 28–33.

Mueller-Vollmer, Kurt, ed. *The Hermeneutics Reader*. New York: Continuum, 1985.

Mullan, Boyd. "Characterisation and Narrative Technique in Grillparzer's *Der arme Spielmann* and Storm's *Ein stiller Musikant*." *German Life and Letters* 44, no. 3 (April 1991): 187–89.

Müller, Heiner. "Brief an Robert Wilson." Supplement to the Program of *DD&D II*. Berlin: Schaubühne am Lehniner Platz, 23 February 1987. Unpaginated.

Naumann, Ursula. *Adalbert Stifter*. Stuttgart: J. B. Metzler, 1979.

Neugebauer, Klaus. *Selbstentwurf und Verhängnis: Ein Beitrag zu Adalbert Stifters Verständnis von Schicksal und Geschichte*. Tübingen: Stauffenberg Verlag, 1982.

Neuhaus, Volker. *Günter Grass*. 2d ed. Stuttgart: J. B. Metzler, 1993.

Neunzig, Hans A., ed. *Hans Werner Richter und die Gruppe 47*. Munich: Nymphenberg, 1979.

———. *Lesebuch der Gruppe 47*. Munich: Deutscher Taschenbuch Verlag, 1983.

Nochlin, Linda. "Why Have There Been No Great Women Artists?" In *Women, Art, and Power and Other Essays*. New York: Harper & Row, 1988. 145–78.

Oates, Joyce Carol. *Bellefleur*. New York: E. P. Dutton, 1980.

Oliver, Kelly. "Keller's Gender-Science System: Is the Philosophy of Science to Science as Science Is to Nature?" *Hypatia* 3, no. 3 (Winter 1989): 137–48.

O'Neill, Patrick. "A Different Drummer: The American Reception of Günter Grass." In Wolfgang Elfe, James Hardin, and Gunther Holst, eds. *The Fortunes of German Writers in America: Studies in Literary Reception*. Columbia: U of South Carolina, 1992. 277–85.

———. ed. *Critical Essays on Günter Grass*. Boston: G.K. Hall, 1987.

O'Sullivan, Maurice J., Jr. "Garp Unparadised: Biblical Echoes in John Irving's *The World According to Garp*." *Notes on Modern American Literature* 7, no. 2 (Fall 1983): section 11.

Page, Philip. "Hero Worship and Hermeneutic Dialectics: John Irving's *A Prayer for Owen Meany*." *Mosaic: A Journal for the Interdisciplinary Study of Literature* 28, no. 3 (September 1995): 137–56.

Pauley, Bruce F. *Hitler and the Forgotten Nazis: A History of Austrian National Socialism*. London: Macmillan, 1981.

Perraudin, Michael. "*Mozart auf der Reise nach Prag*, the French Revolution, and 1848." *Monatshefte* 81, no. 1 (Spring 1989): 45–61.

Petterson, Torsten. "'Eine Welt aus Sehen und Blindheit': Consciousness and World in Stifter's *Abdias*." *Germanisch-Romanische Monatsschrift* 40, no. 1 (1990): 41–53.

Phinney, Kevin. "UT to Stage 9–1/2-Hour Epic Opera" (on *the CIVIL warS*). *Austin American-Statesman*, 27 September 1985: B7.

——. "$4 Million Raised Before Cancellation of Opera." *Austin American-Statesman*, 7 February 1986: B5.

——. "Too Talented to Write Off: Artist's Vision Earns Praise." *Austin American-Statesman*, 12 June 1986: C1.

——. "Wilson, Byrne Theater Begins at PAC." *Austin American-Statesman*, 8 May 1987: D12.

——. "A Little Bit Goes a Long Way: 'Knee Plays' a Good Look at 'warS' Saga." *Austin American-Statesman*, 13 May 1987: B14.

Pickar, Gertrud Bauer, ed. *Adventures of a Flounder: Critical Essays on Günter Grass' Der Butt*. Houston German Studies 3. Munich: Wilhelm Fink, 1982.

Piechotta, Hans-Joachim. *Aleatorische Ordnung*. Gießen: Wilhelm Schmitz Verlag, 1981.

Plumpe, Gerhard. "Diskursive Textstrukturierung: Versuch zu Adalbert Stifters *Bergkristall*." In Helmut Brackert and Jörn Stückrath with Eberhard Lämmert, eds. *Literaturwissenschaft: Grundkurs 1*. Reinbek bei Hamburg: Rowohlt, 1981. 353–79.

Plunka, Gene A. *Peter Shaffer: Roles, Rites, and Rituals in the Theater*. Rutherford, NJ: Fairleigh Dickinson UP, 1988.

Politzer, Heinz. *Franz Grillparzer, oder das abgründige Biedermeier*. Vienna: Verlag Fritz Molden, 1972.

Porter, James I. "Reading Representation in *Der arme Spielmann*." In Clifford Albrecht Bernd, ed. *Grillparzer's "Der arme Spielmann*." 177–205.

Pott, Hans-Georg. "Der 'neue Heimatroman'?: Zum Konzept 'Heimat' in der neueren Literatur." In Hans-Georg Pott, ed. *Literatur und Provinz*. 7–21.

——. *Literatur und Provinz: Das Konzept 'Heimat' in der neueren Literatur*. Paderborn: Ferdinand Schöningh, 1986.

"A Prayer for Owen Meany" [Review]. *Publishers Weekly*, 6 January 1989: 89–90.

Preisendanz, Wolfgang. "Die Erzählfunktion der Naturdarstellung bei Stifter." *Wirkendes Wort* 16, no. 4 (1966): 407–18.

Priestley, Michael. "Structure in the Worlds of John Irving." *Critique: Studies in Modern Fiction* 23, no. 1 (1981): 82–96.

Prikker, Bertel Thorn. "An Interview with Robert Wilson: 'I Just Want to Be Normal.'" *Ricochet* 1 (Fall 1987): 31–37.

Pritchard, William. "Small-Town Saint: A Prayer for Owen Meany." *New Republic*, 22 May 1989: 36–38.

Quadri, Franco. "Robert Wilson oder die Entdeckung der Zeit." In Robert Wilson. *(der deutsche Teil von) the CIVIL warS*. 11–23.

Rabinbach, Anson. *The Crisis of Austrian Socialism: From Red Vienna to Civil War, 1927–1934*. Chicago: U of Chicago, 1983.

Reeve, William C. "Proportion and Disproportion in *Der arme Spielmann*." In Clifford Albrecht Bernd, ed. *Grillparzer's "Der arme Spielmann."* 93–110.

Reilly, Edward C. "The *Anschluß* and the World According to Irving." *Research Studies* (Washington State University) 51, no. 2 (June 1983): 98–110.

———. "A John Irving Bibliography." *Bulletin of Bibliography* 42, no. 1 (March 1985): 12–18.

———. *Understanding John Irving*. Columbia: U of South Carolina, 1991.

Remnick, David. "Hamlet in Hollywood." *New Yorker* 71 (20 November 1995): 66–72.

Richter, Hans Werner. *Im Etablissement der Schmetterlinge: Einundzwanzig Portraits aus der Gruppe 47*. Munich: Hanser, 1986.

Rickels, Laurence A. "*Die Blechtrommel* zwischen Schelmen- und Bildungsroman." *Amsterdamer Beiträge zur neueren Germanistik* 20 (1985–86): 109–32.

Rimmon-Kenan, Shlomith. "Narration as Repetition: The Case of Günter Grass's *Cat and Mouse*." In Rimmon-Kenan, ed. *Discourse in Psychoanalysis and Literature*. 176–87.

———. ed. *Discourse in Psychoanalysis and Literature*. London: Methuen, 1987.

Ritter, Naomi. "Poet and Carnival: Goethe, Grillparzer, Baudelaire." In Clifford Albrecht Bernd, ed. *Grillparzer's "Der arme Spielmann."* 337–51.

Roazen, Paul. *Freud and His Followers*. New York: New York UP, 1984.

Robbins, Bruce. "Oppositional Professionals: Theory and the Narratives of Professionalization." In Jonathan Arac and Barbara Johnson, eds. *Consequences of Theory*. 1–21.

Rockwell, John. "Robert Wilson's Stage Works: Originality and Influences." In Robert Stearns, ed. *Robert Wilson*. 10–31.

———. "Stage: New Work by Robert Wilson (*DD&D II*)." *New York Times*, Arts/Entertainment, 2 May 1987: 12.

Roe, Ian F. "*Der arme Spielmann* and the Role of Compromise in Grillparzer's World." In Clifford Albrecht Bernd, ed. *Grillparzer's "Der arme Spielmann."* 133–44.

Rogan, Richard G. "Stifter's *Brigitta*: The Eye to the Soul." *German Studies Review* 13, no. 2 (May 1990): 243–51.

Ross, Andrew, ed. *Universal Abandon?: The Politics of Postmodernism*. Minneapolis: U of Minnesota, 1988.

Rosovsky, Henry. *The University: An Owner's Manual*. New York: W. W. Norton, 1990.

Rudwick, Martin J. S. *The Great Devonian Controversy: The Shaping of Scientific Knowledge among Gentlemanly Specialists.* Chicago: U of Chicago, 1985.

Rühle, Günther. "Die Vision ins Nichts: Über Bob Wilsons *Death Destruction & Detroit.*" *Theater heute* 4 (April 1979): 6–10.

Runyon, Randolph. "Of Fishie Fumes and Other Critical Strategies in the Hotel of the Text." *Cream City Review* (Milwaukee) 8 (1983): 18–28.

Ryan, Ingrid. "The Memory Perspective in Heimito von Doderer's *Die Dämonen.*" *Perspectives on Contemporary Literature* 9 (1983): 43–50.

Said, Edward W. *Culture and Imperialism.* New York: Alfred A. Knopf, 1993.

——. *Orientalism.* New York: Vintage/Random House, 1978.

——. *The World, the Text, and the Critic.* Cambridge, MA: Harvard UP, 1983.

Sainte-Beuve, Charles-Augustin. *Vie, Poésies et Pensées de Joseph Delorme.* Ed. Gérald Antoine. Paris: Nouvelles Éditions Latines, 1956.

Schäublin, Peter. "Stifters Abdias von Herder aus gelesen." *VASILO* 23, no. 3–4 (1974): 101–13; and 24, no. 3–4 (1975): 87–105.

Schiffermüller, Isolde. "Adalbert Stifters deskriptive Prosa: Eine Modellanalyse der Novelle *Der beschriebene Tännling.*" *Deutsche Vierteljahrschrift für Literaturwissenschaft und Geistesgeschichte* 67, no. 2 (June 1993): 267–301.

Schillinger, Liesl. "Misunderstood as Ever [Review of *Beyond the Flower*]." *New York Times Book Review*, 24 March 1996: 21.

Schmidt-Dengler, Wendelin. "Bibliographie: Sekundärliteratur zu Heimito von Doderer." *Literatur und Kritik* 80 (1973): 615–20.

——. "Heimito von Doderer: Rückzug auf die Sprache." In *Österreichische Literatur der dreißiger Jahre: Ideologische Verhältnisse, Institutionelle Voraussetzungen, Fallstudien.* Vienna: Böhlau, 1985. 291–302.

Schnitzler, Arthur. *Der Geist im Wort und der Geist in der Tat: Vorläufige Bemerkungen zu zwei Diagrammen.* Berlin: S. Fischer, 1927. *The Mind in Words and Actions: Preliminary Remarks Concerning Two Diagrams.* Trans. Robert O. Weiss. New York: Friedrick Ungar, 1972.

——. *Das Haus Delorme* (Performed 1900). In Arthur Schnitzler. *Entworfenes und Verworfenes: Aus dem Nachlaß.* Ed. Reinhard Urbach. Frankfurt/M: S. Fischer, 1977.

——. "Lieutenant Gustl." In *Arthur Schnitzler: Plays and Stories.* Ed. Egon Schwarz. The German Library 55. New York: Continuum, 1982.

Schoenborn, Peter A. *Adalbert Stifter: Sein Leben und Werk.* Bern: Francke, 1992.

Schorske, Carl. *Fin de siècle Vienna: Politics and Culture.* New York: Alfred A. Knopf, 1980.

Seeba, Hinrich C. "Franz Grillparzer: Der arme Spielmann (1847)." In Paul Michael Lützeler, ed. *Romane und Erzählungen zwischen Romantik und Realismus: Neue Interpretationen.* Stuttgart: Reclam, 1983. 386–422.

——. "'Ich habe keine Geschichte': Zur Enthistorisierung der Geschichte vom *armen Spielmann.*" In Clifford Albrecht Bernd, ed. *Grillparzer's "Der arme Spielmann."* 206–32.

Seidler, Herbert. "Adalbert-Stifter-Forschung 1945–1970 (Erster Teil)." *Zeitschrift für deutsche Philologie* 91, no. 1 (1972): 113–57.

——. " Adalbert-Stifter-Forschung 1945–1970 (Zweiter Teil)." *Zeitschrift für deutsche Philologie* 91, no. 2 (1972): 252–85.

——. "Die Adalbert-Stifter-Forschung der siebziger Jahre." *VASILO* 30, no. 3–4 (1981): 89–134.

Sengle, Friedrich. *Biedermeierzeit: Deutsche Literatur im Spannungsfeld zwischen Restauration und Revolution, 1815–1848.* Bd. 1. Stuttgart: J. B. Metzler, 1971; Bd. 2, 1972; Bd. 3, 1980.

Shaffer, Peter. *Amadeus.* New York: Harper & Row, 1981.

——. "Paying Homage to Mozart." *New York Times Magazine,* 2 September 1984: 22–23 ff.

Sheppard, R. Z. "Life into Art: Garp Creator John Irving Strikes Again" [Cover Story]. *Time,* 31 August 1981: 46–51.

——. "The Message Is the Message: A Prayer for Owen Meany." *Time,* 3 April 1989: 80.

Shostak, Debra. "Plot as Repetition: John Irving's Narrative Experiments." *Critique: Studies in Contemporary Fiction* 37, no. 1 (Fall 1995): 51–70.

Shyer, Laurence. *Robert Wilson and His Collaborators.* New York: Theater Communications Group, 1989.

Sjörgren, Christine Oertel. "The Allure of Beauty in Stifter's *Brigitta.*" *JEGP* 81, no. 1 (January 1982): 47–54.

——. "The Frame of *Der Waldbrunnen* Reconsidered: A Note on Adalbert Stifter's Aesthetics." *Modern Austrian Literature* 19, no. 1 (1986): 9–25.

Slawik, Franz. "Literatur von Innen." *Literatur und Kritik* 114 (May 1977): 227–41.

Slaymaker, William. "Who Cooks, Winds Up: The Dilemma in Grass' *Die Blechtrommel* and *Hundejahre.*" *Colloquia Germanica* 14 (1981): 48–68.

Slessarev, Helga. *Eduard Mörike.* New York: Twayne, 1970.

Smith, Barbara Herrnstein. *Contingencies of Value: Alternative Perspectives for Critical Theory.* Cambridge, MA: Harvard UP, 1988.

Spivak, Gayatri Chakravorty. *In Other Worlds: Essays in Cultural Politics.* New York and London: Routledge, 1988.

Stahl, August. "Die ängstliche Idylle: Zum Gebrauch der Negationen in Stifters *Nachsommer.*" *Literatur und Kritik* 167–168 (September-October 1982): 19–28.

Staiger, Emil. "Reiz und Maß: Das Beispiel Stifter." In Lothar Stiehm, ed. *Adalbert Stifter, Studien und Interpretationen.* Heidelberg: Lothar Stiehm Verlag, 1968. 7–22.

——. *Adalbert Stifter als Dichter der Ehrfurcht.* Zurich: Verlag der Arche, 1952.

Stanley, Patricia H. *The Realm of Possibilities: Wolfgang Hildesheimer's Non-Traditional Non-Fictional Prose.* Lanham, MD: UP of America, 1988.

——. *Wolfgang Hildesheimer and His Critics.* Columbia, SC: Camden House, 1993.

Stansbury, David. "getting to A . . . (is very complicated)." *3rd Coast* (December 1986): 50–84.

Stearns, Robert, ed. *Robert Wilson: From a Theater of Images.* Cincinnati: Contemporary Arts Center, 1980. 2d ed., rev., with new material added. New York: Harper & Row, 1984.

Steffen, Hans. "Traumbedürfnis und Traumanalyse: Stifters *Hochwald.*" *Etudes Germaniques* 40, no. 3 (July-September 1985): 311–34.

Stieg, Gerald. "Früchte des Feuers. Der 15. Juli in der *Blendung* und in den *Dämonen.*" In Friedbert Aspetsberger and Gerald Stieg, eds. *Elias Canetti: Blendung als Lebensform.* Königstein/Ts: Athenäum, 1985. 143–75.

Stiehm, Lothar, ed. *Adalbert Stifter, Studien und Interpretationen.* Heidelberg: Lothar Stiehm, 1968.

Stifter, Adalbert. *Abdias.* In *Studien* 1, part 5. 235–342.

——. "Ausstellung des oberösterreichischen Kunstvereines (1867)." In *Vermischte Schriften* (ed. Gustav Wilhelm) 14. 218–19.

——. *Bunte Steine: Journalfassungen.* In *Werke und Briefe* 2, part 2. Ed. Hermut Bergner. Stuttgart: W. Kohlhammer, 1982.

——. *Der Hagestolz.* In *Studien* 1, part 6. 11–142.

——. *Der Hochwald.* In *Studien* 1, part 4. 209–318.

——. *Indian Summer.* Trans. Wendell Frye. New York: Peter Lange, 1985.

——. "Obderennsische Kunstausstellung (1857)." In *Vermischte Schriften* (ed. Gustav Wilhelm). 14: 114.

——. "Der Silvesterabend." In *Vermischte Schriften* (ed. Gustav Wilhelm) 15. 307–17.

——. "Die Sonnenfinsternis am 8. Juli 1842." In *Vermischte Schriften* (ed. Steffen). 14.

——. *Studien: Buchfassungen, 1., 2., und 3. Bd.* In *Werke und Briefe* 1, parts 4, 5, and 6. Eds. Helmut Bergner and Ulrich Dittmann. Stuttgart: W. Kohlhammer. 1, part 4, 1980; 1, parts 5 and 6, 1982.

——. *Vermischte Schriften. Adalbert Stifters Sämmtliche Werke* 14 and 15. Ed. Gustav Wilhelm. 2d ed. Reichenberg: Sudetendeutscher Verlag Franz Kraus, 1933 and 1935.

——. *Vermischte Schriften. Gesammelte Werke in vierzehn Bänden* 14. Ed. Konrad Steffen. Basel and Stuttgart: Birkhäuser Verlag, 1972.

——. "Vorrede" and "Einleitung." In *Bunte Steine.* 9–16 and 17–20.

———. *Werke und Briefe: Historisch-Kritische Gesamtausgabe.* Ed. Alfred Doppler and Wolfgang Frühwald. Stuttgart: W. Kohlhammer.

———. *Witiko: Eine Erzählung. Werke und Briefe* 5, parts 1, 2, and 3. Eds. Alfred Doppler and Wolfgang Wiesmüller. Stuttgart: W. Kohlhammer, 1984, 1985, and 1986.

Stifter, Adalbert, and J. Aprent. *Lesebuch zur Förderung humaner Bildung.* Ed. Richard Pils. Graz: Akademische Druck- und Verlagsanstalt: 1982.

Strand, John. "The Dinner Party." *Art International* 13 (Winter 1990): 26.

Sullivan, William J. "Peter Shaffer's *Amadeus*: The Making and Un-Making of the Fathers." *American Imago* 45, no. 1 (Spring 1988): 45–60.

Swales, Martin. "'As ashamed of the story as if I had written it myself . . . ': Reflections on the Narrator in *Der arme Spielmann*." In Clifford Albrecht Bernd, ed. *Grillparzer's "Der arme Spielmann."* 66–78.

———. "Doderer as a Realist." *Books Abroad* 42, no. 3 (Summer 1968): 371–75.

Swales, Martin, and Erika Swales. *Adalbert Stifter: A Critical Study.* Cambridge and New York: Cambridge UP, 1984.

Symington, Rodney. "Doderer's Cannae: History as Metaphor, Metaphor as History (with unpublished diary notations)." In Jeffrey B. Berlin, Jorun B. Johns, and Richard H. Lawson, eds. *Turn-of-the-Century Vienna and Its Legacy: Essays in Honor of Donald G. Daviau.* Riverside, CA: Edition Atelier, 1993. 459–79.

Thanner, Josef. "Causality and the Ideological Structure of *Der arme Spielmann*." In Clifford Albrecht Bernd, ed. *Grillparzer's "Der arme Spielmann."* 311–21.

Thomas, Eberle. *Peter Shaffer: An Annotated Bibliography.* New York: Garland, 1991.

Thomé, Horst, "Sozialgeschichtliche Perspektiven der neueren Schnitzlerforschung." *Internationales Archiv für Sozialgeschichte der deutschen Literatur* 13 (1988): 158–87.

Thompson, Bruce. *Franz Grillparzer.* Boston: Twayne/G. K. Hall, 1981.

Thompson, Christine E. "Pentheus in *The World According to Garp*." *Classical and Modern Literature* 3, no. 1 (Fall 1982): 33–37.

Thornton, E. M. *The Freudian Fallacy: An Alternate View of Freudian Theory.* Garden City, NY: Dial Press/Doubleday, 1984.

Tismar, Jens, *Gestörte Idyllen.* Munich: Carl Hanser Verlag, 1973.

Toman, Lore. "Posthume Einladung zum Dichter Heimito von Doderer." *Modern Austrian Literature* 14, 1–2 (1981): 97–100.

Tomkins, Calvin. "Onward and Upward with the Arts" [On Max Neuhaus]. *New Yorker*, 24 October 1988: 110–20.

———. "Time to Think." In Robert Stearns, ed. *Robert Wilson*: 54–95.

Towers, Robert. "The Raw and the Cooked" [Review of *A Prayer for Owen Meany*]. *New York Review of Books*, 20 July 1989: 30–31.

Townsend, Martha A. "*Amadeus* as Dramatic Monologue." *Literature/Film Quarterly* 14, no. 4 (1986): 214–19.

Tuchman, Gaye. "Women and the Creation of Culture." In Marcia Millman and Rosabeth Moss Kanter, eds. *Another Voice.* 171–202.

Tunner, Erika. "Zum Sehen geboren, zum Schauen bestellt." *Etudes Germaniques* 40, no. 3 (July-September 1985): 335–48.

Turner, Bruce Irvin. *Doderer and the Politics of Marriage: Personal and Social History in "Die Dämonen."* Stuttgart: Akademischer Verlag Hans-Dieter Heinz, 1982.

"Überall ist Texas: Ein Gespräch mit . . . Robert Wilson." *Süddeutsche Zeitung* 70 (Saturday-Sunday, 23–24 March 1996): 13.

Veblen, Thorstein. *The Higher Learning in America: A Memorandum on the Conduct of the Universities by Business Men.* New York: Sagamore, 1957.

Vobejda, Barbara. "The Great Books Debate: Colleges and Universities Ask What Does It Mean to Be an Educated Person." *Washington Post Education Review*, 7 August 1988: 4, 16–17.

Wall, James M. "Owen Meany and the Presence of God." *Christian Century* 106, no. 10 (22–29 March 1989): 299–300.

Walsh, Michael. Reported by William Blaylock. "A Tree Grows and Grows: Robert Wilson's 'opera,' *the CIVIL warS*, unfolds brilliantly." *Time*, 21 May 1984: 85–86. Varied slightly for the European edition of *Time*, 28 May 1984: 58.

Walter-Schneider, Margret. "Das Licht in der Finsternis: Zu Stifters *Nachsommer.*" *Jahrbuch der deutschen Schiller-Gesellschaft* 29 (1985): 381–404.

———. "Das Unzulängliche ist das Angemessene: Über die Erzählerfigur in Stifters *Nachsommer.*" *Jahrbuch der deutschen Schiller-Gesellschaft* 34 (1990): 317–42.

Weber, Dietrich. "Doderers Wien." *Literatur und Kritik* 193–94 (April-May 1985): 122–31.

———. *Heimito von Doderer.* Munich: C. H. Beck, 1987.

———. *Heimito von Doderer: Studien zu seinem Romanwerk.* Munich: C. H. Beck, 1963.

———. "Die vielen Fälle Doderer und der Fall Doderer: Ein Plädoyer." *Wirkendes Wort* 35, no. 4 (July-August 1985): 202–8.

Weber, Samuel. *Institution and Interpretation.* Minneapolis: U of Minnesota, 1987.

Weininger, Otto. *Geschlecht und Charakter.* Vienna: Wilhelm Braumüller, 1927.

West, Cornel. "Theory, Pragmatism, Politics." In Jonathan Arac and Barbara Johnson, eds. *Consequences of Theory.* 22–38.

Whitinger, Raleigh. "Elements of Self-Consciousness in Adalbert Stifter's *der Nachsommer.*" *Colloquia Germanica* 23, no. 3–4 (1990): 240–52.

Wiese, Benno von. "Adalbert Stifter: *Abdias*." In *Die deutsche Novelle von Goethe bis Kafka: Interpretationen II*. Düsseldorf: August Bagel Verlag, 1962. 127–48.

Wiesmüller, Wolfgang. " Die politische Rede als Medium der Geschichtsdeutung in Stifters *Witiko*." *Etudes Germaniques* 40, no. 3 (July-September 1985): 349–65.

Willson, A. Leslie. "'You just don't know!': An Interview with Günter Grass (Berlin, 26 April 1982)." *Dimension* 16, no. 1 (1987): 8–25.

Wilson, James Q., and Richard Hernstein. *Crime and Human Nature*. New York: Simon & Schuster, 1985.

Wilson, Robert [b. 1941]. *Death Destruction & Detroit: Ein Stück mit Musik in 2 Akten. Eine Liebesgeschichte in 16 Szenen*. Trans. into German by Peter Krumme and Bernd Samland. Berlin: Schaubühne am Halleschen Ufer, Spielzeit 1978–79 Premiere 12 February 1979.

———. *Death Destruction & Detroit₂*. Berlin: Schaubühne am Lehniner Platz, 1987.

———. *(der deutsche Teil von) the CIVIL warS: a tree is best measured when it is down*. Cologne: Schauspiel, 1984.

———. and David Byrne. *the Knee Plays [libretto]*. Ed. Robert Stearns. Minneapolis: Walker Art Center, 1984.

———. and Umberto Eco. "A Conversation." *Performing Arts Journal: 43* 15, no. 1 (January 1993): 87–96.

———. and Heiner Müller. "*the CIVIL warS* — a construction in space and time: Ein Gespräch." In Robert Wilson. *(der deutsche Teil von) the CIVIL warS*. 41–55.

Wilson, Robert [1846–1893]. *The Life and Times of Queen Victoria*. London: Cassell, 1887.

Wirsing, Sibylle. "Argos, der ganz Auge ist: Über den Schauspieler Otto Sander." In Peter von Becker and Henning Rischbieter, eds. *Theater 1979: Jahrbuch der Zeitschrift "Theater Heute."* Seelze: Friedrich Verlag, 1979. 10–11.

Wirth, Andrzej. "Bob Wilsons Diskurs des totalen Theaters: Eine kommunikations-ästhetische Strukturanalyse." *Theater heute* 4 (April 1979): 11–16.

Wittkowski, Wolfgang. "Grenze als Stufe: Josephinischer Gradualismus und barockes Welttheater im *Armen Spielmann*." In Clifford Albrecht Bernd, ed. *Grillparzer's "Der arme Spielmann."* 145–76.

Witzling, Mara R. "Through the Flower: Judy Chicago's Conflict between a Woman-Centered Vision and the Male Artist-Hero." In Suzanne W. Jones. *Writing the Woman Artist: Essays on Poetics, Politics, and Portraiture*. Philadelphia: U of Pennsylvania, 1991. 196–213.

Wolff, Helen. "Heimito von Doderer." *Books Abroad* 42, no. 3 (Summer 1968): 378–79.

Woolf, Virginia. *A Room of One's Own*. New York: Harcourt Brace, 1929.

Wootton, Carol. "Literary Portraits of Mozart." *Mosaic* 18, no. 4 (Fall 1985): 77–84.

"The Writing of Heimito von Doderer." Trans. Vincent Kling. *Chicago Review* 26, no. 2 (1974); special issue.

Wymard, Eleanor B. "'A New Version of the Midas Touch': *Daniel Martin* and *The World According to Garp.*" *Modern Fiction Studies* 27, no. 2 (Summer 1981): 284–86.

Wyss, Dieter. *Psychoanalytic Schools from the Beginning to the Present.* New York: Jason Aronson, 1973. 5th, expanded ed. in German. Göttingen: Vandenhoeck & Ruprecht, 1977.

Yates, W. E. *Grillparzer: A Critical Introduction.* Cambridge: Cambridge UP, 1972.

Young, Robert M. *Mind, Brain and Adaptation in the Nineteenth Century.* Oxford: Clarendon, 1970.

Ziak, Karl. *Des Heiligen Römischen Reiches größtes Wirtshaus: Der Wiener Vorort Neulerchenfeld.* Vienna: Jugend und Volk, 1979.

Zilboorg, Gregory, with George W. Henry. *A History of Medical Psychology.* New York: W. W. Norton, 1941.

Index

Abbott, Scott H., 66
Adams, Jeffrey, 63
Amadeus, 2, 41, 54-60, 64
Amann, Klaus, 32
Anderson, Benedict, 10
Anglican Church, 72-76
anorexia, 75
Anschluß, 16, 18, 33, 67
The Apartment, 101
Apperzeptionsverweigerung, 15, 20, 33
Arac, Jonathan, 106
—, and Barbara Johnson, 214
Aragon, Louis, 86
Arens, Katherine, 130, 152
Arker, Dieter, 82
Armstrong, Paul B., 229
Ashcroft, Bill, Gareth Griffiths, and Helen Tiffin, 10
Astaire, Fred, 101, 102
Bach, Johann Sebastian, 100, 167
Bachem, Michael, 23
Balanchine, George, 91
Barker, Andrew E., 17
Barthes, Roland, 22, 228
Bayreuth, 101
Begemann, Christian, 131
Belgum, Kirsten L., 123
Berkeley, Busby, 95, 99, 102
Bernd, Clifford Albrecht, 155
Bhabha, Homi K., 10
Biedermeier, 41, 121, 154, 178
Bildungsroman (= educational novel), 65, 66, 67, 68, 71, 72, 74, 79-81, 127
Birrell, Gordon, 155
Bloom, Allan, 210
Bloom, Harold, 11
Böll, Heinrich, 49, 54, 64
Boring, Edwin G., 130
Bottomore, Tom, and Patrick Goode, 151
Bourdieu, Pierre, 3
Bové, Paul A., 211
Bowler, Peter J., 152
Boyer, John W., 151
Brahm, Otto, 133

Brecht, Bertolt, 162
Brecht, Stefan, 86, 87, 93
Brentano, Franz, 142
Breton, André, 86
Broce, Gerald, 130
Brombert, Victor, 229
Brooklyn Academy of Music, 87
Browning, Robert M., 155
Burke, Kenneth, 228, 229
Byrne, David, 89, 105, 106

Cage, John, 86, 104
Caillois, Roger, 214, 215
The Caine Mutiny, 100
Campbell, Colin, 210
Canada, 73-76, 83
capital, cultural, 224
Carr, Francis, 64
The Case of the Midwife Toad (see also Kammerer, Paul), 142, 148
Casablanca, 100
Céline, 35
Certeau, Michel de, 11, 38
Chadbourne, Richard M., 153
Chaplin, Charlie, 93
character, characterology, 132-153
Chevalier, Maurice, 101
Chicago, Judy, 91, 182-209
—, works by:
    "The Birth Project," 185, 192, 193, 198, 200, 201, 202, 207
    "The Dinner Party," 182, 183, 185, 192, 193, 195, 198, 200, 201, 202, 205, 207, 209
    "Holocaust Project," 182, 201, 205, 207, 208
    "Pasadena Lifesavers," 184
    "Rainbow Shabat," 205
    Through the Flower (= Beyond the Flower), 184, 195, 205
    "Womanhouse," 185
—, and Donald Woodman, 206
Christo, 91, 182-209
—, works by:
    "Dockside Packages," 187
    "5600 Cubic Meters Package," 189
    "Iron Curtain," 187
    "Pont Neuf Wrapped," 187
    "The Running Fence," 187, 188, 190, 195, 196, 197, 208